GLOBAL FOCUS

GLOBAL FOCUS

U.S. FOREIGN POLICY

AT THE TURN OF THE MILLENNIUM

Edited by

MARTHA HONEY
TOM BARRY

St. Martin's Press
New York

GLOBAL FOCUS

Library of Congress Cataloging-in-Publication Data

Global focus : U.S. foreign policy at the turn of the millennium /
edited by Martha Honey and Thomas Barry.
    p.   cm.
  Includes bibliographical references and index.
  ISBN 0-312-22581-4 (cloth). — ISBN 0-312-22771-X (pbk.)
    1. United States—Foreign relations administration.   I. Honey,
Martha. II. Barry, Tom, 1950– .
JZ1480.G59   2000
327.73—dc21   99-41010
                                                  CIP

First edition: February, 2000

10 9 8 7 6 5 4 3 2 1

CONTENTS

LIST OF FIGURES

ACKNOWLEDGMENTS

THE COMMON WISDOM IS THAT PRODUCING AN edited volume is more grueling than writing a book from scratch. This has not been our experience. With first hand experience as both authors and editors, we note one striking difference: writing is a solitary and often lonely occupation, while editing involves lots of human contact and interchange. Now that this volume is nearly done and we can step back, our overall sense is that we have been enormously fortunate to have had such fine collaborators.

Global Focus: U.S. Policy at the Turn of the Millenium is a product of the Foreign Policy In Focus project, a joint endeavor between the Institute for Policy Studies (IPS) and Interhemispheric Resource Center (IRC). Initiated in 1996, Foreign Policy In Focus pairs two think tanks—one inside the Washington Beltway and the other 2,000 miles away on the Continental Divide in Silver City, New Mexico. The project aims to critique U.S. foreign policy while at the same time forging new principles, practices, and parameters for a U.S. global affairs agenda. We do this through frequent policy briefs, special reports, forums, a website, an electronic listserve, and a biennial book.

To produce a book that addresses the central issues of U.S. foreign policy at the turn of the millennium, we have assembled an extensive network of foreign policy analysts and activists. We are grateful that some of this country's most insightful foreign policy experts agreed to write original chapter for this book. As editors, we found our exchanges with the chapter authors both personally enjoyable and intellectually stimulating.

While the writers in this volume are its public face, equivalent to the actors in a stage play, *Global Focus*, like any large production, has involved a small battalion of behind the scenes "stagehands." Each chapter was peer reviewed by other experts who generously shared their knowledge and helped to refine and deepen the analysis. We would like to thank these 53 peer reviewers (listed in alphabetical order at the end of the Acknowledgments) who volunteered their time to comment on the various chapters in the *Global Focus*.

The Foreign Policy In Focus staff at both IPS and IRC handled the nuts and bolts of the production process and deserve the largest credit for making this volume both professional and attractive. Erik Leaver, who began working on the book while at IRC and then moved over to IPS, energetically, competently, and calmly applied his intelligence and computer skills to oversee production of the figures and essays and assemble the manuscript. He coordinated the charts and tables, researching and creating many of them. He worked closely with us, the editors, as well as with many of the writers in determining the book's final shape and content.

Nancy Stockdale sat at command central, managing and tracking the flow of chapters to and from the writers, editors, peer reviewers, and copy editors. With both persistence and good humor she competently handled all the administrative details of the book as well as tardy writers, unresponsive reviewers, and cranky editors. Chuck Hosking, who proofed each piece, served as a superb copy editor, detecting and correcting grammatical errors, awkward and unclear writing, and factual mistakes or inconsistencies. He has saved the writers and editors from many potentially embarrassing faux pas. Grant Moser used his drafting and artistic skills to produce the camera-ready layouts for the figures.

Special thanks goes to Linda Rhoad who joined the project during its final hectic months and, with great skill and expertise, ferreted out missing information from the Web, publications, and government bureaucrats. Tim McGivern, who also came on board toward the end but with great enthusiasm, used his writing skills to compile a number of the essays. Meena Bhandari provided assistance in the earlier stages of the project, overseeing IPS interns and helping to assemble materials for the charts. Others at IPS, most notably Sarah Anderson, Phyllis Bennis, John Cavanagh, and Miriam Pemberton, took time from their own work to help with editing and critiquing a number of the chapters. In addition, interns and work study students at both IRC and IPS—Dean Coil, Brent Earnest, Samara Freemark, Ryan Hughes, Maiah Jaskoski, Lindsey Osborne, Roopa Purushothaman, Ryan Stinnett, and Will Thomas—helped with fact checking and research, particularly for the figures.

We are also grateful to the executive directors of our two institutions, John Cavanagh at IPS and Debra Preusch at IRC, who provided institutional support, resources, and guidance to *Global Focus*. In addition, our spouses, Tony Avirgan and Debra Preusch, put up with our long hours and weekend work, giving us encouragement and handling many of our family responsibilities during our peak periods of work. This book would never have gotten off the drawing board without the financial support of the John D. and Catherine T. MacAuthur Foundation and its wonderfully supportive program officer, Mary Page. And finally, we are extremely pleased that St. Martin's Press offered to publish this volume and has agreed to do so as a collaborative undertaking with our two institutions and the Foreign Policy In Focus project.

CHALLENGES AND CONUNDRUMS OF A NEW GLOBAL AFFAIRS AGENDA

Tom Barry

WORLDWIDE, COMPUTERIZED COUNTERS ROLL OVER, calendars are replaced, and the digits of time advance. It is the mechanical, inexorable march of time, but these years and these numbers are different—they are infused with significance. Planetary history in 2000–2001 is turning from one century to another, from the end of one thousand years into a new millennium. At this juncture, as society and government are thrust into our next historical era, it is a time for reflection and resolution.

Global Focus: U.S. Foreign Policy at the Turn of the Millennium is a product of this reflection and a forum for new resolutions about global affairs. Produced by Foreign Policy In Focus (a joint project of the Institute for Policy Studies and Interhemispheric Resource Center), this volume of collected chapters aims to lay out the principle challenges of managing global affairs in this new stage of human history—with a special emphasis on the critical role of the U.S. government and its citizens. *Global Focus* attempts both to evaluate the dominant agenda and to lay out an alternative one. The chapters in the first part of the book address the major themes of U.S. foreign policy—budgetary considerations, national security, global economic policy, multilateralism, and the new environmental challenges—while the chapters in the second half examine how these foreign policy issues play out region by region. In addition to the main contribution in each chapter, there are shorter, more focused essays along with charts to paint a statistical overview of the United States in global affairs. Gathered together in this volume, these original contributions by some of the country's most insightful and innovative foreign policy analysts serve as a foundation for constructing a new U.S. global affairs agenda.

The challenges and conundrums of international affairs are diverse and manifold, but three major features of the global map stand in bold relief. Most striking is the degree to which the planet's citizens and their governments are buffeted by many of the same economic, environmental, and political forces. Although common trends are making the world a smaller place and affirming the sense that we are all global citizens, the concept of the planet as a global village hides as much as it illustrates about the new state of global affairs. Hidden behind the one-world scenario is the deepening global divide between the economically privileged, market-skilled, and internet-wired on one side (metaphorically and largely geographically, the global North) and the disadvantaged, unskilled, and unconnected on the other side of the world (the global South). The third outstanding feature of this world map is the commanding position of the United States in global politics, military affairs, ideology, culture, information technology, trade, and investment.

COMMON CHALLENGES AND CONUNDRUMS

The United States, while clearly standing alone because of its hegemonic reach, enters the new millennium confronting many of the same conundrums and challenges as other nations. Most apparent and pressing are those associated with rapid economic integration that pit workers and businesses in America against others worldwide. Increasingly evident at all latitudes and longitudes is the steady deterioration of ecological systems that have sustained the population and the economic growth of the last millennium. Politically, too, today's global citizens and their governments share many of the same concerns about the new constraints on national sovereignty, the appropriate role for nongovernmental actors, and the direction of global governance.

Production, marketing, and finance—aided by new communications technology—have been increasingly integrated by globe-girdling corporations and banks. Globalization has made the world a smaller place but one deeply split by sharp economic divides. Economic globalization—backed ideologically by the neoliberal "Washington Consensus"—has swept across the planet. But the predictions that liberalized markets would in their wake bring prosperity and democratic reform are now being widely questioned. The downside of globalization—economic polarization, financial contagion, environmental plunder, and the destruction of social contracts—have become the defining characteristics of today's global economy.

The world's population, North and South alike, is also waking up to a world of environmental limits. Northern—especially U.S.—patterns of consumption have brought the planet to the brink of environmental disaster. Population growth and rapid economic expansion in many parts of the South threaten to push the planet over the edge. Recognizing their common plight, the world's nations gathered in 1992 for the Earth Summit in Rio de Janeiro and came up with a common agenda of sustainable development. Unfortunately, as David Hunter notes in chapter 5, "virtually every major environmental indicator is worse today," and the summit's "rich body of treaties, action plans, and other instruments have not reversed global environmental decline."

Fortunately, both the policy community and the public recognize that the degradation of the global environment—destruction of rainforests, pollution of seas, holes in the ozone cap—threaten U.S. national interests and, as such, are appropriate U.S. foreign policy concerns. The State Department includes the advancement of international sustainable development as a foreign policy priority, but this new commitment is hampered by old limitations. Myopically, the Washington policy community has avoided measures that might adversely impact the short-term welfare of U.S. consumers and businesses. As with other aspects of global affairs, however, a strong argument can be made that U.S. national interests and U.S. national security are served by a more enlightened U.S. international environmental policy.

As the cold war ended, the ideological and military rivalry that determined political allegiances the world over suddenly dissipated, leaving countries and their peoples free to determine their own political direction. Initially, the possibilities seemed endless, exhilarating. But a more peaceful and just international order has not emerged. Instead political disorder and disintegration—as evident in a rash of ethnic conflicts, civil wars, and failing states—have characterized the era. The cloud of nuclear war was temporarily lifted. But in the absence of any commitment by the "great powers" of the Security Council to take the lead in abolishing nuclear weapons, the capacity to unleash nuclear catastrophe has spread to new states. The principle of multilateralism, long held hostage to the standoff between the socialist and capitalist power blocs, could have been a bedrock principle of a post–cold war future in which nations, acting together, created a "new world order." But like this now-empty phrase popularized by President George Bush, multilateralism seems an empty promise. As it has played out, multilateralism has been more a cover for militarism than a means of effective global governance. In his chapter examining the U.S. budget for international affairs, Robert L. Borosage writes: "In sharp contrast to its military spending, the U.S. devotes comparatively few dollars to foreign diplomacy, international assistance, and support for international institutions."

After celebrating the end of the cold war, we have yet to positively identify the new political era. More than a decade after the fall of the Berlin Wall, the political tag of today's world remains defined by the past. From New York to Berlin, New Delhi to Cairo, we are all still living in the political interregnum of the post–cold war era.

THE INDISPENSABLE NATION

Secretary of State Madeleine Albright is right: the United States is the "indispensable nation." Although the broad political, economic, and environmental context is much the same the world over, America is the only country with the power and influence to shape the course of global affairs. No other country or grouping

of nations has emerged to assume the kind of global leadership routinely prac-
ticed by the United States. In the last decade, America has used its superpower
status to extend its economic and military dominance and has repeatedly demonstrated its willingness to use this power unilaterally to meet perceived threats to
its hegemony.

To a large degree, how the U.S. government defines its "national interests"
and regards its "national security" determines the way it exercises its leadership.
Thus far it has opted for a narrow definition of national interests and a broad definition of national security. Increasingly, the United States regards its national interests as the economic interests of corporate America: what is good for
U.S.-based global corporations is good for America. More difficult to define is the
current concept of national security, although it clearly extends far beyond the
U.S. government's sovereign right to defend national borders. During the cold
war the United States defined national security largely in terms of containing
communism and fortifying the "free world."

The collapse of the Soviet Union did not result in any downsizing of national
security doctrine; on the contrary, U.S. national security was globalized. Today the
major components of U.S. national security include the right to maintain overwhelming U.S. military superiority, to intervene decisively throughout the world,
and to identify and target threats to global stability. William D. Hartung, notes in
chapter 2, "Military-Industrial Complex Revisited," that the United States seeks to
"retain the capability to serve as a sort of 'globocop,' charging to the rescue to restore order, stability, and 'free markets' when they are threatened by the forces of
evil and chaos."

Washington has taken advantage of the unipolar conditions of the first
post–cold war decade to assert and extend its dominance rather than to support the
institutions and international relations necessary to decrease dependence on U.S.
might. In chapter 4, Charles W. Maynes calls this "negative leadership." He argues
that because the United States currently enjoys such a surplus of power, "it is now
possible for Washington to have a very ambitious foreign policy and still remain
unilateral in its approach toward the outside world. The United States is perhaps
now the only country in the world that can, to a very significant measure, get its
way internationally if it is absolutely determined to bend others to its will." In the
process, Washington has dashed the near-term prospects for building a world
order distinguished by multilateralism and compromise. As a result, most other
nations have come to resent and distrust U.S. leadership.

If U.S. policymakers and citizens are to establish a more responsible U.S.
global leadership—sometimes referred to as a more "benevolent hegemony"—the
first step is a major overhaul of the current working definitions of U.S. national
interests and U.S. national security. Fortunately, there is a vibrant debate among
activists and scholars outside the hidebound foreign policy establishment about
what U.S. national interests truly are and what national security should rightly
mean. In addressing such issues as the need for more effective global governance,
an expanded role for nongovernmental voices in foreign policy, and the prevention of ecological collapse, citizen groups are charting the path toward a new
global affairs agenda.

GLOBAL GOVERNANCE

Americans can be proud of the U.S. leadership role in establishing the institutional structures of global governance. Recognizing the need for institutions that would foster collective security and global economic development, the United States guided the formation of the United Nations, the World Bank, and the International Monetary Fund. In addition, U.S. leadership in the aftermath of World War II was central in creating an international framework for trade that broke down mercantile structures and helped prevent mutually destructive trade wars. The failures and flaws of the post–cold war system of global governance are all too apparent, but the continuing need for structures of global governance are just as self-evident.

The cold war's end has offered the United States a new opportunity to use its leadership to redesign the architecture of global governance to overcome structural weaknesses and meet the new challenges presented by economic globalization and the rise of civil conflicts. Unfortunately, thus far this opportunity has been squandered—on both the collective security and economic fronts. With his announcement of the creation of a "new world order" at the start of the Persian Gulf War, President Bush demonstrated the shallow, triumphal, benighted character of America's post–cold war leadership. Initially the Clinton administration offered hope of a more enlightened vision with its embrace of "assertive multilateralism." In practice, however, Clinton's version of a new U.S. internationalism became that of an "indispensable nation" that shunned or manipulated the United Nations, recklessly resorted to military responses, and blithely assumed that what was good for the U.S. economy was good for the world.

An early criticism of the Clinton administration was that it had no foreign policy vision. Some joked that the sum of Clinton's foreign policy experience had been gleaned at the International House of Pancakes. In office, however, Clinton became the most globally traveled president in U.S. history, and the most interventionist, sending U.S. troops on more foreign missions than any of his predecessors. Yet although the Clinton administration never articulated a cohesive global affairs agenda, through its actions and policies the Clinton administration demonstrated a clear sense of purpose in matters of global governance—particularly on commercial and financial matters but increasingly on military and strategic fronts as well. Clinton, reflecting the prevailing conviction of the Washington foreign policy establishment, advanced an aggressive free trade agenda as the only viable set of rules for international economic engagement.

Despite experiencing some setbacks, notably the defeats of fast-track authority in 1997 and 1998, the administration relentlessly (and to a large extent successfully) promoted the extension of free trade governance, mainly through the World Trade Organization (WTO) but also bilaterally and regionally. The short-range and self-aggrandizing character of U.S. international economic leadership revealed itself at the outset of the financial crisis in Asia. Instead of using its influence to strengthen the foundations of international financial governance, Washington regarded the crisis mainly as another opportunity to break down barriers blocking the advance of U.S. capital. As John Gershman observes in chapter

12, "The Clinton administration, recognizing an opportunity to advance U.S. corporate interests, responded to the Asian crisis with a mad rush to pry open sectors of Asian economies previously sheltered from foreign participation." Referring to this same type of opportunism in U.S.-Russia policy, John Feffer writes in chapter 9: "If the U.S. government had wanted to destroy Russia from the inside out, it couldn't have devised a more effective policy than its so-called strategic partnership. From aggressive foreign policy to misguided economic advice to undemocratic influence-peddling, the U.S. has ushered a cold peace on the heels of the cold war."

The main thrust of U.S. leadership in the global economy has not been to build a framework of global decision making but to use trade agreements and the WTO to dismantle forms of national governance that regulate trade and investment flows. Although the liberalization schemes of the "Wall Street–Treasury" complex have resulted in a booming U.S. stock market and sustained growth, these are not the recipes for long-term economic stability either at home or abroad.

Before the global economy stumbles disastrously as a result of financial crisis contagion or deflation and before antiglobalization fever gives way to nationalist reaction, Washington policymakers would be wise to heed the ample warning signs and move away from what William Minter calls its "free market fundamentalism." As Minter outlines in chapter 11, the Clinton administration zealously pursued a "trade over aid" policy in Africa. In chapter 8, Richard Kaufman and Janine Wedel describe how "during the 1990s, both U.S. bilateral and multilateral aid policies toward Central and Eastern Europe were largely shaped by a doctrine prescribed by the multilateral banks and by the supply-side economics school of thought."

The challenge is for Washington to build a new consensus on global commercial and financial engagement—one that will give governments a measure of flexibility to protect vulnerable sectors and to control destabilizing capital flows. In his essay, David Felix proposes a new reform agenda that would update the Bretton Woods financial architecture, "helping to restore some of the stable, equitable growth of yesteryear, while supplying some of the institutional building blocks for erecting a genuinely integrated global economy in the future." Scholars and activists at home and abroad are supplying the blueprints for the main components of this new consensus, such as fundamental reform of the Bretton Woods institutions and trade agreements that advance dignified jobs and healthy communities.

Yet a clear and present danger is that the United States and other developed nations will back new rules that mainly protect living standards at home while ignoring the pressing need to address the widening income and technology gap between North and South. Meeting the challenges of the global economy will mean creating a good name for global economic governance—which will never happen as long as Washington allows corporate America to dictate the rules of the world economy. As John Cavanagh observes in chapter 3, "Utilizing their trade associations, pressure groups, and thousands of well-paid lobbyists, corporations have been able to shape U.S. policy so they are the prime beneficiaries."

Globalization—perceived threats of foreign workers, cheap imports, foreign capital, and so forth—has become a convenient scapegoat for the failure to build constituencies for reform of national economic policy. Clearly, there is a need for improved global economic governance that does not undermine national development strategies that are sustainable, equitable, and that contribute to commonly beneficial international economic integration. At the same time, however, domestic legislation is needed that puts full employment, income distribution objectives, workers' rights, public infrastructure investment, and educational and health services at the top of the policy agenda. For the United States, the prescription—"thinking globally and acting locally"—has special relevance given America's modeling impact on the global economy. A renewed and expanded commitment to the social democratic management of the economy at home is the essential first step for any effective new leadership role abroad.

Although the U.S. government has aggressively pursued the expansion of global economic governance through the WTO and regional integration agreements, it has been less enthusiastic about global governance that aims to maintain collective security and uphold international norms. This differentiated posture is easily explained, given that Washington believes that U.S. national economic interests—namely the welfare of U.S. corporations and investors—are well served by the current instruments of global economic governance. It is true, of course, that occasionally the U.S. government excepts itself from the international rules in the name of national security or to protect a politically powerful economic sector. However, for the most part, the United States plays by the international economic rules that it has been so central in shaping.

In contrast, U.S. exceptionalism is the main feature of its relationship with the political manifestations of global governance. One might logically have expected that the United Nations—gridlocked for decades by the cold war—would have become a stronger international institution after the Soviet demise. But rather than acting to help realize the UN's vast potential, Washington chose to continue its policy of working in concert with the UN only when it was convenient. Largely as a result of Washington's disregard for UN authority and the U.S. reluctance to meet its financial obligations, the United Nations has withered rather than blossomed since the collapse of the Soviet Union.

Instead of a real commitment to construct a new world order based on multilateralism rather than superpower politics, the U.S. government has established itself as the final arbiter of international peace and security. It has appointed itself as the archangel of international peace, sweeping down against all the Lucifers of the underworld whenever it deems fit. Unlike either the gunboat diplomacy era, when the United States intervened abroad mostly to protect its direct economic interests, or during the cold war, when the United States intervened in the name of protecting the "free world" against communist advances, today Washington has assumed a grander imperial mission. The economic and political stability of the entire planet is now its purview, which includes striking down rogue angels and unleashing its holy wrath on terrorists, drug traffickers, and other threats to world order. In chapter 11 on the Middle East, Stephen Zunes, points out, "The United States applies strict interpretations of international law and UN resolutions to governments the U.S. opposes and ignores these laws and resolutions when they target governments the U.S. supports." Focusing on U.S. policy in Latin America and the Caribbean, Coletta Youngers, in chapter 6, paints this picture of new U.S. militarism and interventionism:

> Militarized antidrug efforts undermine regional trends toward democratization and demilitarization and put U.S. assistance into the hands of human rights violators. Rather than taking advantage of the end of the cold war to redefine and limit local military roles, the U.S. government is expanding those roles. Insisting that militaries become involved in internal counternarcotics programs endorses local militaries in maintaining internal public order—precisely when Latin American governments are trying to keep local forces in the barracks—and strengthens the military at the expense of civilian institutions.

Recognizing that, acting alone, it cannot accomplish its mission of maintaining this post–cold war order, the U.S. government has launched a vast global network of police and military training programs while entrusting NATO with an expanded regional role. As Robert Greenberg notes in his essay, the Kosovo bombing "signaled an undeclared shift in NATO's mission in post-Soviet Europe" and implies that "NATO alone—not the UN, OSCE, or EU—could secure the peace of Europe." Addressing the fissures in the transatlantic alliance as a result of U.S. arrogance, Jonathan Bach in chapter 7 on U.S. policy in Western Europe concludes: "Washington is increasingly succumbing to a narrow view of the possibilities of multilateralism. The result, ironically, is not disengagement from international events but quicker recourse to unilateral or uncompromising actions. We see this trend today both in military undertakings marked by growing disregard for international consensus and in economic posturing to control the shape of globalization."

The United States as global peacekeeper is untenable: morally, financially, and politically. Washington is not an impartial arbiter and enforcer of global peace and security. It is a globocop but a selective one. No longer does it maintain the pretension of being willing to "bear any burden" or "pay any price" but, instead it has become highly selective about where and when it intervenes. Evaluations of U.S. national interests and the potential for U.S. casualties are primary considerations. Don't count on the globocop to stop genocide in a backwater state like Rwanda, where U.S. interests are few.

As the U.S. government finds itself overextended and despised in world opinion for its superpower hubris, America's post–World War II commitment to multilateralism in the cause of world peace should be revisited. Paying its UN dues and respecting the UN process are Washington's required first steps. But greater leadership will be needed to meet the multiple challenges of global peace and security.

On a regional level, Washington itself must encourage the transition away from U.S. dominance: by encouraging European Union governments in their new efforts to forge a common foreign policy and collective security regimen, by either abolishing NATO or looking eastward to include Russia, and by promoting the establishment of an Asian common security agreement that would include both

Japan and China. Globally, the challenge is to use U.S. influence to jump-start structural reform at the UN, which is sorely needed to make it a more credible and effective institution. In other words, U.S. leadership is required to help establish the processes and methods that will diminish its central role in global governance and make room for a multipolar world—one in which U.S. leadership is valued more for its wisdom than feared for its raw power.

Closely related to collective security governance is respect for international norms like human rights. No other country is as outspoken about civil liberties and democracy as the United States. The State Department's annual human rights reports offer regular and often harsh criticism of abusive practices around the world, and the president and other administration officials routinely upbraid other heads of state for human rights abuses at summits and regional forums. However, at the same time, no other nation is so responsible for the failure of the international community to establish respect for civil liberties as a fundamental norm. After a half century the United States still has not ratified one of the two Geneva human rights accords, and recently Washington has sought to undermine accords banning land mines, prohibiting the use of child soldiers, and establishing an international criminal court. Rather than being an operative principle of U.S. foreign policy, advancing human rights is part of the U.S. foreign policy toolbox, increasingly used during the past couple of decades, although only selectively and rarely against countries regarded to be strategically or economically important. The credibility of U.S. human rights policy is further undermined by U.S. unwillingness to subject itself to scrutiny of its own practices.

Although an institutional framework is critical to global governance—whether economic, political, or military—the widespread acceptance of international norms such as basic human rights and core labor rights is also a fundamental component. Rather than obstructing attempts to strengthen international norms and insisting on U.S. exceptionalism, the United States should recognize that its broader national interests would be well served by efforts to extend these dimensions of global governance.

A critical component of the U.S. leadership challenge is to build public support for global governance. In part, this will mean giving up some U.S. control over these institutions and encouraging a new leadership role for major powers like Japan and Germany as well as Southern nations. It is likely, however, that the United States will get more than it gives in any expansion of global governance. Given its pervasive economic interests and increasing dependence on international transactions, the United States stands to benefit from the kind of global governance that keeps national economies afloat in times of crisis, encourages sustainable development, fosters equitable economic growth in the South, and keeps trade disputes from degenerating into destructive protectionism or conflict. Similarly, regional collective security arrangements—together with a more effective UN peacekeeping capacity—would free the U.S. government (and its taxpayers) to shift budget priorities from military obligations to programs that meet domestic needs and promote the general welfare of the global community.

The United States should also be acting globally to advance international environmental norms and to help less privileged nations meet those norms. But the key role the U.S. government and its citizens can play is to alter America's unsustainable patterns of consumption—and in that process advance the development of environmental technology and more sustainable systems of production.

THE NGO CHALLENGE

Foreign policy and global affairs have never been the exclusive realm of presidents, generals, and diplomats. The outrage, concern, and vision of citizen groups historically have played a fundamental role in shaping the U.S. role in foreign affairs. As World War II raged, for example, peace organizations and churches provided the visionary and practical foundation for U.S. proposals to create the United Nations.

Although advances in communications technology and economic globalization place new constraints on national sovereignty, nonstate actors have expanded their influence in global affairs—and, in doing so, have assumed a powerful role in global governance. The emergence of nongovernmental organizations as visionaries and instruments of change is perhaps the most hopeful development of this new era. Progressive activists in international networks have proven to be the key actors in setting new directions regarding issues of international security (land mines treaty, small arms trade, arms sales code of conduct), human rights (child soldiers, international criminal court, truth commissions), sustainable development (rain forest conservation, climate change, trade and environment), global economy (social clauses, corporate codes of conduct, debt), and global governance (accountability, transparency). To a large degree, citizen diplomats are forging the global affairs agenda of the twenty-first century.

Previously operating as external pressure groups shaping foreign policy and public opinion, NGOs have become central actors in this new era. Taking to the streets, citizens of East and West Berlin tore down the iron curtain. Since then "civil society" has been demanding a place at the table in international economic, political, and military negotiations. Yet in pressing for the restructuring of international negotiations and institutions to include a formal place for nongovernmental actors, civil society proponents should recognize the attendant risks. Already business associations, for example, have moved into the opening created by social justice and environmental NGOs, asserting that they express the demands and aspirations of civil society. With their easier access to funds, such groups may be better placed to take advantage of the "power shift" that has brought NGOs into global governance.

As NGOs press for a formal role in foreign policy decision making and in international institutions—asserting that such participation will democratize global affairs—their own lack of democratic, transparent, representative structures and processes is increasingly being called into question, and rightly so. Compounding this problem is the disproportionate numbers and power of NGOs from the North. The power shift in this context can accentuate North-South inequities, especially when Northern NGOs and Northern governments work in concert. Although the United States is not so directly affected as less powerful states, U.S. citizens and policymakers should be concerned that NGOs can serve as a cover for privatization and weakening of state structures. Direct and indirect U.S. funding of foreign NGOs, while largely for worthy ends, may undermine local political processes and development, elevating nonrepresentative civil society organizations while sidelining political parties and popular organizations that might otherwise serve as agents of change.

Setting the directions of U.S. foreign policy in the twenty-first century needs to be a more inclusive process, one that takes full advantage of the visionary qualities and determination of the global NGO networks. Their close connections with the grass roots, their new internationalist convictions, and their nontraditional sense of national interests and national security make NGOs valuable collaborators in forging a new global affairs agenda.

A NEW GLOBAL AFFAIRS AGENDA

A common observation at the outset of the post–cold war era was that no one— not in government, not in the think-tank world, not in the activist community— had a principled, coherent vision of what exact role the United States should play in global affairs. As a new millennium begins, the problem with the U.S. global affairs agenda is different. The basic principles of a new "grand strategy" for a responsible U.S. foreign policy have been advanced by a diverse community of activists, advocacy groups, scholars, and a few policymakers. But the Democratic and Republican leadership have dismissed this visionary proposal in favor of an agenda pieced together from old policies and practices.

The prevailing U.S. foreign policy agenda, likely to continue into the next administration, is marked by five main features. It is (1) retrograde, (2) driven by special interests, (3) guided by short-term objectives, (4) interventionist and above international law, and (5) domineering.

Most striking is its retrograde character. Despite all the political hype about leading the country into the next century, Washington's foreign policy establishment is more comfortable dredging up policy from the past than pursuing new initiatives. Examples include the resurrection of the "Star Wars" missile defense system, the revival of the cold war relic NATO, and the renewal of the "open door" economic imperialism of the late nineteenth century, which permitted America's forced entry into foreign markets.

A second distinguishing feature is the degree to which foreign policy is dominated not by strategists and diplomats but by special interests. Military contractors seek to keep the military budget high and arms exports rising, and pharmaceutical companies demand that poor nations use trademark drugs rather than less expensive generic ones in the name of protecting intellectual property rights. Thus, substantive campaign finance reform represents a threat to the current direction of U.S. foreign policy.

The short-term thinking that characterizes U.S. foreign policy, particularly the global economy and environmental policies, reflects the narrow interpretation of U.S. national interests in Washington. Obscuring the benefits of a long-term strategy to foster broad-based sustainable development, the annual profit reports of U.S. corporations are given foremost consideration.

Increasingly sophisticated (but not always accurate) arms technology has allowed the United States to intervene militarily (in Panama, Iraq, Sudan, Kosovo, etc.) with little risk to U.S. troops and with little regard for international law. Emerging from the cold war with no foes, the United States now swaggers across the international arena, relying more on the politics of domination than of compromise. Its domineering presence—sparking resentment and damaging prospects for multilateral global governance—has not given rise to other global leadership, affirming the U.S. conceit that the twenty-first century will be another American century.

During the 1990s the outlines of an alternative agenda gradually came into focus. As within the official foreign policy community, there exist within the reform community many differences about tactics and even different interpretations of the operative principles. The alternative agenda contrasts sharply from the official one. However, one would be mistaken to assume that the contrast is between realism and idealism. Although the new global affairs agenda is certainly visionary, it addresses the unresolved foreign policy issues of our era in a practical way. At a time when the U.S. Treasury Department is holding the course on failed financial liberalization policies, the reform agenda offers pragmatic alternatives to address financial contagion, capital flows crises, and the chaos resulting from unregulated speculative investment. The main prescription is the highly practical suggestion that foreign economic policy be guided not by a narrow ideology benefiting a corporate elite but by its commitment to benefit the broad majority. Similarly, the overriding critique of the current political and military projections of U.S. power is that they are not based on any holistic assessment of what constitutes U.S. interests or security.

In large measure the new global affairs agenda is based on the principles first set out in the U.S. Constitution, namely that the U.S. government should "provide for the common defense" and "promote the general welfare." Rather than projecting military power abroad, the Defense Department should be primarily concerned about military threats against U.S. borders and U.S. citizens. Since the United States faces no powerful enemies, there should be a major retrenchment in the U.S. military mission and budget. Promoting the general welfare will mean a major change in direction in U.S. foreign policy—away from a narrow corporate interpretation of U.S. interests toward an assessment of potential impacts on the health, welfare, and happiness of all Americans.

But the new global affairs agenda, while wary of U.S. interventionism and considerate of the best interests of Americans, is hardly an inward-looking vision of the future. President George Washington's advice that the United States avoid foreign "entanglements" was well taken at the time, but today's world is inextricably integrated. The challenge is not to untangle ourselves but to support the methods and institutions of global governance that foster peace and sustainable development around the globe.

Global Focus: U.S. Foreign Policy at the Turn of the Millennium attempts to set forth some of the best thinking about the state of U.S. foreign policy and about an alternative agenda. This process of detailing a new global affairs agenda is a necessary first step. Still more challenging is the task of advancing and implementing such an agenda. Success requires efforts on multiple fronts. Perhaps most important is the educational and outreach work necessary to ensure public support for a reform agenda that posits a new, more expansive vision of U.S. national interests. Strong political leadership is also essential, but even more important will be unrelenting citizen activism that forces politicians to listen and act. Finally, little is possible without the tireless educational lobbying work of the advocacy organizations that, issue by issue, move the reform agenda forward in Washington.

As the millennium turns, the prospects for a new era of international peace and sustainable development seem remote. Although there are some hopeful signs, such as the rise of NGO activism and new consciousness about environmental deterioration, most indicators are negative. Issue by issue, region by region, the authors of these chapters address the central conundrums and most pressing challenges, each pointing to the kind of responsible U.S. leadership that can help turn the world around.

CHAPTER 1

MONEY TALKS: THE IMPLICATIONS OF U.S. BUDGET PRIORITIES

Robert L. Borosage

ACCORDING TO A RECENT REPORT BY THE COUNCIL on Foreign Relations, "[T]he average American believes we spend 18 percent of the federal budget on foreign affairs, while thinking we should spend only 6 percent. In reality, foreign affairs spending, the bully pulpit of America's strength overseas, is now only 1 percent of the federal budget—a little more than one penny of every federal tax dollar."[1]

This argument has been the centerpiece of Secretary of State Madeleine Albright's campaign for more funds for international activities. "That 1 percent," she argues, "may well determine 50 percent of the history that is written about the era." But although the secretary's cause is a good one, her argument is profoundly misleading, for it excludes the bulk of U.S. international spending—the military budget. Americans basically have it about right when the military is included. The United States spends about 17 percent of its total budget on national security and international activities, with the military consuming 94 percent of the total sum. (See figure 1–1.) Indeed, the military captures almost one-half of the entire federal discretionary budget—money for everything the government does, from the Federal Bureau of Investigation to Head Start and from education to healthcare, excluding only mandatory spending, primarily interest on the national debt and entitlements like Social Security and Medicare.[2]

Facts, Ronald Reagan once said, are stubborn things. And numbers are easy to distort. But looking at how the U.S. spends its money on international and national security affairs gives a good sense of our priorities—what we invest in and what we choose to neglect, and what the implications are for U.S. foreign policy.

Figure 1.1

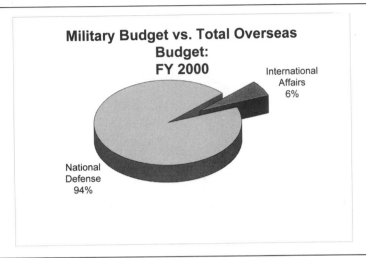

Military Budget vs. Total Overseas Budget: FY 2000

International Affairs 6%

National Defense 94%

Source: Office of Management and Budget, Executive Office of the President, *The Budget for Fiscal Year 2000, Historical Tables of the 2000 U.S. Government Budget* (Washington, DC: U.S. Government Printing Office, 1999).

THE COST OF THE MILITARY

In fiscal year (FY) 1999, the United States spent over $276 billion on its military.[3] This figure includes outlays of the Pentagon, the Department of Energy nuclear weapons programs, and more than $27 billion spent on the intelligence agencies— about half on tactical military intelligence and half for intelligence agencies, including the Central Intelligence Agency (CIA) and the National Security Agency. With this budget, the Pentagon fields a military force without rival in the world. It sustains over 1.4 million men and women in active duty plus another 870,000 in the reserves. Standing forces include 10 active Army divisions, three Marine divisions, 13 active and seven reserve Air Force fighter wings, and 12 aircraft carrier battle groups (11 active), plus around 7,200 deployed nuclear warheads capable of being launched from the ground affixed to MX and Minuteman missiles, by sea from Trident submarines, and by air from B-52 and B-2 bombers. The Pentagon has basically completed its post–cold war drawdown and, with minor reductions, plans to sustain this force structure indefinitely.[4] The Pentagon budget also includes over 770,000 civilian employees, almost 40 percent of total executive branch civilian personnel.

The $276 billion does not include the cost of military pensions or the Veteran's Administration—another $43 billion in FY 1999—nor the military's share of the national debt, a good portion of which was amassed either in active wars or in the massive Reagan military buildup in the 1980s. Loan guarantees offered by the Defense Department to promote arms sales are also an obligation not included in that national security figures.

When you think of big government, this is it. The military establishment issues over half of all government paychecks. It makes about two-thirds of government purchases of goods and services. It sponsors 53 percent of all government research and development.[5] It is the nation's second largest healthcare insurer and provider and the largest day care provider. It runs the world's largest educational enterprise. It manages over 5,000 properties on lands with a total land area about the size of the State of Ohio.[6] Outside of China, it is without rival as the world's largest bureaucracy.

It is also without question the largest source of waste, fraud, and abuse in the federal government. It employs over 40,000 accountants and budget analysts to manage over 250 accounting systems. In 1998, the General Accounting Office reported that the Pentagon was unable to account for $250 billion of more than $1.2 trillion worth of property, equipment, inventory, and supplies.[7] Yet it continues to disperse billions of dollars without records of what it is purchasing. As conservative Republican Senator Charles Grassley has said: "We have financial chaos in the Pentagon. We have meaningless accounting numbers. We have meaningless cost estimates."[8] The Pentagon also provides the pork, or pet projects, that both conservatives and liberals can love. Senator John McCain estimates that $5 billion in pork-barrel special interest projects—primarily weapons or construction projects that the Pentagon did not ask for—were larded into the FY 1999 defense budget.

Each year, the General Accounting Office (GAO) publishes reports on what it calls "at risk" agencies, where mismanagement raises the risk of waste, fraud, and abuse. In 1999, the GAO reports that after "decades of neglect," the Pentagon has a financial management system that "is unable to properly account for billions of dollars in assets . . . is unable to make sound resource decisions . . . consistently pays more and takes longer to develop [weapons] systems that do not perform as anticipated . . . continues to make erroneous, fraudulent and improper payments to contractors . . . [and whose] inventory management system is ineffective and inefficient."[9] The GAO's auditors could not match about $22 billion in signed checks, $9 billion in supplies and material could not be located, and contractors received $19 million in overpayments. *Defense Week* summarized: "[T]he Pentagon doesn't know what it can send to troops, can't avoid buying more of something that the military already owns, and can't tell how much its programs actually cost."[10]

Congress not only condones this endemic waste, it adds to it. It has blocked additional rounds of base closings that Defense Secretary William Cohen estimates might save $2 to $3 billion per year. It happily supports, without question, the Pentagon's grossly inflated estimates of readiness, weapons, and force needs. Between 1994, when Republicans took control of Congress, and mid-1999, it has added a total of $30 billion to the Pentagon's own requests. Despite the "financial chaos," the Pentagon does not hesitate to demand more money, which the Republican Congress and the Democratic president rush to provide.

MEETING THE THREAT OF PEACE

Not surprisingly, with the end of the cold war and the collapse of the Soviet Union, military spending began to wane—in real (inflation adjusted) dollars, as a

percentage of the budget, and as a percentage of the overall economy or gross national product. (See figure 1–2.) But the cuts have been remarkably limited given
the Soviet breakup: 1999 allocations, adjusted for inflation, are roughly 85 percent
of the average level spent on the military from 1976 to 1990.[11]

However, because the economy has been growing, the relative burden of sustaining this military establishment is less than in the decades of the cold war. As
advocates of more military spending like to point out, we now spend a smaller percentage of our budget and our gross national product (GNP) on the military than
at any time since before World War II. The bipartisan budget agreement forged
by President Clinton and the Republican Congress projected that military spending (in inflation-adjusted dollars) would continue to decline slowly through the
year 2002. In response, both the president and Congress have pledged to increase
spending in both nominal and real dollars.[12]

That we *can* more easily afford this level of military spending does not address
the question of whether we *should* support it—whether we need to spend this
amount—nor does it consider what we forgo at home and abroad in order to devote such resources to the military.

In reality, Washington is spending far more on its military than is needed for
defense. Alone, the U.S. accounts for about one-third of the world's military expenditures and more than all other NATO allies combined. (See figure 2–2.) We
spend over three times as much as the most exaggerated estimate of Russian
spending, over four times that of China. Indeed, with our allies and friends, we account for about three-fourths of global military spending. Eight of the world's ten
largest military budgets are those of our allies.[13]

Figure 1.2

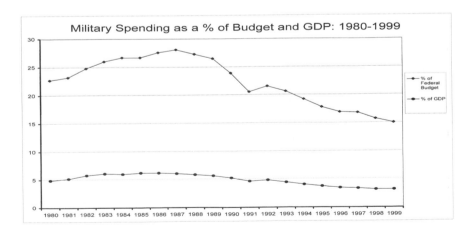

Source: Department of Defense, *National Defense Budget Estimates for FY 2000* (Washington, DC:
Office of the Under Secretary of Defense, March 1999). Available on the Internet at: http://www.
dtic.mil/comptroller.

Moreover, the decline in U.S. military spending is often exaggerated. In dollar terms, the cutbacks have essentially succeeded in reversing the Reagan buildup, which doubled the military budget in the early 1980s—the largest peacetime military buildup in recorded history. In 1999, in constant dollars, the United States will spend more on its military than it did during the cold war under Richard Nixon and Gerald Ford and about as much as it did under Jimmy Carter in 1980 before Reagan was elected.[14]

No threat or potential threat justifies this spending. During the cold war, often exaggerated estimates of Soviet and Chinese military spending and arms buildups were used to conjure up readiness scares and justify large military expenditures.[15] Today there is no such external justification. The United States, as former chair of the Joint Chiefs of Staff Colin Powell noted in 1991, is "running out of demons. I'm down to Fidel Castro and Kim Il Sung."[16] The Soviet Union is no more. The Russian military is literally disintegrating. We are threatened far more by Russia's weakness—its fear of collapse, its peddling of weapons and knowledge in desperation—than by its strength. The Chinese, for all the brouhaha about their buildup, spend an estimated $40 to $65 billion on their military.[17] They lack a modern air force, a blue-water navy, and any semblance of modern communications. Russia and China together account for about 15 percent of global military spending.

The so-called rogue nations that the Pentagon identifies as potential adversaries—Iran, Iraq, Sudan, Libya, Syria, Cuba, North Korea—collectively spend about $15 billion on their militaries each year, under 2 percent of global spending.[18] All of these relatively small countries lack a modern industrial base, cannot produce advanced weapons, are in economic crisis, and have been cutting spending on their militaries in past years.

DIPLOMACY STARVED

In sharp contrast to its military spending, the United States devotes comparatively few dollars to foreign diplomacy, international assistance, and support for international institutions. The total net outlays in FY 1999 will be around $15 billion, less than 1 percent of the $1.66 trillion federal budget.[19] This budget pays for the vast majority of the U.S. civilian role abroad. It includes 150 different account funds, ranging from food aid, to the State Department's antiterrorism programs, to the U.S. contributions to multilateral financial institutions such as the World Bank and its affiliated regional banks. Major items include the State Department, with its worldwide infrastructure of embassies, missions, consulates, and an overseas staff of more than 35,000. Also included are the U.S. Agency for International Development (AID) and bilateral assistance programs, the United States Information Agency (USIA) and a range of activities called "public diplomacy," the Commerce Department's trade offices, as well as the Peace Corps and other humanitarian programs. The funding encompasses assistance to the Newly Independent States (once part of the Soviet Union), U.S. nonmilitary aid commitments to Bosnia, security aid to Israel and the Middle

Figure 1.3   U.S. Official Development Assistance Compared
             with Other Nations: 1997

	1997 ODA ($U.S. millions)	ODA/GNP %
Australia	1,061	0.28
Austria	527	0.26
Belgium	764	0.31
Canada	2,045	0.34
Denmark	1,637	0.97[a]
Finland	379	0.33
France	6,307	0.45
Germany	5,857	0.28
Ireland	187	0.31
Italy	1,266	0.11
Japan	9,358	0.22
Luxembourg	95	0.55
Netherlands	2,947	0.81
New Zealand	154	0.26
Norway	1,306	0.86
Portugal	250	0.25
Spain	1,234	0.24
Sweden	1,731	0.79
Switzerland	911	0.34
United Kingdom	3,433	0.26
United States	6,878	0.09
Total DAC	48,324	
Average per country		0.4

Source: "Official Development Assistance Flows in 1997," Organization for Economic Cooperation and Development, February 8, 1999. Available on the Internet at: http://www.oecd.org/dac/htm/dacstats.htm.
[a]Denmark introduced the new system of national accounts, ENS 95, in 1997. This led to an upward revision of GNP which, combined with other technical factors, caused a downward adjustment of the final Danish ODA/GNP ratio to 0.97 percent in 1997.
Note: The high-income members of the Organization for Economic Co-operation and Development (OECD) are the main (though not the only) source of external finance for developing countries. These members form the Development Assistance Committee (DAC). The DAC exists to help its member countries coordinate their development assistance and to encourage the expansion and improve the effectiveness of the aggregate resources made available to developing and transition economies. In this capacity DAC monitors the flow of all financial resources, but its main concern is official development assistance (ODA). DAC has three criteria for ODA: It is undertaken by the official sector. It promotes economic development or welfare as a main objective. It is provided on concessional terms with a grant element of at least 25 percent on loans.

East, and support for the Export-Import Bank and the Overseas Private Investment Corporation.[20] (The figure does not include the $14.5 billion U.S. quota increase for the International Monetary Fund [IMF] or the $3.4 billion credit commitment to the IMF's New Arrangements to Borrow program, still pending before Congress. IMF appropriations are considered monetary exchanges—

with the IMF providing the U.S. with special drawing rights—and thus are not considered budget outlays.[21])

Secretary Albright is surely right to suggest that this total is shamefully inadequate. The United States is the world's wealthiest nation—and its largest scofflaw. As of mid-1999, our debt to the United Nations totals over $1.6 billion in back dues, and we owe more than $600 million to the international financial institutions (including the Global Environmental Facility). The United States provides less of its wealth to support the impoverished abroad than any other industrial country. The United States spends less than one-tenth of 1 percent of its gross domestic product (GDP) on official development assistance, and about the same amount on other aid-related activities (including peacekeeping). The Organization for Economic Cooperation and Development's Development Assistance Committee (DAC) average is about four times as much, or four-tenths of 1 percent. And the official target of the United Nations is that donors provide seven-tenths of 1 percent in aid. (See figure 1–3.)

Despite having by far the world's largest economy, the United States is no longer the world's largest aid provider. Economically troubled Japan provides more aid in absolute dollar terms, giving $9 billion in 1997; the United States, Germany, and France each provided around $6.5 billion. These numbers are falling rapidly: since 1995 aid from these four countries has dropped 6 percent in real dollars, and total DAC support has dropped 18 percent.

Moreover, U.S. spending on international affairs when measured in constant dollars has been declining steadily since 1980. (See figure 1–4.) From 1992 through 1998, funding dropped an average of about 6 percent annually. Under the projected balanced budget agreements, international affairs funding is slated to be cut another 13 percent by 2002, and U.S. overseas development assistance could drop to about one-tenth of the global total. By 2002, international affairs spending will be about half of its 1980 to 1995 average in constant 1998 dollars and at its lowest level since 1955.[22]

At a time of dramatically increasing U.S. investment, trade, travel, communications, and exchanges abroad, the State Department has been forced to close diplomatic missions and AID programs, to delay building consulates in the new states forming from the former Soviet Union and Yugoslavia, and to postpone expansion in China as provinces open up. Under President Clinton, the State Department has cut more than 2,000 employees, closed more than 30 embassies and consulates, and deferred long-overdue modernization of computers and communications, to say nothing—as noted after the bombings in Tanzania and Kenya—of recommended security improvements. Foreign assistance programs have fallen 30 percent since 1991 in constant dollars.

Of the funding that does exist, a striking portion is consumed by security or military concerns and commitments. From 1992 to 1998, fully one-third of international affairs spending was devoted to supporting international security and peacekeeping activities, including security assistance to Egypt and Israel and UN peacekeeping operations.[23] Foreign military financing programs—grants, loans, and loan guarantees to foreign governments to purchase U.S. military weapons— continue to be the single largest component of security assistance contained in the international affairs budget. (See figure 1–5.)

Figure 1.4   International Affairs Budget Decline: 1980–1998
(constant 1998 $U.S. millions)

Year	Outlay
1980	27,865
1981	25,304
1982	21,533
1983	19,531
1984	25,360
1985	24,744
1986	20,921
1987	16,899
1988	14,663
1989	12,877
1990	17,677
1991	19,303
1992	18,824
1993	19,571
1994	18,819
1995	17,645
1996	14,137
1997	15,487
1998	13,109

Source: Office of Management and Budget, Executive Office of the President, *The Budget for Fiscal Year 2000, Historical Tables of the 2000 U.S. Government Budget* (Washington, DC: U.S. Government Printing Office, 1999).

Similarly, our bilateral assistance programs are skewed toward security concerns rather than economic, development, and social needs. Support for Egypt and Israel consumes 82 percent of all security-related costs and almost 25 percent of all international affairs spending. Assistance to Bosnia, following the commitment of U.S. troops, is the single largest program of U.S. aid in East Europe and the former Soviet Union. "Hot spots"—such as Somalia, Bosnia, and Haiti—attract significant portions of a declining pool of money, with AID shifting funds from ongoing programs to meet demands essentially generated by military commitments. The anomaly is apparent: Israel, with a per-capita GDP of over $12,000, receives over $3 billion in bilateral assistance each year, while all of sub-Saharan Africa, with a per-capita GDP of under $500, receives a total of about $165 million.[24]

Even the State Department's budget reflects similar priorities: funding will swell in the wake of events such as the bombings of the U.S. embassies in Kenya and Tanzania, but the increased funding will be devoted largely to fortifications rather than to modernizing communications, increasing political reporting, or adding consulates to help handle the burgeoning traffic of tourists and businesspeople.

Only about 30 percent of the total FY 1999 budget of $22.5 billion for international affairs actually goes to bilateral assistance programs, the foreign aid that

Figure 1.5   Breakdown of International Affairs Budget: 2000

	(*$U.S. millions*)
Foreign Operations	
Multilateral Assistance	1,816
Agency for International Development	2,611
Other bilateral assistance	1,425
International Security Assistance	6,232
Export and Investment Assistance	725
Other assistance	1,292
Wye Middle East Peace Process	500
Commerce, Justice, State, and Related Agencies	
Department of State	5,408
Broadcasting Board of Governors	452
Other programs	50
Department of Agriculture	787
Labor, Health and Human Services, Education	13
Total	21,311

Source: Secretary of State, *Congressional Presentation for Foreign Operations: Fiscal Year 2000* (Washington DC: Department of State, 1999), pp. 50–54.

is routinely criticized as excessive and wasteful. Of the total $7.3 billion dollars requested in FY 1999 for the U.S. Agency for International Development, about $867 million went to Food for Peace programs, $1.4 billion for aid to East Europe and the Newly Independent States (formerly the Soviet Union), $205 million for International Disaster Assistance, and $3.8 billion for programs included in such funding categories as Child Survival and Disease, Development Assistance, and Economic Support Funds. The remainder is allocated for AID operating expenses.[25]

Were Washington to match the aid level of our allies, significant additional resources would be available for international assistance. If the United States spent, as our allies average, 0.4 percent of its GDP on overseas development aid, it would quadruple its outlays from $6.8 billion to over $27 billion per year. If it invested as generously as Sweden does—nine-tenths of 1 percent of GDP—U.S. aid would rise to about $76 billion a year.

IMPLICATIONS: THE GLOBOCOP

Whenever any politician—whether conservative or liberal, interventionist or isolationist—speaks on the U.S. role in the world, one phrase recurs like a ritual mantra: "Of course, the United States cannot police the world." We are the "indispensable nation," Secretary Albright trumpets, but we cannot "police the world." Pentagon staffers routinely referred to General John Shalikashvili, the now-retired chair of the Joint Chiefs, as "globocop," even while President Clinton proclaimed, "We cannot and should not try to be the world's policeman."[26] The president's incantation pays tribute to public sentiment, for poll after poll shows that large majorities of Americans oppose the notion of the United States policing the globe, but the general's sobriquet is closer to the truth.

Pentagon planners say that U.S. force structure is determined primarily by the self-assigned mission of being ready to fight two regional conflicts at the same time—without allies and on opposite sides of the world—with North Korea and Iraq as the central examples. (See essay 2–1: Military Strategy Under Review.) But we fought only three major wars throughout the cold war, and we face North Korea and Iraq—the designated adversaries for Pentagon planning—with the support of allies. North Korea now has difficulty feeding its troops. Iraqi military strength was decimated in the Gulf War and after, U.S. air patrols erased one-fifth of the Iraqi air defense system in early 1999 without anyone paying much attention. The two-war mission—an inconceivable response to an implausible threat—is used to justify a force still girded for the cold war, laden with the tanks, heavy armor divisions, nuclear warheads, and weaponry designed for another age. No wonder Pentagon analyst Franklin Spinney has described this strategy as a "marketing device for a high Pentagon budget."[27]

The two-war theory—confirmed and reconfirmed in official mission and enshrined in Pentagon planning—is perhaps an understatement of the Pentagon's actual role of a permanent world police force. In day-to-day operations, the U.S. military spans the world. The scope of its activity is staggering. The Pentagon maintains 100,000 troops in Asia (primarily in Japan and South Korea) and another 100,000 in Europe, with the capacity to reinforce them immediately. The troops in Asia, the administration has now announced, will stay even if the two Koreas unite. The Pentagon sustains 15,000 troops in rotating station in the Persian Gulf, a direct contradiction to the pledge made by President George Bush before the war that no U.S. forces would stay in the region. The Pentagon also rotates over 50,000 active-duty and reserve personnel through Latin America every year.[28] (See figure 1–6.)

And the forces permanently deployed abroad are but a small portion of the U.S. presence. The United States, as Secretary of Defense Cohen reported in his 1999 annual report to Congress, is "the only nation in the world able to project overwhelming military power worldwide."[29] He further stated that it is the "only country in the world that can organize effective military responses to large-scale regional threats" while "participating in smaller-scale contingencies and dealing with asymmetric threats like terrorism."[30]

The defense secretary says the United States is committed to the "unilateral use of military power" to do "whatever it takes to defend" vital interests. Vital interests, he reports, include not simply defense of the United States but also "preventing the emergence of hostile regional coalitions or hegemons, ensuring uninhibited access to key markets, energy supplies and strategic resources, deterring . . . aggression against U.S. allies and friends," and "ensuring freedom of the seas, airways and space." The writ extends to every continent and every ocean.[31]

The annual reports of the various military branches give some indication of the pace and scope of the U.S. effort to police the globe. The secretary of the

Figure 1.6 Presence of American Troops Abroad: 1998

Region	Number of Troops
Former Soviet Union and Central Asia	105
Sub-Saharan Africa	281
Latin America and Caribbean	12,614
North Africa, Near East, and South Asia	34,043
East Asia and Pacific	95,015
Europe	112,457
Total	254,515

Source: "Worldwide Manpower Distribution by Geographical Area," Department of Defense, December 31, 1998. Available on the Internet at: http://web1.whs.osd.mil/mmid/military/miltop.htm.

Army reports that in 1997, the Army averaged 31,000 active and reserve soldiers deployed in over 70 countries, not counting those in Europe and Asia. In May 1997, worldwide deployments reached the 100-country mark for the first time in history.[32]

The secretary of the Navy reports that each day of the year more than 50,000 sailors and Marines and over 100 ships are deployed around the world. Naval forces provide "near continuous presence in four major regions—the Mediterranean Sea, the Arabian Gulf/Indian Ocean, the Western Pacific and the Caribbean." Naval carrier battle groups also police sea lanes, with what the Department of Defense (DOD) calls "operational assertions" challenging other nation's claims to territorial seas. In FY 1998, these operations challenged the claims of 27 countries from Albania to Yemen.[33]

The Air Force secretary reports that its total force is designed to protect people and facilities "anywhere in the world." A snapshot of its actions include continued sorties over Bosnia; Operation Southern Watch and Northern Watch over Iraq; counterdrug operations in South America; disaster relief in North Dakota and Minnesota, Italy and Indonesia; evacuations of civilians in Cambodia, Albania, and former Zaire; support for West African states; Cuban flotilla operations; medical evacuation of the president of Ghana; support for Kurdish refugees; as well as 20 exercises with 25 Partnership for Peace countries in Europe, including CENRAZBAT 97, a combined exercise with forces from the United States, Kazakhstan, Uzbekistan, Kyrgyzstan, Russia, and Turkey.[34]

The arms of U.S. training reach far beyond these Air Force joint exercises. In 1998, the DOD contributed to the training of over 8,000 foreign military members from about 100 countries through the International Military Education and Training (IMET) program.[35]

In addition, more than a dozen intelligence agencies maintain "plumbing in place"—a network of agents and assets that spans the globe, particularly in less developed nations—as well as managing covert actions large and small focused on varying targets across the world. Given that the intelligence agencies failed to predict either the collapse of the Soviet Union or the Indian nuclear tests, complaints about the quality of their intelligence are well founded. But our commitment to surveillance is unparalleled: the United States spends more on its intelligence budget alone—over $27 billion in 1999—than all but five countries in the world spend on their entire military establishments.

The Unites States is engaged militarily across the world every day, in areas most Americans cannot find on the map. As former Senator Richard Russell once said, "The more ability we have to go someplace to do something, the more likely it is that we will go there and do it." America's military currently has both the ability and the fiat to go anywhere and to do almost anything.

President Clinton came to office at the end of the cold war, the first baby-boom president, a product of the anti–Vietnam War sentiment, and a skeptic of U.S. intervention. Yet in his administration alone, in a time of relative peace and prosperity, U.S. forces have been engaged in more strikes and interventions—Somalia, Haiti, Bosnia, Kosovo, Iraq, Afghanistan, and Sudan—than most presidents would have dared at the height of the cold war. In fact, by March 1999, when NATO air strikes against Yugoslavia began, Clinton had notified Congress 46 times that he was deploying U.S. troops abroad to face "imminent hostilities," as required by the 1973 War Powers Act. In contrast, President Gerald Ford notified Congress that he was sending troops only 4 times, Carter 1 time, Reagan 14, and Bush just 7 times.[36]

Clinton's behavior reflects the post–cold war elite conceit—shared widely among national security managers and within the Pentagon—that the United States is, as Secretary Madeleine Albright puts it, the "indispensable nation." Whatever sentiment existed for giving the Europeans more responsibility for policing Europe ended with their failure in Bosnia. The United States chose to expand NATO's membership and mission and to reassert its role as commander of NATO forces rather than dismantle that structure at the end of the cold war. In Asia, as well, the 1998 face-off against China in the Taiwan Straits was graphic demonstration of an increasing U.S. commitment to global policing. In Latin America, the U.S. military has expanded its drug interdiction roles, revived its arms sales and training programs, lifted the ban on the sale of high-tech weaponry, and increased its police aid and training programs. The military complains that it is strained by the surging tempo of peacekeeping, peace enforcement, drug interdiction, and other missions, since it considers these as extra tasks beyond its existing commitment to be ready to fight two major regional conflicts at once.

Although most Americans oppose the notion of the Unites States patrolling the world and tend to be appalled when U.S. soldiers are slain in conflict in obscure nations, the interventionist temper of U.S. policy has support across partisan and ideological lines in establishment political and foreign policy circles. In the late 1990s, the Republican leadership in Congress insisted on more money for the military and criticized the Clinton administration for being too passive toward Iraq, North Korea, China, terrorists, and drug peddlers. Liberal human rights advocates criticized the administration for its ignominious withdrawal from Somalia, its failure to intervene against genocide in Rwanda, and its unwillingness to move earlier to stop the violence in Bosnia. Secretary Albright helped advance her career by publicizing her criticism of General Colin Powell for his caution regarding intervention—his Vietnam-grounded reluctance to send men into peacekeeping missions of indeterminate nature and indefinite duration. The gulf between popular and elite opinion often tempers the tactics of U.S. policy (prompting a reliance on high-tech weaponry rather than troops and placing an emphasis on avoiding casualties), but it has no effect on the tempo of routine, global policing.

THE PRIVATIZATION OF U.S. DIPLOMACY

Given America's global military presence and economic prowess, the impoverishment of U.S. public diplomacy and aid budgets has not greatly eroded Washington's influence around the world. In essence, the United States has privatized its "soft powers."[37] Corporate communications and computer capacity outstrip that of the State Department. Private economic data and reporting are often far more current than U.S. intelligence agency information. U.S. culture is spread less through cultural exchanges than through Big Macs and Hollywood movies.

Given the dearth of public assistance, needy countries are consigned to wooing private investment from private banks, corporations, and speculators. Most poor countries have meager natural resources, small internal markets, inadequately educated populations, rudimentary infrastructures, and suffer from political instability—limiting their commercial attractiveness. For the handful of developing countries that can entice external private investment, private capital flows—and private debts—far exceed pubic flows. (See figure 3–3.) But burdened by debt and policed by the IMF and the World Bank, they must focus on exports to service their debts. U.S. public economic assistance merely reinforces the model. Thus, the great bulk of U.S.-backed resources are dispersed not in grants through the public assistance budget but in loans via the IMF (and to a lesser extent the World Bank and other international banks) at times of crisis, to reassure foreign investors by ensuring that foreign debts are repaid. Washington's assistance budget is dominated not by AID but by what has been labeled the Wall Street–Treasury Department complex.

With limited resources, bilateral assistance programs have increasingly either been subordinated to security concerns or provided as a carrot to spur export-led development models. As Benjamin Nelson of the General Accounting Office noted in the careful language of official reports, "AID appears to have established as a priority the importance of influencing domestic policy in the recipient countries."[38] U.S. foreign aid is concerned less with serving basic needs in desperate countries than with cheerleading the market-based reforms that we export.

The starvation of U.S. diplomatic and aid budgets contributes to and reflects the United States default after the cold war regarding the development of innovative public aid programs and strong, multilateral institutions. Any hope that the United Nations might develop into a truly multinational peacekeeping force has been frustrated. Instead UN activities have been cribbed by the United States failure to pay its debts.[39]

The harsh contrast between the treatment accorded Russia after the cold war and that provided Germany, Japan, and the European allies after World War

II reflects the starvation of public aid commitments. Whereas Germany received assistance to rebuild, leeway to control its markets, and cash to revive employment, Russia—facing a far greater challenge—was bludgeoned into opening its markets and making the ruble convertible immediately. Assistance was limited, contingent, and parsimonious. Russia was treated more like Germany after World War I than Germany after World War II, and the devastating aftereffects reflect this treatment. The United States devoted about 2 percent of its annual GDP to the post–World War II Marshall Plan—far more than the entire U.S. aid and international affairs budget now consumes.

Similarly, both Grenada and Haiti—the two microstates where the United States directly intervened to change regimes—found that Washington was afterward unwilling to supply the kind of public assistance needed to foster equitable development. Given Washington's indifference, hopes for increased U.S. private investment evaporated. Honduras, El Salvador, Costa Rica, and Nicaragua were virtually abandoned once the frenzied focus of the cold war passed. Even after the region was wracked in 1998 by Hurricane Mitch in one of the worst natural disasters of the century, U.S. assistance was slow and limited. The president traveled through Africa to celebrate the emerging democracies there, but he could offer them little more than free advice: attract foreign investors. No wonder his agenda received a public rebuke from then–South African President Nelson Mandela, the one leader of sufficient global stature to speak candidly.

As the Asian financial crisis spread to Russia, Brazil, and elsewhere, the limits and perils of this strategy became clear. "America has wanted global leadership on the cheap," Harvard economist Jeffrey Sachs, an architect of the U.S. policy in Russia argues.

> It was desperate for the developing world and post-communist economies to buy into its vision, in which globalization, private capital flows and Washington advice would overcome the obstacles to shared prosperity, so that pressures on the rich countries to do more for the poorer countries could be contained. In this way, the United States would not have to shell out real money to help the peaceful reconstruction of Russia or to ameliorate the desperate impoverishment and illness in Africa.[40]

Sachs is surely right about the limits on U.S. aid. With an expanded budget for international affairs and aid, the United States might lead the way toward bolstering the UN and international peacekeeping capacity, enlisting the industrial nations in providing poor nations with debt relief, funding programs to eradicate unnecessary disease and hunger, redressing global warming, and relieving Russia of its misery. The effects would be both sweeping and vital in building a more prosperous and peaceful world.

But Sachs is wrong about the money. The United States is "shelling out real money" on foreign affairs—but it is being spent on military activity, not on diplomacy, institution building, or assistance. Again the contrast to the Marshall Plan and the end of World War II is instructive. At the same time, the United States demobilized and cut the military budget by 90 percent in three years, freeing up resources for a major commitment to the Marshall Plan. Ten years after the end of the cold war, the U.S. budget remains close to its average cold war level.

DOMESTIC INVESTMENT DEFICITS

The cold war ended with the United States running massive deficits, largely the result of the lethal Reagan combination of cutting taxes while doubling the military budget during peacetime from 1981 to 1984. With the collapse of the Soviet Union, there was widespread hope that reduced U.S. military spending would enable America to begin to make long-deferred domestic investments and to bring the budget into balance.

Deficit reduction took first priority, and the total discretionary budget—all of government except entitlements and interest on the debt—has been reduced both in real dollars and as a percentage of GDP since the early 1980s. But the emphasis on deficit reduction and the continued high levels of military spending have forestalled any major progress on the domestic investment deficit.

Most economists agree that public investment—spending on education and training, physical infrastructure from roads and rail lines to sewers, and nonmilitary research and development—is vital to economic growth. But over the past two decades, federal support for virtually all categories of public investment has declined. Measured as a share of total economic output (GNP), federal spending on public investment has fallen by more than a third and is slated to shrink another third over the next ten years.

Moreover, social justice is a dream deferred, even in the world's richest nation. One in five children live in poverty in the United States, the worst child poverty level of all the industrialized nations. Four million U.S. children endure hunger or food shortages on a daily basis. Clearly, food stamps do not cover all needy children. One-fourth of mothers and infants eligible for nutrition and healthcare are not covered. Head Start, the preschool program for children from low- and moderate-income families, is universally hailed as a success. Yet despite the promises of both the Bush and Clinton administrations, only one in three eligible children is enrolled in the program.[41]

The General Accounting Office estimates that one-third of U.S. schools, serving some 14 million students, are in need of substantial repair or replacement. It estimates that the cost of bringing schools up to code would total $112 billion—ironically, the same figure that President Clinton announced he would add to the $1.7 trillion military spending planned in 1998 for the next six years.[42]

Economist Dean Baker, of the Economic Policy Institute, estimates the shortfall in core public investment areas at about $66 to $95 billion a year.[43] That sum would enable the government to provide Pell grants for university education to all eligible college students (only about half of the low-income students who qualify are currently able to receive grants). It would match U.S. investment in training with the average level that the other industrialized nations spend as a percentage of their gross domestic product. It would extend Head Start to all eligible students and provide federal education aid to qualified elementary students. It would provide funds to improve U.S. roads and mass transit in conjunction with a growing economy. The investments the Environmental Protection Agency says are needed in sewage and drinking water treatment could be afforded.

Where would the money come from? If the United States devoted the same portion of its GDP to the military as the other NATO allies do (on average), it would free up about $100 billion a year to invest at home. And America would still retain, by far, an unrivaled military force. Clearly, investing $100 billion each year in education and training, research and development, infrastructure, alleviating childhood poverty, and eliminating hunger and family homelessness would produce remarkable benefits in both economic growth and social decency.

AN ACQUIESCENT PUBLIC

America is a rich country. If taxes or deficits were raised, it could afford to police the world, sustain an active foreign assistance program, and invest in vital social and economic needs at home. But no leader of either political party has made the case for doing this. Instead, U.S. leaders are forced to make choices about priorities. And thus far they have chosen to sustain a bloated military at the cost of starving both domestic infrastructure and foreign assistance and diplomacy.

Many in the national security establishment blame these skewed priorities on the provinciality and lurking isolationism of the American people. In reality, opinion research suggests almost the reverse. Most Americans are both more skeptical of global intervention and more supportive of the United Nations than are the foreign policy elites. U.S. citizens prefer multilateral over unilateral action; they are uncomfortable with the United States policing the world. Given the choice, the American people prefer aid to the poorest of the world's poor over the high levels of assistance—mainly military—that flow to Israel and Egypt.

Most Americans have confidence in the military as an institution, particularly after the victory in the Gulf War. They want the United States to have a strong military. According to a 1995 poll by the Center for the Study of Policy Attitudes at the University of Maryland, almost three-fourths of the country agrees that "because the U.S. has global interests, it is important for the U.S. to maintain a large military with the capacity to project its forces around the world."[44]

But there is no driving demand for more spending on the military. Indeed, when people are asked what spending should be devoted to, military comes near the bottom of the list. In a November 1998 bipartisan poll, voters wanted to see more government investment in education, healthcare, job training, and Social Security with a deemphasis on military spending.[45]

As Americans gain more information about federal spending—data on how much other nations spend on their militaries and details about the level of congressional pork-barrel spending—the majorities supporting cuts in defense spending will grow larger. Researcher Steven Kull of the Center for the Study of Policy Attitudes found, for example, that when told how federal spending was allocated, 80 percent of those polled favored reducing the military budget, urging cuts averaging a whopping 42 percent of current spending.[46]

The frustration for all reformers is that most Americans are not prepared to stand up strongly on these issues, deferring to the judgments made in Washington. While caring about domestic concerns, such as violence and healthcare, the public does not perceive the trade-off between military spending and domestic investment. Only dramatic events and concerted effort—such as the Americans held hostage in Iran or the collapse of the Soviet Union and the end of the cold war—are sufficient to move majorities to demand either more or less spending for foreign affairs.

Given an acquiescent public, elite opinion and the military-industrial-intellectual complex wield enormous clout. Bureaucratic inertia—reinforced by the built-in lobby of military forces, veterans, contractors, base-dependent communities, and conservative legislators—renders either reform of the Pentagon or dramatic reductions in military spending very difficult. The powerful military lobby makes it easier to increase spending in the wake of an international crisis such as the Kosovo war than to decrease it in the absence of any serious threat.

THE ELITE DEFAULT

At the end of the 1980s, with the breakup of the Soviet Union, a broad elite consensus developed for a fundamental redefinition of U.S. security, accompanied by dramatic cuts in military spending. In 1991, the Carnegie Endowment for International Peace convened a select body, including conservatives such as former Defense Secretary James Schlesinger, Reagan defense planner Richard Perle, former Joint Chiefs chair Admiral William Crowe, and others. They endorsed a document calling for a "fundamental overhaul" of the "present system," with greater emphasis on "domestic renewal." They called for further cuts in military spending to pay for domestic reinvestment in education and training, an "overhaul" of the international system of trade and finance, and a renewed "commitment to help poor nations" and to "invest in the future of the former Communist countries." In short, the Carnegie group urged the United States to lead an effort to cut global defense expenditures to half of their 1988 peak.[47]

When President Clinton became the first president elected after the cold war, he had a rare opportunity for proposing that a change in priorities is vital to our national security. Having campaigned on "the economy, stupid," he was in a perfect position to explain to the country that the nature of our true security had changed with the end of the cold war, that economic challenges pose greater concern than military threats, and that political and diplomatic arrangements require more attention than military alliances.

Clinton's central task was to make our budget priorities fit the new realities. But burdened by questions about his avoidance of the draft in Vietnam and mortified by the clamor around gays in the military, the president wanted to avoid a major debate about national security and military spending. So Defense Secretary Les Aspin's misnamed 1993 Bottom Up Review, designed to project U.S. military needs and strategy, reaffirmed the basic outlines of the military structure developed by George Bush—when the Soviet Union was still intact. The two-war strategy was ratified as well as the U.S. commitment to global policing. Overlapping roles and missions were not challenged. Baroque weapons designed for the cold war arms race went forward anyway. With the approval of Colin Powell, chair of the Joint Chiefs, a small amount was pared from the projected Bush defense budgets, but that was it. Since that time, elite opinion has shifted, and the opportunity for scaling back the military has vanished. Conservatives and the Pentagon began lobbying for more military spending. Support for further reductions eroded among the national security elite, editors, and columnists.

As a result, the current debate on global priorities is remarkably circumscribed. Secretary of State Albright and the administration have tried to make the case for greater spending on international affairs. Yet what is notable about their quest is its modesty, not its ambition; liberal establishment voices are content with pleading that international spending should be sustained at current levels. In 1997, for instance, the Brookings Institution and the Council on Foreign Relations convened another prestigious commission to report entitled "Financing America's Leadership," making the case for greater investment in diplomacy and foreign assistance. The task force called for an incremental increase of funding for international affairs of "one-tenth of one percent" of the federal budget, with spending rising from $19 to $21 billion per year.[48]

At the same time, the consensus both inside and outside the administration has resolved that military spending must go up, not down. The president has signed off on a commitment that spending on new weapons will be increased to $60 billion a year by 2002, up from $49 in FY 1999. The United States will spend more money on research, development, and purchase of new weapons each year than any other country spends on its entire military. The Republican Congress has invited the Joint Chiefs to lay out their wish list, with a growing consensus that spending must rise by $15 to $25 billion per year over the previously projected increases of the next several years. Likewise, the president has called for adding $112 billion over six years.

COMMON SENSE

The current course ought to be vulnerable to public criticism, simply because Pentagon spending levels are ridiculously high. The United States could save $100 billion a year and still maintain the strongest military in the world. Experts like former Reagan defense planner Lawrence Korb suggest the Pentagon could save $40 billion a year and still maintain its current global posture of being prepared to fight two regional conflicts at once. Moreover, the Pentagon will continue to provide reformers with scandals about weapons that do not work, finances that are mismanaged, and contractors that are ripping off taxpayers. And the Pentagon will continue to place American soldiers in obscure corners of the world, with little understanding or support among the broader U.S. public.

With currently projected budget surpluses certain to be consumed by a combination of bolstering Social Security and Medicare and cutting taxes, discretionary spending will remain under a tight lid. In a world of constraints, the large and expanding Pentagon budget should logically generate opposition. Environmentalists concerned about sustainable development, global warming, and the funding of alternative energy in poor nations find the Pentagon budget an obstacle to their ability to obtain funding. Human rights and development groups concerned with global advancement, healthcare, and conflict prevention will compete with the Pentagon for scarce funds. Domestic groups—teachers, parents, advocates of children, the poor, the cities, the disabled—will find the rising military budget a direct threat to their ability to gain investments vital to the future health of U.S. society. A president could make a compelling case to the American people for new priorities, but such leadership is unlikely. The military-industrial complex that Dwight D. Eisenhower warned against is powerful and entrenched. A bipartisan conservative congressional bloc seeks more, not less, military spending.

Thus, any move to change priorities will have to come from outside Washington. Some efforts are now under way to at least begin the debate. Groups such as Peace Action have started to put greater emphasis on Pentagon spending. Ben Cohen, the founder of Ben and Jerry's Ice Cream, has gathered hundreds of business executives into a group entitled Business Leaders for Sensible Priorities and has launched a multiyear campaign to arouse citizens to the opportunity to change priorities. Global campaigns for debt relief, disarmament, and curbing arms trafficking have begun to gain some momentum. The remarkable citizen victory culminating in a land mine treaty despite the initial opposition of virtually every national government and military shows the potential for independent action.

But as the century ends, the opportunity posed by the end of the cold war seems to be slipping away. The Clinton administration has given a bipartisan cast to an international policy inevitably skewed toward military engagement. Other priorities—at home and abroad—remain starved of funds, attention, and momentum. In 1992, the authors of the Carnegie Endowment report concluded that the end of the cold war was a "rare opportunity" and, above all, "a time to change the way we think about the world and the way we conduct our affairs at home and abroad."[49] Tragically, that challenge posed so clearly in the early 1990s has not yet been fulfilled by the decade's close.

MILITARY-INDUSTRIAL COMPLEX REVISITED: HOW WEAPONS MAKERS ARE SHAPING U.S. FOREIGN AND MILITARY POLICIES

William D. Hartung

INTRODUCTION: BACK TO THE FUTURE?

The conjunction of an immense military establishment and a huge arms industry is new in the American experience. The total influence—economic, political, and even spiritual—is felt in every city, every state house, and every office of the federal government In the councils of government, we must guard against the acquisition of unwarranted influence, whether sought or unsought, by the military-industrial complex.

> President Dwight D. Eisenhower
> Farewell Address to the Nation
> January 17, 1961

CONTRARY TO INITIAL EXPECTATIONS, the military-industrial complex did not fade away with the end of the cold war. It has simply reorganized itself.

As a result of a rash of military-industry mergers encouraged and subsidized by the Clinton administration, the "big three" weapons makers—Lockheed Martin, Boeing, and Raytheon—now receive among themselves over \$30 billion per year in Pentagon contracts. This represents more than one out of every four dollars that the Defense Department doles out for everything from rifles to rockets.[1]

If they get their way, the new military-industrial behemoths will receive billions more in the years to come. The Clinton administration's five-year budget plan for the Pentagon calls for nearly a 50 percent increase in weapons procurement, from $44 billion per year now to over $63 billion per year by 2003. (See figure 2–1.) On issue after issue—from expanding the North Atlantic Treaty Organization (NATO), to deploying the Star Wars missile defense system, to rolling back restrictions on arms sales to repressive regimes—the arms industry has launched a concerted lobbying campaign aimed at increasing military spending and arms exports. These initiatives are driven by profit and pork-barrel politics, not by an objective assessment of how best to defend the United States in the post–cold war period.

In order to achieve an effective, affordable defense, it will be necessary to rein in the power and profits of the Pentagon and the military contractors. But before looking at the recent activities of the arms lobby, it is important to reflect on just how misguided the Pentagon's current spending priorities really are.

MISSION IMPLAUSIBLE: TWO-WAR STRATEGY AND THE UNITED STATES AS "GLOBOCOP"

President Eisenhower's warning about the "acquisition of unwarranted influence" by the military-industrial complex is as relevant today as it was in 1961. Despite the dissolution of the Warsaw Pact and the breakup of the Soviet Union, the U.S. military budget is higher today than it was when Eisenhower gave that speech. At $290 billion per year, the U.S. military budget (in constant dollars) remains near the peacetime cold war average that prevailed during the prime period of U.S.-Soviet rivalry, from roughly 1950 to 1989. This is astonishing considering that Russia has slashed its weapons procurement budget by 77 percent since 1991 and that Russian forces could barely prevail over a rebel army in Chechnya (inside its own borders), much less project force against neighboring countries.[2]

Absent a robust Russian military, where is the threat that justifies spending over a quarter of a trillion dollars per year on war and preparations for war? The Pentagon's answer is simple: there is no longer one powerful superpower adversary to contend with, but U.S. forces still need to be equipped to fight two major regional conflicts simultaneously against "rogue states" like Iraq and North Korea.[3] (See essay 2–1: Military Strategy Under Review.) And getting hundreds of thousands of troops to these faraway places requires spending almost as much as the United States spent during the cold war—or so the Pentagon claims.

This "two-war" scenario is implausible in the extreme. As Michael Klare, Director of Peace and World Security Studies at Hampshire College, has masterfully demonstrated in his book, *Rogue States and Nuclear Outlaws*, Colin Powell devised the two-war strategy once he realized that the United States was "running out of enemies" large enough to justify spending hundreds of billions on the Pentagon every year. Klare also demonstrates that the two "major regional conflicts" that are the building blocks of the Pentagon's new spending scenario both involve theoretical regional adversaries that are far better armed and equipped than existing regional powers like Iraq or North Korea.[4]

Figure 2.1

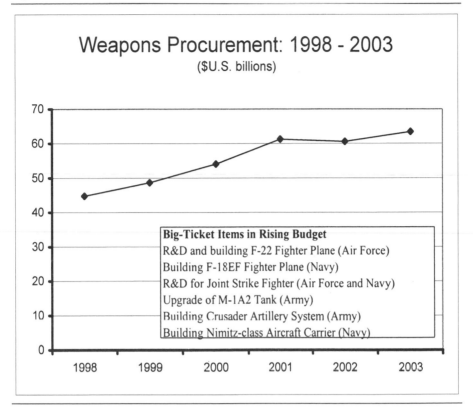

Weapons Procurement: 1998 - 2003
($U.S. billions)

Big-Ticket Items in Rising Budget
R&D and building F-22 Fighter Plane (Air Force)
Building F-18EF Fighter Plane (Navy)
R&D for Joint Strike Fighter (Air Force and Navy)
Upgrade of M-1A2 Tank (Army)
Building Crusader Artillery System (Army)
Building Nimitz-class Aircraft Carrier (Navy)

Source: Department of Defense, FY 1999 Budget Request, and William Hartung.

Klare is not alone in suggesting that the new threats to U.S. security have been greatly exaggerated. Pentagon budget analyst Franklin Spinney has bluntly asserted that "the Pentagon's two-war strategy is just a marketing device to justify a high budget." Merrill McPeak, who served as Air Force Chief of Staff during and after the 1991 Persian Gulf War, has also weighed in on this issue: "We should walk away from the two-war strategy. Neither our historical experience nor our common sense leads us to think we need to do this. We've had to fight three major regional contingencies in the past 45 years—Korea, Vietnam, and Iraq. One comes along every 15 years or so—two have never come along simultaneously."[5]

For those who question whether conflicts like Vietnam or the Gulf War were essential to U.S. security, McPeak's estimate of one major conflict every 15 years can be extended to one every 20 to 30 years. And, as we will discuss later, the U.S. military budget could be sharply reduced if our government would take concerted action to prevent conflict. A preventive strategy would be far cheaper and more effective than the current approach of marshaling huge, expensive forces to prepare for contingencies that are unlikely to occur. This point is borne out by the Spring

1999 war in Kosovo, where it has become painfully evident that the costly application of high-tech military force is the wrong tool for dealing with ethnic conflicts and civil wars. By forcing the withdrawal of human rights monitors and humanitarian organizations that had been operating in the province, the NATO bombing campaign actually made it easier for Serb forces to drive ethnic Albanians out of Kosovo at gunpoint. And by intervening in an internal conflict without seeking the consent of the United Nations Security Council, the United States and its NATO allies confronted one illegitimate use of force—ethnic cleansing in Kosovo—with another—NATO's unauthorized bombing campaign. Meanwhile, relatively inexpensive measures that might have stopped the killing in Kosovo sooner, such as a beefed-up monitoring presence by the woefully underfunded Organization for Security and Cooperation (OSCE) in Europe or a well-funded UN peacekeeping effort—were cast aside in favor of an ill-considered air war.[6]

Lawrence Korb, a top official in the Reagan Pentagon who now serves as the director of studies at the Council on Foreign Relations, has argued that even if one accepts the proposition that U.S. forces need to be ready to fight two major regional conflicts at once, there is still room to make major cuts in the current Pentagon budget. Korb notes that the United States currently spends 19 times more on its military forces than all of the Pentagon's so-called rogue states—Iran, Iraq, Sudan, Libya, Syria, Cuba, and North Korea—combined. (See figure 2–2.) Korb also asserts that the Pentagon completely discounts the military capabilities of such key U.S. regional allies as Israel and South Korea, which would reinforce U.S. military power in a major regional conflict in the Middle East or Asia. Once we take into account the relative weakness of the rogue states and the strength of our allies, Korb suggests that there is room to trim at least $40 billion from our current Pentagon budget, even if we accept the highly unlikely scenario of needing to fight two major conflicts at one time.[7] The point about the relative strength of the United States and its allies is underscored by the fact that the United States and its key allies (NATO, Japan, and South Korea) now account for 62 percent of total global military spending, up from roughly one-half in the mid-1980s.[8] In short, despite repeated calls for higher military spending to remedy the alleged "readiness crisis" facing U.S. forces, the United States and its allies currently account for a much higher share of global military spending than they did at the height of the Reagan military buildup in the mid-1980s.

By exaggerating the current threat to U.S. security, the Pentagon is carrying on a long and dishonorable tradition. In fact, in the early 1990s it was revealed that U.S. projections of Soviet military power had been wildly overstated for years as a result of misleading intelligence supplied by people like Aldrich Ames, the CIA agent who was convicted of spying for the Soviet Union. Similarly, in the 1970s, the conservative Committee on the Present Danger pressed the CIA to do a slanted "Team B" assessment of Soviet military power that helped pave the way for Ronald Reagan's unprecedented peacetime military buildup of the 1980s.[9] (See essay 2–2: The Intelligence Apparatus.)

The increasing flow of illegal drugs from Latin America (See essay 2–3: Militarization of the U.S. Drug Control Program), terrorist bombings of U.S. embassies in Kenya and Tanzania (August 1998), missile tests by Iran (July 1998) and

Figure 2.2

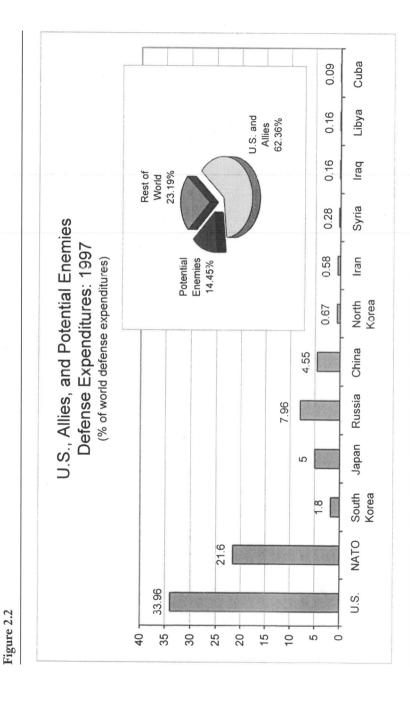

U.S., Allies, and Potential Enemies
Defense Expenditures: 1997
(% of world defense expenditures)

Source: The Military Balance, 1998/99, International Institute for Strategic Studies (London: 1155, 1998).

North Korea (August 1998), and NATO's air war in Kosovo (inaugurated on March 24, 1999) have prompted politicians and media pundits to demand that the Pentagon be given more money in order to beef up its national security policies. It is essential to offer a compelling alternative to the exaggerated threats and misguided spending priorities that military hawks are promoting in the hopes of dramatically increasing the Pentagon budget, bringing it back to the record-high, Reaganesque levels that prevailed in the mid-1980s. (See figure 2–3.)

If the current threats to U.S. interests do not justify spending $290 billion a year on the Pentagon, much less increasing the military budget, as conservatives are suggesting, what is driving these enormous expenditures? First and most obviously, the main beneficiaries of cold war military spending—including the Pentagon, the major military contractors, and key members of Congress who routinely steer military dollars to their districts—have been working overtime to keep the military gravy train running. Beyond this institutional pressure for permanently high military spending, there is also a strategic rationale—the notion that the United States should retain the capability to serve as a sort of "globocop," charging to the rescue to restore order, stability, and "free markets" when they are threatened by the forces of evil and chaos. Although it is true that in a number of key instances, such as Somalia and Rwanda, the United States has abandoned the task of policing violent conflicts due to public concern about U.S. casualties, the Pentagon's strategy and budget remain focused on retaining a capability for global force projection. And in those areas where there are critical resources or potential U.S. investments at risk—such as the Persian Gulf and the oil-and-gas-rich former Soviet Republics of Central Asia—the Pentagon is busily at work providing arms and training, arranging access to bases, and (in the case of the Persian Gulf) prepositioning troops and equipment in readiness for a possible military intervention at some future date. If we were to abandon the outdated notion that the United States needs to maintain the capability to project force to every corner of the globe and focus instead on developing better diplomatic, economic, and cultural relations with other nations, we could afford to cut tens of billions of dollars from our bloated military budget.[10]

NEW MILITARY MEGACOMPANIES: CORPORATE OR NATIONAL INTERESTS?

In the 1950s, when General Motors was the nation's top automaker and its chief executive officer, Charles Wilson, was tapped to be President Eisenhower's secretary of Defense, Wilson responded to critics who were concerned that he and his company had too much power by saying "what's good for General Motors is good for America." Today, the nation's top weapons maker is Lockheed Martin, which was created by merging Lockheed with Martin Marietta, Loral Defense, the General Dynamics combat aircraft division, and scores of other military companies to create a $35 billion behemoth that received over $18 billion in Pentagon contracts.[11] Lockheed has facilities in 447 cities and 45 states and operates in 56 nations and territories around the world. In recent years, Lockheed Martin and its

Figure 2.3 Intelligence Agencies: Estimates of Budget and Personnel 1998

The National Intelligence Community nominally consists of 13 agencies, grouped under the National Foreign Intelligence Program (NFIP) and the Joint Military Intelligence Program (JMIP). NFIP includes those agencies or subagency programs that support national policymakers (i.e. the president and other national leaders). JMIP includes those agencies or subagency programs that support defense-wide intelligence needs as opposed to the needs of an individual military service. Nearly all intelligence agencies and programs are within the Defense Department.

In addition, there are hundreds of free-standing, relatively small programs that support tactical intelligence needs (the requirements of individual combat units). These are grouped under the Tactical Intelligence and Related Activities (TIARA). Some TIARA programs are executed by other nonintelligence agencies, which is why the aggregate agency budgets do not equal the entire intelligence budget. A number of other agencies perform intelligence and counterintelligence functions; they are identified in italic in this table.

Organization	Budget ($U.S. billions)	Staff
Tactical Intelligence & Related Activities (TIARA)	over $10	a
National Foreign Intelligence Program (NFIP)		
Central Intelligence Agency	$3.1	16,000
Community Management Staff	$0.1	278
Defense Department:		
Defense Intelligence Agency[b]	$0.9	8,500
National Reconnaissance Office[c]	$6.2	1,700
National Security Agency[d]	$3.6	21,000
Army Intelligence & Security Command[b]	$1.0	13,000
Office of Naval Intelligence (ONI)	$1.2	16,000
Marine Corps Intelligence Activity	(incl. in ONI)	(incl. in ONI)
Air Intelligence Agency	$1.5	15,000
Energy—Nonproliferation & National Security	$0.04	300
Justice—Federal Bureau of Investigation	$0.5	2,500
State—Bureau of Intelligence & Research	$0.2	300
Treasury		
Office of Intelligence Support	a	a
Financial Crimes Enforcement Network	$0.02	150
Secret Service	$0.03	300
Joint Military Intelligence Program (JMIP)		
(all within Defense Department)		
National Imagery & Mapping Agency	$1.2	9,000
Defense Airborne Reconnaissance Office	$0.77	20
Defense Support Project Office	$0.99	20
Other Defense Department Agencies		
Defense Investigative Service	$0.35	3,000
Naval Criminal Investigative Service	$0.02	350
Advanced Research Projects Agency	a	a

(continues)

Figure 2.3   *(continued)*

Organization	Budget ($U.S. billions)	Staff
Other Departments		
Transportation		
Coast Guard Intell Coordination Center	$0.02	220
Justice		
Drug Enforcement Administration	$0.25	1,000
Totals	over $27.00	over 100,000

Source: Compiled by John Pike, Federation of American Scientists, July 1998. Available on the Internet at: http://www.fas.org/irp/agency/budget1.htm.
Note: With very few exceptions, the budgets of these agencies are not publicly acknowledged, and thus it is necessary to estimate, by various means, their annual budgets and personnel levels, which is no mean task. We generally believe that all our estimates are accurate with about a 5% margin of error.
[a]No estimate available.
[b]Part of General Defense Intelligence Program (GDIP).
[c]The operations of the National Reconnaissance Office (NRO) are governed by the National Reconnaissance Program (NRP).
[d]NSA is the largest component of the Consolidated Cryptologic Program (CCP), which also includes signals intelligence programs in other national agencies.

allies in the weapons industry have pushed aggressively for favorable treatment from the federal government in the form of special subsidies, lucrative contracts for big-ticket weapons systems, and wholesale changes in U.S. policies on arms sales and military technology transfers. (See figure 2–4.) Given the tremendous growth of these military conglomerates, one way to look at the development of U.S. security policy as we approach the twenty-first century is to echo the question that critics raised about General Motors in the 1950s: Is what is good for Lockheed Martin good for America?

In gauging the power and influence of our new, "improved" military-industrial complex, it is instructive to look at how the military merger boom came about in the first place. Early in the Clinton administration, Defense Secretary Les Aspin and Undersecretary of Defense William Perry decided to encourage mergers of defense firms. First, at a meeting that Lockheed Martin's Norman Augustine refers to as the "last supper," Perry bluntly told industry executives that the Pentagon would not be ordering enough ships, planes, and tanks to support the number of major military contractors that had been sustained by the Reagan military buildup of the 1980s.[12] Perry's judgment reflected two realities. First, weapons procurement budgets, while still high by historical standards, were dropping significantly from the lavish levels they had reached during the Reagan years. This meant that the Pentagon budget could no longer support the same number of major contractors in the style to which they had become accustomed in the years of the Reagan military boom. And second, the Pentagon was in the process of slowing down the production lines for current-generation systems, such as the

Figure 2.4 Subsidies to Defense Industry for Arms Sales

Annualized average for 1996 and 1997	*$U.S. millions*
Foreign Military Financing (FMF) Program: Adminstered by the Defense Department, This program provides grants to foreign countries to buy American military equipment. Since 1994, more than 24 countries have recieved FMF grants.	3,318
Excess Defense Articles: This Defense Department program gives away surplus weapons stocks or sells them at deep discounts. The cost calculation is based on the difference between the market value of the items and their eventual selling prices.	750
Economic Support Funds: Adminstered by USAID and ostensibly a fund for balance-of-payments supports, 90 percent of the program's funds go to major U.S. weapons clients Israel, Egypt, and Turkey, to help them offset the costs of arms pruchases.	2,042
Eximbank Loan Subsidies: The Commerce Department subsidizes the costs of outstanding military-related Eximbank loans.	34
Forgiven/Bad Loans: Costs incurred on defaulted military-realted loans.	1,000
Waiver of Recoupment Fees: Congress decided in 1995 to allow the Pentagon, at its discretion, to waive a 3 percent to 25 percent fee once required on weapons exports. Recoupment fees were intended to reimburse the government for development costs of the weapons sold.	200
Air Show and Expos: The Pentagon subsidizes overseas promotional events and demonstrations for potential weapons buyers.	34
Personal Cost: Currently there are 6,500 full-time federal workers enaged in promoting and financing weapons exports.	410
Total	7,788

Source: William D. Hartung, *Welfare for Weapons Dealers 1998: The Hidden Costs of NATO Expansion* (New York: World Policy Inatitute, March 1998).

F-16 fighter and the M-1 tank, to make room for next-generation systems, such as the F-22 and the Joint Strike Fighter (JSF). The official rationale behind the merger movement was that it would cut overhead by reducing the number of underutilized factories in the military industry. But, as will be discussed later, companies and their allies in Congress have fiercely resisted closing weapons production lines, preferring instead to lay off workers even as industry profits hit near-record levels and industry executives earn fat bonuses and inflated salaries.

The strategy that Perry and his Pentagon colleague, John Deutch, who went on to direct the CIA during 1995–96, chose for consolidating the weapons industry was dubbed "payoffs for layoffs" by such critics as Representative Bernie Sanders (I-VT). At the urging of then Martin Marietta CEO Norman Augustine, in the summer of 1993 Perry and Deutch signed off on a new policy under which the Pentagon would partially underwrite defense industry mergers by picking up the costs of moving equipment, dismantling factories, and providing golden parachutes for top executives. In a classic example of the "revolving door" between the defense industry and the Pentagon, Perry and Deutch had to get a conflict-of-interest waiver from Secretary Aspin before they could give the green light to the new merger subsidy policy. (Both men had worked as paid consultants for their old friend Norman Augustine at Martin Marietta just prior to joining the Clinton administration.) Augustine himself became the new CEO and received $8.2 million in bonus money as a result of the Lockheed/Martin Marietta merger, which was announced just three months after Perry and Deutch cleared the new merger subsidy policy. Augustine's lobbying for the merger subsidies, which has yielded his company over $855 million in taxpayer money, prompted one former Pentagon official to observe "when it comes to corporate welfare, you'd better look out for St. Norman Augustine."[13]

The Pentagon claims that using taxpayer money to subsidize military mergers will cut overhead and save money by, as Augustine puts it, allowing companies to run "three full factories instead of six half-full factories." In reality, as research by Harvey Sapolsky of the Massachusetts Institute of Technology has demonstrated, the Pentagon has not shut down a single major weapons production line since the end of the cold war. And even if Lockheed Martin cuts some overhead costs by closing factories and laying off workers, there is no guarantee that the same company that brought us the $600 toilet seat in the 1980s and pioneered in the arts of bribery and influence peddling in the 1970s is going to pass on its savings on overhead to U.S. taxpayers. So, while it may never provide lower weapons prices for the Pentagon, the 1990s bout of government-backed merger mania in the military industry has accomplished one thing: it has resulted in a slightly leaner, considerably meaner, and much more politically powerful corporate military sector. As John Pike of the Federation of American Scientists has noted, a company like Boeing, which since its absorption of McDonnell Douglas has over 250,000 employees, leaves a huge "political footprint" that gives the company immense clout on Capitol Hill. Similarly, after the Lockheed/Martin Marietta merger was consummated, Lockheed Martin put out a slick brochure that bragged openly about its "facilities in all 50 states."[14]

The geopolitical reach of the new defense megafirms has been reinforced by millions of dollars in campaign cash. In 1997–98 the top six U.S. military companies spent over $6 million in contributions to candidates and political parties, and Lockheed Martin was "leader of the PACs" (political action committees) among weapons contractors. In fact, from 1991 to 1997, defense companies made more political donations than that other well-known merchant of death, the tobacco lobby, by a margin of $32.3 million to $26.9 million. In addition to these hefty campaign donations, America's six biggest defense contractors spent an astonishing $51 million on lobbying in 1997 and 1998. These lobbying funds go for items like maintaining armies of lobbyists and public relations people in Washington, producing slick materials to present to Congress, and running ads touting company products in Capitol Hill publications.[15]

Last but not least, the consolidation of the weapons sectors gives arms companies greater leverage over the Pentagon, because the Department of Defense has so few options left when it comes to purchasing a major weapons system. In the spring of 1998, when the Pentagon awarded a $1.6 billion contract to do the so-called systems architecture for a National Missile Defense system (the latter-day successor to Ronald Reagan's Star Wars plan), the competition pitted Boeing against a partnership called United Missile Defense, which was a teaming arrangement composed of Lockheed Martin, TRW, and Raytheon. When Boeing won the competition, TRW and Raytheon immediately switched teams and became major subcontractors for Boeing on the project. Given the fact that three of the four major players were going to have a big payday regardless of which company won the competition, how likely is it that TRW and Raytheon officials were racking their brains for innovative approaches to the problem at hand?[16]

Similarly, in the field of combat aircraft, Boeing is a partner with Lockheed Martin on one major system (the Air Force's F-22 stealth fighter plane) and a competitor on another (the next-generation Joint Strike Fighter). These interlocking business relationships create a climate in which it often makes more sense for the defense megafirms to team up and use their unprecedented political clout to increase the Pentagon budget pie than to compete to produce cost-effective systems for existing programs. And that's just what they've been doing.

BUYING WEAPONS THAT THE PENTAGON NEVER REQUESTED

One way that firms such as Lockheed Martin and Boeing fatten their bottom lines at the expense of our long-term security is by using their connections on Capitol Hill to force the Pentagon to buy weapons that were not included in the department's original budget request. This add-on game is a bipartisan pursuit. Former House Speaker Newt Gingrich always kept an eye out for Lockheed Martin, which has a plant near his former district in Marietta, Georgia, but House Minority Leader Dick Gephardt has been just as aggressive in seeking funds for the McDonnell Douglas division of Boeing, the largest employer in his St. Louis area district. Senate Majority Leader Trent Lott was a master at steering military projects to his home state of Mississippi, but Democratic Senator Daniel Inouye of Hawaii almost matched Lott's lobbying prowess: Inouye inserted 31 projects for his home state—worth over $258 million—into the FY 1999 Pentagon budget.[17]

Spreading Pentagon contracts around to the districts of powerful legislators has been a routine practice for decades, but defense budget politics have taken a unique twist in the 1990s. Since 1994, when the Republicans took control of both Houses of Congress, Congress has added billions to the Pentagon budget every year beyond what the Department of Defense requested. This is a role reversal from the Reagan years, when liberals in Congress were always trying to shave a few billion off from the President's Pentagon budget request. According to the nonpartisan Center for Strategic and Budgetary Assessments, Congress added a total of roughly $20 billion to the Pentagon budget during fiscal years 1996 to 1998. And despite cries from the military and Pentagon budget hawks regarding the "readiness crisis" that is afflicting U.S. forces, three-quarters of this $20 billion windfall was earmarked for weapons projects that benefit major arms makers, not for maintenance, training, pay, or other items that would improve the safety and quality of life of our men and women in uniform.[18]

The add-on game is designed to increase the revenues of major contractors by extending the production runs of weapons systems that the Pentagon had hoped to terminate. The payback for legislators is twofold: not only do they get hundreds of thousands of dollars in campaign contributions from the contractors, but they also get to claim credit for high-profile, job-producing weapons projects in their districts. This self-serving process has serious costs. First, it wastes billions of dollars in taxpayer funds that could be put to more productive uses rebuilding our schools or restoring our environment. Second, it undermines our security by distorting the spending patterns within the Pentagon budget.

Take the C-130 transport plane, which is built by Lockheed Martin just outside of Gingrich's Marietta, Georgia, district. Since 1978, the U.S. Air Force has requested a total of just five C-130s, but Congress has purchased 256 of them. This ratio of 50 planes purchased for every one requested by the Pentagon may well be a record in the annals of pork-barrel politics. Senator John McCain (R-AZ) has remarked that Congress has purchased so many surplus C-130s that "we could use them to house the homeless." The C-130 has been promoted over the years by everyone from former Senate Armed Services Committee chair Sam Nunn (D-GA) to former National Guard and National Reserve subcommittee chair Sonny Montgomery (R-MS) to House Speaker Gingrich to Senate Majority Leader Lott. The added planes are generally placed with National Guard units based in the states of key members. For example, of the more than two dozen C-130s that Congress has added to the budget in recent years, more than half of them will be based at Kessler Air Force Base in Lott's home state of Mississippi.[19]

The C-130 add-on is an example of "the waste that keeps on wasting." For one thing, Congress has been buying them at such a rapid clip that since 1991, the Air Force has been forced to retire 13 perfectly usable C-130s with more than a dozen years of useful life left. Second, because Congress does not budget funds to operate the added C-130s, the Pentagon will have to come up with over $1 billion to maintain the unrequested C-130s over the next six years, funds that may have to deplete allocations for pay, or training, or other so-called readiness accounts of the sort that the Joint Chiefs of Staff have been claiming are underfunded.[20]

The C-130 is one of dozens of unnecessary items that members of Congress from key committees have been cramming into the Pentagon budget during the Clinton/Gingrich era. Even in 1998, when Congress was allegedly operating under a balanced budget agreement that was supposed to cap the military budget at roughly $270 billion, Trent Lott managed to slip in a down payment on a $1.5 billion helicopter carrier for the Marines (to be built in his hometown of Pascagoula, Mississippi) and $94 million for a spaced-based laser program that he hopes to have located in the state. The Texas delegation slipped in a few more F-16 fighters (built at Lockheed Martin's Fort Worth facility), and Connecticut will benefit from the addition to the Army's budget of no fewer than eight extra Sikorsky Black Hawk helicopters. In June 1998, Senator McCain released a list of $2.5 billion in unrequested projects that members of the Senate had added to the Pentagon's FY 1999 budget; he described the add-ons as the "worst pork" that he had witnessed in the Pentagon budget process in years. In the last-minute maneuvering between the White House and Capitol Hill on the FY 1999 federal budget, the congressional leadership added an astounding $9 billion to the Pentagon's funding, including an extra $1 billion for Star Wars research. Then, to add insult to injury, in May of 1999 Congress more than doubled President Clinton's already generous $6 billion supplemental budget request to pay for the war in Kosovo, adding billions in unrequested military funds that had nothing to do with sustaining NATO's bombing campaign and everything to do with opening up room in the budget for more military pork targeted to the states and districts of key members of Congress.[21]

SHAPING POLICY, OR HOW
TO WRITE YOUR OWN TICKET

Beyond joining with key legislators to insert specific items into the Pentagon budget, companies like Lockheed Martin are also actively engaged in the business of shaping U.S. foreign and military policies to meet their needs. This more sinister form of lobbying can involve changing the terms under which major contractors are reimbursed, such as the payoffs-for-layoffs subsidies for defense industry mergers that Norman Augustine engineered prior to the Lockheed/Martin Marietta merger; or eliminating royalty fees that foreign arms customers had been paying to reimburse the U.S. Treasury for the cost of weapons systems that were developed at taxpayer expense (a move that is costing the Treasury roughly $500 million per year); or creating billions of dollars of new grants and government-guaranteed loans to support the export of U.S. weaponry; or lifting long-standing arms control curbs, such as the ban on the sale of advanced combat aircraft to Latin America. In other instances, contractors have weighed in heavily in favor of controversial programs or policies that stand to benefit them. The most immediate examples of this kind of lobbying are the Star Wars missile defense program, which has received on average an extra $1 billion per year as a result of lobbying by Pentagon contractors and conservative research and advocacy groups, and the push for NATO expansion, which benefited from considerable time, effort, and money from Lockheed Martin, Boeing, and Textron, which see expanding NATO as a golden opportunity to open up a new, government-approved, taxpayer-subsidized market for their wares. (See essay 2–4: NATO at 50.) A few examples of specific industry lobbying campaigns will illustrate how the big three arms makers have been using their newfound political clout.

PEDDLING WEAPONS ABROAD: LIFTING THE LATIN
ARMS BAN, PROMOTING NATO EXPANSION

As the Reagan weapons-buying binge of the 1980s begins to wind down, U.S. weapons manufacturers began to focus more attention on foreign markets as a way to sustain their profit margins. Because foreign sales often involve transfers of

more "mature" technologies in which the bugs have been worked out of the production process, and because the research, development, and initial production
runs on the system have been paid for by U.S. taxpayers (in the form of Pentagon
contracts), weapons exports are often more profitable than sales of weaponry to
the Pentagon. This quest for easy profits has driven virtually all major weapons
producing companies worldwide to make a concerted effort to boost their exports.
U.S. companies have fared the best, cornering 40 percent to more than 50 percent
of the total global arms market in the 1990s. (See figure 2–5.) Given this impressive market dominance, companies like Lockheed Martin and Boeing have found
that the only way to expand their exports beyond current levels is to change U.S.
government policy. The changes they want involve either opening up new markets, by eliminating existing restrictions based on the human rights or proliferation record of potential recipient states, or seeking new government subsidies that
can be used to create more cash-paying customers (i.e., foreign clients that use
U.S.-taxpayer–supplied "cash" to buy U.S. weapons).

The industry's successful campaign to lift a 20-year-old ban on exports of advanced U.S. combat aircraft to Latin America is a prime example of how its lobbying machine operates. First the industry prevailed on Defense Secretary Perry to
advocate that the Clinton administration lift the ban and send U.S. Air Force F-
16s to do demonstration flights at the March 1996 air show in Santiago, Chile.
Prior to the show, the Pentagon had also arranged for some Brazilian generals to
do test flights in F-16 planes deployed with the Puerto Rican National Guard.
Then aerospace lobbyists generated letters to then Secretary of State Warren
Christopher from 38 senators and 78 members of the House of Representatives

Figure 2.5

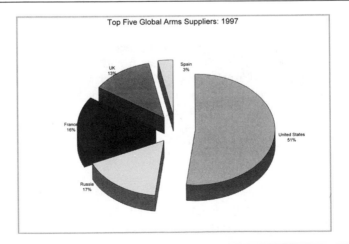

Source: SIPRI Arms Transfer Project, "The 30 Leading Suppliers of Major Conventional Weapons,"
updated July 17, 1998. Available on the Internet at: http://www.sipri.se/projects/armstrade/atsup93-
97.html.

urging him to support the lifting of the ban. *Time* magazine reporter Douglas Waller described the lobbying letters as the "more million-dollar letters," because the members of the House and Senate who signed onto the appeal to Christopher received a total of more than $1 million in PAC contributions from major weapons-exporting companies. The industry representatives followed up by holding White House meetings with presidential counselor and confidant Mack McLarty and an aide to Vice President Al Gore.[22]

According to an account by Merrill Goozner of the *Chicago Tribune*, a Lockheed Martin brochure touting the Latin arms market as "a $3 to $15 billion opportunity over the next 10 years" was even slipped under the hotel door of former Costa Rican president and Nobel Peace Prize winner Oscar Arias during one of his business trips. Dr. Arias has been working with the Carter Center, the Council for a Livable World, and a coalition of DC-based public interest groups to promote a moratorium on new sales of advanced weaponry to Latin America as a first step toward promoting regional discussions on conflict prevention and force reductions. But so far, the power and money of the arms lobby has sidetracked this commonsense proposal, which would do far more for the future security and stability of Latin America than would hawking expensive military hardware.[23]

On the issue of NATO expansion, the role of U.S. contractors was not to change administration policy but rather to reinforce a questionable policy decision. The Clinton administration decided to expand NATO for a variety of reasons, such as consolidating free market democratic reforms in East and Central Europe and recruiting new allies to help keep the peace in Bosnia and other hot spots. But given the obvious downsides of expanding the alliance—such as alienating Russia, stalling further efforts at U.S.-Russian nuclear arms reductions, and initiating an open-ended, costly commitment to rearm the new member states—the Clinton administration needed allies to help it sell the NATO expansion concept to Congress and the public. By far the most important players in the pro-NATO expansion lobby were organizations of Polish, Hungarian, and Czech Americans along with major arms manufacturers including Lockheed Martin and Textron, who took an aggressive stance in support of this costly new commitment.

Corporate lobbying for NATO expansion took several forms. Most important, Lockheed Martin lent out one of its vice presidents, Bruce Jackson, to serve as president of the U.S. Committee to Expand NATO, a lobbying and public education group housed at the offices of the conservative American Enterprise Institute. The committee sponsored ad campaigns, congressional briefings, speeches, articles, and white papers promoting the "widest possible" expansion of NATO. Jackson claims that his role at the Committee to Expand NATO is a "hobby," but the nature of his work suggests otherwise. For example, in the summer of 1997, when the U.S. Committee sponsored a dinner at which 12 U.S. senators were briefed on NATO expansion by Secretary of State Albright, Jackson invited Lockheed Martin board member Bernard Schwartz, who, coincidentally, was the largest individual donor of soft money to the Democratic Party during the 1995–96 election cycle. Schwartz's presence was a clear signal to the senators present that supporting NATO expansion would be a good way to garner support for their campaign coffers. To reinforce that message, a few weeks after the NATO dinner Schwartz sent a $50,000 check to the Democratic Senatorial Campaign Committee.

Other pro-NATO expansion activities pursued by U.S. weapons firms included financial contributions by Lockheed Martin, Textron, and McDonnell Douglas to proexpansion ethnic organizations like the American Friends of the Czech Republic and several Romanian foundations promoting that nation's candidacy for NATO membership; political funding to help pass the public referendum on NATO expansion that was held in Hungary in 1997; and all manner of wheeling and dealing in East and Central Europe in order to convince the top leadership in Poland, Hungary, the Czech Republic, Romania, and other NATO "wannabe" nations that buying U.S. weapons would be the best way to curry favor with the U.S. government and win its support for their NATO candidacies. It is important to note that many people in East and Central Europe, including democratic leaders such as Vaclav Havel of the Czech Republic and Lech Walesa of Poland, were supportive of NATO expansion based on long-standing fears of Russia, which made them a receptive audience for the NATO expansion proposal.

When the Senate finally voted on NATO expansion in early 1998, it passed by a vote of 81 to 19. But due to public concerns about the costs of future NATO expansion—by one estimate the total cost of multiple rounds of expansion could reach as much as $500 billion over 12 to 15 years, or at least $2,500 for every American household—the next round of NATO entrants may not be invited to join until 2001, not 1999 as originally planned. This delay offers critics of NATO expansion an important political opening to marshal the forces that will be needed to hold back the arms lobby and the executive branch from going further down the dangerous and costly path of expanding a cold war alliance that has no clear purpose in the post–cold war world.[24]

By the time that NATO held its fiftieth anniversary celebrations in Washington in April of 1999, the costs of expanding the alliance had been outpaced by the price tag for the air war against Yugoslavia, which has been costing roughly $1 billion per month. Restocking the U.S. and allied arsenal with Raytheon Tomahawk cruise missiles, Boeing Joint Direct Attack Munitions (JDAM), and Lockheed Martin F-16 and F-22 fighter planes will provide billions in new contracts for the big three weapons makers; and if the public does not demand that the president and the Congress pursue a preventive strategy in the wake of the Kosovo fiasco, these billions in replacement contracts may be just the down payment on a massive feeding frenzy for the military industrial complex. The weapons manufacturers are mindful of the "benefits" of the Kosovo conflict; in fact, Lockheed Martin vice president Bruce Jackson took to the pages of the Capitol Hill newspaper *Roll Call* to urge Congress to amply fund the war effort. Meanwhile, back at the arms bazaar, Boeing, Raytheon, and United Technologies plunked down $250,000 each to serve on the official "Host Committee" for the April 1999 NATO fiftieth anniversary meetings in Washington, as a way to get the inside track on meeting the NATO foreign policy bureaucrats and defense ministers who will be making the decisions on whether to stock up on U.S. military hardware in the years to come.[25]

PUSHING WEAPONS AT HOME:
THE STAR WARS LOBBY

One of the most amazing lobbying stories of recent times involves the work done by the Pentagon, contractors such as Lockheed Martin and Boeing, and right-wing think tanks such as the Heritage Foundation and the Center for Security Policy (founded by former Reagan Pentagon official Frank Gaffney) to keep Reagan's Star Wars program alive—despite radical changes in the world security environment, which have rendered its original mission obsolete, and a string of uninterrupted technical failures. Fifteen years and $55 billion have gone down the drain since Reagan first gave his Star Wars speech in March 1983, and the Soviet Union, whose nuclear missiles were supposed to be the main target of Reagan's cherished missile defense system, no longer exists. Undaunted, the Star Warriors have devised a new mission for missile defenses: to protect us against attacks by "rogue states" like Iraq and North Korea, which do not even have missiles that can reach American territory. And even when a major component of Star Wars fails—such as Lockheed Martin's troubled Theater High Altitude Area Defense system (THAAD), which two foreign in tests conducted during this decade—the Star Wars lobby in Congress shouts for more money.[26]

The nerve center of the Star Wars lobby is Gaffney's Center for Security Policy (CSP), a think tank and advocacy organization that puts out roughly 200 press releases per year (under the more authoritative name of "national security decision briefs") touting missile defenses, increases in the military budget, and other stock right-wing themes. Since its inception in 1988, Gaffney's group has received over $2 million in corporate donations, mostly from companies such as Lockheed Martin and Boeing, which are major Star Wars contractors. Gaffney's CSP also has no fewer than five Lockheed Martin executives on its board, not to mention vintage Star Warriors such as weapons physicist Edward Teller and his protégé, George Keyworth, who served as Reagan's science advisor when the Star Wars scheme was first being hatched. The CSP also has close links to other conservative think tanks like the Heritage Foundation and Empower America, both of which have representatives on the CSP board. During the fall of 1998, the Star Wars lobby made a concerted effort to win over one more senator to Mississippi Senator Thad Cochran's Defend America Act, which would require deployment of a National Missile Defense system. Toward that end, Empower America ran misleading radio ads in the State of Nevada in an effort to convince residents that the reluctance of their two Democratic senators, Harry Reid and Richard Bryan, to vote for a largely useless and massively expensive missile defense system meant that they were against "defending our families" from nuclear attack. In the short term, these prodigious efforts on the part of the Star Wars lobby were in vain. Due in part to a public backlash against the tactics used by special prosecutor Kenneth Starr and the Republican congressional leadership in the Monica Lewinsky scandal, the Republicans failed to pick up a seat in the Senate in the 1998 elections, and Democratic incumbents such as Harry Reid and Barbara Boxer of California, who had been specifically criticized for opposing Star Wars, were reelected.

Despite these apparent setbacks in the 1998 elections, the Star Wars lobby did not give up; by the spring of 1999, both the Senate and the House had been persuaded to pass legislation modeled on the Cochran bill which stated that it is the policy of the U.S. government to deploy a National Missile Defense as soon as it is "technologically feasible." While arms control advocates such as Senator Carl Levin (D-MI) tried to soften the blow by sponsoring amendments calling for the United States to continue to pursue nuclear weapons reductions with Russia, the passage of the two Star Wars resolutions were clearly a major propaganda victory for conservative missile defense boosters and their corporate sponsors.[27] (See essay 2–5: Living (Still) with Nuclear Dangers.)

FIGHTING BACK:
PROMOTING A PREVENTIVE STRATEGY

The best way to fight back against the arms lobby's new push for increases in military spending and arms export subsidies is by promoting an alternative strategy for preventing conflicts and limiting the violence level at which they are waged. To do so means uniting behind concrete, commonsense demands.

Stopping the Spread of Deadly Weaponry

The International Campaign to Ban Land Mines, whose key organizer, Jodie Williams, won the 1997 Nobel Peace Prize, is a prime example of what non-governmental organizations can do to shape the international security agenda in a positive direction. When the campaign was launched less than a decade ago, few people had even heard of the land mine problems. But after a few years of persistent campaigning and public education by veterans groups, organizations of handicapped individuals, human rights advocates, doctors, relief organizations, and arms control groups, more than 100 governments were persuaded to support the Oslo agreement to eliminate antipersonnel land mines. (By the spring of 1999, 81 nations had already ratified the accord, enough to make it an official treaty.) The campaign was given a huge boost by the work of Senator Patrick Leahy (D-VT), who prevailed upon his colleagues in the Senate to impose a moratorium on U.S. exports of antipersonnel land mines. The land mines campaign succeeded because it was able to drive home the immense human consequences of these senseless and indiscriminate weapons. The millions of innocent civilians who have been killed and wounded by land mines finally found their voice in the land mines campaign, which was largely championed by citizen organizations, with important assistance from key governments such as Canada and Norway.

The same organizations that have put the land mines issue squarely on the international agenda are now zeroing in on so-called small arms or light weapons—the rifles, hand grenades, and light vehicles that are the stock-in-trade of the world's ethnic killing fields. Because small arms are standard issue with most armed forces of the world, and because the issue intersects with the controversial issue of domestic gun control, the small arms fight will no doubt be longer and more complex than the land mines campaign. But to the extent that progress can be made in limiting the access of combatants to their weapons of choice, the cause of peace and disarmament will be advanced exponentially. At a May 1999 peace conference in the Hague, the global campaign to curb small arms was officially launched under the umbrella of the International Action Network on Small Arms (IANSA).[28]

A second strand of work against the arms trade is the global campaign for a Code of Conduct on arms sales. The Code of Conduct, which is embodied in legislation sponsored by Representative Cynthia McKinney (D-GA) and Representative Dana Rohrabacher (D-CA), calls for sharp restrictions on arms sales to human rights abusers, undemocratic governments, and nations involved in aggression against their neighbors. In the United States, the bill passed the House of Representatives in the summer of 1997 and has been championed in the Senate by Senator John Kerry (D-MA). In the meantime, the European Union (EU) has passed its own Code of Conduct, which, although lacking the specifics some arms control advocates were seeking, nonetheless represents a first step toward making human rights a priority in the arms sales decisions of EU members. Last but not least, Oscar Arias has created a Nobel Laureates Commission (including other peace prize winners such as Elie Wiesel, Betty Williams, José Ramos Horta, and the Dalai Lama) that is pressing for an international Code of Conduct on arms sales modeled on the McKinney/Rohrabacher bill.[29]

Abolish Nuclear Weapons

Building on the work of the Canberra Commission—a panel of former government officials and top military personnel that included General Lee Butler, the former head of the U.S. Strategic Air Command—the movement to abolish nuclear weapons has gained new momentum in recent years. Galvanized by Jonathan Schell's latest book, *The Gift of Time: The Case for Abolishing Nuclear Weapons*, the Abolition 2000 campaign has rallied around the goal of eliminating nuclear weapons as soon as is practically possible.

In the United States, the campaign is supporting legislation to eliminate funding for so-called subcritical nuclear weapons testing—a $40 billion, ten-year program that would allow the U.S. government to violate the spirit of the Comprehensive Test Ban treaty by designing new weapons by computer—and is encouraging a sense of Congress resolution that would press the executive branch to move toward abolition of U.S. nuclear forces. The value of the nuclear abolition movement lies not only in progress toward eliminating existing arsenals of mass destruction but also in providing the best hope of establishing a higher international norm to mitigate against the development of future nuclear weapons and be persuasive to new nuclear powers such as India and Pakistan, countries that have long pointed to the hypocrisy of the U.S. government's "Do as I say, not as I do" approach to the development and possession of nuclear weapons.[30]

Cut the Military Budget

Nearly a decade after the fall of the Berlin Wall, the U.S. military budget is still $276 billion, which equals the peacetime cold war average. This excessive spending causes two kinds of problems: first, it depletes scarce funds that could be used for more worthwhile purposes such as education, healthcare, transportation, and other job-creating activities with far more economic payoff than building weapons. Second, when the most powerful nation in the world continues to put the majority of its surplus resources into outmoded weapons instead of preventive diplomacy, peacekeeping, or other more constructive approaches, it sends the wrong signal by implying that force is still the ultimate arbiter of international disputes.

Efforts to reduce the military budget are now gathering force on two fronts. In the United States, an organization called Business Leaders for Sensible Priorities has brought together 500 business executives to work on a multiyear publicity campaign designed to achieve a $40 billion reduction in the Pentagon budget by the year 2001, with the resulting funds to be invested in more pressing domestic needs. On a global scale, Oscar Arias has been working with organizations such as the Washington-based Center for International Policy and the New York-based Council on Economic Priorities to promote reductions in military spending worldwide. This effort is linked to a series of UN-supported security talks aimed at reducing arms and increasing mutual cooperation and confidence among potential rivals in regions of tension.

And a new proposal has emerged from the Institute for Defense and Disarmament Studies, the World Order Models Project, and the Union of Concerned Scientists under the ambitious title "Global Action to Prevent War." The proposal outlines a series of four treaties that would be phased in over a 40- to 50-year period with the goal of eliminating nuclear weapons, radically reducing conventional arms production and sales, and establishing a global mechanism for cooperative peacekeeping and conflict prevention designed to render war obsolete. Ambitious as it may be, the unique strength of the Global Action to Prevent War proposal is that it provides a long-term vision for peace and security that can compete for public attention with the dire worst-case scenarios that the Pentagon and the weapons contractors have been using to drive up weapons spending and fuel arms races for the past five decades. Until the international community learns how to plan for peace rather than prepare for war, the arms makers and military hawks will always have the upper hand in debates about how to use our common resources.[31]

All of these campaigns—to limit the arms trade, to abolish nuclear weapons, and to reduce global military spending—are examples of conflict prevention in practice. If they can be linked to new ways of solving security dilemmas—both through international law, as embodied in a World Court and an International Criminal Court that should have the support of all of the world's major powers and through international cooperation, utilizing better-funded, more democratically structured arrangements for international and regional peacekeeping—then the era of stockpiling weapons to "solve" security problems may be brought to an end. The sooner all this happens, the better.

NOTES

1. William D. Hartung, "Military Monopoly," *The Nation*, January 13/20, 1997.
2. U.S. budget figures are from Elizabeth Hecter and Steven Kosiak, "Conference Report on the FY2000 Appropriations Bill," Center for Strategic and Budgetary As-

sessments, October 18, 1999, and the Office of the Undersecretary of Defense (Comptroller), *National Defense Budget Estimates for FY 1998* (Washington, DC: U.S. Department of Defense, March 1997). Estimates on Russian military spending in the post–cold war period vary considerably, but the figures on massive cuts in weapons procurement have been widely cited. As the conservative International Institute for Strategic Studies has noted in its most recent analysis: "The major threat to the Russian armed forces in 1997 was not military, but financial. A dire lack of funding was compounded by delays and genuine difficulties in implementing urgently needed structural reforms." See International Institute for Strategic Studies, *The Military Balance 1997–98* (London: IISS, 1997), p. 101.

3. William S. Cohen, Secretary of Defense, *Report of the Quadrennial Defense Review* (Washington, DC: U.S. Department of Defense, May 1997).

4. Michael T. Klare, *Rogue States and Nuclear Outlaws: America's Search for a New Foreign Policy* (New York: Farrar, Straus, and Giroux, 1995).

5. The quotes from Franklin Spinney and Merrill McPeak are from Mark Thompson, "Why the Pentagon Gets a Free Ride," *Time*, June 5, 1995.

6. On the prospects for cutting military spending dramatically under a more cooperative, preventive approach to security, see Janne E. Nolan, ed., *Global Engagement: Cooperation and Security in the 21st Century* (Washington, DC: The Brookings Institution, 1994). On the costs of the war in Kosovo and the benefits of preventive approaches, see William D. Hartung, "Beyond Kosovo: Preventive Diplomacy," *The Nation*, May 10, 1999.

7. Lawrence J. Korb, "Our Overstuffed Armed Forces," *Foreign Affairs*, November/December 1995, pp. 22–34.

8. Statistics on the share of global military spending accounted for by the United States and its allies are calculated by the author based on data contained in annual reports of the U.S. Arms Control and Disarmament Agency, *World Military Expenditures and Arms Transfers*, Department of State, Washington, DC, from the editions covering 1987 and 1998.

9. On the "Team B" report, see Anne Hessing Cahn, *Killing Detente: The Right Attacks the CIA* (University Park, PA: Pennsylvania State University, 1998).

10. On increased U.S. troop presence in the Persian Gulf since the 1991 war with Iraq, see Caryle Murphy, "Engulfed in a War That Won't End," *Washington Post*, July 30, 1995; on U.S. efforts to increase capabilities for projecting force into Central Asia, see David Brindley, "Asia's Big Oil Rush: Count Us In, GIs Arrive in Longest Airborne Mission Ever," *U.S. News and World Report*, September 29, 1997, which describes a U.S. military exercise that involved parachuting the 82nd Airborne Division and the chief of the U.S. Atlantic Command into Kazakhstan as a way to show the flag.

11. Figures are from Lockheed Martin's annual report for 1996. For further background on the Lockheed Martin merger, see William D. Hartung, "St. Augustine's Rules: Norman Augustine and the Future of the American Defense Industry," *World Policy Journal*, Summer 1996, pp. 65–73.

12. Norman R. Augustine, "Reshaping an Industry: Lockheed Martin's Survival Story," *Harvard Business Review*, May-June 1997, pp. 83–94.

13. The quote is from Hartung, "St. Augustine's Rules"; for the full story on the "payoffs for layoffs" phenomenon, see the excellent series of articles by Patrick J. Sloyan in *Newsday*, including "Sweet Deal from Pentagon: Top Brass OK $60 Million Break to Ex-Employer, Martin Marietta," June 30, 1994; "Layoff Payoff: Pentagon Pays $31 Million to Bosses for Merger that Wipes Out Jobs," March 17, 1995; and "Big Blunders, Then Big Bonus: Defense Firms Rewarded After $2.3 Billion in Disasters," November 1, 1995. For statistics on the relative fate of production workers and

executives in the military industry as a result of the merger boom, see Charles M. Sennott, "CEO Salaries Rise as Jobs Are Lost," *Boston Globe*, February 11, 1996, p. B-12.

14. See Hartung, "Military Monopoly" and "St. Augustine's Rules"; and Lockheed Martin, "Investor's Fact Sheet," Spring 1996.

15. On campaign spending and lobbying by defense contractors, see Katharine Q. Seelye, "Arms Contractors Spend to Promote an Expanded NATO," *New York Times*, March 30, 1998; and William D. Hartung, *Peddling Arms, Peddling Influence: Exposing the Arms Export Lobby* (New York: World Policy Institute, October 1996), and *Peddling Arms, Peddling Influence Update* (New York: World Policy Institute, April 1997).

16. On Star Wars contractors and the Star Wars lobby, see William D. Hartung, "Reagan Redux: The Enduring Myth of Star Wars," *World Policy Journal*, Fall 1998, pp. 17–24.

17. On add-ons, see Business Leaders for Sensible Priorities, "Midnight Pork: It's What's for Dinner," fact sheet, September 1998; John Isaacs, Council for a Livable World, "Items of Interest in the Omnibus Appropriations Bill," memorandum, October 22, 1998; Taxpayers for Common Sense, "$50 Million for Mississippi Pork," *The Waste Basket*, Vol. 3, No. 25, August 3, 1998; Charles R. Babcock, "Congress Fattens Defense Bill with $4 Billion in Pork," *Washington Post*, August 15, 1998; and Pat Towell, "No Chance for a Nonfat Bill as Special Projects Flourish," *Congressional Quarterly Weekly Report*, August 22, 1998, p. 2292.

18. Data on add-ons provided by Steven Kosiak, Center for Strategic and Budgetary Assessments, based on analysis of the relevant appropriations and authorization bills in the House and Senate during the FY 1996 to 1998 time frame.

19. Walter Pincus, "Cargo Plane with Strings Attached: Congress Funds and Stations C-130s Unwanted by Pentagon," *Washington Post*, July 23, 1998.

20. Ibid.

21. Statement of Senator John McCain for FY 1999 National Defense Authorization Bill S. 2057, (available at http://www.senate.gov/~McCain/def99.htm) and John Isaacs, "Items of Interest"; on the Kosovo supplemental, see Council for a Livable World, "Kosovo Supplemental Appropriations Bill: Republicans Load Up the Bill for a War Most Oppose; Layaways for Pork in Fiscal 2000," press advisory, April 30, 1999 (available at http://www.clw.org/ef/kosovo_advisory.html); and Tim Weiner, "Bill on Emergency Spending Hits $15 Billion at the Finish," *New York Times*, May 14, 1999.

22. On lobbying to lift the ban on fighter sales to Latin America, see Hartung, "Peddling Arms, Peddling Influence Update"; Douglas Waller, "How Washington Works: Arms Deals—The Inside Story of How the Pentagon and Big Defense Contractors Got the President to Open the Way for Weapons Sales to Latin America," *Time*, April 14, 1997; and Thomas Cardamone, Council for a Livable World, "Arms Sales to Latin America," *Foreign Policy In Focus*, Vol. 2, No. 53 (Washington, DC and Albuquerque, NM: Institute for Policy Studies and Interhemispheric Resource Center, December 1997).

23. On the moratorium proposal, see Cardamone, "Arms Sales," note 22; on Lockheed Martin's lobbying of Oscar Arias, see Merrill Goozner, "Nobelists Press for Weapon Sales Curbs," *Chicago Tribune*, May 29, 1997.

24. For a full run-down on corporate lobbying for NATO expansion, see "Desperately Seeking Subsidies: Arms Industry Lobbying," in William D. Hartung, *Welfare for Weapons Dealers 1998: The Hidden Costs of NATO Expansion* (New York: World Policy Institute, 1998), pp. 223–30; or two magazine pieces summarizing this material: William D. Hartung, "NATO Boondoggle," *Progressive*, May 1998, pp. 22–24; or William D. Hartung, "Pentagon Welfare: The Corporate Campaign for NATO Expansion," *Multinational Monitor*, March 1998, pp. 9–13.

25. For more on the costs of the Kosovo conflict and the potential benefits to weapons contractors, see William D. Hartung, "The Costs of NATO Expansion Revisited: From the Costs of Modernization to the Costs of War," *World Policy Institute* issue brief, April 21, 1999 (available on the Internet at: http://www.worldpolicy.org/arms/april99.html). On the role of arms manufacturers in hosting the NATO fiftieth anniversary summit, see Sam Loewenberg, "Stocking Up for the Next War," *Legal Times*, April 5, 1999.

26. On technical glitches and cost overruns in the Star Wars program, see Hartung, "Reagan Redux: The Enduring Myth of Star Wars"; Stephen I. Schwartz, ed., *Atomic Audit: The Costs and Consequences of U.S. Foreign Policy Since 1940* (Washington, DC: Brookings Institution), pp. 269–70 and 290–98; and William D. Hartung, "Spacey Missile Defense," *The Nation*, July 27/August 3, 1998.

27. On the passage of Cochran-style, pro–Star Wars bills in the House and Senate, see Craig Cernello, "Senate, House Approve Bills Calling for NMD Deployment," *Arms Control Today*, March 1999; and Elizabeth Becker, "House Approves Star Wars Defense Program," *New York Times*, May 21, 1999.

28. For an introduction to the small arms issue, see Jeffrey Boutwell, Michael T. Klare, and Laura W. Reed, eds., *Lethal Commerce: The Global Trade in Small Arms and Light Weapons* (Cambridge, MA: AAAS, 1995); Michael Renner, *Small Arms, Big Impact: The Next Challenge of Disarmament* (Washington, DC: Worldwatch Institute, October 1997); and British American Security Information Council, *Campaigns and Projects on Light Weapons*, BASIC Report 98.3 (Washington, DC: BASIC, April 1998). BASIC also coordinates an international network of researchers, activists, and government officials concerned with the light weapons problem. For more details, consult the BASIC website on the Internet: http://www.basicint.org. There are now dozens of groups now working on the small arms issue, so this short listing is by no means complete.

29. For an overview of efforts to limit arms sales, see David Isenberg, "Controlling U.S. Arms Sales," *Foreign Policy In Focus*, Vol. 1, No. 4 (Washington, DC and Albuquerque, NM: Institute for Policy Studies and Interhemispheric Resource Center, November 1996).

30. On nuclear abolition, see Jonathan Schell, *The Gift of Time: The Case for Abolishing Nuclear Weapons* (New York: Henry Holt, 1998); and Joseph Rotblat, ed., *Nuclear Weapons: The Road to Zero* (Boulder, CO: Westview Press, 1998). The Abolition 2000 campaign to eliminate nuclear arsenals is in the process of launching a U.S. campaign that will be up and running in 1999; for background on that effort, see Alistair Millar, "The Urgency of Our Mission," *Inforum*, Winter 1998, No. 23, p. 3 (available from Fourth Freedom Forum, 803 N. Main St., Goshen, IN 46528).

31. See Randall Forsberg, Jonathan Dean, and Saul Mendlovitz, "Global Action to Prevent War: A Program for Government and Grassroots Efforts to Stop War, Genocide, and Other Forms of Deadly Conflict," published jointly by the Union of Concerned Scientists, the Institute for Defense and Disarmament Studies, and the World Order Models Project, May 15, 1998.

MILITARY STRATEGY UNDER REVIEW

Carl Conetta and Charles Knight

IN MAY 1997, DEFENSE SECRETARY WILLIAM COHEN submitted to Congress the Quadrennial Defense Review (QDR)—the Pentagon's third attempt to outline a post–cold war military strategy. The QDR surveys America's defense needs through the year 2015, provides a strategic justification for defense programs, and sets out guidance for regional military policy. Outstanding among its prescriptions is an expanded role for the military in U.S. foreign policy and a distinct elevation of national military objectives.

While the cold war strategy sought parity with the Soviet Union as key to deterrence, the new strategy sees permanent global military superiority as necessary to maintaining U.S. world leadership. The QDR proposes that the U.S. armed forces be developed and used to do three things: respond to crises, shape the strategic environment in ways favorable to U.S. interests, and prepare now for possible future threats. This means less emphasis on existing threats and more on future, hypothetical ones. The QDR warns of unnamed future "peer" competitors and the proliferation of revolutionary new weapons and military techniques.

"Environment shaping" prescribes a more active peacetime use of military power, discouraging other nations from even trying to compete militarily with the United States. Key to achieving this novel "preemptory" deterrence is the maintenance of a robust U.S. regional presence, a daunting degree of U.S. military superiority, and a technological edge that no prospective competitor could hope to diminish.

The new military strategy carries forward key elements of its predecessor, the 1993 Bottom Up Review (BUR), including a need for the ability to fight and win two major regional wars at once. However, the QDR postulates that this requirement is a generic one, not tied to what military planners had viewed as the most probable theaters of hostility, the Persian Gulf and northeast Asia. As the QDR puts it, a generalized two-war capability is "the sine qua non of a superpower."

There are a number of problems with the QDR, which ties U.S. leadership to permanent global military superiority. As CIA director George Tenet observed in 1998 Senate testimony, military threats to vital U.S. interests are declining; instead today's challenges include global economic instability, communal violence, and the dislocations associated with weakened and collapsing state. The QDR's new strategy puts too much emphasis on large-scale wars that are increasingly unlikely or speculative.

The result is a "new era" military very much like the old and almost as large. Shortchanged, however, are the actual operations that the military is undertaking today—primarily peace operations, as in Bosnia. A greater focus on these would produce a military different from the one the QDR envisions. It would have more light units and military police in its active component, for instance. Failing to give peace operations their due results in the paradox of a 1.4 million-person military that has trouble keeping 40,000 troops deployed in such operations.

Further, the QDR's reliance on military power to stem the emergence of new threats impinges on one of the State Department's principal functions. The 1998 National Defense Panel (NDP), which Congress commissioned to critique the QDR's strategy, strongly argued that the foremost tools for enhancing regional stability should be diplomacy and development assistance, not forward-deployed military units. In treating leadership as synonymous with military superiority, the new strategy will bolster the legitimacy of military power as a routine policy instrument. This stance is likely to inspire imitation among friends and foes alike and contribute to a process of gradual global remilitarization and repolarization.

Finally, the QDR favors multinational arrangements in which the United States predominates. As the war in Kosovo demonstrates, this means a preference for exclusive military clubs, such as the North American Treaty Organization (NATO), rather than inclusive institutions, such as the Organization for Security and Cooperation in Europe (OSCE). The OSCE not only emphasizes nonmilitary solutions but also includes Russia as a full member—and as a potential counterweight to U.S. influence.

A U.S. military strategy that is suited to today's challenges and opportunities would put greater emphasis on nonmilitary security instruments and invest more in building inclusive multilateral security institutions. This requires a reallocation of resources and responsibility among the different agencies and instruments of U.S. security policy. Traditional military power and the Pentagon should play a smaller role than during the cold war. Plans to conduct two major counteroffensives in an overlapping timeframe should be abandoned.

Today, the U.S. international affairs budget—which covers all forms of diplomatic activity, foreign assistance, arms control, and participation in international organization—is less than 7 percent as large as the Pentagon budget. This ratio has not changed significantly since the cold war, but it should. Development assistance is often the most effective tool for enhancing long-term regional stability. Despite its great expense, the 1947 Marshall Plan paid high dividends as a security and stability-building measure. Compared to 40 years of post–World War II defense spending, it came cheaply.

The cold war's end has offered a singular opportunity to extend security cooperation across lines of political division and to make progress in demilitarizing international relations. U.S. policy should fully exploit this opening in three ways: first, by investing in inclusive security organizations, such as the United Nations and the OSCE; second, by encouraging the reduction of national arsenals and tightening the limits on arms transfers; and third, by progressively restricting the role of armed forces in foreign policy.

America's stance should be one of progressive multilateralism: rely on multilateral instruments where they exist and are effective; where they do not exist, build them. "Stability assistance" together with support for regional security cooperation and demilitarization form the heart of an appropriate "environment-shaping" strategy for the new era. The country's best hope lies in a diversified security and military strategy—one that works hard to change the rules of the game and that appreciates the real source of America's long-term strategic flexibility: its economy, its political culture, and its people.

THE INTELLIGENCE APPARATUS

Kit Gage

IN 1947, CONGRESS PASSED THE NATIONAL SECURITY ACT that created the Central Intelligence Agency (CIA) to coordinate factual, unbiased intelligence gathering and to produce analysis essential to foreign policy decisions. Although the act did not expressly authorize covert operations, Section 102(d)(5) stated that the CIA would "perform such other functions and duties related to intelligence affecting the national security as the National Security Council may from time to time direct."

The U.S. national security elite seized on this vague clause to justify the CIA's notoriously interventionist activities. Covert operations, an almost irresistible option for a U.S. president, quickly evolved into a major foreign policy instrument. Covert actions are, almost by definition, illegal and often run counter to laws, treaties, and stated U.S. foreign policy objectives. CIA covert operations have ranged from fomenting political opposition to manipulating elections, from orchestrating coups to assassinating heads of state.

Agency officials under false "cover" (diplomatic, business, missionary, academic, etc.) covertly employ and supervise foreign "assets," "agents," "operatives" and "contract employees." The CIA pays informants to report on government corruption, criminal activity, and internal dissent. Often, however, the informants are directly involved in these activities and either withhold information or simply expose the competition. Because CIA officials abroad operate under cover and it is a crime to reveal their identity, all Americans working abroad are put at risk. Despite protests by all leading journalist organizations, the CIA continues to employ journalist cover "in exceptional circumstances."

Since 1974, when several CIA scandals became publicized, the president has had to sign off on covert projects. After a presidential finding, congressional intelligence committees are informed of the action "in a timely manner," generally in advance of the action. Both Presidents Bush and Clinton, for instance, signed findings directing the CIA to create conditions to overthrow Iraqi President Saddam Hussein, and Congress appropriated funds.

Congress has created a dozen other intelligence programs. Individual intelligence budgets are secret and must be estimated, although the total aggregate amount—currently around $27 billion annually—has recently been released. Despite the collapse of the Soviet Union, the overall U.S. intelligence budget has nearly doubled since 1980. After a brief downturn, it is again climbing as spies try to carve out new fields monitoring and countering "rogue" states, terrorists, drug trafficking, and economic espionage. The current budget is $10 billion higher than all other U.S. foreign relations programs (diplomacy, aid, and information) combined, and spies reportedly outnumber diplomats in some U.S. embassies.

These spy agencies collect intelligence data via electronic and satellite surveillance. Such activities have major privacy, foreign policy, and other consequences not well debated in public. In recent years, the Federal Bureau of Investigation (FBI), with virtually no public or congressional oversight and often in competition with the CIA, has expanded its mission overseas, including its covert operations.

While the House and Senate Intelligence committees approve budgets and activities of the spy agencies, committees are sworn to secrecy in almost all matters. Committee staff are routinely vetted by the intelligence agencies. Only rarely, such as in the historic Church and Pike Committee hearings in the mid-1970s and in the 1987 Iran contra hearings does the public get a peek behind this curtain of secrecy. In the wake of the newspaper exposé linking the CIA to the crack cocaine epidemic in the United States, the CIA inspector general admitted in a March 1998 House hearing that between 1982 and 1995, the Agency had had legal permission from the Justice Department to employ agents and assets who were drug traffickers and money launderers. Despite this shocking revelation, no congressional committee followed up with public hearings.

The CIA often arms and trains assets in methods of torture and assassination, in clear violation of U.S. and international laws. Sometimes these assets use these "skills" against the United States. For example, Osama bin Laden, the Muslim fundamentalist financier who was named by the CIA as the mastermind of the August 1998 bombings of the two U.S. embassies in East Africa, was trained in the 1980s in CIA-run guerrilla camps in Afghanistan.

While the stated foreign policy goal of the United States is to promote political and economic freedom, the CIA has instigated bloody coups in Iran, Guatemala, Indonesia, and Chile; paramilitary operations in Cuba, Indochina, Afghanistan, Angola, and Central America; and destabilization campaigns against governments in Guyana, Australia, Grenada, Jamaica, and Greece. Much of central Africa's current slide into regional war is rooted in the CIA-assisted 1960 assassination of popular Congolese leader Patrice Lumumba and in the decades of U.S. support for Mobutu Sese Seko, Zaire's devastatingly corrupt and brutal dictator.

Even the most benign function of intelligence agencies—information collection—is frequently flawed. As late as 1989, the CIA failed to forecast the Soviet Union's collapse, and in 1979, the Agency did not predict the overthrow of the Shah of Iran, nor the seizure by militant students of the U.S. embassy and 66 U.S. diplomats in Tehran. The CIA has also knowingly relayed false or tainted information to policymakers on a grand scale. In the late 1980s, exaggerated CIA estimates of Soviet military strength led the U.S. government to authorize millions of dollars for unneeded weapons systems.

Executive and congressional reforms border on the ludicrous. An executive order permits spying within the United States as long as it is not "intended to influence United States political processes, public opinion, policies or media." The spy agencies can give intelligence "assistance to coup attempts against political leaders who are then assassinated as long as assassination is not the stated goal of the coup."

Not surprisingly, CIA efforts to police itself have been a dismal failure. In 1992, CIA spy Aldrich Ames was arrested as a Soviet double agent. Ames had, he admitted, sold the CIA's "crown jewels" by betraying more than 100 U.S. intelligence operations. This led to the execution of at least ten of the CIA's most important penetration agents in the Soviet Union. Yet then-CIA director James Woolsey issued only the mildest slap on the wrist—11 letters of reprimand—to CIA officials responsible for Ames.

The CIA—often described as a "shadow government"—and other parts of the intelligence apparatus urgently need public and congressional scrutiny and major overhaul. Reforms should include:

1. A ban of covert operations as incompatible with constitutional democracy
2. Use of diplomats to gather intelligence openly and use of public source information for analysis, except in rare instances
3. Release of budget details and general program information
4. Drastic cutbacks in budgets and staff and clear designation of narrowly defined functions to correspond with the real post–cold war needs of the United States
5. Genuine congressional oversight of intelligence activities
6. Release of all historical files.

In today's world, the United States needs to pursue diplomatic and multilateral solutions and to seek to resolve disputes through international laws and institutions.

MILITARIZATION OF THE U.S. DRUG CONTROL PROGRAM

Peter Zirnite

AT A TIME WHEN FLEDGLING CIVILIAN GOVERNMENTS IN LATIN AMERICA are struggling to keep security forces in check, the United States has enlisted the region's militaries as its pivotal partners in international drug control. This militarization, which begins at the U.S.-Mexico border, is undermining recent trends toward greater democratization and respect for human rights while doing little to stanch the flow of drugs into the United States.

Washington's militarization of its antidrug efforts is the product of a U.S. drug control strategy that historically has emphasized reducing the supply of illegal narcotics rather than addressing the demand for drugs. In 1971, three years after the first declared "war on drugs," President Richard Nixon took a crucial step toward militarization by proclaiming drug trafficking a national security threat. "Protecting the national security" has remained the rallying cry for providing more money and firepower to wage the war on drugs. Since the 1970s, U.S. spending on the drug war has risen from less than $1 billion to more than $16 billion annually.

In the early 1980s, President Ronald Reagan raised the curtain on a rapid expansion of U.S. antidrug efforts, justifying the expansion, in part, by developing the narco-guerrilla theory by positing ties between the Colombian cartels and Cuba, leftist guerrillas in Colombia, and the Sandinistas in Nicaragua. The purported guerrilla-drug link has been used to legitimize the Pentagon's gradual shift in Latin America from the cold war against communism to the drug war against communist-linked guerrillas.

The National Defense Authorization Act of 1989 designated the Pentagon as the "single lead agency" for the detection and monitoring of illicit drug shipments into the United States. Soon after, President George Bush announced his Andean Initiative, to stop the cocaine trade at its source. This opened the door to a dramatic expansion of this role and to a significant infusion of U.S. assistance to police and military forces in the region.

U.S. policymakers view local militaries as the most capable and reliable allies in the war on drugs. Although counternarcotics operations are a law enforcement function reserved in most democracies for civilian police, the United States prefers to use military forces. When Washington does recruit police, it provides them with heavy arms and with training in combat tactics that are inappropriate to the role that police should pay in a civilian society.

The militarization of counternarcotics efforts in Latin America not only undermines efforts to promote human rights and democracy, it also threatens regional security. In Colombia, where the line between fighting drug trafficking and combating insurgents is blurred, Washington risks becoming mired in the hemisphere's longest-running guerrilla war, possibly widening that conflict into neighboring countries. In Mexico, U.S. helicopters supplied for antidrug work were used to ferry troops to quell the rebellion in Chiapas. Such dangers are likely to be heightened regionwide by a disturbing trend—an increasing amount of U.S. aid is being provided under Pentagon programs that are exempt from civilian oversight and human rights legislation.

During the Clinton administration, the vast majority of the Pentagon's international drug spending has still gone to detection and monitoring operations in the Caribbean and

Gulf of Mexico transit zones. In late 1993, President Clinton shifted the emphasis of military operations, at least in terms of energy, if not spending, from interdicting cocaine as it moved through the transit zones into the United States to dismantling the so-called air bridge that connects coca growers and coca paste manufacturers in Peru and Bolivia with Colombian refiners and distributors. As a result, drug traffickers quickly abandoned air routes in favor of the region's labyrinth of waterways.

Today, the bulk of Washington's international antinarcotics spending goes to Latin America and the Caribbean, where thousands of U.S. troops are deployed annually in support of the drug war, operating ground-based radar, flying monitoring aircraft, providing operation and intelligence support, and training host-nation security forces.

Ironically, the decision to engage armed forces as its principal allies in the drug war has meant that the Pentagon is now providing counternarcotics assistance to militaries implicated in both human rights violations and drug-related corruption, including those in Colombia, Peru, Guatemala, and Mexico.

Despite this militarization and the massive funding for Washington's drug war, illegal drugs still flood the United States. In fact, illegal drugs are more readily available now, at a higher purity and lower cost, than they were when the drug war was launched.

That militarization of antidrug efforts continues apace underscores a critical point: the Clinton administration lacks a broad, clearly defined strategy for strengthening civilian governments and reducing the role of the armed forces in the region. Given the problems and risks associated with Washington's militarization of its antinarcotics programs in Latin America, the U.S. government should cease financial and political support for Latin American military involvement in drug control operations. But Washington lawmakers, fearful of being labeled "soft" on drugs, are moving in the wrong direction.

It is time that Washington recognize that its war on drugs has been a failure, at home and abroad. An alternative approach requires redefining drugs and drug policy in terms of public health rather than national security. Such a redefinition would focus on the domestic roots of the problem—consumer demand. Reducing demand for drugs requires greater attention to treatment, education, and prevention—all more cost effective, the research suggests, than law enforcement. A domestic-based strategy does not require abandoning all international efforts. The United States should put greater controls on money laundering, precursor chemicals, and firearms as well as on development alternatives for the poor at both ends of the drug network—in the growing regions of Latin America as well as in the inner cities and border regions of the United States.

NATO AT 50

Tomás Valásek

THE NORTH ATLANTIC TREATY ORGANIZATION (NATO), composed of 17 European nations, the United States, and Canada, is the world's most powerful military alliance. Created under U.S. leadership in 1949, NATO served during the cold war as a defensive alliance to protect the West against Soviet aggression.

In April 1999, when NATO celebrated its fiftieth anniversary at a gala gathering in Washington, the alliance was embroiled in the Kosovo conflict, its first-ever military engagement. This military campaign served to transform NATO into an offensive police force with authority extending beyond its geographic borders and within sovereign nations.

NATO's move into uncharted security waters raised questions reaching well beyond the immediate conflict. It circumvented the United Nations, sidelined more inclusive European security organizations, antagonized Russia and China, short-circuited diplomatic efforts, and stalled nuclear disarmament agreements. It clearly signaled, however, NATO's willingness to interfere in affairs of sovereign states in defense of Western values.

Kosovo represented the latest change in NATO's decade-old transformation effort. The 1989 collapse of the Soviet Union and demise of the Warsaw Pact invalidated NATO's original mandate and, for a time, prompted a search for a new approach to European security. However, before completion of a comprehensive review of the need for NATO, the alliance was thrust into a peacekeeping role in the Balkan wars. When the activities of the United Nations and the European Union failed to prevent escalation of the violence in Bosnia, NATO was called on to deliver punitive strikes against the Bosnian Serb aggressor forces. NATO troops entered the country in December 1995 to safeguard implementation of the Dayton peace agreement. In June 1998, NATO countries extended the mandate of the Stabilization Force (SFOR) in Bosnia indefinitely.

In July 1997, primarily at U.S. urging, NATO decided to invite three former Warsaw Pact countries—Hungary, Poland, and the Czech Republic—to join. Nine other former communist countries are lined up, seeking membership. Estimated costs of NATO expansion range widely, from $1.5 billion to over $500 billion, depending on the number of new members, time frame, and level of military upgrades. Historically, the United States has provided the largest share of funds, troops, and weapons for NATO's activities, and the U.S. portion of expansion costs could reach one-third to one-half of the total amount spent. In addition, the United States deploys approximately 100,000 troops on European soil, and there are no plans to bring them home. All of these factors will play a significant role in assessing the true cost of NATO expansion to the United States. One big winner is, as Bill Hartung outlines in Chapter 2, the weapons industry manufacturers.

NATO's expansion activities, coupled with its peacekeeping duties in the Balkans, have become the alliance's raison d'être. But they have also damaged America's relations with Russia and have contributed to the radicalization of the Russian political scene. NATO's attempts at damage control—such as the signing of the NATO-Russia Founding Act, a largely unimplemented document on cooperation—have failed to weaken Moscow's opposition. In 1999, NATO air strikes against Serbian targets intensified Russian distrust and anger, prompting the Yeltsin government to threaten nuclear retaliation while simultaneously attempting to broker a peace agreement. When the NATO bombing was halted, Russia unilaterally moved a small military unit into the Pristina airport, creating a temporary impasse with NATO. Almost simultaneously, the Russian armed forces began large-scale military maneuvers, described by the *Moscow Times* as "a sign that Russia remains deeply suspicious of NATO."

Another thorny issue is NATO's authority to act without UN approval. NATO's 1949 founding treaty, among other documents, obligates the allied nations to act only in accordance with the principles and procedures of the United Nations. In practice, however, the Security Council failed to act swiftly and effectively during the Bosnia and Kosovo crises. Before launching air strikes against Serbian targets, the NATO nations, citing a probable Russian veto, did not even try to obtain an explicit Security Council authorization. And Clinton administration officials have argued that NATO should be allowed to operate even when formal authorization from the UN Security Council cannot be obtained.

But the Kosovo conflict has raised serious concern about NATO's future. Will the alliance intervene against non-NATO sovereign states in the future and, if so, under what circumstances? In Kosovo, NATO was ostensibly defending values enshrined in the UN Declaration of Human Rights. Its military action, however, violated the rights of a sovereign country and endangered relations with Russia and China, both of which have serious internal problems and worry that Kosovo may be used to justify interventions into their territories.

Although a revitalized NATO is likely to remain the dominant security organization in Europe, there is a need to clarify the alliance's relations with the Organization for Security and Cooperation in Europe (OSCE), the United Nations, and other security bodies and to divide responsibilities among these institutions. NATO countries have the manpower, but the allied troops are not trained in prevention and monitoring duties. In contrast, the OSCE specializes in conflict monitoring and prevention, arms reduction, and postconflict reconciliation—all areas outside NATO's current expertise.

Any new arrangement needs to give European nations an opportunity to assume responsibility over security on their continent. Tensions over NATO's Kosovo operation helped lead to the European Union's decision to adopt responsibility for security issues and lessen its dependence on the U.S. military. A stronger European role in Europe's military affairs would enable the United States both to reduce its military presence and to decrease its expenditures on military operations in Europe. In the future, European-led operations also promise to relieve some of Russia's concerns with the dominant role of the United States in an expanded NATO. Through these possibilities for reform, a win-win situation may yet be achievable.

LIVING (STILL) WITH NUCLEAR DANGERS

Lisa Ledwidge

THE NUCLEAR ARMS RACE BETWEEN THE UNITED STATES and the Soviet Union during the cold war led to the manufacture of well over 100,000 nuclear weapons, involved over 2,000 nuclear weapons tests, and released large quantities of radioactive and other hazardous materials into the earth's air, soil, and water.

Currently, the United States possesses about 12,000 nuclear weapons, Russia, 22,000. The other declared nuclear weapons states—Britain, China, and France—now possess a combined total of approximately 1,300 nuclear weapons. Additional countries suspected or known to possess or to have deployed nuclear weapons include India, Israel, Pakistan, and possibly North Korea.

With the collapse of the Soviet Union in 1991, a rare window of opportunity emerged to reverse course and eliminate nuclear weapons. There has been modest progress toward this goal, including implementation of the U.S.-Russian Strategic Arms Reduction Treaty (START I) and negotiation and signature of both the START II agreement and a global Comprehensive Test Ban Treaty. But the momentum on these and other nuclear risk-reduction measures has ground to a halt, leaving the potential for nuclear catastrophes from accidents, proliferation, and terrorism.

ACCIDENTAL NUCLEAR LAUNCH

Currently, more than 5,000 U.S. and Russian nuclear weapons are set on hair-trigger alert, meaning that each president has less than 15 minutes after detecting a possible attack to decide whether to order a counterstrike. This quick-decision posture increases the risk that a nuclear weapon could be launched in response to a false alarm or malfunction. The risk is exacerbated by Russia's aging command and control system (the communication links in its nuclear chain of command), Y2K and other potential communications problems, and political tensions between the United States and Russia over, for instance, expansion of the North American Treaty Organization (NATO) and the bombings of Yugoslavia.

The risk of war by miscalculation was dramatically illustrated when, on January 25, 1995, President Boris Yeltsin came within minutes of ordering a nuclear counterstrike against the United States, because Russian radar operators mistook a research rocket launched from the coast of Norway for a U.S. ballistic missile.

NUCLEAR PROLIFERATION

"Horizontal" proliferation to countries such as Iran, Iraq, and North Korea has been the main focus of U.S.-led nonproliferation efforts. However, these efforts have been undermined by "vertical" proliferation among the five official nuclear powers. This nuclear double standard was highlighted in May 1998, when sanctions were imposed on India and Pakistan for conducting nuclear tests, while the five nuclear powers continued to modernize their own nuclear arsenals.

Vertical proliferation is exemplified in the United States by the "Stockpile Stewardship and Management" program, which involves laboratory testing and computer simulations of nuclear weapons explosions for the purpose of maintaining both the existing U.S. nuclear arsenal and the infrastructure for designing and producing new nuclear weapons. The five major nuclear weapons states, as well as India, all have such "virtual" research and development nuclear weapons programs.

Stockpile Stewardship and similar programs, which serve to maintain America's nuclear arsenal, appear to violate the 1968 Nuclear Nonproliferation Treaty (NPT), to which each declared nuclear weapons state is a party. In 1996, the International Court of Justice at The Hague agreed in spirit. In a unanimous advisory opinion, the court reaffirmed Article VI of the NPT, which stipulates that "each of the parties to the Treaty undertakes to pursue negotiations in good faith on effective measures relating to cessation of the nuclear arms race at an early date and to nuclear disarmament."

NUCLEAR TERRORISM

Although military production of nuclear materials has slowed, the global stockpile of commercial plutonium—which can also be used to make nuclear weapons—is growing rapidly. Technologies such as reprocessing nuclear fuel and using plutonium fuel in civilian reactors are expanding the global stockpile and circulation of bomb materials and increasing the possibilities that they will be stolen or diverted. The widespread use of commercial nuclear power also complicates efforts to stem the spread of nuclear weapons-usable material.

Russia's economic crisis heightens the risk of nuclear materials being sold on the black market. From 1992 through 1994, there were at least eight reported seizures of weapons-usable material originating from the former Soviet Union.

To reduce the most imminent dangers posed by nuclear weapons, the U.S. government should take the following steps:

1. Institute unilateral measures to remove all nuclear missiles from hair-trigger alert. De-alerting could be done, for instance, by shutting off power to missiles, removing warheads from delivery systems, or other measures that build in more time for verification of communications data. And de-alerting has precedent. In 1991, President George Bush unilaterally de-alerted hundreds of U.S. nuclear missiles and bombers; a week later Russian president Mikhail Gorbachev followed suit.
2. Withdraw the 150 U.S. nuclear weapons stationed in various NATO countries near Russia. No other country has nuclear weapons stationed beyond its borders. Their withdrawal would help set the stage for resuming U.S.-Russian cooperation on a broad range of issues and would help allay Russian concerns about NATO's expanding role in Europe.
3. End nuclear weapons research and development, which has the potential to contribute to the development of new nuclear weapons. Halt laboratory testing and computer simulations of nuclear weapons explosions, stop the production of plutonium pits, and scrap plans for the production of tritium for weapons.
4. Halt activities that could increase the volume and circulation of weapons-usable nuclear materials. For instance, work with other countries to end reprocessing and reactor-based plutonium programs; put all weapons-usable nuclear materials into non–weapons-usable forms, placing them in secure, accountable, and verifiable storage under international control; and phase out nuclear power.

Although these are essential steps, the only real solution to the dangers posed by nuclear weapons is their total and permanent elimination. The United States, as the world's sole superpower, must take the lead. The political will required for the United States to initiate the elimination of nuclear weapons is not likely to emerge from Washington but rather from individuals, groups, and communities pressuring for abolition.

CHAPTER 3

U.S. LEADERSHIP IN THE GLOBAL ECONOMY

John Cavanagh

WHO IS RIGHT?

IN A DECEMBER 1998 *WALL STREET JOURNAL*/NBC NEWS survey, 58 percent of Americans polled indicated that "foreign trade has been bad for the U.S. economy."[1] (See figure 3–1.) Similar U.S. public opinion surveys in recent years register growing public apprehension over the current course of corporate-led economic globalization. Yet expanding trade and overseas investment has been the Clinton administration's central strategy both for job growth and for addressing a rapidly changing global economy. This fundamental divide between U.S. government policy and U.S. public opinion represents a monumental challenge for the crafters of U.S. foreign policy at the onset of a new century.

Especially over the past two decades, U.S. policy toward the global economy has been guided by a rigid free trade formula. The administrations of Reagan, Bush, and Clinton have pursued policies at home and abroad based on the premise that free markets will bring prosperity and democracy. Accordingly, in countries such as China and Nigeria, U.S. policy has focused more on liberalizing markets than on improving human rights or enhancing democracy.

The Clinton administration has been dogged in its pursuit of new free market institutions and rules precisely at a moment when evidence is growing that such measures bring enormous gains to a highly visible minority but hurt the majority of people and the environment in both the United States and the rest of the world. Though the damages are currently greater in other countries than in the United States, as the U.S. trade deficit soars, manufacturing jobs are being purged, social

Figure 3.1 U.S. Public Rejects Trade

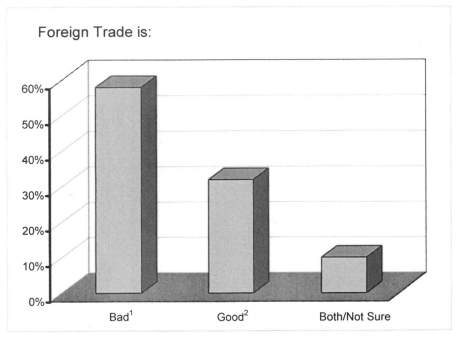

Foreign Trade is:

U.S. Public Rejects Trade

Source: Wall Street Journal/NBC News poll published in the *Wall Street Journal*, December 10, 1998.
[1]Bad for U.S. economy because cheap imports hurt wages and jobs.
[2]Good for U.S. economy because it creates foreign demand, U.S. economic growth, and jobs.

services are cut, and quality of life is declining for many.[2] Likewise, the global financial crisis that has brewed since mid-1997 has deepened U.S. public distrust of globalization policies.

The public rejection of free trade should not mask the discord among the dissenters around what should replace it. Conservative nationalists and small entrepreneurs favor protectionism. A growing alliance of labor, environmentalist, farm, and consumer activists prefer what they often call "fair" or "responsible" trade. Similarly, a rising number of North and South religious groups and development organizations call for fundamental debt reduction and a better deal for poor countries. These various groups unite in opposition to the dominant model of economic globalization but splinter in what they endorse.

Regardless of these differences, if the majority of the public is correct in its skepticism about the global economy, then the time is ripe for the U.S. government to change its global outlook. The United States would do well to adopt a "new internationalist" approach to the global economy, taking leadership in reshaping the rules of the world market to maximize the number of winners and to ensure that the global economy serves workers, communities, and the environment both at home and abroad. At the same time, U.S. policy toward the world market should "protect" standards and regulations designed to improve the quality of life at home while advancing food security, energy conservation, and other sustainability goals. This implies that certain aspects of the global economy should be halted (e.g., trade in hazardous products, arms to dictators, and goods like water that are part of the "global commons") or curtailed (e.g., "hot money"). The new internationalism, then, aims to maintain and improve the quality of life in the United States while ensuring that the foreign projection of U.S. economic and political power also advances sustainable and equitable development abroad.

This approach diverts strongly from the options that the conventional globalization debate poses. Most corporate-led globalization proponents argue that the only alternative to globalization is destructive protectionism. Growing numbers of people are challenging this narrow range of choices. Unrestrained globalization and protectionism are by no means the only options. The twenty-first century requires new paths that encourage exchanges of goods, capital, and people that enhance the social and environmental common good and that discourage or stop those exchanges that undermine healthy communities, a clean environment, and dignified work. Fortunately, these new paths are being paved by thousands of organizations all around the world.

THE CURRENT POLICY

Whenever the occasion arises, President Clinton and like-minded proponents of free trade in the think tank, business, and academic communities recite a now-familiar litany: Thanks to several hundred market-opening trade agreements—including the rule-transforming North American Free Trade Agreement (NAFTA) and World Trade Organization (WTO)—U.S. exports have grown at breathtaking speed, as have U.S. jobs in export industries. And, while the rest of the world has been shaken by financial crisis, the U.S. economy in the waning years of the twentieth century has remained the global bright spot of growth and stability.

Media magnate Mortimer Zuckerman trumpeted America's success in a 1998 *Foreign Affairs* essay: "The American economy is in the eighth year of sustained growth which transcends the 'German miracle' and the 'Japanese miracle' of earlier decades. Everything that should be up is up—Gross Domestic Product (GDP), capital spending, incomes, the stock market, employment, exports, consumer and business confidence. Everything that should be down is down—unemployment, inflation, interest rates."[3] As fascinating and revealing as what Zuckerman includes in his measurements is what he omits: economic inequality and falling job security and benefits, weaker consumer protection, environmental decay.

The Clinton policies represent a smooth continuation of those of his Republican predecessors and build on the efforts of all post–World War II presidents to reduce trade barriers around the world. With the emergence of the governments of Ronald Reagan, Margaret Thatcher, and Helmut Kohl in the early 1980s, there was a growing consensus in rich-country governments and business circles that free trade, free investment, deregulation, and privatization were the best route to growth. At that time, most developing countries still favored a stronger state role in development, fearing that unfettered markets in a world of unequal nations would put them at a disadvantage.

Yet by the late 1970s, many developing countries lost substantial leverage over their economic destiny as rapidly rising external debts to Western banks came due at a moment of historically high interest rates and oil prices. Washington, working with Japan, Germany, the United Kingdom, and other rich governments, pressed developing countries into the free market paradigm as a condition for new loans and to ensure continuing payment of previous debts. The International Monetary Fund (IMF) was given the role of global policeman to enforce the free market policies, and the World Bank imposed similar reforms through its new policy-oriented "structural adjustment" loans. By the end of the 1990s, most developing countries outside the East Asian "tigers" had been obligated to liberalize trade and investment policies (although some, such as Brazil, India, Saudi Arabia, and Iran, resisted in parts of their economies). In 1989, John Williamson, then of the pro–free trade Institute of International Economics, dubbed this move toward liberalization, deregulation, and privatization as "the Washington Consensus," and he elaborated ten sets of policies around which he saw elite agreement.[4]

In the 1990s, the Clinton administration triggered an acceleration of corporate-led globalization in all three major arenas of global economic policymaking. (See essay 3–1: Corporate Welfare and Foreign Policy.) In trade, the administration completed Republican projects with the passage of NAFTA in 1993 and the WTO in 1994. In investment, a flurry of negotiations was launched for a Multilateral Agreement on Investment (MAI) and for regional agreements along the NAFTA model. And in finance, the multilateral agencies, in tandem with the U.S. Treasury Department, pressed for financial liberalization in South Korea, Thailand, the Philippines, Mexico, Brazil, Russia, and elsewhere.

The acceleration of corporate-led globalization in the 1990s stems from a disproportionate (and growing) concentration of political power and influence in the hands of global corporations. Utilizing their trade associations, pressure groups, and thousands of well-paid lobbyists, corporations have been able to shape U.S. policy so they are the prime beneficiaries. On a global scale, U.S. firms in the 1990s tended to benefit more from the new rules than firms of other countries due to U.S. corporate dominance of so many sectors, from cigarettes to high technology to biotechnology. Some of the wealth amassed by globalization has trickled down to U.S. citizens through the steady growth of the economy, especially to the mounting number of Americans who have some investment in the stock market.

One of the most disturbing outcomes of this march toward ever greater global corporate mobility is that the power balance between corporations and workers has markedly shifted in favor of corporations. University of Massachusetts economist Arthur MacEwan explains:

> The deregulation of the international economy has meant a much greater freedom for capital movement but not a much greater freedom for labor movement.

Since "freedom" means having alternatives, and having alternatives means having power, a system that enhances the freedom of capital relative to the freedom of labor means giving capital more power relative to labor. The fact, for example, that NAFTA allows firms to move essentially at will among the countries of North America, but provides no such option for labor, nor for the organizations of labor (unions), means that it is an agreement that enhances the power of capital relative to labor.[5]

WINNERS AND LOSERS
UNDER THE CURRENT POLICY

Three leading think tanks, Brookings Institution, Progressive Policy Institute, and Twentieth Century Fund, began a 1998 book entitled *Globaphobia* as follows: "It is one of the paradoxes of the modern age. America has been leading the world to encourage more integration of national economies. Yet just as we appear to be succeeding, increasing numbers of Americans appear to be expressing growing doubts or worries about this process of 'globalization.'"[6] The goal of that book as well as many other pro–free trade works in recent years was "to demonstrate that the fear of globalization—or 'globaphobia'—rests on very weak foundations."[7]

Accordingly, the central question that should guide U.S. policy toward the global economy is: Do the majority of people in the United States and abroad benefit or lose from the deregulated market approach to globalization?

The position of most globalization supporters is that consumers everywhere gain from the liberalization of trade and investment, and that most workers gain as well. Yet in the battles over NAFTA and the WTO, growing numbers of groups have challenged these assertions from two quite diverse quarters. The nationalist right—led by Pat Buchanan in the United States and his counterparts elsewhere and supported by small business—argues that most small entrepreneurs and workers are hurt by globalization, and that sovereignty and culture are undermined. These forces have kindled populist passions with the argument that protectionism leads to prosperity. By the late 1990s, roughly 60 to 70 Republican members of Congress belonged to this camp.

A second group—comprising unions, environmentalists, small farmers, and citizen leaders such as Jesse Jackson and Ralph Nader—argues that free trade undermines workers, the environment, farmers, and sovereignty and thus deepens inequality. In the United States, this view is shared by most Democratic members of Congress, led by David Bonior (Michigan) and Richard Gephardt (Missouri), with their call for "fair trade." Portions of this left coalition did, at times, intersperse their internationalist posture with more nationalist arguments about the safety of imported foods and the dangers of Mexican truck drivers on U.S. roads.

Both sets of critics have amassed strong evidence that the policies of the elite consensus have benefited a small number of highly mobile corporations and hurt most equality, the environment, workers and consumers:

- *Equality:* United Nations studies show that, with a handful of exceptions, growing *inequality* has accompanied trade and investment liberalization over the past 15 years in most countries. Likewise, researchers at the Institute for Policy Studies have noted a growing divide between the wealth of the world's billionaires and the world's poorest since the early 1990s. In the most recent year for which data are available, the combined wealth of the world's 447 billionaires is greater than the income of the poorest half of the world's people.[8] Growing inequality, globalization opponents argue, is a direct outgrowth of the rising disparity in power between corporations and workers. The growing imbalance is a result of the ability of globalized corporations to threaten and shift operations to a location with lower wages or standards. This mobility allows corporate managers to bargain down wages and working conditions, thus exacerbating income inequality.

*   *Environment:* Many developing countries, from Chile and Brazil to the Philippines and Indonesia, have been endowed with abundant natural resources. In these and many other countries, the elite consensus emphasis on leading "development" with exports has translated into some combination of tearing down forests, overfishing, rapid depletion of minerals, and poisoning of land by agrochemicals. The long-term costs of this brand of growth are not factored into the various measures of success, yet the next generations in these countries will spend much of their energy coping with erosion, depleted fishing banks, and increasingly unproductive soil. This is not to suggest that these countries were pursuing environmentally sustainable policies before the pressure for increased trade and investment liberalization. But liberalization has accelerated the plunder of resources in many countries.

In the United States, corporations can increasingly use the threat of moving production elsewhere to water down U.S. environmental regulations. For example, an official of Boise Cascade, a timber giant that had already moved some of its mills from the United States to Mexico, boldly stated in the congressional debate over logging rights that "The number of timber sales granted by the government will determine our decision to move south."[9] This kind of intimidation helped the logging industry pressure Congress into passing a law in 1995 to allow increased logging and to suspend environmental protections in national forests.

Northern environmentalists also express concern about the rising power of the World Trade Organization, which gives nations the power to challenge perceived barriers to trade and investment, including health, safety, and environmental laws. (See essay 3–2: The World Trade Organization.) Since the United States and other Northern nations have relatively strong environmental regulations, the WTO represents a largely negative forum where other nations challenge those laws as unfair trade practices. Among the more controversial of the 125-plus WTO rulings thus far are the following two examples. The first WTO ruling involved a challenge by the Venezuelan and Brazilian governments on behalf of their oil industries against the United States. They charged that an Environmental Protection Agency (EPA) regulation governing the cleanliness of gasoline discriminated against oil imports into the United States. The WTO ruled against the United States and, in 1996, the Clinton administration agreed to abide by the ruling rather than face trade sanctions.

In another controversial ruling, in 1998, the WTO ordered the United States to lift a ban on shrimp imports from nations that do not adequately protect sea turtles. In the United States, the shrimp industry is required to use devices on its nets to prevent drownings of endangered sea turtles. Thailand, Malaysia, India, and Pakistan had complained that the U.S. ban unfairly discriminated against their shrimp industry.

- *Workers:* Factories have sprung up in southern China, Indonesia, Brazil, Malaysia, and dozens of other countries. Indeed, an average of more than one factory each day has been opening along Mexico's 2,000-mile border with the United States since the advent of NAFTA in 1994. Yet workers in most of the third world's new global factories are denied basic rights to organize and strike. And in the United States, companies use the threat of moving production to China or Mexico to bargain down wages and benefits.

What about the quantity of jobs? Globally, there is a severe crisis of unemployment and underemployment; in its *World Employment Report 1998–99*, the International Labor Organization estimated that 25 to 30 percent of the world's workers were underemployed and about 140 million workers were fully unemployed. In the United States, despite low overall unemployment, liberalized trade also claims victims. Free trade advocates often boast about jobs created by U.S. exports while ignoring the jobs lost to increased imports. But if consumers switch from a U.S.-made product to one made elsewhere, this does result in lost U.S. jobs and, often, to poorer-quality jobs in the United States. This trend has become a major concern as the U.S. trade deficit has grown for six consecutive years. Moreover, though U.S. jobs in export industries tend to pay better than the average U.S. job, so do industries that face intense import competition, where jobs are currently being lost. This is because both import and export jobs are concentrated in manufacturing, while more U.S. jobs overall are in the lower-paying service sector. When the Washington-based Economic Policy Institute compared U.S. industries where exports and imports were growing most rapidly, it found that wages were higher in the import-competing industries than in the export sectors.[10]

Free trade backers often shrug off complaints of lost U.S. jobs, citing the overall low U.S. unemployment rate. Yet the U.S. Labor Department reports that only about 35 percent of dislocated workers find new jobs that pay as well or better than their old ones. Many of the fastest-growing job categories are the less desirable ones; indeed Labor Department projections indicate that the fastest-growing U.S. job category is cashiers, who made $6.58 per hour on average in 1996. Institute for Policy Studies' monitoring of U.S. workers who lost jobs due to NAFTA-related trade and investment dislocations also indicates that a disproportionate number of U.S. workers hurt by trade and investment are people of color, women, or located in rural areas.[11]

- *Consumers:* Although globalization boosters will often admit that free trade and investment can have a negative impact on inequality, the environment, and workers, they invariably argue that these impacts are greatly offset by the overwhelmingly positive impact of global markets on consumers. The *Globaphobia* authors put it this way: "Consumers benefit from trade not only because imported goods can be (and often are) cheaper than their domestically produced counterparts, but also because the competition provided by imports, or the mere threat of imports, keeps domestic producers from charging excessive prices."[12]

Yet how many consumers are really benefiting? There is no question that globalization has expanded the variety of goods available in the marketplace. It is also true that roughly a third of U.S. imports come from poorer countries, where workers earn a fraction of U.S. wages. (See figure 3–2.) Hence, these goods often enter the United States at prices far below the price of U.S.-made goods.

But a key question is how frequently these firms sell cheaper goods to consumers at lower prices instead of selling them at normal or even higher prices to keep the benefits of trade for themselves. Evidence suggests that in sectors of the economy where small producers predominate, such as clothing, consumers often find that increased trade lowers prices. Many firms in certain other sectors, such as steel and computers, have also kept prices low. However, in sectors where a handful of large global firms dominate—such as autos, grains, pharmaceuticals, and chemicals—increased trade often does not lower prices.

In the United States, for example, General Motors decided to expand production of its "Suburban" sports utility vehicle in 1994. Instead of investing in its Suburban plant in Janesville, Wisconsin, or adding capacity at another U.S. plant, the company built a new facility in Silao, Mexico, to produce for the U.S. market. By 1996, GM was producing almost as many Suburbans in Mexico as in Wisconsin. In the process, General Motors' wage bill plummeted, since its Mexican workers made $1.54 per hour versus the $18.96 per hour paid to GM's U.S. workers (in 1996). Yet the price of Suburbans bought in the United States jumped from an average of $22,750 in 1994 to $27,250 in 1996.[13]

This debate over winners and losers is one of the most important empirical policy issues of our time. In addition to the factors of equality, workers, the environment, and consumers, there are likewise debates over the impact of globalization policies on food security and safety, culture, and the viability of communities. Clearly, the argument here is that the number of losers is substantial and that the gap between the winners and losers is growing. And that is certainly the perception of the majority of Americans.

THE NEW MAJORITY TO SLOW DOWN AND RESHAPE GLOBALIZATION

By the late 1990s, the debate over U.S. policy toward the global economy had expanded from an almost exclusive focus on trade and investment policy to increasing concerns about short-term finance. As the recent global financial crisis spread, the long-standing elite argument that free markets lead to development began unraveling.

Figure 3.2 Geographic Breakdown of U.S. Imports and Exports: 1991–1998 ($U.S. billions)

	1991	1994	1998
U.S. Exports to Asia	130.6	161.0	187.6
U.S. Imports from Asia	210.2	291.3	367.6
U.S. Trade Balance with Asia	−79.6	−130.3	−180.0
U.S. Trade Balance with China	−12.7	−29.5	−56.9
U.S. Trade Balance with Japan	−43.4	−65.7	−64.0
U.S. Exports to Western Hemisphere	148.6	207.0	298.8
U.S. Imports from Western Hemisphere	153.5	216.4	318.2
U.S. Trade Balance with Western Hemisphere	−4.9	−9.3	−19.4
U.S. Trade Balance with Mexico	2.1	1.4	−15.8
U.S. Trade Balance with Canada	−5.9	−14.0	−16.7
U.S. Exports to Africa	8.8	9.2	11.2
U.S. Imports from Africa	14.0	14.1	15.8
U.S. Trade Balance with Africa	−5.2	−4.9	−4.6
U.S. Exports to Europe	123.5	123.5	170.0
U.S. Imports from Europe	104.0	136.6	202.9
U.S. Trade Balance with Europe	19.4	−13.1	−32.9
Total U.S. Exports	421.7	512.6	682.1
Total U.S. Imports	488.5	663.3	911.9
Total U.S. Trade Balance	−66.7	−150.6	−229.8

Source: Compiled from data from U.S. Department of Commerce, International Trade Administration, May 1999.

At the onset of a new century, the Washington Consensus is now severely discredited and threatened by two dynamics. First, free trade and investment policies have generated widespread human suffering and environmental degradation, which, in turn, have spawned an increasingly effective citizen backlash in both Northern and Southern nations since the early 1990s. Second, deregulated finance flows have engendered extreme volatility in the financial markets of numerous developing and newly industrialized nations, such as Indonesia and South Korea, and have precipitated severe economic downturns.

Although outside criticism of the elite consensus has been growing throughout the 1990s, the consensus among governments, economists, and multilateral institutions held quite firm until the Asian financial crisis spread globally in 1998.[14] The roots of the crisis lie in the World Bank, the IMF, and the U.S. Treasury pressuring governments around the globe during the 1990s to open their stock markets and financial markets to short-term investments from the West. Quick injections of capital from mutual funds, pension funds, and other sources did propel growth in the 1990s, but they also encouraged bad lending and bad investing. Between 1990 and 1996, the volume of private financial flows entering poorer nations skyrocketed from $44 billion per year to $244 billion.[15] Roughly half of this was long-term direct investment, but most of the rest was footloose, moving from country to country at the tap of a computer keyboard. (See figure 3–3.)

Figure 3.3   Long-term Financial Flows to Developing Countries: 1990–1998
($U.S. billions)

	1990	1994	1998[a]
Official flows	56.9	45.5	47.9
Private flows	43.9	178.1	227.1
International capital markets[b]	19.4	89.6	72.1
Foreign direct investment	24.5	88.5	155.0
Net long term resource flows	100.8	223.6	275.0

Source: World Bank, *Global Development Finance 1999* (Washington, DC: The World Bank Group, 1999), p. 14.
[a]Preliminary figure. Total flows in 1998 dropped significantly from 1997 due to the global financial crisis.
[b]Bonds, loans, and portfolio equity flows.

When Western investors got spooked in Thailand, Indonesia, and several other countries in mid-1997, the "hot money" panicked and left much faster than it had arrived. Big-time currency speculators deepened the crisis by betting against the currencies of the crisis nations. Currencies and stock markets from Korea to Brazil nose-dived, and as these nations stopped buying everything from oil to wheat, prices of these products plummeted as well. As the financial crises have spread from foreign exchange accounts at central banks to the industrial centers of the Indonesian, Russian, and other affected economies, there has been widespread pain, dislocation, death, and environmental ruin. The International Confederation of Free Trade Unions predicted that more than 27 million people would be unemployed in the five worst-hit Asian nations (the Philippines, Indonesia, Malaysia, Thailand, and Korea) by the end of 1999.[16]

Fiddling while Asia burns, U.S. Treasury secretary Larry Summers—continuing the approach of his predecessor Robert Rubin—proclaims the lofty rhetoric of constructing "a new global financial architecture" while continuing to advocate mere cosmetic changes, such as increasing information disclosure and flow among nations. Yet since real economies have collapsed, two sets of elite actors have broken away from the status quo positions of the IMF and the U.S. Treasury Department.

One faction supports free markets for trade, but not with respect to short-term capital. This group is led by such prestigious free trade economists as Jagdish Bhagwati of Columbia University, Paul Krugman of MIT, Jeffrey Sachs of Harvard, and World Bank chief economist Joseph Stiglitz. Bhagwati argues that capital markets are by their nature unstable and require controls. Krugman has outlined the case for exchange controls as a response to crisis. Henry Kissinger, with his focus on promoting long-term over speculative investment, also falls within this group.[17] As dramatic as some of these proposals are and as heated as the debate may sound, overall the group largely seeks to restore the consensus by allowing national exchange and/or capital controls under certain circumstances.

Not surprisingly, these critics also tend to disagree with portions of IMF structural adjustment programs. Prominent economists such as Jeffrey Sachs, one of the architects of the U.S.-promoted economic restructuring in Russia, have faulted the IMF for recessionary policies in Asia that turned a liquidity crisis into a financial panic and triggered economic collapse in a growing list of nations. They press for a major revision of IMF policies in favor of openness and creating more space for different policy responses to meet the needs of the moment.

The other set of dissidents argues for the abolition of the IMF. They view the problem as IMF interference in markets by bailing out investors, an activity that eliminates the discipline of risk in private markets (a phenomenon this faction calls "moral hazard"). This camp is led by such long time free trade institutions as the Heritage Foundation and the Cato Institute (whose concern about publicly funded aid institutions in nothing new) as well as some free market economists, such as Milton Friedman of the University of Chicago. The group's ranks have recently swelled with such well-known and vocal converts as Citibank's Walter Wriston, former Secretary of State George Shultz, and former Treasury Secretary William E. Simon.[18]

These two main offshoots of dissent within the consensus have been bolstered by new center-left governments in many European countries, which are also raising their voices to question parts of the consensus. For example, the French government helped stall efforts to further liberalize investment flows. Voices in the Canadian parliament (with counterparts in Europe) are exploring an international tax on foreign currency transactions, to discourage the overwhelming majority of transactions, whose intent is purely speculative. Most Western European governments support at least limited versions of capital controls, and many press for explicit management of exchange rates.

Most of these elite dissenters share a strategic goal: to salvage the overall free market thrust of the Washington Consensus by modifying earlier positions in favor of unregulated capital flows. And although the debate is heated between these groups and the IMF/Treasury pillar, the arguments are largely over revisions to the consensus.

Still, the language some use in their critiques is raising questions about the wisdom of the theoretical foundations of the Washington Consensus and about the narrow interests that it serves. Free trade champion Bhagwati—echoing President Eisenhower, who warned of the military-industrial complex—has decried free capital mobility across borders as the work of the "Wall Street–Treasury complex." By this he means the powerful men who move from Wall Street financial firms to the highest echelons of U.S. government and back, and who, in Bhagwati's words, form a clique that is "unable to look much beyond the interest of Wall Street, which it equates with the good of the world."[19]

In addition to these internal critics, however, the Washington Consensus faces continued attack from the same groups that led the opposition to its free trade agenda, as anti-free trade coalitions of all political stripes have expanded their critiques to encompass financial flows. These groups point out that the financial crisis has exacerbated the social and environmental crises endemic to the elite consensus.

On the environmental front, the more progressive critics are sounding the alarm that among the nations worst hit by the financial contagion are four of the six "emerging market" countries with the largest remaining tracts of forest: Brazil,

Russia, Indonesia, and Mexico. With their economies now deeply integrated into the international market, all four feel pressure to increase their foreign exchange reserves by exporting timber resources. In 1998, this author witnessed firsthand the environmental effects of the crisis in the Philippines; the pressure to increase export earnings prompted the government to rush through a series of investment projects that threaten vast environmental damage. These and related concerns helped propel elements of the progressive coalition in at least 15 countries to obstruct the elite consensus attempt to standardize liberalized foreign investment rules across the globe in the proposed "Multilateral Agreement on Investment."

On the economic front, although the opposition of the political right and left to the corporate-driven global economy arises from different visions of alternatives to the Washington Consensus, the two strange bedfellows have, on key occasions, joined forces to block further momentum of the free trade agenda. Evidence of the success of this joint tactical alliance is seen in the congressional defeats of "fast-track" trade authority and in public opinion polls revealing that the U.S. public is opposed to fast-track and NAFTA by roughly a two-to-one margin.

In addition to the acrimonious public debate over "free trade," citizen groups in both the North and South have exposed the adverse development impacts of the World Bank and the IMF, the two institutions that most zealously enforce Washington Consensus policies. (See essay 3–3: The World Bank and the IMF.) After two decades of prodding the World Bank to address the impact of its policies on the environment, women, the poor, and workers, several hundred nongovernmental groups convinced World Bank president James Wolfensohn to carry out a multicountry comprehensive review of the bank's policies. Labeled the Structural Adjustment Policy Review Initiative (SAPRI), the effort has helped to document the abuses of the structural adjustment, free market model.[20]

A NEW ALTERNATIVE

Many free trade proponents begin their critique of opposition views with a ringing condemnation of "the alternative: protectionism." The *Globaphobia* book of Brookings, the Progressive Policy Institute, and the Twentieth Century Fund is typical: it suggests that "protectionist remedies" are the only alternatives posed by critics.[21]

Again, the public is more sophisticated. In a November 1996 poll by BankBoston, only 23 percent of Americans labeled themselves "protectionists," and only 25 percent accepted the label "free traders." More people—45 percent—called themselves "fair traders." And in that poll, 73 percent said that "labor and environmental issues should be negotiated as part of trade agreements."[22]

With the crumbling of the elite consensus and widespread popular discontent, there is a vibrant debate over what the U.S. posture toward the global economy should be. Many positions advanced are far from protectionist. Ironically, one of the elite critics, World Bank chief economist Joseph Stiglitz, has attempted to steer the debate in a broader direction, even as his institution operationally remains more cautious. Stiglitz encourages the development of a "post–Washington

Consensus" that moves beyond the narrow goal of economic growth to the more expansive goals of sustainable, equitable, and democratic development, but his institution, the World Bank, has yet to move in this direction.

In the United States, as in other Northern and Southern forums, unions, environmental groups, farmer organizations, and others are sketching the outlines of a new U.S. role in the global economy. Central to these efforts is the reorientation of U.S. policy away from the Wall Street–Treasury complex toward a broader definition of national interest. Mindful of the needs of U.S. workers, consumers, farmers, and others at home, this redefined vision recognizes that the greatest threat to the security of all of us is the wealth disparity, erosion of labor standards, and environmental degradation around the world—bred by corporate-led globalization. (See essay 3–4: Repairing the Global Financial Architecture.)

Although critics both North and South share many concerns about the direction and impact of economic globalization, there are oftentimes sharp differences about the remedies. Within the South, both among citizen groups and governments, there is deep concern, for example, that Northern governments, environmental groups, and labor activists may use noneconomic standards to maintain an unequal playing field in international trade, to restrict Southern exports, and to protect jobs in the North.

A broader internationalist agenda requires a varied approach to globalization. Some aspects should be stopped, including trade in such harmful products as arms, toxic wastes, and drugs. Other aspects should be curtailed, such as speculative capital flows and agreements that give new rights to corporations without commensurate responsibilities. And some facets of globalization should be reshaped, such as antitrust laws, enforceable corporate codes of conduct, and tougher enforcement of internationally recognized labor and environmental rights.

A broader agenda also requires a thorough rethinking of U.S. policy in the realms of trade, investment, and finance. With respect to trade, the goal should be to craft a policy that helps U.S. workers and communities while advancing the rights and health of workers and communities abroad. There will be tensions as jobs shift both within countries and across borders. But if the United States and other countries managed trade relations to advance certain common principles, then trade and investment could better serve viable communities, a healthy environment, and dignified work. When feasible, managed trade should grant consumers choices that offer good quality and low prices, but not at the expense of the other goals of viable economies.

Managed trade should allow countries to protect their citizens against products manufactured by abusing workers or the environment in other countries. Concretely, it could be argued that the best part of the $57 billion 1998 U.S. trade deficit with China is rooted in the denial of Chinese workers' basic rights to organize and strike and in the violation of core environmental standards. Hence, the United States should encourage China and other trading partners to respect core labor rights, and Washington should attempt to establish international trading rules that incorporate labor, environmental, and human rights standards.

As the United States and other countries shift toward more managed trade, the management could focus on:

- Promoting food safety and food security in order to protect farmers and peasants
- Protecting sectors deemed vital to each country's development strategy, its environment, and its people
- Providing safeguards when currency fluctuations undermine otherwise competitive industries
- Providing safeguards that allow countries to react with tariffs and quotas when domestic industries experience destabilizing fluctuations or when overall trade deficits become unsustainable

These policies fall under the overall rubric of a "new internationalism," because the overarching goal is not to favor workers or communities in one country over another but rather to strengthen the role of all governments in protecting worker, community, and environmental improvement over narrow corporate interests. U.S. policy should not seek preferential treatment for U.S. workers or U.S. industries, except when there are clear violations of internationally accepted norms, or when one of the above principles of managed trade applies. In such cases, under such policies, some will be displaced. Governments have the responsibility to intervene with far more effective "safety net" programs of training and education as well as policies to promote domestic investment, full employment, and better labor laws facilitating union organizing.

At the core of a new agenda on global finance is a reorientation of financial flows from speculation to long-term investment in the real economy at the local and national level.[23] A premium needs to be put on creating maximum space for local and national governments to set exchange rate policies, regulate capital flows, and eliminate speculative activity. And mechanisms should be installed to keep private losses private.

Such goals require new action at the international, national, and local levels. A priority at the international level is the creation of an international bankruptcy mechanism independent of the IMF. When a country cannot repay debts, this mechanism would oversee a debt restructuring that requires public and private sharing of costs. The United Nations Conference on Trade and Development is examining ways that such a mechanism could prevent liquidity crises from becoming solvency crises. For instance, if Brazil or any other country was teetering on the brink of deep financial crisis, it could go to this facility rather than to the IMF.

With such a facility in place, the IMF could return to its smaller and more modest original mandate of overseeing capital controls, not capital account liberalization, and providing a venue for open exchange of financial and economic information. Citizen groups (led by religious coalitions in many countries), rallying under the banner of Jubilee 2000, have also argued that current debt reduction initiatives should be expanded substantially to cover a sizable amount of bilateral and multilateral debt, and that debt reduction should be delinked from IMF and World Bank conditions. (See essay 3–5: Multilateral Debt.)

Finally, at the international level, many are reviving a 1978 proposal by Nobel Prize winner James Tobin of Yale University, who suggested a tiny global tax on foreign currency transactions as a deterrent to part of the emerging casino of speculative capital flows.[24] In today's flourishing casino, Tobin's proposal would discourage harmful speculation and could generate revenues that might be deployed to a wide array of needs, from environmental cleanup to social investments. Some have suggested shifting part of the revenue back to the tax-imposing governments as an incentive to them for adopting the tax.

At the national level, there is renewed enthusiasm for ensuring that the rules and institutions of the global economy create maximum space for national governments to regulate capital movements. Look at the countries that are not getting destroyed in the crisis: India, China, Chile. Each has capital controls that discourage short-term "hot money" while encouraging long-term productive investment. More and more national and local governments are talking about incentives to channel outside capital to meet local opportunities and needs and to direct mutual and pension fund investments toward productive local activity. For example, unions in Quebec and other parts of the world are taking control of pension funds for local investment.

In trade and investment, a multiyear process between U.S. unions and citizen groups and their counterparts across the Americas has begun to craft an "Alternatives for the Americas" framework for a new approach to U.S. policy.[25] The goal is to shift integration from an emphasis on exports based on the plunder of resources and the exploitation of workers to sustainable economic activity that roots capital locally and nationally. Such an approach rejects the undemocratic "fast track" authority in the United States. Instead it supports the development of a democratic and accountable process for negotiating trade and investment agreements in the United States and throughout the hemisphere. Among the many challenges of implementing such a new internationalist agenda is the need to keep the United States from using its disproportionate power to advance standards and rules that protect its own citizens and economic sectors while keeping its less affluent trading partners undeveloped and disadvantaged.

The alternative agenda includes the following three highlights:

- *Harmonize labor and environmental standards upward:*

  The commitment to apply and respect basic workers' rights should be included in any hemispheric agreement as an obligatory requirement for membership in the accord. The precedence of environmental accords signed by the governments of the Americas should be established in the negotiations around, and agreement on, investment and trade. Environment and sustainability should not be limited to a single area of economic-financial accords, but rather [should] be addressed as an overarching dimension and perspective throughout any such agreements.[26]

  Representatives of citizen organizations in the South accept this call as part of a grand bargain wherein groups in the North agree to advocate measures to close the growing gap between North and South.

- *Close the gap between rich and poor countries through debt cancellation delinked from IMF conditions:*

  In the Western Hemisphere, the most effective way to level the playing field would be through a substantial reduction of the debts owed by low-income

countries. Therefore the FTAA [Free Trade Area of the Americas] should include the negotiation of a reduction of the principal owed, lower preferential
interest rates, and longer repayment terms. Orthodox structural adjustment
conditions demanded by the World Bank and the IMF should be abandoned
as they have manifestly failed to resolve the debt crisis and have caused enormous hardship for the poorest sectors of the population.[27]

In fact, a Development GAP (Group for Alternative Policies) study of 71
countries that have adopted World Bank–and IMF–dictated structural adjustment programs, in part to reduce their debts, found that debt as a portion of gross domestic product (GDP) grew on average by nearly 50
percent.[28] The alternative approach, urging that debt reduction be decoupled from IMF conditions, departs significantly from the Clinton administration's current strategy. The administration is supporting increased
debt relief but tying such relief to strict adherence to IMF and World
Bank conditions.

• *Strengthen respect for migrant worker rights:*

All governments should sign and/or ratify the 'International Convention on
the Protections of the Rights of All Migrant Workers and Members of Their
Families' (1990), and a similar instrument should be created for the Americas. This convention must be part of the international legal framework for all
trade and financial negotiations.[29]

All of this debate and activity around finance, trade, and investment is reigniting the legitimacy of a state role in development. Whatever comes of the global financial crisis, the widespread fear of an unregulated casino economy able to
devastate economies overnight is also destroying the Washington Consensus's rejection of an activist role by the state. Although most elite participants in the debate allow for a government role only in the realm of short-term financial flows,
this concession lets the government genie out of the bottle. If most now acknowledge that governments are needed to check markets in one realm, perhaps there
can be a more intelligent discussion about what role governments might play in
other aspects of the rapidly globalizing economy.

Citizen groups are growing strong enough to stall the implementation of elite
consensus policies, as seen in the fights over fast track and the Multilateral Agreement on Investment (MAI). In private discussions among think tanks that have
been at the center of the consensus, there is a begrudging acknowledgment that
the Washington Consensus has lost much of its legitimacy with the public and that
there is a need to factor more labor and environmental concerns into the policy.
Yet the growing strength of citizen opposition does not yet translate into an ability
to create a new overall consensus. Too much of the elite still clings to the basic
precepts of the old consensus.

The emerging era of no overall consensus on the U.S. role toward the global
economy can be healthy and vibrant, notwithstanding the vast human suffering
around the world among victims of the financial casino. If there is any lesson from
these past two decades, it seems to be that an elite consensus on the best approach
toward globalization is dangerous.

Most of the new citizen debate over globalization focuses on the theme of democracy. In country after country, citizen organizations are demanding an end to the customary practice of governments consulting primarily with corporate representatives. They are demanding that global institutions—and the negotiations setting their rules—be transparent, accountable, and inclusive. They are insisting that globalization not undermine the democratic prerogative of national and local governments to decide limits and priorities in economic matters. As workers, environmentalists, farmers, women, and others demand to be heard, the contours of the global economy of the twenty-first century are being redrawn.

NOTES

1. Jackie Calmes, "Despite Buoyant Economic Times, Americans Don't Buy Free Trade," *Wall Street Journal*, December 10, 1998. In the same poll, almost three-quarters responded that immigration "should not increase, because it will cost U.S. jobs and increase unemployment."
2. See the Development Group for Alternative Policies website (http://www.igc.org/dgap) for documentation on the impact of free market regulations on Southern nations.
3. Mortimer Zuckerman, "A Second American Century," *Foreign Affairs*, May/June 1998.
4. John Williamson, "The Progress of Policy Reform in Latin America," *Policy Analyses in International Economics*, No. 28 (Washington, DC: Institute for International Economics, January 1990). Williamson's 1990 monograph built on a paper entitled "What Washington Means by Reform," which he presented at a conference in La Paz, Bolivia, in 1985.
5. Personal communications, Arthur MacEwan, March 5, 1999.
6. Gary Burtless et al., *Globaphobia: Confronting Fears About Open Trade* (Washington: Brookings Institution, Progressive Policy Institute, and Twentieth Century Fund, 1998), p. ix.
7. Ibid., p. 7.
8. Calculated by author using data from the United Nations Development Program and *Forbes* magazine in 1996.
9. Quoted in *Sierra Magazine*, July/August 1996, p. 22.
10. Robert Scott, Thea Lee, and John Schmitt, "Trading Away Good Jobs: An Explanation of Employment and Wages in the U.S., 1979–1994," Economic Policy Institute, October 1997.
11. Data published in Sarah Anderson, John Cavanagh, and Thea Lee, *A Field Guide to the Global Economy* (New York: New Press, 2000).
12. Burtless et al., *Globaphobia*, pp. 20–21.
13. Data supplied from Steve Beckman, an international economist with the United Auto Workers, 1999.
14. See Lance Taylor, "The Revival of the Liberal Creed—The IMF and the World Bank in a Globalized Economy," *World Development*, Vol. 25, No. 2, 1997.
15. Figures from the World Bank, quoted in John Cavanagh and Sarah Anderson, "International Financial Flows: The New Trends of the 1990s and Projections for the Future," Institute for Policy Studies, April 1997, p. 6.
16. See International Confederation of Free Trade Unions, *ICFTU Online*, January 21, 1999. Available on the Internet at: http://www.icftu.org.

17. Henry Kissinger, "Perils of Globalization," *Washington Post*, October 5, 1998.
18. William E. Simon, "Abolish the IMF," *Wall Street Journal*, October 23, 1997.
19. Jagdish Bhagwati, "The Capital Myth," *Foreign Affairs*, May/June 1998, p. 12.
20. See the Development GAP, Structural Adjustment Participatory Review International Network website at http://www.igc.org/dgap/saprin/index.html.
21. Burtless et al., *Globaphobia*, p. 7.
22. BankBoston, "Poll Shows Public Believes Trade Pacts Cost U.S. Jobs," Press Release, November 7, 1996.
23. The proposals that follow are drawn from "A Call to Action: A Citizen's Agenda for Reform of the Global Economic System," which was drafted at a December 1998 meeting sponsored by Friends of the Earth, the International Forum on Globalization, and the Third World Network. For a detailed analysis of alternative proposals regarding global finance, see Robert A. Blecker, *Taming Global Finance: A Better Architecture for Growth and Equity* (Washington, DC: Economic Policy Institute, 1999).
24. James Tobin, "A Proposal for International Monetary Reform," *Eastern Economic Journal*, Vol. 4, 1978, pp. 153–59.
25. Alliance for Responsible Trade, Common Frontiers, Red Chile por una Iniciativa de los Pueblos, Red Mexicana de Acción Frente al Libre Comercio, and Reseau Québécois sur l'Integration Continentale, "Alternatives for the Americas: Building a People's Hemispheric Agenda, Discussion Draft #2," November 1998.
26. Ibid., pp. 15, 19.
27. Ibid., p. 36.
28. The study by the Washington-based NGO was released in April 1999. It found "a positive correlation between the number of years that a country has an adjustment program in place and an increase in debt as a percentage of GDP. The average (mean) increase in the debt/GDP ratio among those countries studied was 49 percent."
29. Alliance for Responsible Trade et al., "Alternatives for the Americas," p. 25.

CORPORATE WELFARE AND FOREIGN POLICY

Janice Shields

THE U.S. GOVERNMENT DOLES OUT MORE THAN $167 BILLION annually in what critics dub "aid for dependent corporations (AFDC)." An analysis of government documents done for the Center for Study of Responsible Law shows that this corporate welfare includes: (1) cash payments by government to businesses; (2) government provision of below-cost products and services (such as loans and insurance) to businesses; (3) tax breaks for businesses; (4) laws—and changes in laws—that help business bottom lines; and (5) government purchases of goods and services from businesses at inflated prices (though laws are supposed to prevent this).

U.S. aid for international investors, exporters, and importers exceeds $32 billion annually and benefits such "needy" recipients as General Motors, Citibank, Archer Daniels Midland, and Boeing. The Market Access Program (MAP), for example, uses taxpayer money to reimburse corporate foreign advertising costs. The Overseas Private Investment Corporation (OPIC) supplies loans and insurance to companies investing abroad, while the Export-Import Bank provides insurance and financing programs to U.S. exporters. Federal tax law allows exporters to exempt a portion of revenues from taxation. The Sugar Program, which limits U.S. sugar imports, increases the sweetener industry's income by keeping supplies lower, leading to higher prices. In addition to the bevy of arms export programs (See figure 2–4), there are agriculture export subsidies and export guarantee programs, fishing subsidies, dairy export incentive programs, and travel and tourism subsidies.

The validity of corporate arguments supporting their welfare programs is often questionable. For example, some executives claim that subsidies and tax breaks are needed to create or maintain U.S. exports and jobs. Proponents of MAP contend that these subsidies generate $16 in revenue for every $1 in taxpayer costs. Yet several General Accounting Office studies could not document any increase in exports due to MAP expenditures. Similarly, the Congressional Research Service could not confirm the job creation claims of OPIC beneficiaries. The tax break that allows U.S. corporations to defer payment of more than $1.3 billion annually in U.S. taxes on foreign earnings until remitted actually encourages U.S. companies to locate overseas.

Corporate welfare may also harm international relations, especially when companies force countries to compete against each other to attract businesses by offering more subsidies and tax breaks or when countries use subsidies and tax breaks to retaliate against each other's policies. For example, the U.S. Secretary of Agriculture recently threatened to provide Export Enhancement Program bonuses to American flour exporters as a signal to the European Union that the United States was concerned about European flour subsidies.

Both progressives and conservatives are campaigning to cut corporate welfare, though they seek different outcomes. Progressives argue that the money should be used instead to provide housing, food, medical care, and education for truly needy families and children. Conservatives want to downsize government by cutting corporate welfare.

If these subsidies are not cut, each government agency that disburses corporate welfare and each company recipient should be required to provide detailed annual public reports disclosing the amount of welfare disbursed/received, how the welfare was used, and how the taxpayer expenditure benefited the company and the public. Corporate welfare programs should be periodically reviewed and, if costs exceed public benefits, eliminated. Government agencies doling out corporate welfare should bar companies with bad labor, environmental, and social records from obtaining benefits; "AFDC" recipients should be required to follow codes of good corporate conduct and to refund the corporate welfare they receive if they fail to meet their commitments, such as creating promised jobs.

THE WORLD TRADE ORGANIZATION

Aileen Kwa

IN JANUARY 1995, THE WORLD TRADE ORGANIZATION (WTO) replaced the General Agreement on Tariffs and Trade (GATT), which was created in 1947. WTO is much more powerful because of its institutional foundation and its dispute settlement system. Countries that do not abide by its trade rules are taken to court and can eventually face retaliation. The logic of commercial trade pervades the WTO. The development goals articulated when GATT was first formed—to raise living standards, ensure full employment, and expand real income—have been put aside or are wrongly assumed to be the natural consequences of increased trade.

As of the end of 1999, the WTO has 132 members (nearly the whole world except China, some communist countries, and a number of small nations) with another 31 in the process of accession. Of the total membership, 98 are developing countries, including 27 nations categorized as the least developed countries.

While supporters argue that the WTO gives developing countries expanded access to industrialized country markets, critics charge that trade liberalization undermines long-term development prospects for Southern nations. One of the commonly used yardsticks to measure the success of the WTO is the volume of world trade. The results seem excellent, with world trade up 25 percent in the last four years. But the least developed countries (LDCs) represent 20 percent of the world's population, and they generate a mere 0.03 percent of the trade flows.

Although purportedly a democratic institution, with three-quarters of its membership from developing countries, the WTO is dominated by the leading industrialized countries and by the corporations of these countries.

Over the years, transnational corporations have successfully lobbied for GATT/WTO to cover more areas. The WTO's agenda now includes agriculture, services, intellectual property rights, and electronic commerce; other proposed new issues are investment, government procurement, and competition policy.

Developing countries have little power within the WTO framework. The agenda of the WTO, the implementation of its agreements, and the much-praised dispute settlement system all serve to advance the interests of developed countries. Rules uniformly applied to WTO members have brought about inequalities because developing countries have fewer human and technical resources. Hence they often enter negotiations or the dispute settlement system less prepared than their developed country counterparts. Furthermore, the basis on which the system is run—whether a country is violating free trade rules—is not the most appropriate for their development needs.

The LDCs are marginalized in the world trade system, and their products continue to face tariff escalations. Trade negotiations are based on the principle of reciprocity or trade-offs. That is, one country gives a concession in an area, such as the lowering of tariffs for a certain product, in return for another country acceding to a certain agreement. This type of bartering benefits the large and diversified economies, because they can get more by giving more.

Washington has used the WTO to promote free trade principles only in sectors that benefit the U.S. economy; in other sectors, such as textiles, protectionism reigns. Recent United Nations' studies confirm that tariffs still hamper developing nations' attempts to export new products such as beef, cigarettes, clothing, footwear, and wood articles to the United States and other developed countries. As Martin Khor of the Third World Network frequently puts it, the U.S. agenda is "liberalization if it benefits me, protectionism if it benefits me, what counts is my commercial interest."

Using creative calculations and interpretations, the U.S. has managed to use WTO agreements to institutionalize subsidies to U.S. agroexporters while prohibiting developing country governments from using subsidies to support for their own disadvantaged farmers. Under the WTO's "Green Box" policies, direct income subsidies to U.S. agroexporters are exempted from reductions on the specious grounds that they are "decoupled" from production or are somehow "non-trade distorting."

U.S.-led WTO agricultural policies will not meet the food needs of a growing world population. These policies promote food availability through trade and discourage countries from developing food self-sufficiency. Most developing countries are short of foreign exchange and cannot afford to buy food from the world market, despite low pricing and availability.

Instead, the WTO should consider its top priority to be the development needs of its members. Sections of agreements that work to the disadvantage of developing countries must be changed, including agriculture, textiles, and the dispute settlement system.

The WTO should emphasize greater self-sufficiency of economies nationally and regionally. Domestic markets, rather than foreign markets, should be the main stimulus of growth. Resources should be used sustainably to support local and national communities. People and the preservation of the environment, rather than capital, should be the primary objectives of any expansion of global trade. Countries must be free to choose if they want overseas investments and, if so, what kind of investments. They must also be able to decide on their tariff rates and other trade barriers in order to protect their industries, as the developed countries have been doing.

The dispute settlement system must consider the development needs of countries (especially the most vulnerable), not just whether free trade rules have been violated. For instance, in the 1998–99 dispute over the banana trade, the WTO ruled in favor of the U.S. over the European Union's traditional arrangement of preferential access for Caribbean banana exporting countries—a ruling that may have devastating economic consequences for Caribbean economies that depend solely on banana exports.

If developed and developing country farmers are to compete in the same markets, then the $280 billion in annual subsidies that developed countries provide to their farmers should be reduced to the negligible amounts that developing countries provide. Otherwise, developing countries should be allowed to increase the subsidies they provide to their own farmers. Further, if the WTO continues to force all countries down the liberalization path, the protected sectors in the United States must also be liberalized to open up new export markets for developing nations.

The final test of the WTO's success is not the volume of world trade or the extent to which trade barriers have been lowered, but whether and to what extent living conditions in all nations—particularly the developing countries, which constitute three-fourths of its members—are improving.

THE WORLD BANK AND THE IMF:
SHIFTING AGENDAS OF THE
BRETTON WOODS TWINS

Erik Leaver

In 1944, the United States, Britain and other major capitalist powers met at Bretton Woods, New Hampshire, to create two powerful international financial institutions (IFIs) to manage postwar restructuring of Europe and the expansion of the global capitalist economy into developing countries. The World Bank was created to make long-term loans for development projects, while its sister organization, the International Monetary Fund (IMF), was given a mandate to make short-term, general support loans to help countries through temporary currency exchange and balance-of-payments difficulties.

The World Bank's work was complemented with the subsequent creation of four regional multilateral development banks (MDBs) for Latin America (founded in 1959), Africa (1963), Asia (1966), and Europe (1991). These MDBs obtain 80 percent of their funds from the world capital markets and 20 percent from assessing member governments. In contrast, the IMF depends solely on quota payments from member countries.

Voting in the IFIs is proportional to assessment fees, which means that the United States, Britain, Germany, France, and Japan control more than 40 percent of the votes in the World Bank and IMF. The United States, as the largest contributor, has always wielded the most influence within these two institutions, which are both headquartered in Washington, DC.

While the overarching objective of both the World Bank and the IMF has always been the integration of low-income countries into the global capitalist market, their lending strategies have shifted and expanded over time. The World Bank was not created to be an anti-poverty agency; rather it argued that as developing countries mature into modern industrial economies, living standards would rise and wealth would trickle down to the poor. By the 1960s, it was clear this strategy was not working; therefore, the World Bank moved to reach the poor directly by making loans for education, housing, and other social services, although borrowing countries were still required to repay in hard currency. As a result, World Bank lending grew dramatically, from less than $1 billion dollars a year in the late 1960s to over $12 billion in 1981.

In the 1970s, the IMF's mission also expanded. When the dollar was delinked from the gold standard, the IMF's original purpose of assisting with currency exchange problems was lost and it began acting as a short- and long-term creditor and, like the World Bank, an economic policy adviser. The IFI-encouraged heavy borrowing by developing countries, combined with rising oil prices, helped precipitate the debt crisis in the early 1980s, causing another shift in IFI lending policies. With Brazil and several other major countries facing bankruptcy, the World Bank, for the first time, began making balance-of-payment loans, further blurring the distinction between the two organizations.

Both institutions also began conditioning their balance-of-payment loans on "structural adjustment policies" (SAPs), which required that the borrowing country convert to a free market, export-oriented economy and adopt reforms intended to reduce inflation, promote exports, meet debt-repayment schedules, lower inflation, and decrease budget deficits. SAPs prescriptions force governments to adopt wide-ranging policy reforms, including cutbacks in government spending (invariably for health, education, housing, and other social services), increases in interest rates, removal of trade barriers, liberalizing imports, privatizing government-owned enterprises, and promotion of foreign investment and trade.

Virtually all developing countries—particularly in Latin America and Africa, and increasingly in the transition countries of East and Central Europe—have implemented or are implementing SAPs. Beginning in the 1980s, MDBs and many U.S. bilateral aid programs also linked their loans and development assistance to SAPs. While SAPs have also largely succeeded in shrinking government budget deficits, eliminating hyperinflation, and maintaining debt payment schedules, they have failed to create a base for sustainable, balanced economic development; instead they have weakened local industries, increased dependency on food imports, gutted social services, and widened the gap between rich and poor.

In addition, for most borrower countries, foreign debt has increased. In a 1999 study of 71 countries that have operated under at least three years of SAPs, the Development GAP found "two-thirds saw their debt burdens increase during the adjustment period" and the "longer these countries implemented the neoliberal programs, the worse their debt burdens typically became." The fact that no government has ever defaulted on a World Bank or IMF loan reflects not the quality of these loans but the power of the IFIs. Borrowers dare not default because the World Bank's and IMF's imprimatur has become essential for any international loan. In addition, the World Bank makes it possible for borrowers to meet repayment schedules by routinely making new loans to pay old ones. This so-called defensive lending papers over both the growth in debt among borrowers and the poor quality of the World Bank's lending practices.

A large proportion of World Bank loans are failures: nearly one-third of its projects and adjustment loans do not meet the minimum standard for economic productivity, and 56 percent are unlikely to be sustainable, according to the World Bank's own internal evaluation. Yet the borrowing countries alone bear the burden of failure; the World Bank does not forgive bad loans or share any responsibility for failures.

In 1995, the World Bank announced yet another agenda shift, declaring that the "private sector is now a recognized area of emphasis." Between 1990 and 1997, private capital flows to the developing world increased from $42 billion to $256 billion, surpassing the amount of money available through the World Bank and government aid programs. SAPs policies contributed to this trend toward "trade not aid" and "private not public" as the route to poverty alleviation and development.

Two rapidly growing World Bank divisions, the International Finance Corporation (IFC) and the Multilateral Investment Guarantee Agency (MIGA), exclusively finance and underwrite private companies. The bulk of their funds go to foreign not local companies, involve natural resource extraction not renewable resources, and emphasize roads over mass transit. In addition, the World Bank has set lower standards and less rigorous environmental and social disclosure policies for private sector loans than for those to governments.

In the 50-plus years since Bretton Woods, the World Bank and the International Monetary Fund have gone through periodic face-lifts, but their mission—to incorporate developing countries into the capitalist economy—has remained the same. Today, as never before, these institutions are being challenged by staff from within, by both borrower and lender governments, and by citizen movements around the globe that argue it is time to modernize both the architecture and the mission of these powerful financial twins.

REPAIRING THE GLOBAL FINANCIAL ARCHITECTURE: PAINTING OVER CRACKS VS. STRENGTHENING THE FOUNDATIONS

David Felix

THE LIFTING OF CONTROLS ON INTERNATIONAL CAPITAL MOVEMENTS over the past quarter century has been paralleled by a succession of international financial crises, the current one being the most extensive and virulent to date. "By any standard," observes Gerald Corrigan of Goldman, Sachs and former president of the New York Federal Reserve Bank, "the frequency and consequences of these events are simply too great." There is now, therefore, general consensus that something needs to be done to reduce the incidence of such crises. In the jargon of financial bureaucrats, the "world's financial architecture" needs reforming.

Beyond that, consensus fragments. The reform agenda of the International Monetary Fund (IMF)—and of the central bankers and finance ministers of most of the major industrial powers who dominate the IMF—would extend free capital mobility while at the same time trying to enable developing countries to handle volatile capital flows more effectively. The alternative approach—restraining the freedom of financial capital to move globally in order to reduce its power to deter countries from pursuing autonomous economic policies—is not on that agenda. But this alternative approach is evoking support among academic economists and grass-roots groups in both developed and developing countries, and, since political feasibility is an essential requisite, it is infiltrating official circles.

Because each approach requires collective action restricting national sovereignty, there will be trade-offs between different types of freedom. To induce free but more stable capital flows, proposals on the IMF agenda would standardize tighter bank regulations and require each country to enforce them. Other schemes would increase the power of the IMF to oversee the economic policies and performances of developing countries and ensure that these countries provide accurate data to international investors, eschew capital controls, and avoid defaulting on their foreign debts. Propositions under the alternative approach call for coordinated measures—international tax and/or regulatory agreements—to minimize evasion and policy discordance.

Proposals demanding a much greater surrender of national sovereignty have also been put forth: a global central bank, a uniform bankruptcy code enforced by international bankruptcy courts, and other ambitious institutional innovations of global reach. These ideas have didactic value by identifying distant possibilities, but they clearly lack a serious political constituency either among the power elite or the grass-roots. What follows is an attempt to draw from the two approaches, liberalizing and restraining capital, specific proposals that in combination would improve global welfare and also have some chance of being adopted.

AN ALTERNATIVE PACKAGE OF ARCHITECTURAL REFORMS:
BRETTON WOODS LIGHT

The components of the package to be outlined have been circulating as separate reform proposals—some on the IMF and/or Group of Seven (G-7) reform agendas, others struggling against Washington and IMF resistance. Combined they are an updating of the Bretton Woods architecture commensurate with today's changed economic and political environment. They would help restore some of the stable, equitable, economic growth of yesteryear while adding institutional building blocks for erecting a genuinely integrated global economy in the future. The components are:

1. A target zone arrangement to limit exchange rate fluctuations between the Big Three currencies: the dollar, euro, and yen.
2. A uniform tax on global foreign exchange turnover (a.k.a. the Tobin tax).
3. Increasing capital requirements on interbank loans in the Basle Capital Accords.
4. Equalizing the prices of over-the-counter derivatives with those on the organized futures markets by imposing appropriate capital requirements on the derivative-issuing banks.
5. Curbing the tax and regulatory evasions of offshore havens.
6. Reauthorizing developing countries to impose capital controls as needed.

Limiting fluctuations between the Big Three currencies is a looser version of the Bretton Woods exchange-rate regime, which relied on the fixed-dollar price of gold. This time the Big Three central banks would agree to intervene jointly in the foreign exchange market to keep fluctuations within chosen limits, and, with open capital markets, they would also have to subordinate other policies to this task. Moreover, the ease with which rampaging capital flows shattered the 1987 Louvre target zone agreement and the exchange rate mechanism (ERM) in 1992 makes it clear that curbing such rampaging is essential. A global Tobin tax would not only help perform this task but would also substantially reduce the subordination of other national policies required to sustain the target zone.

The Tobin tax is a "market-friendly" alternative to direct capital controls, since the tax leaves the screening out of hot money flows to the markets. Around 80 percent of the $1.5 trillion daily foreign exchange volume comprises legs of round-trip transactions spanning a week or less. Most relate to arbitraging and open speculation by banks, investment houses, hedge funds, and the like that are taking high-volume, short-term positions to exploit transitory, usually small, profit margins. A small tax would cut deeply into these margins and slash the return on capital.

On the other hand, the tax bite on the profit margins from trade and foreign direct investment, which involve much longer round trips, would be minimal and would be offset by the reduced exchange risk and hedging costs that would result from stabilizing Big Three rates. The transaction tax revenue would increase official resources for intervening to stabilize exchange rates while providing more scope for national economies to implement full employment and other welfare goals without being sandbagged by anticipatory capital flight. As Nobel economist James Tobin noted when offering his tax proposal over two decades ago, it would slow the reaction speed of the globalizing financial markets, allowing time for welfare-oriented policies to manifest results.

Increasing capital requirements on interbank loans in the Basle Capital Accords and on over-the-counter derivatives would further reduce financial rampaging. The interbank market has been the major channel for moving funds to conduct arbitraging and speculative gambits, and over-the-counter derivatives have been elements in risky strategies by hedge funds, which fuel contagion, that is, a crisis in one country instigating capital flight from an array of countries. Higher capital requirements raise the costs of the financial leveraging that underpins the massive movement of funds for arbitraging and speculation. And curbing the abuse of offshore havens that evade taxes and regulations would, of course, facilitate the enforcement of the above four components.

Finally, sanctioning capital controls by developing countries would reduce their vulnerability to capital flows that could otherwise overwhelm their thin financial markets. Article VI of the IMF's Articles of Agreement already authorizes capital controls, but the IMF has honored this fundamental part of its charter only in the breach. Instead, the IMF has been pressuring countries to avoid capital controls. The reauthorization of Article VI would call off the dogs.

OBSTACLES TO IMPLEMENTATION

In combination, the six components of the alternative reform agenda reinforce each other's effectiveness. And although implementation raises technical issues requiring further study, the main obstacles are political. In the case of the target zone and the Tobin tax, the challenge is how to get these proposals on the official reform agenda for study. In the case of the other four components, which are already on the agenda, it is how to overcome, as American University economist Robert Blecker argues in *Taming Global Finance*, "the least common denominator approach that emphasizes financial interests and is unlikely to deviate substantially from the views of the U.S. Treasury." The adoption of this reform package depends on a buildup of political pressure sufficient to force finance ministers and central bankers, who currently monopolize the reform agenda, to put unemployment and income inequality ahead of facilitating trading opportunities and capital movements. That is made more difficult because the main media rely almost exclusively on spokespeople from financial houses to interpret global financial events, and those spokespeople predictably take the banker's point of view.

The pressures for change are, however, mounting. At the Group of Seven meeting of finance ministers in March 1999, the French, German, and Japanese ministers tried to put the Big Three target zone proposal on the agenda. Washington quickly shot down this proposal. But with double-digit European unemployment and the deterioration of the Japanese economy persisting, the need to create a more propitious financial environment for expansionary policies becomes more compelling.

Washington has gone to great lengths to keep the "market-friendly" Tobin tax off the agenda. The United States squelched the attempt by the United Nations Development Program (UNDP) to promote international discussions of the feasibility and benefits of the Tobin tax. This did not keep a Canadian coalition of nongovernmental organizations, academics, and unions from obtaining a 2-to-1 vote for a House of Commons resolution in March 1999 urging the Canadian government to "enact a tax on financial transactions in concert with the international community." The finance minister has promised, accordingly, to introduce the Tobin tax proposal before the Group of Seven. A French grass-roots movement is demanding comparable action from the French government and has organized sister movements in other European Union countries.

There is no such grass-roots activity in the United States as yet. Partly this may reflect the fact that the U.S. economy has thus far benefited in various ways from the global crisis. These include seignorage profits—the difference between the face value of the bills and the minor cost of printing them—totaling about 0.5 percent of gross domestic product. Over two-thirds of U.S. currency is held outside the United States. Some is drug money, but mainly it is the increasing use of the dollar as a store of value by middle-income households upset by the instability of local currency.

Another boon to the U.S. economy has been the flight to U.S. bonds by foreign investors, whose share of all private holdings of U.S. bonds rose from 21 percent at the beginning of 1995 to 38 percent at the end of 1998. In addition, developing countries, which in 1997 already held 55 percent of global official reserves—mainly U.S. treasury notes—though transacting only 25 percent of world trade, have been desperately trying to regain the confidence of the financial markets by increasing their dollar reserves. This has meant curtailing imports and emphasizing exports, which has severely depressed world prices for their chief exports: primary goods and labor-intensive manufactures. Thus the United States has been able to increase its foreign liabilities to cover its rapidly growing trade deficit without having to raise interest rates, as the rest of the world has to do, in order to get foreigners to hold its currency and securities.

The dark side is that U.S. residents whose income and wealth derives from owning financial assets or who are employed in skilled jobs in the nontraded goods sector have garnered the lion's share of the benefits. In contrast, workers in the exporting and import-competing industries have lost high-paid jobs and have had to migrate to lower-wage, service sector jobs. Feeling their profits squeezed by unusually low prices, agriculture, mining, steel, and other material producing industries with political clout are joining with labor in demanding import protection. Washington's attempt to ride both its high horses—free trade and free capital mobility—is becoming politically precarious.

MULTILATERAL DEBT

Soren Ambrose

MULTILATERAL DEBT IS THAT PORTION OF A COUNTRY'S EXTERNAL DEBT burden owed to international financial institutions (IFIs) such as the International Monetary Fund (IMF), the World Bank, and the regional development banks—all institutions owned by consortia of governments. For the world's poorest countries, almost all of which have serious debt problems, multilateral debt looms larger than other debts in view of the IFIs' status as "preferred creditors," accorded them because of their mission as providers of core development and balance-of-payment loans supported by the international community. This status means that payments to the IFIs must be given the highest priority, over private and bilateral (government-to-government) debt. Until the IMF gives its stamp of approval, which usually requires adherence to the economic policies it recommends, poor countries generally cannot get credit or capital from other sources. And until a country has signed onto an IMF program, it cannot apply for bilateral debt relief from the "Paris Club" of creditor countries.

Significant growth of multilateral debt began with the Latin American debt crisis of the early 1980s, when Mexico, Argentina, and Brazil all came to the brink of defaulting on their debts. The IMF and the World Bank responded with massive loan packages conditioned on implementation of structural adjustment programs (SAPs)—packages of neoliberal economic reforms. Private debts were converted into multilateral debt, as countries used the funds acquired from the IFIs to pay off the banks that would no longer loan to them. Consequently, governments faced with no other way to keep capital flowing have, after falling into debt, been forced to implement one SAP after another, despite these programs' repeated failures to deliver countries from poverty or debt.

The multilateral debt of the world's low-income countries (with per capita gross national product [GNP] below $785) increased by some 544 percent in the period between 1980 and 1997, from $24.1 billion to $155.3 billion. This debt currently constitutes 32.75 percent of their countries' total long-term debt burden (versus about 25 percent in 1980). Multilateral debt of middle-income countries (with GNP between $785 and $9,600) increased by 481 percent between 1980 and 1997. Multilateral debt, then, is a problem for the entire developing world, but a particularly acute one for the poorest countries concentrated in sub-Saharan Africa. In fact, debt servicing takes up about 20 percent of sub-Saharan Africa's export income.

The human impact of debt is felt in two ways: through the diversion of national resources to debt servicing, and through the effects of economic programs designed by outsiders to transform local economies to a "globalized" model in which debtor countries are supposed to produce and export whatever garners the most hard currency. The policies that foster this economic role have benefited Northern corporations and investors but have been devastating for all but those small segments of the Southern wealthy classes positioned to profit from them. Thus, in the global South, income and wealth gaps have widened, illiteracy and disease have spread, women's burdens and domestic violence have shot up, environmental devastation has worsened, unemployment has increased, thousands of businesses have failed, and farmers have been forced to sell their land and work for large landowners or on marginal lands.

A major concern for IFIs and creditor nations is that outright debt cancellation would result in their loss of leverage over poor countries. In 1998, in the wake of Hurricane Mitch's devastation, Honduras and Nicaragua, the two worst-hit countries and two of the world's most indebted nations, asked for substantial debt relief. The U.S. Treasury gave loss of leverage as its reason for refusing to consider either bilateral or multilateral debt relief.

In recent years, however, particularly in the wake of the Asian financial crisis, there have been growing calls for abating or canceling the multilateral debt of the poorest countries. In 1999, Congress debated several debt relief bills, and both President Clinton and Vice President Gore verbally endorsed debt relief for the most impoverished countries, possibly financed by sales of some of the IMF's estimated $30 billion in gold stocks.

The United States played a positive role in shepherding through the World Bank and the IMF a modest and restricted debt relief scheme known as the Heavily Indebted Poor Countries (HIPC) Initiative. Under this complex plan, adopted in 1996, the unsustainable debt burdens of the poorest countries are reduced to sustainable levels if those countries successfully adhere to "sound economic policies"—an IFI euphemism for implementation of SAPs. To qualify for HIPC, a country must fulfill six years under SAP prescriptions before relief of multilateral debt is actually granted. At that time, all creditors will give matching relief to reduce the country's debt to a "sustainable" level. Critics of HIPC charge that it offers a cruel paradox to poor countries—they must first further cut government spending even before the IFIs are willing to grant any relief. Only five countries are to receive any relief under HIPC before 2000—Uganda, Mozambique, Mali, Bolivia, and Guyana—and they have found the debt scheme to be worth relatively little.

One sincere response to the debt issue, a global movement called Jubilee 2000, calls for the cancellation of poor countries' unpayable debts by the beginning of the new millennium. This effort has gradually gained momentum, with national campaigns currently in some 40 countries. For countries that have endured decades of severe indebtedness, poverty, and subordination to the IFI's economic policies, cancellation of substantial portions, if not all, of the outstanding debt is necessary if their resources are ever to become available for development and if their people are ever to gain a sense of ownership of their economic destiny.

Jubilee 2000 argues that IFIs should be forced to accept—through a change in their bylaws, if necessary—the option of writing off debts. The U.S. government should ideally take the lead in such a program of cancellation, first by canceling the bilateral debt owed it by the poorest countries and then by using its position at the IFIs to urge them to do the same for multilateral debt.

CHAPTER 4

AMERICA'S FADING COMMITMENT TO THE WORLD

Charles William Maynes

SINCE WORLD WAR II THE UNITED STATES HAS LED the effort to develop and support a number of international institutions to grapple with international problems that are difficult for a single government to resolve or that no single country has an interest in solving by itself, such as: questions of peace and security, development and growth issues, trade, and a host of functional problems like air safety, telecommunications, and the environment. Until roughly the mid-1970s, there was no greater champion of these institutions than the United States, which demonstrated its endorsement through its financial support of the United Nations, World Bank, International Monetary Fund, and a host of functional institutions.

In recent years, this postwar tradition has come under attack, primarily, one must add, from America's political elite rather than from its ordinary citizens. That elite began to sour on international institutions, which they viewed as dominated by third world governments, when in the early 1970s the United States suffered a number of painful setbacks at the hand of third world states. Vietnam inflicted a military defeat on the United States in Indochina. The oil-producing states inflicted an economic defeat on the United States with the oil embargo of 1973. And Iran humiliated the United States politically when Iranian students occupied the American embassy in Tehran and the United States could do little in retaliation, its massive military power notwithstanding.

Although the Carter administration attempted to reaffirm America's commitment to international institutions, the Reagan administration (exploiting the political elite's anger against the third world, which had built up in response to the setbacks of the early 1970s) was able to make the "anti-Americanism" of third world-dominated institutions a key political issue within the nation's conservative movement. That movement was already predisposed to view international institutions with hostility because of fears that the decisions and actions of these international institutions would derogate from national sovereignty: that is, faceless bureaucrats of another nationality would make decisions affecting the American people.

Today we have arrived at a point where, for the first time since the end of World War II, one can imagine an American repudiation of the Roosevelt-Truman-Eisenhower legacy of liberal internationalism. Early in the second term of the Clinton administration, the United States was in arrears to every major international body except the North Atlantic Treaty Organization (NATO). This, despite the fact that the United States holds the largest voting block in the International Monetary Fund (18 percent) and the World Bank institutions (ranging from 15 to 22 percent). As of March 1999, the United States owed over $1.6 billion in back dues to the UN—or 61 percent of all arrears. Congress was threatening to withhold payment unless these organizations agreed to a number of reforms that did not enjoy majority support from other countries. Although public opinion polls demonstrated that the general public did not share the hostility of many in the political elite toward international institutions, there was little public outcry against Congress for withholding payment.

Meanwhile, the end of the cold war had breathed new life into traditional American isolationism. With no great security threat from abroad, American conservatives were even less likely to accept the constraints of international institutions and obligations. With no need for allies, why accept the constraints necessary to lure and mollify them?

The extraordinary range of American military power also undermined any postwar commitment to multilateralism. With America towering over others militarily, could we not do what we wanted? Was there a need to accept the constraints of alliance and membership? Why not act as we saw fit to protect American interests, the views of allies and friends notwithstanding?

In these new circumstances, what balance should exist between multilateralism and unilateralism? The question has become acute as domestic attacks on multilateralism have intensified, foreign discontent with American unilateralism has grown, and allied fears of nascent American isolationism have begun to surface.

MULTILATERALISM VERSUS UNILATERALISM

It is difficult to determine the appropriate balance in American foreign policy between multilateralism and unilateralism without specifying what kind of foreign policy the United States wishes to carry out in the post–cold war world. After all, the more isolationist a foreign policy the country adopts, the more unilaterally it can act. But it does not necessarily follow that the more ambitious a foreign policy the United States embraces, the more multilateral it must be. Because the United States currently enjoys such a surplus of power, it is now possible for Washington to have a very ambitious foreign policy and still remain unilateral in its approach toward the outside world. The United States is perhaps now the only country in the world that can, to a very significant measure, get its way internationally if it is absolutely determined to bend others to its will. What is required is a sufficient commitment of political, economic, and military resources.

In Europe, for example, the United States is able to pursue what we might call a unilateralist internationalist policy on political and security issues. By devoting roughly half of its enormous military budget to the defense of Europe, the United States has managed to acquire a position of almost total dominance in NATO. America's European allies are willing to accept this degree of U.S. control because America's defense commitments enable the Europeans to forgo massive defense expenditures of their own. In effect, the payment they make in lieu of larger defense expenditures is to throw a multilateral cloak over American unilateralism. In so doing, they provide multilateral legitimacy to American unilateral action. Elsewhere in the world, American unilateralism is more exposed for what it is. No one doubts that American policy toward Cuba, for example, is the product of a unilateralist foreign policy, and in the eyes of others it lacks legitimacy.

For the purposes of this chapter examining America's choices between multilateralism and unilateralism, the following assumptions about the likely course of American foreign policy under either Democratic or Republican administrations seem realistic:

- First, the United States will not seize what some have called our "unipolar" moment to set up an imperial regime. That is to say, the United States will not strive for the policy of "hegemony" that the editors of the conservative weekly, *The National Standard*, have been urging the nation to adopt.
- Second, the United States will not adopt a full-blown policy of isolationism, championed by conservatives like presidential candidate Pat Buchanan. It will not withdraw its troops from most foreign bases. It will not abandon its alliances. It will not adopt a protectionist trade policy.
- Third, the main debate in American foreign policy will be over how Washington should adapt the policy it has followed since 1945 to the new post–cold war conditions. Formally, the United States will announce its continued commitment to a policy of friendly alliances, open trade, and a democratic ideology. At the same time, Washington will probably become more demanding of its allies in terms of material support for America's own foreign policy goals, less indulgent of others' trade discrimination against it, and since the end of the cold war freer to press for commitment to its democratic ideology in all cases where the country in question is not in a position to resist.

What all this means, more specifically, is that in the security field, the United States will insist that its allies not only finance the war, such as they did in the effort against Iraq, but that they also help in actually fighting the war. It is quite probable that America's allies will rebuff such pressure and that their refusal to bow to American demands will place great strains on America's alliance system. In the trade field, it means that the United States is likely to show more resistance to maintaining its traditional, compliant role of importer of last resort, even though the now-globalized world economy may require it to play such a role.

The United States will continue to pursue the spread of the ideology of elected democracy. In this regard, it will remain more Wilsonian in its approach to international affairs than Rooseveltian (Teddy), although its foreign policy will be an uneasy mix of Wilsonian triumphalism and balance-of-power realism. In other words, whenever the price is not too high in terms of direct damage to core U.S. interests, future American administrations are likely to be more motivated by democratic ideals than by power politics. They will press small countries that cannot resist to democratize and open their markets. They will be more modest in their demands of a large power like China.

On the assumption that these predictions of future American behavior are correct, what kind of multilateralism should the United States embrace? It should have the following characteristics:

- Be stronger but more responsive to the demands of member states
- Be more democratic but more reflective of the altered balance of power internationally
- See its mandate as protecting not just the bureaucracy itself but the people it is supposed to serve

Instead, the Bush and Clinton administrations decided to proceed down a more familiar path. The United States has struggled to retain every institutional advantage it enjoyed during the height of the cold war and pressed forward to improve its position in the name of "exporting" security and welfare to those formerly trapped behind the Iron Curtain. Institutions, domestic and foreign, configured to fight the cold war—the Defense Department, the Central Intelligence Agency, and NATO—have remained at cold war financial and organizational levels. The institutional foundations of the new world order have begun to look very much like the institutional foundations of the now-defunct cold war order.

This approach, however, faces a very special problem. The more honest among those who called for the United States to move beyond its cold war level of commitments to approach something resembling global hegemony recognize that such a policy would require a massive increase in the current international affairs budget. For a variety of domestic reasons, Washington has recently found money for international purposes hard to come by. In this post–cold war era, how can America pay for its foreign policy of calculated advance and enlargement of its responsibilities? How can it gain the acquiescence, if not the support, of others no longer inclined to blindly follow the U.S. lead now that the Soviet threat has disappeared?

U.S.-CONTROLLED MULTILATERALISM

The answer the political elite in the United States has given to these questions has been a new form of multilateralism: America will turn to international institutions to solve the problems of money and legitimacy, but it will not accept all the obligations of membership. The reasoning behind this approach is that international organizations institutionalize burden sharing and legislate compliance, and if the United States can gain these without hindering its own margin of maneuver, so much the better. By nature of membership in international institutions, all members must contribute to the overall program. Through their membership, all states also bestow legitimacy on the decisions taken—even those they oppose.

The system worked well for a while. During the Gulf War the United States called the shots and presented the bill to others. Indeed, in the case of the Gulf War, the United States even made money out of the effort. Washington was also able to persuade United Nations (UN) members to provide troops and money to support the U.S.-led intervention in Haiti. It convinced the Security Council to impose sanctions on Libya. UN members shared the cost of the very expensive international intervention in Cambodia—U.S.-conceived and organized.

The Clinton administration looked at this pattern and in its early days began to talk of "assertive multilateralism" as its new foreign policy doctrine. Under American direction, international organizations would manage the new post–cold war world. The American leadership position in most international organizations would permit Washington to set the policy, gain legitimacy for its decisions through the institutional endorsement of others, and secure common financing for a Washington-approved objective.

In some respects, of course, the new multilateralism was the old unilateralism by another name. In its new emphasis on international organizations, the United States gave no assurance that its own actions would be limited by the decisions of the institutions it now claimed were so important. Indeed, even to hint that the United States might be bound by international obligations—as it insisted others should be—was to risk a political firestorm. This point surfaced regularly and was confirmed in the negotiations that attempted to create an international criminal court, where the United States insisted that because now it was the world's sole superpower, it should not be subject to the same rules as others. (See essay 4–1: International Criminal Court.) The United States also insisted that other societies permit UN human rights investigators to enter their territory to document human rights abuses, but it was dismissive of UN efforts to study the flawed American record with regard to capital punishment where in practice those of color receive one standard of justice and those who are white receive another. (See essay 4–2: Human Rights and U.S. Policy.) What is astonishing is not simply the administration's position but the lack of reaction to it. Who can blame Clinton for wanting to avoid an unnecessary political battle with members of Congress opposed to UN investigations of U.S. practices? Why, however, was the American media so silent on this obvious double standard? (See figure 4–1.)

The U.S. decision to intervene in the Somali crisis ended all talk of assertive multilateralism. Here again, the United States set the policy while seeking legitimacy and financing from others. Initially, President George Bush sent U.S. troops into Somalia, bypassing the UN Security Council. This was soon viewed as a blunder. The United States was picking up 100 percent of the bill, well into the billions, which clearly could have been a collective obligation. So the United States passed the baton back to the United Nations. To ensure American control, the former deputy head of the National Security Council, an American admiral, was put in charge of the new multilateral effort. He remained in close contact with Washington, which never relinquished command of the U.S. troops participating in the UN operation.

Figure 4.1 Human Rights Regulations in U.S. Foreign Relations

Human Rights Regulations in U.S. Foreign Relations

The cornerstone of U.S. human rights legislation consists of three sections in two Authorization Acts, which are relatively permanent aspects of law: the Foreign Assistance Act and the International Financial Institutions Act. Another three sections relating to human rights legislation are contained in the Foreign Operations Appropriations Act, which must be reintroduced each year. This legislation ties grants of military and economic assistance to the human rights policies of recipient governments.

Foreign Assistance Act

Section 116a: "No assistance may be provided under this part to the government of any country which engages in a consistent pattern of gross violations of internationally recognized human rights such as torture or cruel, inhumane, or degrading treatment or punishment, prolonged detention without charges, or other flagrant denial to life, liberty, and the security of person, unless such assistance will directly benefit the needy people in such country."

Section 502b: "The United States shall, in accordance with its international obligations as set forth in the Charter of the United Nations and in keeping with the constitutional heritage and traditions of the United States, promote and encourage increased respect for human rights and fundamental freedoms throughout the world."

International Financial Institutions Act

Section 701: "The United States Executive Directors of the institutions listed in subsection (a) (International Bank for Reconstruction and Development, the International Development Association, International Finance Corporation, the Inter-American Development Bank, The African Development Fund, The Asian Development Bank, and the African Development Bank) are authorized and instructed to oppose any loan, any extension of financial assistance, or any technical assistance to any country that illustrates a pattern of gross violations of internationally recognized human rights such as torture or cruel, inhumane, or degrading treatment or punishment, prolonged detention without charges, or other flagrant denial to life, liberty, and the security of person; or, provides refuge to individuals committing acts of international terrorism by hijacking aircraft unless such assistance is directed specifically to programs which serve the basic human needs of the citizens of such country."

Foreign Operations Appropriations Act

Section 508: "None of the funds appropriated . . . [by] this Act shall be . . . expended to finance directly any assistance to any country whose duly elected head of government is deposed by military coup or decree: Provided, That assistance may be resumed to such country if the President determines . . . that subsequent to the termination of assistance a democratically elected government has taken office."

Section 568 [known as the Leahy Amendment]: "None of the funds made available by this Act may be provided to any unit of the security forces of a foreign country if the

(continues)

Figure 4.1 *(continued)*

Secretary of State has credible evidence that such unit has committed gross violations of human rights. In the event that funds are withheld from any unit pursuant to this section, the Secretary of State shall promptly inform the foreign government of the basis for such action and shall, to the maximum extent practicable, assist the foreign government in taking effective measures to bring the responsible members of the security forces to justice so funds to the unit may be resumed."

Section 551: "None of the funds appropriated . . . by this Act may be available to any foreign government which provides lethal military equipment to a country the government of which the Secretary of State has determined is a terrorist government. . . . The prohibition . . . with respect to a foreign government shall terminate 12 months after that government ceases to provide such military equipment."

Despite the strength of these regulations, each law contains various exceptions. Thus, economic aid does not have to be terminated if "such assistance will directly benefit the needy people in such country" (Foreign Assistance Act, Section 116a and International Financial Institution Act Section 701) Moreover, the president may continue security assistance to a gross violator if he certifies to the Congress "that extraordinary circumstances exist warranting provision of such assistance" or if the Secretary of State determines that the country is taking effective measures to bring the culprits to justice (Foreign Assistance Act, Section 502b and Leahy Amendment).

U.S. human rights law would be substantially strengthened by the passage of the Code of Conduct on U.S. Arms Transfers and Military Assistance, which would "prohibit United States military assistance and arms transfers to foreign governments that are undemocratic, do not adequately protect human rights, are engaged in acts of armed aggression, or are not fully participating in the United Nations Register of Conventional Arms."

Sources: Thomas Buergenthal, *International Human Rights in a Nutshell* (St. Paul, MN: West Publishing Co., 1988), pp. 232–236; "A Guide to the Laws Prohibiting U.S. Aid to Human Rights Violators Abroad," Center for International Policy, 1991.

Soon, in large measure because of its unilateralist approach to its multilateral obligations, the United States overreached. Under orders from Washington, the American force in Somalia, without informing the UN command, directed its troops to attempt to seize a Somali warlord. In the ensuing struggle, the U.S. troops—without any backup from other UN forces who were in the dark about the operation—suffered casualties. American citizens watched in horror over live TV as Somali mobs dragged the naked corpse of a U.S. Ranger through the streets of Mogadishu. Suddenly, the costs of trying to run the world in a post–cold war environment became apparent. A firestorm erupted in the Congress, and the United States was forced to withdraw from Somalia in humiliation. (See essay 4–3: The United States and Abuse of the United Nations.)

Administration critics immediately began to launch vehement attacks on multilateralism, which amounted, they said, to subcontracting American foreign policy to the United Nations or some other international body. Quickly, the administration's attitude toward multilateralism went from its being the approach of preference to that of an occasionally useful tool. U.S. officials began asserting that the United States would attempt to follow the multilateral path when it could but the unilateral path when it must. In other words, the United States alone would decide when it would work with others. It would not accept for itself the binding commitments it wished to impose on others.

Washington's approach to the war in Kosovo fits this pattern. The United States, in effect, imposed its vision of multilateralism on its allies. Countries such as France, Germany, and Italy strongly preferred that the alliance attempt to gain legitimacy for its actions against Belgrade through a UN Security Council mandate. Washington knew it needed a multilateral cloak to cover its unilateral policy preferences, but it insisted that the operation be routed through NATO, which it controls, as opposed to the UN, which it does not. (See essay 4–4: Humanitarian Intervention: A Dangerous Doctrine.)

Washington won this policy dispute at the beginning of the war. The conflict's end, however, may give America's allies some quiet comfort. To bring the war to a conclusion without a ground campaign, Washington needed diplomatic assistance from Moscow, which insisted that the UN Security Council provide final blessing to the peace settlement.

This American trend to dictate to others the form of multilateralism it prefers can be seen in the U.S. approach to both economic and political issues. When the major American policymakers considered U.S. membership in the World Trade Organization, they threatened to call for a reconsideration of membership if the new body were to rule against the United States three times. In the case of the UN-approved sanctions against Iraq, Washington insisted that all member states comply; whereas in the case of the UN-sanctioned arms embargo against the successor states of the former Yugoslavia, the United States repeatedly threatened to violate the embargo if others would not follow its policy lead.

At this point, critics of multilateralism are high in the saddle. The United States has shown increasing hostility toward almost every international organization except NATO—the one it completely dominates. It is true that the administration opposes this negative stance toward international institutions, but the pressure from Congress is so great that in this case Congress, not the administration, is determining U.S. foreign policy.

Congressional hostility to international institutions ought in theory to end the debate over multilateralism versus unilateralism. It remains acute for one simple reason: Congress is unwilling to fund the ambitious foreign policy that it and the administration want to pursue. Washington must have the financial support of others to continue on its current course. That requires a bow to multilateralism. It also needs the legitimacy that flows from their support, because it knows that acting unilaterally will extract a high price politically. That requires a certain respect for multilateralism. The U.S. effort to curb the nuclear ambitions of North Korea is an excellent example of these points. Initially, some U.S. officials were inclined to try to solve the problem unilaterally through a preemptive military strike. But it soon became apparent that U.S. military action would not enjoy the support of South Korea and Japan—the two nations the United States was ostensibly protecting from the North Koreans. A negotiated settlement became imperative. Here, however, Washington faced an impasse. The North Korean goal was economic assistance; it would not halt its nuclear program without it. Meanwhile, for both political and economic reasons, the United States would not provide North Korea with any significant assistance.

Washington therefore turned to a multinational mechanism involving Japan and South Korea to finance an agreement that they themselves had played only a minor role in negotiating. In the final agreement, South Korea and Japan pledged billions of dollars compared to only millions from the United States. The fate of this agreement has been jeopardized repeatedly not only by provocative North Korean actions like missile tests through Japanese air space but by the repeated U.S. failure (from the beginning) to live up to its end of the agreement. The administration has had difficulty gaining approval for the small amount of aid the United States committed itself to provide. It has also refused to open U.S. markets to North Korea as promised in the agreement.

It is ironic that the tenure of Madeleine Albright, the first secretary of State to serve as the permanent U.S. representative to the United Nations, may well mark the lowest point in Washington approach toward multilateralism since the end of World War II. When Albright again becomes a private citizen, the United States is likely to remain massively in arrears to the United Nations (or to have paid only on condition that no U.S. dues be used for abortion advocacy), behind in its obligations to the international financial institutions, and at the lowest point of political elite support for these institutions within Washington since 1945. Clinton might rightly plead that he had made an effort to reverse congressional attitudes, but the record makes clear that this has not been a high priority of his administration.

THE REAGAN LEGACY

How did America come to this position? The turning point was the Reagan administration and its initial hostility toward international organizations.

Other administrations had had their difficulties with various international institutions, particularly the United Nations. Current mythology notwithstanding, the United States was never entirely comfortable with an activist role by the United Nations, even in the days of the now secularly sainted Dag Hammarskjold. Any secretary general who proves too independent will not be palatable to American tastes. The United States has always preferred the head of the UN to be more secretary than general. Like the Soviet Union, the United States has usually preferred a secretary general who would concentrate on management, not international diplomacy. Only in emergencies where Washington officials have had little alternative have they changed their minds.

The legendary difficulties between Washington and Boutros Boutros-Ghali during his term as secretary general stem primarily from the fact that in the post–cold war world, the United States is even less inclined to seek an interlocutor. It wanted a secretary general to announce support and help secure it from others; it does not want a secretary general to show diplomatic initiative. Boutros-Ghali felt that his responsibilities as secretary general barred him from offering any nation, even the United States, such automatic support.

Any objective assessment would reveal that Boutros-Ghali generally followed a very pro-American line while he was secretary general, but he was perhaps the most independent of all the secretary generals since Hammarskjold, and he paid for this independence by losing American confidence—and thus his job. His public calls for the members of the Security Council to live up to their responsibilities and attempt to halt the genocidal struggle in Rwanda were particularly unsettling to the Clinton administration, which after the debacle in Somalia was determined to avoid further involvement in African civil wars. (Although it must have given Boutrous-Ghali little comfort, the president did admit during his historic visit to Africa in 1997 that the outside world should have done more to halt the slaughter.)

The Clinton administration is not the first to find it difficult to secure congressional funding for international organizations. Every administration has found it a perils-of-Pauline experience to persuade Congress to fund the U.S. share of international development and cooperation efforts. These enduring problems notwithstanding, the Reagan administration marked a departure, because, with its rise to power, occasional executive branch discontentment with the policies or performance of international institutions gave way to conceptual hostility. The official U.S. representative to the United Nations, Jeane Kirkpatrick, publicly denounced the world body as a "socialist" bastion of anti-Americanism. Senior Treasury Department officials publicly questioned the value of international development institutions. In the monetary field, the administration embarked on an economic policy of high interest rates at home (designed to fight inflation) and paid no attention to the international ramifications. Indeed, the Latin American debt crisis can be directly traced in a significant measure to the fact that the Reagan Treasury believed the United States had no obligation to be concerned about the international impact of U.S. interest policies. In effect, during that period, the United States ceased regarding itself as the steward of the international system, a role it had played since 1945. The Brady plan to deal with the Latin American debt crisis—named after the then U.S. Secretary of the Treasury—marked a return by the Bush administration to that earlier stewardship role.

The Clinton administration—not by choice but in response to congressional pressure—has moved closer to the early Reagan view than did even the Bush administration.

The Reagan legacy of unilateralism has become dominant, at least within the political elite, and is having a profound influence on the conduct of American foreign policy. This legacy is, of course, in harmony with many of the more enduring themes of American history, which partially explains its power. American unilateralism, in fact, is simply American isolationism in another form. The essence of American isolationism, after all, was not a pacific America. Indeed, during America's most isolationist phase in the last century, the country was at its most bellicose and imperialistic, launching military actions against indigenous peoples across the country and against Canada, Mexico, and a host of Central American and Caribbean states. Rather the essence of American isolationism has been the freedom of action the American Republic enjoyed. No alliance tied it down. Geography allowed it to ignore the preferences of others. George Washington warned against entangling alliances because America would no longer be in control of its own fate. It could be drawn into quarrels against its will and interests.

In today's multilateral world, America has tried to square its unilateralist tradition with its multilateral commitments by insisting that the United States dominate the alliances it joins. In this new world, provided America still calls the shots, it will still retain control over its own fate, concerns of allies or demands of international obligations notwithstanding. In other words, the United States does not have to be isolationist to be unilateralist. Following this logic, Washington will never "subcontract its foreign policy" to an international body, as conservative critics of the Clinton administration have charged it was doing by seeking UN sanction for its actions. The United States will always insist on controlling or ignoring any international body in which it is involved. Following the August 1998 terrorist attacks on the U.S. embassies in East Africa, for instance, the United States retaliated by unilaterally bombing a suspected guerrilla camp in Afghanistan and a pharmaceutical factory in Sudan. Then President Clinton lectured the United Nations about the need for collective response to the threat of global terrorism. (See essay 4–5: International Terrorism.) Perhaps one explanation for the U.S. political elite's growing dissatisfaction with the United Nations is that although the United States is clearly the dominant power in the organization and gets its way most of the time, it does not get its way all of the time. From this standpoint, the United Nations affronts a fundamental premise of American foreign policy: namely, that the United States must control its own fate in a way that no other power in modern history ever has.

THE CHALLENGE OF THE NEW AGENDA

If historic American attitudes toward foreign policy help to explain the increasingly suspicious official U.S. view of international institutions that it does not dominate, the changing nature of the international agenda has only compounded U.S. concern with multilateralism. With the end of the cold war, there seems no reason why the international community should not be much more active in the field of peace and security—except that greater activism might entail U.S. commitments in parts of the world not central to traditional American concepts of national interest. The changing character of the world economy is progressively lifting from the hands of national governments the power to shield their citizens from economic adversity. Open borders, massive capital flows, and mounting levels of international trade, together with volatile exchange rates, have exposed the workers of every country to sudden shifts in fortune. Governments can do little to serve as a buffer.

Proposals to deal with these developments by strengthening international institutions cause anxiety on both the right and the left within the American political establishment. On the right, the fear is of a loss of sovereignty; on the left, the concern is a loss of democracy.

Both wings of the antimultilateralist coalition, in fact, have a case to make. The global market is eroding sovereignty. The market is steadily tightening a vise on national governments, leaving less and less room for maneuver. Globalization is also eroding democracy. The free market rules, not national parliaments. In recent years, France has repeatedly elected governments that have promised they would use the powers of office to reduce unemployment. Once elected, these governments find that they are powerless to influence economic policy because of France's membership in the European Union and its commitment to an open market.

Although the size of America's economy gives it a somewhat larger margin for maneuver, Bill Clinton learned how much the world had changed when he entered the White House. To balance the budget and protect the value of the dollar internationally, he was forced to scrap most of the promises he had made to the voters. The consequence of keeping these promises might have been a falling exchange rate, which would have then persuaded the Asians—who had helped finance the Reagan deficits—to withdraw their money. So campaign promises gave way to market reality. James Carville, the political operative who helped Clinton reach the White House, has stated that if he could be born again, he would want to return as a bond dealer because they, not politicians, now run the world.

The democratic deficit inherent in the rise of multilateralism increases to the degree that states attempt to cope with disruptions in international markets by asking international organizations to play a larger role. Almost all international institutions are elitist, removed from ordinary people and controlled by a handful of bureaucrats within the organizations and key ministries of the member governments. To the degree that these institutions are accorded responsibilities that were previously the domain of nation-states, a serious issue of democratic accountability arises.

In Asia, the International Monetary Fund and a handful of national technocrats makes decisions adversely affecting the fate of hundreds of millions of people. In theory, only elected representatives should make such fateful decisions. Along the Mexican border, expert panels are making decisions that enrich some and impoverish others. Florida's tomato growers understand this and have successfully lobbied to block key provisions of NAFTA.

In Bosnia, the U.S. commander of NATO troops is making decisions regarding the use of troops from other countries that previously only their own governments would have made. For Americans, the democratic deficit in the management of NATO is less because it is an American-controlled institution. There is, however, a democratic deficit for other members, which has been a traditional French complaint about NATO.

The supporters of multilateralism face a dilemma. They are correct that many of the problems of globalization can be addressed only through stronger and more effective international organizations. In the military field, future international institutions must provide the intrusive inspection capabilities necessary to police arms control agreements. As efforts to control weapons of mass destruction become more serious, these institutions will achieve a degree of intrusiveness heretofore undreamed of. This point was recognized during negotiations regarding the chemical weapons treaty. To control chemical weapons, one must be in a position to police every fertilizer plant in the world—a daunting task. (See figure 4–2.)

In the economic field, a one-world economy will increase the need for capable international institutions that can monitor and regulate this new global commerce. Democratic states cannot allow the lives of their citizens to be overwhelmed suddenly by global economic developments over which they have no control. They will either raise barriers to protect themselves, or they will have to cooperate to master these new forces.

In the environmental field, cross-border pollution and other environmental problems beyond the capability of any one country to solve also call for more capable international institutions. Consequently, multilateralism is here to stay, its

Figure 4.2   Status of Major Arms Control Treaties

Comprehensive Test Ban Treaty (CTB)

Signed by United States:	September 24, 1996
History of Negotiations:	Negotiations on banning nuclear weapons testing began under President Eisenhower but were derailed by the downing of an American U-2 spy plane over the Soviet Union in 1959. Intermittent negotiations throughout the Cold War but no real progress until 1996. Negotiations concluded September 1996.
Key Elements:	Bans all nuclear weapons test explosions for all time. Creates a mutilayered verification system to detect cheating.
Status in World:	Enters into force when all 44 nations with seismic monitoring stations on their territory ratify the CTB. India and Pakistan, both of whose ratifications are necessary for the treaty to enter into force, conducted a series of nuclear tests in 1998. Both countries are slowly making progress toward signing the treaty. Nations that have ratified can meet in 1999 to determine how to speed up the ratification process.
Status in United States:	President submitted CTB to U.S. Senate in September 1997 for its advice and consent to ratification. In October 1999 the U.S. Senate failed to ratify the CTB. Technically, the test ban treaty remains at the Senate desk and can be called up at any time. But in reality, it will take a newly elected president to resurrect and bring the test ban treaty before the Senate again with any hope of approval.

Amendments to the Anti-Ballistic Missile Treaty (ABM)

Signed by United States:	September 26, 1997
History of Negotiations:	ABM Treaty between United States and Soviet Union entered into force, October 3, 1972. Protocol was added, July 3, 1974. Negotiations on delineating between theater missile defense systems and ballistic missile defense systems began in 1995. One agreement on interceptor velocity for theater missile defense and an agreement on treaty succession to the newly independent republics was reached at the Helsinki Summit in March 1997. These two agreements, plus an additional agreement on interceptor velocity, were signed on September 26, 1997.
Key Elements:	Three separate agreements: (1) On September 26, 1997, the United States, Russia, Ukraine, Belarus, and Kazakhstan signed a memorandum of understanding extending the treaty to the Soviet Union successor states. This agreement will go to the Senate. (2) The United States and Russia signed a "part 1" demarcation on September 26, 1997, distinguishing national missile defenses from lower-velocity theater missile defenses. This agreement will go to the Senate. (3) The United States and Russia signed a "part II" demarcation agreement on September 26, 1997, distinguishing national missile defenses from higher velocity theater missile

(continues)

Figure 4.2 *(continued)*

	defenses. Once agreed upon, "part II" will also go to the Senate.
Status in United States:	ABM Treaty under attack by conservatives in the U.S. Senate who want to abrogate the ABM Treaty and build a national missile defense system. Modifications to the treaty must be approved by the Senate, but the administration has not sent them to the Senate for consideration. A U.S. decision to deploy a National Missile Defense may destroy the treaty.

Landmine Treaty (Ottawa Treaty)

History of Negotiations:	Approximately 100 nations negotiated a treaty in 1997 to ban land mines and replace the flawed Convention on Conventional Weapons.
Key Elements:	Would ban the production, use, and transfer of antipersonnel land mines and require their destruction.
Status in World:	Negotiations completed in Oslo on September 18, 1997. Treaty entered into force on March 1, 1999. 135 nations have signed the treaty; 81 have ratified.
Status in United States:	United States was unable to get exceptions in the treaty for "smart" mines that self-destruct and for mines on the Korean Peninsula. Clinton administration has stated that it will not sign the treaty until alternative defenses are developed.

Modifications to Strategic Arms Reduction Treaty II (START II)

Signed:	January 3, 1993; modifications agreed to March 1997 and signed September 27, 1997.
History of Negotiations:	START II originally signed by Presidents Bush and Yeltsin in 1993; Presidents Clinton and Yeltsin agreed to a framework agreement to START III at the Helsinki summit in March 1997, negotiations of which will begin after the Russian Duma has ratified START II.
Key Elements:	START II reduces U.S. and Russian strategic nuclear forces to between 3,000 and 3,500 delivery vehicles each by 2003. Deadline for completing reductions extended to 2007, but warheads must be deactivated by 2003.
Status in World:	U.S. Senate approved ratification January 26, 1996. Ratification by Russian Duma still pending.
Status in United States:	Modification of START II awaiting Senate advice and consent to ratification.

Strategic Arms Reduction Treaty III (START III)

History of Negotiations:	Presidents Clinton and Yeltsin agreed to a framework for START III at the March 1997 Helsinki Summit. The U.S. and Russia are "discussing" a new treaty but not formally "negotiating" a new agreement. The U.S. position is that formal negotiations cannot begin until the Russian Duma ratifies START II.
Key Elements:	Reduces U.S. and Russian nuclear arsenals to between 2,000 and 2,500 delivery vehicles. Calls for destruction of nuclear warheads. (Previous agreements only required that

(continues)

Figure 4.2 *(continued)*

Status in World:	warheads be taken off of delivery vehicles and retired.) Negotiations to begin once Russian Duma ratifies START II.
Status in United States:	Once signed, ratification must be approved by U.S. Senate.

Strategic Arms Reduction Treaty I (START I) Extension

History of Negotiations:	Russia and the United States are negotiating an indefinite extension of the 15-year START I agreement.
Key Elements:	Makes START I limits of 6,000 warheads per side and 4,900 ballistic missiles permanent.
Status in World:	Treaty between Russia and the United States has been in force since 1991.
Status in United States:	Once signed, ratification must be approved by U.S. Senate.

South Pacific Nuclear Weapons Free Zone (Treaty of Rarotonga)

Signed by United States:	March 25, 1996
History of Negotiations:	Treaty was opened for signature by the five nuclear-weapons states in August 1986. Moscow signed in May 1988; China signed in January 1989. The United States, however, did not want to undercut its French allies, who were continuing their testing program in the South Pacific.
Key Elements:	Bans the manufacture, acquisition, testing, and stationing of any nuclear explosive device in the South Pacific as well as the dumping of radioactive wastes at sea.
Status in World:	Entered into force December 11, 1986.
Status in United States:	Awaiting transmittal by President to the Senate for its advice and consent to ratification.

African Nuclear Weapons Free Zone (Treaty of Pelindaba)

Signed by United States:	April 11, 1996
History of Negotiations:	The Organization of African Unity formally expressed a desire for a nuclear-free Africa in July 1964. Opened for signature April 11, 1996; culmination of a 32-year effort to ban nuclear weapons from the African continent.
Key Elements:	Bans the research, development, manufacturing, stockpiling, acquisition, testing, possession, control, or stationing of any nuclear explosive device in Africa. Also prohibits dumping of radioactive waste in the zone. The United States does not want to preclude option of using nuclear weapons against an alleged Libyan chemical weapons production facility but has not stated opposition to the treaty.
Status in World:	Enters into force after 28 countries ratify. Five countries, including South Africa, have ratified.
Status in United States:	Awaiting transmittal by President to Senate for advice and consent to ratification.

Law of the Seas Treaty

Signed by United States:	July 19, 1994
History of Negotiations:	Negotiated from 1973 to 1982. Opened for signature in 1982.

(continues)

Figure 4.2 *(continued)*

Key Elements:	Creates a comprehensive framework governing the use of the ocean and its resources.
Status in World:	Entered into force November 16, 1994. One hundred countries have ratified.
Status in United States:	Submitted to Senate in October 1994 for its advice and consent to ratification.

Amendments to the Convention on Conventional Weapons (CCW)

Signed by United States:	May 3, 1996
History of Negotiations:	Convention was opened for signature in 1980. The United States signed April 8, 1982; entered into force, December 2, 1983; Senate approved ratification, March 24, 1995. Treaty needs to be strengthened significantly.
Key Elements:	The original convention places restrictions on the use of land mines. The amendments will require that all land mines delivered outside of marked areas self-destruct 30 days after their placement.
Status in World:	Amendments enter into force six months after 20 members to the CCW provide notification of their consent to be bound by the amendments.
Status in United States:	Adopted in Senate by unanimous consent on May 20, 1999.

Fissile Material Cutoff Treaty

Key Elements:	Would cap the amount of fissile material available for nuclear explosives. Could bring unsafeguarded programs of non-NPT states under some international restraint for the first time.
Current Status:	Preliminary talks under way in Geneva.

Biological Weapons Convention

History of Negotiations:	The convention was approved on April 10, 1972; U.S. Senate approved ratification on December 16, 1974; Convention entered into force, March 26, 1975.
Key Elements:	Prohibits development, production, and stockpiling of bacteriological and toxin weapons. Members required to destroy their biological weapons arsenals. Duration is indefinite. Needs stronger verification protocol.
Current Status:	Conference ongoing to strengthen convention and create verification process similar to Chemical Weapons Convention.

Treaties Already Ratified

Chemical Weapons Convention (CWC)

Signed by United States:	January 13, 1993
History of Negotiations:	Bilateral negotiation between the United States and Soviet Union under President Nixon. International negotiations began under President Reagan. Opened for signature
Key Elements:	Would ban the development, production, transfer, and stockpile of toxic chemicals for use in warfare. Provides the most intrusive verification regime of any arms control agreement in history.

(continues)

Figure 4.2 *(continued)*

Status in World:	Entered into force April 29, 1997. Over 170 countries have signed the CWC and over 100 countries have ratified it.
Status in United States:	The U.S. Senate approved ratification 74–26, on April 24, 1997.

Amendments to the Conventional Forces in Europe Treaty (CFE)

Signed by United States:	May 31, 1996
History of Negotiations:	CFE Treaty signed on November 19, 1990; entered into force July 17, 1992. Amendments agreed to May 31, 1996. Further negotiations are under way in Vienna to adapt the treaty to new security environment. In July 1997, 30 countries announced the outline of the new agreement.
Key Elements:	Post–Soviet Union amendments resolve level of Russian troops along the southern flank in the Caucasus and Ukrainian troop levels on their southern flank.
Status in World:	Enters into force pending approval by all states of the CFE by May 15, 1997.
Status in United States:	Submitted to the Senate April 7, 1997; on May 14, 1997, the Senate voted 100–0 for the amendments.

Protocol on NATO Expansion

Key Elements:	Expands North Atlantic Treaty Organization (NATO) alliance to include Poland, Hungary, and the Czech Republic. Other former Warsaw Pact states likely to be invited to join in the future.
Status in World:	At the NATO summit meeting in Madrid on July 8–9, 1997, NATO voted to accept Poland, Hungary, and the Czech Republic. New member states were formally admitted in March 1999.

Convention on Nuclear Safety

Signed by United States:	September 20, 1994
History of Negotiations:	Negotiated 1992 through 1994.
Key Elements:	Would create international standards for the safety of land-based nuclear reactors. Lacks meaningful enforcement mechanism.
Status in World:	Entered into force October 24, 1996. Sixty-five countries have signed, twenty-five have deposited their instruments of ratification.
Status in United States:	Senate approved ratification on May 25, 1999.

Source: John Isaacs, "Status of Arms Control Treaties," *Council for a Livable World Education Fund,* November 1999. A June 1999 version, "Treaties that May Be Considered by the United States Senate in the Next Two Years" available on Internet at: http://www.clw.org.

growing defects notwithstanding. In all these fields, greater responsibility for international organizations seems essential for the peace and welfare of the world community. Yet the issues of sovereignty and freedom reveal serious flaws in the approach the world is currently taking. Reforms are obviously needed.

THE CHALLENGES

Reformers, however, face two major challenges, one conceptual and one ideological. As the great Israeli statesman Abba Eban has pointed out, behind the original conception of international organizations lies a belief that states will agree to act dispassionately and fairly in judging the international actions of others. Trade disputes will be decided on their merits. Aggression will be judged according to the facts, unbiased by alliances. There should be a single standard by which human rights violations are judged.

In other words, the founding fathers of the United Nations believed (or at least hoped it could become the case) that members of the General Assembly and the Security Council would not use a double standard in judging the actions of others. It is clear, however, that even the most democratic state will exercise a double standard in its assessments of the actions of friends. The United States will apply one standard in judging the domestic and international actions of Israel in the West Bank, or Britain in Northern Ireland, or Turkey in its Kurdish areas, and quite another standard in judging the actions of Syria in Lebanon, or Russia in Latvia, or Iran anywhere.

The ideological challenge facing the United Nations stems from recent shifts in attitudes toward government in general. After 1945, until perhaps 1975, the dominant ideology of noncommunist governments might be described as social democratic. The astonishing accomplishments of governments during World War II convinced everyone that governments could act for the common good. Their accomplishments during the war period seemed to put in the shadows the deeds of private business, still tarnished by the performance of the economy during the Great Depression. Ordinary citizens in most countries came to believe that it was entirely appropriate for governments to involve themselves directly in the economic management of their societies. This attitude influenced the way people looked at international organizations. If governments could achieve important economic and social objectives domestically, then through cooperation in international institutions they could attempt similar feats internationally. Given this orientation, the international community launched a number of important development programs designed to accomplish results in the developing world similar to those achieved in the industrialized world.

Today, popular belief in the social democratic approach to public policy problems has almost entirely collapsed. Growing pockets of resistance to the market-dominated policy framework exist, and sudden economic disaster may greatly swell their numbers. Nevertheless, the general assumption today is that only the market economy can solve economic and even social problems.

This is manifestly not true, but it would be foolish to deny the radically changed nature of public ideology in democratic countries. This change in the intellectual climate has profound consequences for efforts at international cooperation. If social democracy is bankrupt domestically, does it not follow that it will be bankrupt internationally? Can we pretend to solve in Haiti the very problems that we have come, regrettably, to agree we cannot solve in Harlem or West Virginia?

In short, we have arrived at the end of an era. It is now necessary to reformulate the mission of international institutions to reflect this change in the intellectual climate. International institutions need not only reform, they need also acquire a new ideology.

THE FUTURE

Historically, the paramount role of government has been to provide physical security, by stopping the invader at the borders. Since the end of World War II, for most states the primary role of government has been to reduce economic uncertainty in the lives of ordinary citizens. Although many governments were not in a position to fulfill this role in any adequate measure, protecting citizens from economic setbacks is still the goal. It is to be accomplished through the provision of emergency aid in times of disaster, both economic and natural, and through the management of the economy at the macro level in normal times.

In recent years because of changing demographics and excessive demands, more by the rich than the poor, the system has become overtaxed. Citizens have come to expect benefits that the economies in which they work cannot support. Nevertheless, the fundamental obligation of governments, both national and intergovernmental, to reduce the degree of uncertainty in the lives of their citizens should remain the foremost obligation of the public sector. The immediate task of intergovernmental institutions in the coming years should be to document the activities of the globalized economy in a way that can enlarge the opportunities for greater democratic control by ordinary citizens. This means that these institutions should use a greater degree of transparency to encourage more effective steps in the field of regulation, beginning with the realm of environmental standards, labor rights, and the protection of children. As argued above, it is simply not possible for either the United States or other countries to cope with the global economy without stronger international institutions. A unilateralist approach will ultimately fail.

At the national level, one of the functions of government is to prevent a race to the bottom, as capital seeks the cheapest and most compliant source of labor. In a globalized market, mechanisms comparable to those at the national level must be developed to prevent a similar race from occurring. Although recent administrations seem to have embraced the invisible hand almost totally in their international economic policy, over the long run, democratic political systems will demand that governments play a larger role internationally in protecting the rights of ordinary workers and citizens.

There is another responsibility that international institutions cannot abandon; namely, the effort pioneered by Woodrow Wilson to establish an institutional alternative to the traditional game of great power politics. This latter approach to international affairs is the most realistic and can never be neglected. It will remain central to the conduct of any foreign policy. Nevertheless, the weakness of the balance-of-power approach to international relations is its record. It is prone to repeated failure, and when it fails, the costs are enormous, as we have learned in this century.

There is no reason to believe that such an approach will not bring similar devastation in the future. It may be that the effort to try to tame the international competitive game among nation-states through the establishment of international norms and laws will continue to prove utopian. It is clear that the United Nations cannot operate as its founding fathers had hoped. Not only will the great powers not work together systematically to prevent aggression, but the response of smaller countries to decisions by the Security Council has never been what the UN's founding fathers anticipated. They expected that when the permanent members of the Security Council could agree on a course of action, the assemblage of power represented by the agreement of the five permanent members would induce the rest of the world to fall into line. In practice, smaller countries learned long ago that they could defy the Security Council with impunity, because it was not in the national interests of the larger states to punish them for their defiance.

The Security Council is, therefore, often faced with the unpleasant choice between accepting the fact that states may defy its decisions or resolving to take steps to compel compliance. Attempting the latter means, in practice, either economic sanctions or the use of military force. The Security Council has shown itself loath to impose either. A close examination of the economic sanctions imposed in recent years reveals that important states usually take steps to protect themselves, even at the risk of limiting the effectiveness of the sanctions. Thus, sanctions against Libya do not prevent oil shipments to Italy. The sanctions against South Africa were carefully designed to protect British firms. The UN sanctions against Haiti were designed to protect American investors with properties in Haiti. (See figure 4–3.)

It is time that a key characteristic of sanctions be recognized: They are effective only at the margin, and they are more effective as a threat than as a weapon. What this means is that sanctions cannot be used to force a government to undertake an action that it knows amounts to national suicide. It is totally unrealistic to expect that sanctions will force Saddam Hussein to leave power voluntarily or even to take any action that he believes will have the same consequential effect. Trade sanctions against China will force it to make concessions at the margin but not to dismantle its entire political system. No amount of economic pressure will force Fidel Castro to take actions that will lead to the downfall of his regime. Sanctions in all these cases should aim lower to be more effective. Sanctions can force Iraq to curb its military power significantly. They can force China to take some steps in the human rights field and make concessions in the economic area. That is far as one can expect sanctions to go, however.

The use of force is even more controversial. Peacekeeping works as long as the intended beneficiaries accept the presence of foreign troops on their soil. The minute the host countries cease to welcome them and the troops must fight to maintain their presence, the will of UN members to persevere disappears. No achievable reform will solve this problem overnight, and for the moment, the hostility of the U.S. Congress to peacekeeping puts limits on what the international community can do collectively in the field of peace and security. (See figure 4–4.)

The current unfavorable political climate does not mean, however, that the world should abandon the multilateral experiment. The United Nations and most international institutions have proven to be marginal institutions, but the margin itself is important. The key objective in the coming years must be to try to enlarge the margin. We do not want to rely solely on the balance of power in an age of spreading weapons of mass destruction.

Figure 4.3   Different Types of U.S. Economic Sanctions

Both the Congress and the president in recent years have increasingly relied on economic sanctions to establish and promote their foreign policy objectives. The Congressional Research Service has documented 228 laws that are currently used or could be used to apply sanctions. In general, sanctions take the general forms:

- Foreign assistance, all or some programs, could be terminated, suspended, limited, conditioned, or prohibited. Foreign assistance to particular organizations that operate in the targeted country could be curtailed. U.S. government arms sales and transfers, military assistance, and International Military Education and Training (IMET) funding could be similarly restricted. Scientific and technological cooperation, assistance, and exchanges could be reduced or halted.
- Both public and private sector financial transactions could be restricted; assets in U.S. jurisdictions could be seized or frozen, or transactions related to travel or other forms of exchange could be limited or prohibited.
- Importation and exportation of some or all commodities could be curtailed by denying licenses, closing off shipping terminuses, or limiting related transactions.
- Government procurement contracts could be canceled or denied.
- Negative votes on loans, credits, or grants in international financial institutions could be cast, or the United States could abstain in voting.
- Trade agreements or other bilateral accords could be abrogated, made conditional, or not renewed. Beneficial trade status could be denied, withdrawn, or made conditional. Trade and import quotas for particular commodities could be lessened or eliminated altogether. The U.S. tax code could be amended to discourage commerce with a sanctioned state.
- Funding for investment, through the Overseas Private Investment Corporation, Trade and Development Agency, or Export-Import Bank, could be curtailed.
- Aviation, maritime, and surface access to the United States could be canceled or denied.
- Certain acts associated with sanctionable behavior could be made a criminal offense—making the targeted individual subject to fines or imprisonment. Additionally, sanctions could be applied against those individuals, businesses, or countries that continue to trade with or support targeted individuals, businesses, or countries.

In 1998, the United States had imposed sanctions against 26 countries, including, Burma, Cuba, Haiti, Indonesia, Iran, Liberia, Nigeria, and Yugoslavia, according to the Institute for International Economics, a conservative think tank. With international sanctions against Iraq causing an estimated 5,000 deaths a month, there is growing public debate about when, where, and under what kind of conditions sanctions should be applied.

Sources: Dianne E. Rennack and Robert D. Shuey, "Economic Sanctions to Achieve U.S. Foreign Policy Goals: Discussion and Guide to Current Law," *CRS Report for Congress,* June 5, 1998, pp. 4, 7–26; Gary Clyde Hufbauer, "The Snake Oil of Diplomacy: When Tensions Rise, the U.S. Peddles Sanctions," *Washington Post,* July 12, 1998.

Figure 4.4   U.S. Role in UN Peacekeeping: 1998

U.S. Troops serving as UN Peacekeepers	583 (5% of total UN peacekeeping troops)
U.S. Financial Contributions to UN Peackeeping	$285 million (31.4% of UN peacekeeping costs)
U.S. Outstanding Dues for Peacekeeping	$1.0 billion

Sources: "Current United Nations Peace Operations & U.S. Troop Levels," Council for a Livable World Education Fund, November 30, 1988, UN Department of Public Information, Interview, June 21, 1999.

HOW CAN WE RESTORE FAITH IN MULTILATERALISM?

For most of the postwar period, the United States offered what might be termed positive leadership in multilateral diplomacy. The United States was willing to make a heavy financial commitment to a variety of institutions, its share of the budget often approaching 50 percent or more. Washington was also willing to bolster diplomatic initiatives with a generous offer of support during the critical, initial start-up period.

Since 1980, the United States has reverted primarily to what might be called negative leadership. It has threatened to punish others if it did not get its way. It has suggested it would withdraw if others did not agree. It has withheld its dues. Other countries have grown tired and resentful of these tactics. Even faced with intense American financial blackmail through the withholding of dues, other members have been unwilling to accept the American position on UN reform, which really amounts to a severe crippling of the UN's potential for development as an important international institution.

We need a new approach. In the field of peace and security, the United States should enter into a period of modest retrenchment internationally. It is not in a position to participate in any more vigorous commitments to constructive multilateralism. It should encourage others, including its allies, to show the way. In the economic and environmental field, U.S. policymakers and citizens must press for the U.S. government to do its share.

The secret to great leadership is not so much radical departures but an ability to take advantage of crises to gain majority support for a course that many have acknowledged all along was sensible but that was deemed politically unrealistic. In the coming years, it seems fairly clear that American unilateralism will encounter growing resistance from our friends and allies. It also seems clear that the rise of the global economy will demand a new approach to multilateralism. A crisis is approaching. We must exploit it to commit the United States to the path of responsible multilateralism for the new century.

THE INTERNATIONAL CRIMINAL COURT

Joe Stork

ON JULY 17, 1998, AFTER FIVE WEEKS OF INTENSE NEGOTIATIONS, 120 states voted in Rome to approve a treaty to establish an International Criminal Court (ICC). Seven states—the United States, China, Iraq, Israel, Libya, Qatar, and Yemen—voted against the treaty. The court, which will investigate and prosecute individuals accused of genocide, crimes against humanity, and war crimes, comes into being once 60 states ratify the treaty. As of mid-November 1999, 5 states have ratified and 89 have signed the treaty, indicating intent to ratify.

The purpose of the ICC is not to replace or substitute for national criminal justice systems but rather to operate when a government is unwilling or unable to investigate and prosecute serious allegations against an individual—including situations where political turmoil renders a national justice system ineffective or when the government itself is responsible for gross abuses. An ICC, if it had existed, could have been the venue for the work of the special tribunals now dealing with the atrocities committed in Rwanda and the former Yugoslavia. It will not have retroactive jurisdiction—it will not be empowered to address the crimes of General Pinochet, for instance, or the Iraqi government's genocide campaign against that country's Kurds. But such a court will be empowered to address such crimes that occur in the future. One of the achievements of the Rome treaty, moreover, was the specific inclusion of crimes against humanity and war crimes that are directed against women, including rape and sexual slavery.

A bloc of like-minded states, including Canada, Germany, South Africa, and Argentina, worked closely with nongovernmental organizations to spearhead the effort for an effective and independent ICC. The Rome conference rejected the position of China and the United States, both of which wanted to subordinate the court to the UN Security Council, where they have a veto.

The Rome treaty rejected attempts to require the consent of all states concerned before the ICC could proceed with an investigation. Any deferral by the Security Council requires a majority vote of that body, without objection from a permanent member, thereby barring the ability of any one permanent member to block jurisdiction. It also gives the prosecutor "ex officio" powers to investigate allegations of crimes not only by referral from the Security Council or states that have ratified the treaty, but also based on information from victims and nongovernmental organizations. The principal weakness of the statute is that in the absence of Security Council referral, either the state of nationality of the accused or the state where the crimes occurred must have ratified the treaty for the court to have jurisdiction. This requirement can impede prosecution where crimes are committed in the context of an internal conflict, and means that nearly universal ratification will be required to overcome this obstacle.

U.S. opposition to the treaty stems mainly from the insistence of the Pentagon on retaining U.S. ability to prevent the prosecution of U.S. military personnel for actions undertaken in the course of duty. Under the treaty, a state that has ratified the treaty could initiate charges against U.S. citizens for war crimes alleged to have been committed on its territory, even if the United States is not party to the treaty. The administration cites the global deployment of U.S. forces, particularly those assigned to peacekeeping and humanitarian intervention missions, to suggest that it ought to have some special dispensation when it comes to accountability.

Such arguments are far-fetched. First, the court's jurisdiction will be limited to genocide, war crimes, and crimes against humanity—levels of atrocity unrelated to isolated and minor offenses committed during a peacekeeping or aid delivery mission. Second, if and when serious crimes and atrocities are committed, it will remain the paramount responsibility of a national judicial or military justice system—which certainly exists in the United States—to investigate and prosecute. Third, the treaty contains numerous checks and judicial review procedures that would prevent an ICC prosecutor from pursuing politically motivated and spurious allegations. Only if there was reasonable evidence that U.S. citizens ordered or committed war crimes or atrocities, and this was not investigated and prosecuted by U.S. authorities, could the ICC assert jurisdiction. This is the point of justice for all.

Although Washington often proclaims a commitment to multilateralism, it many times fails to support multilateral initiatives that may compel a higher degree of accountability to the international community. The United States should support an effective ICC—one that will not be impossibly constrained by the political imperatives of the moment in particular capitals, including Washington. If the Clinton administration declines to take up this challenge, then it may find itself once again—as in the Ottawa land mines negotiations—sidelined by history.

HUMAN RIGHTS AND U.S. POLICY

Joe Stork

THE PERIOD SINCE WORLD WAR II HAS SEEN AN EXPANDING international consensus around fundamental human rights. The United States has played a leading role in this unfolding dynamic, at least with regard to political and civil rights, but this role has been fraught with tension. Assertions that human rights are central to U.S. foreign policy are undermined both by Washington's reluctance to criticize the practices of commercially or strategically important countries and by a strong sense of exceptionalism-that the U.S. constitution and justice system cannot be improved upon and that efforts to hold the United States accountable to international standards are unacceptable infringements on sovereignty.

U.S. diplomats were influential in drawing up the 1948 Universal Declaration of Human Rights and the two primary treaties—the International Covenant on Political and Civil Rights (ICCPR) and the International Covenant on Economic, Social, and Cultural Rights (ICESCR)—that transformed the principles of the nonbinding declaration into treaty-based legal obligations. This leading diplomatic role coexisted alongside a fundamental ambivalence about the promotion and protection of human rights. Although the two covenants were opened for signature in 1966, the United States ratified the ICCPR only in 1992 and still has not ratified the ICESCR. In 1994, the Clinton administration secured ratification of the Convention Against Torture and Other Cruel, Inhuman, or Degrading or Punishment (CAT) and the Convention on the Elimination of All Forms of Racial Discrimination (CERD). But Washington still has not ratified the international conventions on women and children and has not joined any of the major International Labor Organization (ILO) conventions guaranteeing core labor rights to organize and engage in collective bargaining.

This exceptionalism is also manifested in the reservations the United States attached to those treaties it has joined. U.S. ratification of the ICCPR, for instance, included a reservation to the prohibition against executions for crimes committed under the age of 18. In all such ratifications, moreover, the United States has insisted that the treaties are not self-executing—in other words, specific implementing legislation is required—and has refused to introduce enabling legislation. Thus Americans cannot claim any of these extra protections in a U.S. court of law. As a result, those ratifications that have occurred are largely empty gestures in terms of providing any additional enforceable rights for U.S. citizens and residents.

The U.S. constitutional safeguards ensure de facto compliance with international human rights standards in many areas, but the divergences are serious. Some U.S. laws violate international treaties to which the United States is party. The "expedited removal" procedures of the 1996 Immigration Reform Act, for example, conflict with U.S. obligations under the 1951 UN Convention Relating to the Status of Refugees. In April 1998, the United States publicly rejected the finding of the UN Special Rapporteur for extrajudicial executions that the death penalty was being applied in an unfair, arbitrary, and discriminatory manner.

The Clinton administration's foreign human rights policy has been much like that of its predecessors: namely, prioritize human rights when competing concerns are insignificant, or as with China, when public pressure compels a response. A major focus of U.S.

commercial and strategic interests, China engages in a wide range of severe and systematic abuses, and Chinese human rights activists and political reformers keep the issue prominent. In 1993, Clinton issued an executive order linking renewal of trade benefits to human rights improvements. However, in 1994, trade benefits were renewed despite the absence of human rights improvements, and the question of linkage was dropped. To cover its retreat, the administration has asserted a false choice between a policy of isolation and one of engagement, claiming the relationship was too important to be held hostage to a single issue. But when the administration more successfully threatened to end trade concessions over issues such as copyright piracy, there was no clamor from the corporate community about holding the relationship hostage to single issue diplomacy.

The most crippling feature of U.S. human rights policy abroad is its transparent selectivity. Nowhere is this so pronounced as in the Middle East, where human rights concerns are consistently trumped either by questions of military and corporate access or by the "peace process." The exceptions are Libya, Iraq, Sudan, and Iran, where human rights criticism meshes with broader U.S. efforts to stigmatize and delegitimize those governments. Israel and Egypt, which account for 91 percent of global U.S. military and economic aid, and Saudi Arabia, the largest customer for U.S. weapons, are generally insulated from public rebuke, and the United States has made no discernible effort to use its leading role as donor and arms supplier to promote human rights in those cases.

In the key areas of international justice and accountability, the United States has resisted efforts to establish international checks and scrutiny over the legality of its policy decisions. Washington has supported international tribunals dealing with the atrocities committed in Rwanda and in former Yugoslavia, but has worked to cripple the International Criminal Court in order to ensure that no U.S. citizen or policymaker ever comes under its jurisdiction. While signaling support for international efforts to try former Cambodian dictator Pol Pot (before his death) and other Khmer Rouge leaders for genocide, the administration has declined to cooperate fully with Spanish efforts to extradite ex-Chilean dictator Agusto Pinochet to stand trial for "crimes against humanity." Given direct U.S. interest in Pinochet's prosecution for the murder of U.S. citizens in Chile and the 1976 car bomb assassination of former Chilean foreign minister Orlando Letelier and his American assistant, Ronni Moffitt, in Washington, it is difficult to discern any principled basis for this inconsistency, which suggests that embarrassment over revelations of U.S. complicity with Pinochet's reign of terror is the motivation.

What has passed for U.S. human rights policy for most of the last two decades exhibits a disturbing lack of consistency and a large gap between pronouncement and practice. Progress on human rights is subordinated to other concerns or disingenuously deferred as the inevitable outcome of economic liberalization. The United States needs to develop a policy that addresses the major failings of this approach: (1) the selectivity that exempts the foreign policies of allies or strategically important countries from scrutiny or rebuke, and (2) the exceptionalism that demands U.S. exemption from international standards and accountability.

THE UNITED STATES' USE AND ABUSE OF THE UNITED NATIONS

Phyllis Bennis

IN 1998 AND 1999, U.S.-LED BOMBING ATTACKS AGAINST IRAQ and Yugoslavia provided new evidence of Washington's disregard for the United Nations. The UN Charter, signed in 1945, gives the Security Council sole responsibility to authorize the use of force against any country (except in the most urgent need for self-defense). But since the end of the cold war, the United States, reveling in its unchallenged role as a global superpower, has regarded the charter as an option, not an obligation.

The unipolarity of the post–cold war era sorely needs the counterbalance of UN internationalism. But, as French foreign minister Hubert Vedrine told the *International Herald Tribune* in February 1999, "[T]he predominant weight of the United States . . . leads it to hegemony, and the idea it has of its mission to unilateralism."

President Bush's administration began the 1990s by influencing enough Security Council members to make the UN his instrument of choice for legitimating the Gulf War. By the end of the decade, the United States (with Britain) claimed the right to bomb Iraq repeatedly, without even the pretense of UN backing.

The Clinton administration took a further step working overtime to replace the UN's role with that of NATO as both grantor of legitimacy for and implementer of U.S.-led military interventions. Although the earlier Bosnia deployment included at least a semblance of power sharing between the UN and NATO, Washington's response in Kosovo completely sidelined the UN.

The Clinton administration took office in 1992 proclaiming "aggressive multilateralism" as its watchword. But by 1995, then-U.S. ambassador to the UN Madeleine Albright declared, "The UN is a tool of American foreign policy."

Based on a Heritage Foundation assessment claiming Washington's power would be increased by denying money owed to the UN, the United States began withholding significant portions of its UN dues (25 percent of the total) in 1985, during the Reagan administration. Throughout the next 15 years Washington ignored the United Nations as irrelevant, maligned it as incompetent, and undermined its capacity by continuing to ignore U.S. financial obligations.

By mid-1999, Washington's debt to the UN totaled $1.6 billion. Not surprisingly, the UN sought other sources of funding. The $1 billion gift by media mogul Ted Turner, however well motivated, brought to light some of the dangers corporate funding presented. Inevitably, corporations followed suit offering private donations to the UN and its agencies, looking, in return, to "greenwash" records of environmental or labor devastation, or seeking to gain influence through the UN as they bargained with impoverished governments. Some UN agencies themselves reached out to forge new alliances with corporations.

The UN's financial crisis became far more acute during the 1990s, as Washington linked the payment of dues to its own definitions of reform. There are needs for real UN reform—particularly in democratizing the Security Council and building financial transparency. But serious reforms will not be achieved if the United States continues in its attempts to manage the institution unilaterally by withholding dues. By failing to pay its share of the bill, the

United States has placed the existence of the institution in peril. In the past, shortfalls could be met by borrowing from peacekeeping funds. But with the dramatic decline in UN "Blue Helmet" operations after 1995, due largely to U.S. refusal to authorize UN peacekeeping operations, those funds dried up, leaving the world body near bankruptcy.

In late 1999, Congress and the Clinton administration reached a compromise allowing the United States to pay about two-thirds of its dues if the UN itself met a host of unprecedented conditions, including that no U.S. funds support international family planning agencies. Although Clinton resisted the package proposed by conservative members of Congress, he failed to use his 'bully pulpit' to mobilize public pressure and mount an aggressive campaign to get Congress to pay the dues as required under international law. Clinton appointed a special envoy to negotiate with UN members over other congressional demands: that annual U.S. dues be cut from 31 percent to 25 percent of the total UN budget, that there be no growth in the UN budget (even to keep up with inflation), and that the United Nations accept as final the partial U.S. payment. If the United Nations rejects any of these demands, the U.S. dues will remain in arrears and Washington stands to lose its vote in the General Assembly.

Post–cold war realities brought new challenges, including wars within states, the collapse of national governments, massive refugee flows, and human rights catastrophes. By 1999, Washington and London won NATO support to exclude the UN in their decision to wage war in Kosovo and elsewhere in Yugoslavia. When the bombs stopped falling, they left underfunded UN humanitarian agencies to pick up the pieces.

On the other hand, the UN has made significant gains in some areas, and the intersection of it with civil society action strengthened efforts towards new kinds of internationalism despite U.S. resistance. When Washington succeeded in keeping the land mines issue off the UN's agenda, an international citizen campaign, joined by Canada and other states, mobilized to create the Ottawa Convention banning land mines, and later incorporated it back into UN treaty structures. In the arena of international law, in June 1998 the first steps toward forming the newly UN-organized International Criminal Court succeeded despite massive U.S. efforts to undermine its authority.

Kofi Annan of Ghana, the last UN secretary general of the twentieth century, came into office with strong U.S. backing but turned out to have more backbone than Washington had bargained for. In 1996, the Clinton administration campaigned for Annan to prevent a second term for Boutros Boutros-Ghali, who had antagonized U.S. officials by his sometimes back-talking style, despite his willingness to largely follow Washington's agenda.

Instead, Annan, the first sub-Saharan African to hold the position and the first to rise from within the UN Secretariat, was regarded by many to be the first secretary general since Dag Hammarskjold to bring unimpeachable honesty and integrity to the job. But Annan operated within tighter constraints than any of his predecessors and was the first secretary general forced to contemplate the very real possibility of bankruptcy and having to close the doors of some UN agencies regardless of their urgent tasks.

In May 1999, at the 100th anniversary of the Hague Appeal for Peace, 9,000 peace activists convened to create an agenda for a new Appeal for Peace. Closing the ceremonies, Annan told the crowd, "Wars can be ended. Even better, they can be prevented." But, he added, "It takes patient and skillful diplomacy [and] the development of a culture in which statesmen and diplomats alike know . . . the ultimate crime is to miss the chance for peace."

Placing the UN at the center of world affairs will be difficult. The United States does not need the UN to protect its military might or its global reach. But smaller and weaker countries, especially those in the global South, as well as those wealthier Northern countries willing to challenge U.S. domination, will find new allies in civil society, nongovernmental actors, and social movements around the globe. Whether together they can lead the world body to reform and democratize, to reemerge at center stage of a new internationalism designed to counter U.S. domination, remains an ongoing challenge.

HUMANITARIAN INTERVENTION: A DANGEROUS DOCTRINE

Jules Lobel and Michael Ratner

THE RECENT U.S.-LED NATO AIR ASSAULT AGAINST YUGOSLAVIA undertaken with the avowed aim of stopping human rights abuses in Kosovo has been extolled by some as a new model of humanitarian intervention. President Clinton and others have argued that where a nation is committing gross human rights violations against its citizens, other nations or multilateral coalitions have the right to intervene militarily, without the authority of the UN Security Council, to end those abuses. Proponents of this argument believe that the protection of human rights must supersede outdated notions of state sovereignty.

The United Nations Charter clearly prohibits nations from attacking other states for claimed violations of human rights. Article 2(4), the central provision of the Charter, prohibits the "threat or use of force against" another state. There are only two exceptions to this prohibition. Article 51 allows a nation to use force in "self-defense if an armed attack occurs against" it or an allied country. The charter also authorizes the Security Council to employ force to counter threats to or breaches of international peace. This has been interpreted to allow individual nations to intervene militarily for humanitarian reasons, but only with the explicit authorization of the Council. This occurred in Somalia, Rwanda, Haiti, and Bosnia. In Kosovo, the United States and NATO never sought explicit authorization in the Security Council, and there was no claim of self-defense.

One important reason that post–World War II international law has rejected humanitarian military intervention is the potential for powerful states to abuse such a doctrine. The history of humanitarian military intervention is replete with invocations of humanitarian intentions by strong powers or coalitions to conceal their own geopolitical interests. Professors Thomas Franck and Nigel Rodely examined the historical record of such interventions in a 1973 *American Journal of International Law* article entitled "Africa Bangladesh: The Law of Humanitarian Intervention by Military Force" and concluded that "in very few, if any, instances has the right [to humanitarian intervention] been asserted under circumstances that appear more humanitarian than self-seeking and power seeking." The European military interventions against the Ottoman Empire, France, and Spain in the nineteenth century; the Japanese invasion of Manchuria in 1931; as well as Hitler's intervention in Czechoslovakia in 1938 were all justified on humanitarian grounds. The historical record led the International Court of Justice to conclude in 1949 that a right of forcible intervention in the name of international justice "has, in the past, given rise to most serious abuses. . . . [F]rom the nature of things, it would be reserved for the most powerful states."

Nor has the United States been immune from asserting humanitarian reasons to justify military interventions that served its own geopolitical interests. President McKinley's 1898 war message to Congress asserted that the United States was intervening against Spain " . . . in the cause of humanity and to put an end to barbarities, bloodshed, starvation, and horrible miseries [in Cuba]." President Johnson claimed that our Vietnam intervention and Dominican Republic invasion of 1965 were undertaken for humanitarian reasons. President Reagan argued that the interventions against Nicaragua and Grenada in the 1980s were designed to restore freedom and human rights for those people. All of these interventions were arguably undertaken for political and strategic reasons, not for moral and humanitarian purposes.

Thus, the actual history of so-called humanitarian interventions leaves one deeply suspicious of any doctrine that would allow powerful states—or even coalitions of allied nations—the right to intervene unilaterally in the affairs of other states. The UN Charter provides that only the Security Council—an institution representing the nations of the world and not one particular group of countries—can decide whether to use force against a country. Permitting individual states to make those decisions unilaterally and based on their own determinations of human rights abuses would eviscerate the international legal restraints against the use of force. Any powerful nation could always assert a "humanitarian motive" for intervening against a less powerful nation and be subject to virtually no oversight by an international decision-making body.

There is another reason, apart from the problem of pretextual abuses of human rights, that international law has thus far rejected the doctrine of humanitarian intervention. The primary goal of the United Nations is to "save succeeding generations from the scourge of war." The charter thus requires that war be viewed as a last resort, taken only after all peaceful alternatives have failed. The procedural mechanism that the charter employs to further that substantive goal requires that decisions to go to war be made only by a deliberative body of states representing a broad range of constituents: the Security Council.

The Kosovo crisis illustrates the danger of bypassing that procedural restraint. It is possible that the settlement that ended the air war could have been achieved without the use of force. The Security Council might have required deletion of several of the most objectionable aspects of the so-called Ramboullet Agreement and mandated that other peaceful means to resolve the crisis be attempted. Moreover, the greater destructiveness of war that led the charter's framers to choose peace as its central tenet was illustrated by the Kosovo events: many more Kosovars and Serbs were killed and wounded after the air war started than during the prior two years of civil strife and human rights abuses in Kosovo.

Of course, there may be extreme cases of ongoing genocide where the Security Council refuses to authorize force due to one country's veto, yet thousands or millions of lives would be lost unless immediate action is undertaken. In dealing with those cases, it is preferable to recognize that on the rare occasions when a nation is genuinely motivated by human rights considerations to intervene, it is violating the law to save lives. That is a less dangerous alternative than dilution of the prohibition on the unilateral use of force.

INTERNATIONAL TERRORISM

Stephen Zunes

IN SEPTEMBER 1998, A MONTH AFTER THE BOMBINGS of the U.S. embassies in East Africa, President Clinton told the UN General Assembly that international terrorism was a worldwide priority. In recent years, other U.S. presidents have also identified international terrorism as a major security threat.

Random violent acts inflicted against civilians by international terrorists are truly horrific. Yet the fixation on terrorism is grossly out of proportion to its impact: acts of terrorism worldwide have actually declined since the 1970s, and the number of Americans killed by terrorists is quite small compared to deaths from other violent crimes, automobile accidents, or preventable diseases.

Beyond exaggeration, there are other serious problems with Washington's targeting of terrorism. Counterterrorism has been used to justify a series of controversial policies, ranging from tougher immigration laws to high military budgets, restrictions on civil liberties, and arms shipments and training programs for repressive governments abroad.

There is nothing inherent in Islamic, Middle Eastern, Irish, Basque, or other traditions that spawns terrorism. Terrorism is primarily the weapon of the politically weak or frustrated—those who are or believe themselves to be unable to exert their grievances through conventional political or military means. Effective intelligence, interdiction, and certain conventional counterterrorism efforts do have their place. But terrorism's roots are political, so ending it is at least as much a political problem as a security problem.

U.S. foreign policy toward international terrorism is far too focused on unilateral military solutions, including "surgical" air strikes against targets in foreign nations. Although such attacks have played well with the American public because they give the impression that the United States is taking decisive action, in reality the U.S. war against terrorism often has taken the form of foreign policy by catharsis.

In addition, targeting terrorist bases, which are often in close proximity to populated areas, risks casualties among innocent civilians. In 1986, for instance, the United States bombed two Libyan cities, killing more than 60 civilians, in retaliation for suspected Libyan involvement in a terrorist attack that killed two American GIs. Often such air strikes are based on faulty intelligence, such as the April 1993 bombing of a Baghdad neighborhood in reaction to an unsubstantiated allegation of an Iraqi assassination attempt against former President Bush or the August 1998 U.S. bombing of a Sudanese pharmaceutical plant, mistakenly claimed to be a chemical weapons plant controlled by a foreign terrorist leader.

Rather than curbing terrorism, such strikes often escalate the cycle of violence as terrorists seek further retaliation. In 1988, Libyan agents allegedly blew up Pan Am Flight 103 over Lockerbie, Scotland, in retaliation for the U.S. strikes against Libyan cities.

There are serious legal questions as well. The United States claims that Article 51 of the UN Charter allows such military actions against terrorism, but Article 51 deals only with self-defense; neither retaliatory strikes nor preemptive strikes are included. The United States has so far refused to seek prior Security Council approval for preemptive military action.

Still another problem has been the politicization of the terrorism issue. For example, Syria and Cuba remain on the State Department's list of terrorist states, despite the U.S. admission that they have found no evidence of terrorist involvement by either of those countries in more than a decade. More revealing still is the U.S. offer to drop such labels, which would allow for the lifting of certain sanctions, if these governments acquiesce to U.S. demands in unrelated policy areas. Similarly, U.S. officials quietly dropped the "terrorist" label from the Kosovo Liberation Army after the militant secessionist group became key to the military operation of NATO in Kosovo.

The United States itself has sponsored international terrorism. In 1985, CIA director William Casey, with the approval of President Reagan, authorized the car bombing of a suburban Beirut neighborhood that killed 80 people and wounded 200 others, as part of an unsuccessful effort to assassinate an anti-American Lebanese cleric. In addition, the United States has supported governments in Indonesia, Turkey and other Middle Eastern countries, Guatemala, and elsewhere that engage in widespread terrorism against their own populations.

Although there is no foolproof set of policies that will protect the United States and its interests from terrorists, there are a number of policy shifts that would likely reduce the frequency and severity of terrorist strikes. These shifts must be based in part on the understanding that terrorist attacks are generally rooted in social, political, or economic desperation, which must be addressed for antiterrorism efforts to have any chance of success.

The tactics of terrorists can never be justified. But the most effective weapon in the war against terrorism would be to take measures that would lessen the likelihood for the United States and its citizens to become targets. Such a policy change would include an end to unconditional U.S. military, economic, and diplomatic support of governments that invade and occupy neighboring countries, attack civilian targets in villages and refugee camps, or deny people their right of self-determination. For example, a large number of anti-American terrorists in recent years have come from Palestinian and Lebanese families who have been directly harmed by actions of the U.S.-backed Israeli government.

Another policy shift must be away from supporting irregular groups that may be prone to terrorism. Many of the most notorious terrorists in the world today received their training from the CIA as part of U.S. efforts to undermine leftist governments in Cuba, Nicaragua, and Afghanistan. There must also be an end to any direct involvement by any branch of the military, intelligence agencies, or any other part of the U.S. government in acts of terrorism.

International terrorism is a global problem. Unilateral action merely isolates the United States from the allies it needs in the fight against terrorism. The most effective short-term strategy against terrorism involves intelligence and interdiction, which works best when it is part of a transnational effort.

The United States is a target of terrorists in large part due to our perceived arrogance, hypocrisy, and greed. Becoming a more responsible member of the international community will go a long way toward making the United States safer and ultimately stronger.

CHAPTER 5

GLOBAL ENVIRONMENTAL PROTECTION IN THE TWENTY-FIRST CENTURY

David Hunter

INTRODUCTION

IN THE PAST THREE DECADES, protecting the global environment has emerged as one of the major challenges in international relations. No fewer than ten global environmental treaties have been negotiated as well as literally hundreds of regional and bilateral agreements. (See figure 5–1.) Governments have also endorsed dozens of comprehensive action plans, most notably the 400-page *Agenda 21*, which set forth a blueprint for implementing sustainable development. The result is an increasingly complex and broad body of international environmental law and policy. At least on paper, this provides a broad framework for moving toward a more environmentally sustainable future.

Unfortunately, this rich body of treaties, action plans, and other instruments has not reversed global environmental decline. Virtually every major environmental indicator is worse today than it was at the time of the 1992 UN Conference on Environment and Development (UNCED, or the Earth Summit) held in Rio de Janeiro. Climate change has caused the warmest decade in recorded history, the ozone layer continues to deteriorate, species extinction is at the highest rate since the end of the dinosaur era, fish populations are crashing, and toxic chemicals are accumulating in every part of the planet and in every living organism, including humans.[1] This chapter looks first at the promise of the Earth Summit and then proceeds to analyze several critical areas where implementation has fallen short—and where U.S. leadership can make a difference in the new century.

118

Figure 5.1 Major Environmental Treaties and U.S. Status

Basel Convention on Transboundary Movements of Hazardous Wastes

The Basel Convention on the Control of Transboundary Movements of Hazardous Wastes and Their Disposal was adopted in 1989 and entered into force in May 1992. This global environmental treaty regulates the transboundary movement of hazardous wastes and obliges its parties to ensure that such wastes are managed and disposed of in an environmentally sound manner. It also protects the right of states to ban entry of foreign waste within their territories. The United States signed the Basel Convention on March 22, 1989, but has not yet ratified it.

Convention on Biological Diversity

The Convention on Biological Diversity was signed by over 150 governments at the Rio "Earth Summit" in 1992 and entered into force in 1993. It has become the centerpiece of international efforts to conserve the planet's biological diversity, ensure the sustainable use of biological resources, protect ecosystems and natural habitats, and promote the fair and equitable sharing of the benefits arising from the utilization of genetic resources. The Convention was signed on June 4, 1993, but the United States has failed to ratify it.

Convention on Climate Change

Over 150 states signed the United Nations Framework Convention on Climate Change in June 1992 at the Rio "Earth Summit," recognizing climate change as "a common concern of humankind." The Convention aimed to reduce emission levels of "greenhouse gases" to 1990 levels by the year 2000 but failed to set binding goals. The United States signed the treaty on June 12, 1992, ratified it on October 15, 1992, and entered it into force in the United States on March 21, 1994.

Convention on Climate Change: Kyoto Protocol

The agreement sets, for the first time, legally binding limits on the heat-trapping greenhouse gases that cause global warming. Under the protocol, 38 industrialized countries agreed to reduce their overall emissions to about 5 percent below 1990 levels by 2012, with a range of specific reduction requirements for other countries. The U.S. signed the Protocol on November 12, 1998, but has not yet ratified it.

Convention to Combat Desertification (CCD)

The Convention to Combat Desertification in Those Countries Experiencing Serious Drought and/or Desertification, Especially in Africa, the CCD promotes an integrated approach to managing the problems posed by dry-land ecosystems and encourages developed nations to support such efforts internationally. The Convention went into effect in 1996 and has over 120 parties. The United States has signed but not ratified the Convention.

(continues)

Figure 5.1 *(continued)*

Convention on International Trade in Endangered Species (CITES)

CITES establishes international controls on global trade in endangered or threatened species of animals and plants. For example, CITES prohibits all commercial trade in wildlife species threatened with extinction. CITES was ratified by the United States on January 14, 1974, and implemented as the Endangered Species Act. More than 125 countries are members.

Montreal Protocol on Substances that Deplete the Ozone Layer

The Montreal Protocol and subsequent revisions are the primary international regime for controlling the production and consumption of ozone-depleting substances such as CFCs, halons, and methyl bromide. As of June 1994, 136 states, including virtually all major industrialized countries and most developing countries, had become parties to the Protocol. The United States signed the Protocol on September 16, 1987, and ratified it on April 21, 1988. The Protocol and its subsequent revisions modified the original 1985 Vienna Convention for the Protection of the Ozone Layer.

Sources: Department of States, *Major Environmental Agreements*, 1998. Available on the Internet at: http://www.state.gov/www/global/oes/envir_agreements.html. See also, Susan R. Fletcher, "International Environment: Current Major Global Treaties," Congressional Research Report, November 5, 1996.

THE PROMISE OF RIO

The 1992 Rio Earth Summit was heralded as the turning point for global environmental policy. More than 100 countries came to the Rio summit, which sought to merge two critical international concerns—environmental protection and economic development—that had been evolving on different tracks during the 1970s and 1980s. For developing countries, the merger of environment and development was a major improvement over earlier environmental conferences and provided hope for increased North-South cooperation. In addition, the cold war had recently ended, and the rise of a one-superpower world meant that East-West conflicts would not dominate this conference, as they had earlier international environmental efforts.

On paper, at least, the Earth Summit did provide a potential vision for moving toward sustainable development—that is, toward both greater environmental protection and greater economic justice. The Earth Summit yielded two legally binding treaties: the Framework Convention on Climate Change and the Convention on Biological Diversity. Also a product of the summit were a set of nonbinding general principles known as the *Rio Declaration*, a set of nonbinding principles on forest management, and the blueprint for sustainable development entitled *Agenda 21.*[2] The assembled governments also established the Commission on Sustainable Development (CSD) to integrate environment and development into the UN system while providing a forum to monitor the implementation of summit commitments.

Perhaps as important as the formal commitments was Rio's endorsement of the concept of sustainable development. Although the precise meaning of sustainable development was not clarified, governments emerged from Rio knowing that they had at least generally agreed to the further integration of the economy, the environment, and social equity. Beyond that, the constructive ambiguity of the concept *sustainable development* provided a framework that allowed both the North and the South to walk away with something from Rio. Essentially the South received renewed commitments for increased development assistance, a recognition that the North was substantially responsible for global environmental degradation, and a commitment that the North would take the leadership role in addressing global environmental problems. In turn, the North won the South's promised cooperation in addressing environmental issues as long as they were integrated with issues of social and economic development. These reciprocal commitments offered a broader consensus for moving forward on the global environment than did any previous environmental negotiation.

By 1999, however, the momentum from Rio had dissipated and the reciprocal commitments had been largely abandoned. Official development assistance from the North to the South had declined since Rio, and the new emphasis is on private sector flows of capital. (See figure 3–3.) Some Northern countries (including the United States) even maintain that such direct and indirect investment flows make up for declining development assistance by facilitating environmentally sound technologies.

The Rio treaties remain poorly implemented. Negotiations on the climate change regime reflect a deep split between developing and industrialized countries. The Biodiversity Convention, which the United States has never ratified, has had little impact. Perhaps most critically, institutions such as the Commission on Sustainable Development and the preexisting United Nations Environment Program (UNEP), as well as the environmental secretariats, continue to take a backseat to economic powerhouses such as the World Trade Organization (WTO), the World Bank, and the International Monetary Fund (IMF).

Domestically, some countries introduced interesting multistakeholder processes for implementing *Agenda 21*. These include province-wide roundtables in Canada for building consensus for sustainable development and issue-oriented working groups in Chile that brought multiple stakeholders together to make recommendations regarding every chapter of the agenda. Few, if any, countries have gone beyond discussions, however, and embraced sustainable development in ways that fundamentally challenge the systemic orientation toward economic growth— an orientation that ultimately undermines the promise of Rio and is environmentally unsustainable.

LOOKING FOR U.S. LEADERSHIP

More than any other country, the United States is responsible for the existing gulf between Rio's rhetoric of international environmental consciousness and the post-Rio environmental reality. Not only is the United States the world's only remaining economic and political superpower, it is also the largest polluter and the largest user of most important resources. Although the United States is often in the vanguard in recognizing global environmental threats and in calling for a multilateral response, it many times lags in changing its own behavior. Once considered the leader in environmental regulation, the United States now trails well behind Germany and other European countries in adopting new and innovative regulatory approaches such as ecological taxes, extended product responsibility, and the precautionary principle on avoiding probable environmental damage. (See figure 5–2.)

Although a leader in previous environmental conferences and negotiations, the United States (under then President George Bush) almost single-handedly undermined the Earth Summit. Just days before the Rio summit opened, for example, the United States announced that it would not sign the Biodiversity Convention, despite provisionally adopting the draft version at the end of the negotiation session two weeks before. Instead, the United States emphasized the need to conserve the world's forests and offered what was considered a small, $150 million aid package to protect forests in developing countries. Southern leaders immediately labeled this gesture as "greenwash," viewing U.S. support for forest conservation as a cynical effort to shift the focus from the North's responsibility to control industrial pollution to the South's responsibility to conserve forests as carbon sinks. According to press accounts, Malaysia's ambassador Ranji Sathia responded, "The [$150 million] does not impress us. They are just trying to divert attention from their failing elsewhere—for example, in the watering down of the climate change convention and their refusal to sign the biodiversity treaty."

With the ascendancy in 1992 of the Clinton administration, and particularly Vice President Al Gore, most observers thought the United States would claim the mantle of international environmental leadership. Soon after taking office, Clinton signed the Biodiversity Convention, and the Senate ratified the Climate

Figure 5.2   U.S. Consumption of Global Resources

Resource	U.S. as a percent of World
Energy consumption (1995)	24.8
Forestry product consumption (1996)	18.5
Materials consumption (1995)	28.7
Water consumption(1990)	13.7
Population (1999)	4.6

Sources: Energy: U.S. Department of Energy. Energy Information Administration, *International Energy Outlook 1997* (Energy Information Adminstration 1997, Washington, DC); Forest Products: State of the World's Forest 1998 (FAO, 1999); Materials: Information obtained from Minerals Information Team, U.S. Geological Survey, 1999; Water: David Seckler, Upali Amarasinghe, David Molden, Radhika de Silva, and Randolph Barker, Research Report #1, *World Water Demand and Supply, 1990 to 2025: Scenarios and Issues* (Washington, DC: International Water Management Institute, 1998); Population: United Nations Department of International Economic and Social Affairs, *World Population Prospects*, United Nations, New York, 1994).

Convention. The Clinton administration also negotiated and signed the environmental side agreement to the North American Free Trade Agreement (NAFTA), which, although flawed, was an advance over previous approaches to trade and the environment. The Clinton administration can also take credit for elevating environmental concerns within the U.S. State Department by establishing regional environmental offices in selected U.S. embassies around the world, improving the environmental standards of our bilateral development agencies, and building some popular support for the 1997 Kyoto Protocol on climate change.

Still, this is a relatively weak record for two terms in office, reflecting (among other things) the general lack of interest in global environmental affairs by Environmental Protection Agency (EPA) administrator Carol Browner. The EPA has essentially abdicated authority over international environmental affairs to the Council on Environmental Quality in the White House and to foreign policy agencies such as the Department of State and the U.S. Trade Representative.

The lack of high-level, consistent attention to the environment is clearly illustrated by the Clinton administration's failure to parlay the modest gains embodied in the NAFTA environmental side agreement into integrated environment and trade policies in other fora. Clinton's lack of leadership on trade and the environment sparked a progressive coalition of environmental and labor interests that helped defeat the president's 1997 bid for expanding free trade negotiations to Chile and elsewhere.

Regarding climate change, perhaps the most important international environmental issue during Clinton's term, the administration has not played a leadership role either before or after the 1997 negotiations of the Kyoto Protocol. Although the president did elevate the domestic profile of climate change leading up to the Kyoto negotiations, the United States has failed to take significant steps either domestically or internationally to reduce effectively America's impact on the climate system. In particular, Washington's preoccupation with ensuring the creation of a limitless global trading market for carbon emissions has colored the U.S. position on every other issue. As a result, U.S. proposals are consistently less protective of the climate system than are those of the European Union.

Nor has the United States done much domestically to implement sustainable development generally or *Agenda 21* specifically. In 1993, President Clinton established a President's Council on Sustainable Development (PCSD), a high-level advisory committee to outline a national strategy for achieving sustainable development. The PCSD's final report emphasized both broad national goals and local initiatives. The PCSD did not have formal authority, however, and few of its recommendations have been implemented. As John Dernbach, professor of law at Widener University in Harrisburg, Pennsylvania, concluded in 1997, after completing the most comprehensive review thus far of U.S. implementation of *Agenda 21:*

> Five years after Rio, the United States still has no coherent or comprehensive commitment to sustainable development. There has been no concerted effort to progressively integrate governmental decisionmaking on environmental, social and economic issues; no substantial improvement in our existing legal framework to better foster sustainable development; no implementation of satellite systems of social and environmental accounting; and no governmental use of sustainable

development indicators. No agency or individual in the U.S. government even has government-wide responsibility for coordinating or implementing sustainable development policy. Although President Clinton appointed a blue ribbon panel (the PCSD) that produced a sustainable development report with recommendations, there was little effort or interest in implementing those recommendations.[3]

In short, the United States is still without any meaningful strategy or framework for implementing *Agenda 21* or the other Rio commitments. (See figure 5–3.)

Of course, the Clinton administration should not bear all the blame. The Republican-led Congress is perhaps the most hostile to global environmental issues of any in recent history. Ratification of environmental treaties and significant funding for global environmental causes stand little chance of gaining the requisite support in Congress. With respect to climate change, for example, the U.S. Senate passed a resolution effectively tying the administration's hands in negotiating greenhouse gas reductions in the Kyoto Protocol. Congress subsequently prohibited any expenditures for implementing the protocol before Senate ratification—which is unlikely in the foreseeable future. Similar opposition in Congress prevents U.S. ratification of conventions relating to the law of the sea, desertification, and the conservation of biodiversity.

Given the lack of U.S. leadership, global failure to fulfill the Earth Summit's promises is not surprising. Over time, the details of the precise promises have been lost, leaving us with little else than the general concept of sustainable development as the framework for global environmental policy in the next century. The following discussion outlines several priority steps for moving global governance toward sustainable development, including: (1) filling the remaining gaps in international environmental policy; (2) improving the institutional architecture for protecting the global environment; (3) integrating environmental protection with the global economy; and (4) emphasizing the role of individuals and communities in protecting the global environment.

FILLING THE ENVIRONMENTAL POLICY GAPS

Despite the many environmental regimes and action plans negotiated in the past quarter century, important gaps still exist in the international environmental policy framework. The framework has not developed in any systematic or strategic way. Rather it is a collection of numerous treaties, each addressing relatively discrete global or regional environmental issues. Superimposed over these binding treaties are a set of broader, nonbinding declarations or resolutions, such as the Stockholm and Rio declarations. No binding set of general environmental principles currently exists. Moreover, some new or particularly complicated environmental issues still await international attention, a fact that compounds the policy gaps.

Developing a Binding Framework of Environmental Principles

The lack of an overarching binding framework has many implications for the future effectiveness of international environmental policies. In trade and environment

Figure 5.3   International Environmental Law Principles

These principles have been adopted from the Rio Declaration on Environment and Development or the International Union for the Conservation of Nature and Natural Resources (ICUN) Draft Covenant on Environment and Development.

Common Concern. The global environment is a common concern of humanity. (*IUCN Covenant*, Principle 13).

Common but Differentiated Responsibilities. In view of the different contributions to global environmental degradation, states have common but differentiated responsibilities. (*Rio Declaration*, Principle 7).

Duty Not to Cause Environmental Harm. States have the responsibility to ensure that activities within their jurisdiction or control do not cause damage to the environment of other states or of areas beyond the limits of national jurisdiction. (*Rio Declaration*, Principle 2).

Environmental Impact Assessment. Environmental impact assessment shall be undertaken for proposed activities that are likely to have a significant adverse impact on the environment and are subject to a decision of a competent national authority. (*Rio Declaration*, Principle 17).

Global Partnership. States shall cooperate in a spirit of global partnership to conserve, protect and restore the health and integrity of the Earth's ecosystem. (*Rio Declaration*, Principle 7).

Integration. In order to achieve sustainable development, environmental protection shall constitute an integral part of the development process and cannot be considered in isolation from it. (*Rio Declaration*, Principle 4).

Nonrelocation of Harm. States should effectively cooperate to discourage or prevent the relocation and transfer to other states of any activities and substances that cause severe environmental degradation or are found to be harmful to human health. (*Rio Declaration*, Principle 14)

Notification and Consultation. States shall provide prior and timely notification and relevant information to potentially affected states on activities that may have a significant adverse transboundary environmental effect and shall consult with those states at an early stage and in good faith. (*Rio Declaration*, Principle 19).

Peaceful Resolution of Disputes. States shall resolve all their environmental disputes peacefully and by appropriate means in accordance with the Charter of the United Nations. (*Rio Declaration*, Principle 26).

The Polluter Pays Principle. National authorities should promote the internalization of environmental costs and the use of economic instruments, taking into account the approach that the polluter should, in principle, bear the cost of pollution. (*Rio Declaration*, Principle 16).

The Precautionary Principle. Where there are threats of serious or irreversible damage, lack of full scientific certainty shall not be used as a reason for postponing cost-effective measures to prevent environmental degradation. (*Rio Declaration*, Principle 15).

(continues)

Figure 5.3 *(continued)*

Public Participation. Environmental issues are best handled with the participation of all concerned citizens, at the relevant level. (*Rio Declaration*, Principle 10).

Right to Development. The right to development must be fulfilled so as to equitably meet developmental and environmental needs of present and future generations. (*Rio Declaration*, Principle 3).

State Sovereignty. States have the sovereign right to exploit their own resources pursuant to their own environmental and developmental policies. (*Rio Declaration*, Principle 2).

Source: Compiled by David Hunter.

disputes, for example, environmental concerns are at a disadvantage, because the set of rules for international environmental protection is not as clear as the WTO's trade rules. Binding environmental principles could help to achieve more balanced integration between environmental protection and other social goals such as trade. Such principles could also provide a substantive basis for coordinating the activities of the many international institutions that currently claim a role in environmental policy. Finally, binding principles could help in establishing minimum environmental standards—both for private sector activities and for governments—by assisting in the harmonization of domestic environmental laws.

Despite the potential importance of binding principles, the United States has consistently opposed the development of any general environmental covenant. It argues that any covenant negotiated today would not sufficiently protect the global environment, because developing countries would defend their sovereign right to develop. The negotiation of a binding covenant may indeed magnify the overall influence of developing countries, because they do not generally have the financial and human resources to participate effectively in the contemporaneous negotiations of many separate environmental treaties and instruments. In fact, it may be exactly those fears of negotiating on a level playing field that drives U.S. opposition to a covenant rather than a fear that the resulting principles would be too weak.

Instead of pursuing a binding covenant, the United States seems intent on weakening some of the key proposed principles. For example, the United States is one of the few remaining countries still opposing the precautionary principle (which holds that a lack of scientific certainty should not be used to prevent cost-effective action to address potentially irreversible environmental threats). The U.S. approach to environmental regulation requires that there be proven environmental damage *before* control measures are taken.

Washington stands virtually alone in rejecting the precautionary principle—a guideline with significant implications for many global environmental issues. Based in part on the precautionary principle, Europe is championing a much stronger regulatory approach to biosafety issues such as the release of genetically modified organisms (GMOs). To make matters worse, the United States has been threatening to challenge Europe's precautionary approach to GMOs in the World

Trade Organization, basing its argument on the lack of definitive science for justifying GMO trade restrictions.

Getting the Rules Right Regarding the Climate Regime

Climate change may be the single most significant environmental issue of the next few decades. Between 1900 and 1996, global carbon dioxide (CO_2) emissions rose 12-fold, from 536 million to 6.52 billion metric tons. By 1996, U.S. emissions totaled 1.45 billion metric tons or over 22 percent of global emissions—even though the U.S. constitutes less than 5 percent of the total world population.[4] In the Kyoto Protocol, industrialized countries committed to reduce their net greenhouse gas emissions an average of 5 percent from 1990 levels by 2012. In addition, the parties also established an international trading system in carbon emissions. Tons of carbon emissions will soon trade like other commodities throughout the world. To incorporate as many countries as possible, the Kyoto Protocol was necessarily general, leaving many critical issues for future negotiations. By the end of 2000, the Conference of the Parties to the Protocol must address such issues as how to count the carbon sequestered by forests, landfills, and agricultural practices in calculating a country's net greenhouse gas emissions; how to facilitate the trading of carbon emission credits between countries; and how to monitor and enforce such a trading system. Given America's position as the world's supreme carbon emitter and energy user, U.S. leadership in getting these rules right will be critical if the climate regime is to have any hope of responding effectively to the threat of climate change. (See figure 5–4.)

Imposing Liability and Providing Compensation

Few international environmental regimes have addressed the question of liability and compensation for harm caused to the environment. The Montreal Protocol, widely viewed as the model for all international environmental treaties, effectively banned the production and use of most ozone-depleting substances. But it did not hold those responsible for ozone depletion legally accountable, nor did it provide for compensating persons or countries that have suffered from ozone depletion. Even where liability issues have been generally acknowledged in international law—for example, concerning damage caused by transboundary shipments of hazardous wastes—the parties have been deadlocked in trying to operationalize the concept of liability. The United States has often opposed international liability in these contexts, ostensibly out of concern that minimum levels of due process and fairness may be hard to ensure in international forums. However, America's disproportionate responsibility for many global environmental threats and its vulnerability to liability claims also help explain U.S. opposition.

Emphasizing Environmental Restoration

Given how far we have come in damaging the global environment, future international environmental efforts will have to be focused more on environmental

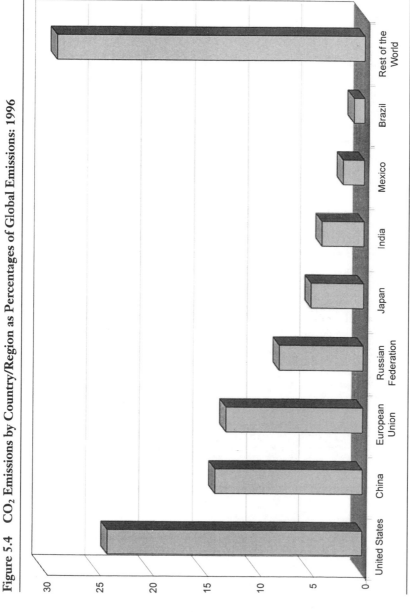

Figure 5.4   CO$_2$ Emissions by Country/Region as Percentages of Global Emissions: 1996

Source: International Bank for Reconstruction and Development/The World Bank, *World Development Indicators 1999* (Washington, DC: The World Bank, 1999).

restoration than protection. Although more expensive and less effective than protecting resources in the first place, restoration sometimes may be the only choice
left. Environmental restoration is now a dynamic part of domestic environmental
management and will undoubtedly begin to inform future global environmental
negotiations. In this country, for example, the increasing trend toward removal of
dams, reintroduction of endangered species, and large-scale restoration projects—
such as the attempt to recover the Florida Everglades—portends a future focus of
international cooperation. (See figure 5–5.)

    As an example, international aid agencies are discussing whether to undertake
a massive effort to restore coastal mangroves and interior watersheds in Central
America. Many mangrove forests have disappeared as a result of shrimp aquacul-
ture, and the region's watersheds have been deforested for export timber. As a result, in 1998, Hurricane Mitch struck with greater devastation. In the hurricane's
wake, political pressure has been building in the region for governments to restore these important ecosystems, so fundamental for the region's environmental
sustainability.

Addressing Persistent Chemicals

In June 1998, negotiations began in Montreal to establish a global convention to
eliminate or manage twelve of the world's worst chemical contaminants, including
dioxins, PCBs (polychlorinated biphenyls), DDT (dichloro-diphenyl-trichloro-
ethane), and other pesticides. These chemicals persist in the environment and ac-
cumulate in human and animal tissues. Many of them have been linked to cancer
and to adverse affects on human endocrine systems. Although most countries con-
cur on how to regulate the 12 chemicals currently identified in the agreement,
major differences exist about how to add new chemicals to the list of globally regulated or prohibited substances. Also critical to any global accord will be the decision about whether countries that are the source of existing stockpiles of

Figure 5.5   Top 10 Countries with the Most Threatened Plant Species: 1997

Country	Number of Threatened	Percent Threatened
United States	4,669	29
Australia	2,245	14
South Africa	2,215	12
Turkey	1,876	22
Mexico	1,593	6
Brazil	1,358	3
Panama	1,302	13
India	1,236	8
Spain	985	2
Peru	906	5

Source: Linda Starke, ed., State of the World 1999 (New York: W.W. Norton & Co., 1999), p. 98.

phased-out chemicals should be responsible for their disposal. The document (to be completed by 2000) has been closely monitored by the chemical industry, which is pressing the United States to narrow the agreement's purview.

Water Shortages

Most experts agree that access to fresh water may be the most important natural resource issue for the next century. Human health, the environment, and even a country's national security depend on access to adequate water supplies. But according to a recent UN report on fresh water, humans are already using "about half" of the 12,500 cubic kilometers of water that is readily available. With world population expected to double in the next 50 years and with water consumption historically increasing at twice the rate of population, our global water situation is bleak. To make matters worse, water is allocated unevenly around the globe. Today, 460 million people or 8 percent of the world's population live in countries already facing serious water shortages. Regional water shortages thus may exacerbate international conflicts and threaten national security if international management efforts are not successful. (See essay 5–1: Environment and Security Policy.) A 1997 UN convention on transnational water uses provides a beginning framework for managing these regional disputes, but long-term financial and political leadership from the United States and other powerful countries will be required for the convention to be successful.

Consumption Levels

The Earth Summit recognized explicitly that achieving sustainability would require addressing both population *and* consumption. (See figure 5–6.) Two years after the Earth Summit, the world's governments came together at the Cairo Population Summit to negotiate a comprehensive plan to curb population growth (See essay 5–2: Population and Environment), but the North has yet to allow any meaningful dialogue on consumption. The United States, in particular, has blocked international efforts to address consumption levels. Domestically, the United States lacks any comprehensive effort to "green" consumption and lags well behind Europe, for example, in adopting green taxes, ecolabeling procedures, "take-back" legislation (requiring industries to take back and dispose of their by-products at the end of their useful life), or other policies aimed at greening consumption. In the new century, no serious effort at achieving sustainable development will be able to avoid tackling the issue of Northern consumption levels and patterns.

IMPROVING THE UN ARCHITECTURE

No single institution legislates or manages international environmental problems. Scores of official and semiofficial organizations and agencies have at least some environmental mandate. In the future, global environmental governance will continue

Figure 5.6   Global Population: 1999

Region	Population (millions)
World	5,982
Total Africa	771
Northern Africa	170
Western Africa	223
Eastern Africa	235
Middle Africa	94
Southern Africa	49
Total North America	304
United States	273
Canada	31
Total Latin America and Caribbean	512
Central America[a]	135
Caribbean	37
South America	339
Total Asia	3,637
Asia excluding China	2,383
Western Asia	186
South Central Asia	1,451
South East Asia	520
East Asia	1,481
Total Europe	728
Northern Europe	95
Western Europe	183
Eastern Europe	306
Southern Europe	145
Total Oceania	30

Source: Carl Haub and Diana Cornelius, *1999 World Population Data Sheet* (Washington, DC: Population Reference Bureau, 1999). Summary available on the Internet at: http://www.prb.org/pubs/wpds99/wpds99a.htm.
[a]Central America includes Mexico.

to involve an array of multilateral, national, and intergovernmental organizations together with citizen groups and treaties. This is as it should be, given that the concept of sustainable development embraces so many different disciplines and issues. But as Professor Dan Esty, a leading international environmental lawyer, has observed: "The difficulty with existing international institutions that address environmental issues . . . is that they have been given narrow mandates, small budgets and limited support. No one organization has the authority or political strength to serve as a central clearinghouse or coordinator."[5]

The UN Environment Program is widely considered the primary international environmental agency. Its mission is to "facilitate international cooperation in the environmental field; to keep the world environmental situation under review so that problems of international significance receive appropriate consideration by governments; and to promote the acquisition, assessment, and exchange of environmental knowledge."[6] In recent years, financial and political support of UNEP has lagged, and most observers question whether it can effectively champion environmental issues within the UN system.

Partly in response to UNEP's weaknesses and partly because of the many different international institutions that exercise at least some environmental authority, governments created the UN Commission on Sustainable Development at the 1992 Earth Summit to coordinate and integrate environmental and economic issues within the United Nations. Unfortunately the CSD's role is limited to providing a political forum for discussion, without any operational mandate or authority. The result is that international environmental governance is still spread across too many institutions with diffuse, conflicting, or weak authorities.

Given these problems in the UN architecture for international environmental governance, there may be no escaping the need for broad institutional reform. Several important leaders have called for such reform. In a 1997 speech to the UN General Assembly, German chancellor Helmut Kohl suggested amending the UN Charter to include sustainable development as one of the two overall purposes of the UN and to establish a global environmental umbrella organization, with UNEP as a major pillar. In addition, Brazil, South Africa, Singapore, and New Zealand have also proposed a new, stronger UN environmental body.

Other specific proposals have been advanced, including the creation of an environmental organization with powers analogous to that of the World Trade Organization. Such an organization could consolidate the different environmental secretariats and UNEP, creating one organization responsible for ensuring the implementation and enforcement of environmental treaties. If a binding set of principles existed, a "World Environmental Organization" could also resolve environmental disputes more efficiently than can the current processes.

Less ambitious, and perhaps more realistic in the short term, would be to strengthen the growing number of regional environmental institutions that are being established to manage shared natural resources. For example, the International Joint Commission between the United States and Canada, which aims primarily at managing the Great Lakes, has been highly regarded as a model for the environmental management of shared watersheds. Regional fisheries management organizations are also emerging in many areas of the world and have been given potentially strong enforcement powers under recently negotiated global fisheries agreements.

INTEGRATING ENVIRONMENTAL
PROTECTION INTO THE GLOBAL ECONOMY

The concept of sustainable development requires the integration of environmental concerns into the fields of international trade, investment, and finance. Since the Earth Summit, environmentalists have made significant advances. Environmental issues are now legitimate concerns for discussion at such organizations as the World Bank and the WTO. Indeed, most of the international financial institutions, such as the World Bank, have adopted new environmental policies and increased their environmental staffs. Even the IMF has created an environmental unit (albeit thus far with only one person).

Despite these policy and staffing advances, the successful practical integration of the environment and the global economy lags far behind. The approach of the international financial institutions (IFIs) continues to emphasize mitigating environmental impacts from poorly designed and inappropriate projects rather than finding ways to proactively promote environmentally sustainable development. More important, the IFIs and trade institutions have not fundamentally reconsidered their general approach to building a global economy in light of the constraints implied by the concept of sustainable development. (See essay 5–3: International Investment Rules and the Environment.) As a result, these institutions have failed to reduce significantly their adverse impact on the global environment.

The Global Financial Architecture and the Environment

In light of the role that foreign capital flight played in precipitating the Asian and Russian economic crises, an increasing number of people have begun to question the dominant global economic prescription offered by the IMF and the World Bank. This prescription has long been promoted by the U.S. Department of Treasury as a critical component of U.S. foreign economic policy aimed primarily at maintaining stability on Wall Street by protecting foreign (i.e., U.S.) capital investments in developing countries. As these capital investments have increasingly become short term and speculative, the social utility of protecting capital flows is increasingly questionable. Speculative, "hot flows" of capital are not intended for long-term productive investments. Protecting the rights of countries to impose capital controls, particularly on short-term investments, may be critical for ensuring both long-term stability and increased benefits from natural resources for local people.

Over the past decade, environmentalists have also shown that the IFIs frequently saddle developing countries with loan conditions that increase the pressures on natural resource exploitation with devastating environmental consequences. Among other things, these structural adjustment policies (SAPs) significantly increase the rate of forest harvesting, mining, and fishery harvests. While these SAPs are increasing natural resource exploitation, many governments are also being directed to reduce public spending, including funds for environmental protection and natural resource management.

To make matters worse, large structural adjustment loan packages heap additional debt onto already heavily indebted countries. Due in large part to civil society pressure in the past few years, some limited debt relief may be on the way for the world's poorest countries. But the United States must take a much greater leadership role in prodding the World Bank and the IMF to make broader and deeper cuts in developing country debt. Such a step could help alleviate the pressures on low-income countries to exploit their environments in order to service their foreign debts.

Greening International Trade

Shortly after the 1992 Earth Summit, the United States, Canada, and Mexico signed the North American Free Trade Agreement. Negotiated by the outgoing Bush administration, NAFTA originally avoided addressing the environmental or labor aspects of free trade. Pressure from environmentalists ultimately led to negotiation of an environmental side agreement, which ostensibly reflected the Clinton administration's increased commitment to integrating the goals of environmental protection and trade liberalization. Following closely on NAFTA, the Clinton administration also promised to green the WTO in a 1993 speech by Vice President Al Gore. Unfortunately, this would later prove to be the high-water mark of the Clinton administration's commitment to integrating trade and the environment.

Despite occasional promises to the contrary, free trade has become the paramount value driving most U.S. international relations under the Clinton administration. Lost is the balanced goal of integrating environment and trade as pronounced at the Earth Summit and subsequently in the environmental side agreement to NAFTA. A case in point is the administration's effort to railroad the so-called fast-track trade bill through Congress in 1997. The president's proposal largely ignored environmental issues and was thus universally opposed by all environmental groups (even those that had previously supported NAFTA). Nor has the United States shown any leadership in promoting sound environmental policies at the WTO. Although the WTO did create a Committee on Trade and the Environment shortly after Vice President Gore's 1993 speech, that committee has been largely ineffectual in catalyzing any meaningful trade and environment policy.

Ultimately, the problem may be that liberalizing trade and investment is too often viewed as a positive goal in its own right. Lost is any critical analysis of whether such liberalization always leads to improvements in human welfare and quality of life. Goals such as environmental protection, human rights, and social equity—which are arguably more closely linked to human welfare than is liberalized trade—have been relegated to the backseat during the drive toward free trade. Only by honestly evaluating the environmental and social impact of liberalizing trade and investment, sector by sector, can we determine whether expansion or contraction of the world trade system is more likely to lead to a sustainable future. Thus the United States should support calls by environmentalists for a thorough analysis of the impacts of current trade policies on environmental sustainability *before* supporting any expansion of liberalized trade and investment policies.

Respecting Global Environment Agreements

IFIs and trade institutions also need to do a better job of mainstreaming concerns about the environment into their day-to-day operations. This general issue is highlighted by the way in which these institutions relate to the multilateral environmental agreements (e.g., the climate change regime or the Montreal Protocol with respect to ozone depletion). The IFIs have yet to prohibit funding projects that exacerbate the very same problems that these global environmental regimes are meant to address.

The U.S. Overseas Private Investment Corporation (OPIC) has recently adopted a hopeful approach, announcing that it would not finance any projects that are inconsistent with certain international environmental obligations—for example, projects that use ozone-depleting substances controlled by the Montreal Protocol, projects that manufacture certain toxic chemicals, or projects affecting sites listed under the UNESCO World Heritage Convention. Yet OPIC continues to finance projects that have a significant negative impact on climate change. Similarly, the WTO still struggles with how to dovetail international trade law with international environmental agreements—although in a recent decision, a WTO dispute panel did agree that international environmental agreements should be taken into account when deciding an international trade dispute.

Balancing Investment Rights with Privileges

In promoting broad investment agreements, such as the proposed Multilateral Agreement on Investment (MAI), the United States and other Organization for Economic Cooperation and Development (OECD) countries tried to formalize into international law a reduction in the power of national and local governments to control the environmental and social impacts of foreign investment. Adoption of "free trade" in investment capital would mean that companies would enjoy all of the benefits of free capital flow and repatriation of profits while accepting none of the environmental and social responsibility inherent in the goal of sustainable development. Sovereign nations should be able to retain the right to regulate how foreign investors operate in their territory and to determine the extent to which local people should be given preferential treatment with respect to local resources. (See essay 5–4: Intellectual Property Rights and the Privatization of Life.) Although this may in some cases lead to reduced environmental protection, ensuring that local people benefit from natural resource exploitation is not only fair but, in the long run, will likely lead to more sustainable development.

Although multinational corporations often operate in developing countries with higher environmental standards than do local companies, multinationals typically follow lower standards than they practice at home. Adhering to lower standards in developing countries raises serious questions of equity and competitiveness. To minimize the impact of lower standards abroad, the United States should ban the export of domestically prohibited technologies and goods and should impose minimum environmental standards on U.S. corporations operating abroad. The United States should also provide fair and equal judicial access to foreign citizens and communities harmed by environmental damage that was caused by U.S. corporate activities.

Greening Technology Transfers

The markets for environmental investments are large and increasing; for example, investments for global pollution control are expected to reach $300 to 600 billion per year by 2000; investments in energy-efficiency projects are expected to total another $250 billion in the next 20 years. Many of these opportunities for environmental investments are being created or stimulated by international and domestic law. For example, the Kyoto Protocol under the climate change regime now requires a reduction in net greenhouse gas emissions in industrial countries, which may in turn create a massive new market for renewable and efficient energy technologies. Transferring these green technologies to developing countries should be a priority of both U.S. and international finance lending. (See essay 5–5: U.S. Trade Policy Backs an Economic Loser: Weapons over Environmental Technology Exports.) Such lending should be earmarked for shifting societies to appropriate, nonpolluting technologies and not simply for improving the efficiencies of fundamentally unsustainable technologies, such as coal-fired power plants or nuclear reactors.

EMPHASIZING NGOS AND THE INTERNET TO PROTECT THE GLOBAL ENVIRONMENT

Perhaps the most promising development for protecting the global environment since the Earth Summit is the rise of a global environmental movement. The number of environmental nongovernmental organizations (NGOs) addressing international issues, particularly in developing countries, has exploded in recent years, as has their capacity to build networks, gather and analyze technical information, and gain the attention of key policymakers. Virtually every country has at least one environmental NGO, many of which actively seek to collaborate with their colleagues from other countries.

Today's communication technology has also increased the effectiveness of the global environmental community considerably. The Internet, in particular, provides a vast opportunity for forming and maintaining global networks, sharing information and experiences, and coordinating international lobbying efforts. In this regard, the most important developments are not in the formation of permanent federations or groups of formal networks but in the ability of temporary networks and campaigns to form, adapt, and dissolve readily. This dynamic process allows for concentrated efforts through new and changing alliances that focus on specific issues. It allows coordinated action in many different countries around the same issue, with little need for expensive infrastructure or costly planning meetings. Success often depends as much on internal diplomacy—the ability to maintain the interest of a large number of NGOs through the use of information technology— as on any external communication strategy. In the Internet world, NGOs may have a slight advantage over corporations in that the informality of the NGO community helps in conducting business through the Internet, and trust can build quickly among NGOs with shared goals and vision.

Protecting Unrestricted Citizen Access to the Internet

Effective Internet use by citizen movements has not gone unnoticed by those who benefit from isolating civil society. Given recent pronouncements by several countries, including Russia and Vietnam, about restricting or monitoring international

Internet communication, and given the ongoing discussions by U.S. law enforcement agencies about obtaining the capabilities to monitor Internet messages,
maintaining unrestricted access to the Internet must be a high priority for the
global environmental movement.

Democratizing International Environmental Law

Traditionally only nation-states have had the right to participate in the making, interpretation, and implementation of international law. This model is being challenged with respect to international environmental law, however, as many nonstate
actors assume more prominent roles. Nowadays nonstate actors—for example,
multinational corporations and NGOs—gather their own information, make their
own alliances, and expect to participate fully in international affairs. To be sure, the
primary impact of NGOs is indirect—through pressuring national governments—
but in recent years NGOs have also begun to participate directly in international
environmental negotiations. For example, the U.S. delegations to international
meetings now routinely include both environmental NGO and industry representatives as unofficial observers. Given that environmental NGOs are generally
more likely to insist on environmental protection than are government representatives, this trend toward the democratization of international environmental law
will generally work to the environment's advantage.

A few forums also now exist that give citizens a more direct role in enforcing
stronger environmental policies. Prodded by NGOs and donor governments, for
example, the World Bank created an inspection panel in 1993. The creation of this
panel marked the first time in history that people harmed by an international institution could seek an investigation into that institution's activities without first involving their government. Although the panel process has become highly
politicized, in almost every instance claimants have received some relief and have
triggered important discussions and debate about reforms at the highest level of
the World Bank. The Asia Development Bank and Inter-American Development
Bank now offer similar mechanisms for citizen-based enforcement. The International Finance Corporation (which is part of the World Bank) also recently created
an ombudsman's office to hear citizen complaints, while it also considers creating
an inspection panel. Another recent citizen forum is the petition process of the
NAFTA Commission on Environmental Cooperation, through which citizens can
question the effectiveness of any NAFTA country's environmental enforcement
efforts. All these citizen forums need to be strengthened and others created to expand the role of citizens in protecting the global environment.

The expansion of citizen rights within the international system will come at a
cost, however. As nation-states relinquish their monopoly on international policymaking, corporations (not just individuals or civil society organizations) will also
gain greater access and power. Already the influence of corporations on formal international governance structures is apparent. Corporations that contribute large
sums of money to the so-called host committees for international meetings, such
as the April 1999 NATO Summit in Washington or the WTO Ministerial Conference in Seattle in late 1999, are promised special access to the delegates. UNEP

has also sought contributions from both environmental groups and industry to help pay for the negotiations of a binding treaty on persistent organic pollutants. Environmental groups will not be able to compete with the chemical industry in a treaty negotiation if financial contributions become the currency for access and political influence.

Developing Minimum and Uniform
International Administrative Procedures

Transparent and accountable procedures in international affairs can temper rising corporate influence. Campaigns to press for increased access to information and to attain citizen rights to participate in international institutions are ongoing simultaneously at many different international institutions. Thus, for example, efforts to ensure minimum levels of transparency and access to information are currently being waged at the WTO, the IMF, the United Nations Development Programme (UNDP), and the multilateral development banks.

A minimum level of citizen-based rights to information, participation, and independent review should be provided at all international institutions. Currently no minimum procedures or standards exist, and civil society ends up duplicating its efforts for improving governance at every institution. To avoid repeating the same battles with each regulatory body, governments should negotiate one international "administrative procedures" treaty covering all the relevant institutions. Models currently exist that can be used for the development of such a treaty—for example, Europe's *Convention on Public Participation in Environmental Decisionmaking*.[7] Since the United States has been a leader in promoting greater transparency and participation at individual international organizations, it should also promote harmonization of minimum standards for international governance through an administrative procedures treaty.

Integrating Human Rights and the Environment

Human rights laws may also present important opportunities for gaining better environmental protection. Intuitively, people support the fundamental human right to enjoy minimum amounts of air and water free of contamination—to grow crops in a stable climate system on land protected from harmful ultraviolet radiation; in short, to live and raise their children in an environment conducive to human life and health.

Regardless of whether the human right to a healthy environment is recognized, however, the relationship between environmental protection and human rights is a natural one. Environmental damage is often worse in countries and in areas where human rights abuses are greatest, particularly where outside forces are driving the exploitation of valuable natural resources—for example, gold or oil— over the objections of local communities. Repression is often the only way to force this type of "development," particularly when little or no benefit is obvious for the local community. Leading environmental activists such as Chico Mendes in Brazil and Ken Saro Wiwa in Nigeria have been killed and many others have been beaten for raising their voices. In many of these instances, the international human rights movement offers the best hope for protection from internal oppression.

CONCLUSION

In hindsight, we can now see that the UN Conference on Environment and Development held in Rio de Janiero never effectively addressed the speed and scale of the global economy. Although UNCED raised questions about unsustainable levels of consumption and emphasized the goal of sustainable development over economic growth, the conference did not herald a significant shift away from the global preoccupation with economic growth. Indeed, at least until the economic crises in Asia, Russia, and Brazil, the 1990s witnessed an unprecedented and uninterrupted drive toward a global economy, with virtually no recognition of the goal of sustainable development.

Globalization is being supported by international policies and institutions that attempt to remove regulatory barriers to the flow of goods, services, and capital. No set of governments or institutions is managing the global economic tide, which is strong and unpredictable. At least with respect to environmental protection, international organizations (both economic institutions and environment and development bodies) lack both the authority and the will to manage the global market for sustainable development. Moreover, agreements such as the MAI, designed to facilitate global markets, undermine national efforts to impose environmental protections.

As we have discussed, scenarios for imposing environmental controls on global markets involve greatly strengthening current global environmental policies and institutional frameworks. Global economic regimes could even be greened from the inside, if leading economic powers made sustainable development a priority. Human rights, too, may provide a mechanism for checking the environmental excesses of the global market economy, although complicated and technical environmental problems are generally more conducive to complex management regimes than to a black-and-white system of minimum rights. Yet whatever mix of these approaches is used to nudge the global economy toward more sustainable development, it will have little chance of success until the United States takes a leadership role in pursuing global environmental protection above unbridled economic growth.

NOTES

1. See also *Programme for the Further Implementation of Agenda 21*, paras. 9–10, adopted by the Special Session of the UN General Assembly, June 23–27, 1997 (concluding that "[f]ive years after UNCED, the state of the global environment has continued to deteriorate)."
2. Legally binding treaties create a legal obligation on all countries who sign and ratify the agreement. Nonlegally binding instruments do not create a legal obligation, although they can set politically or morally important standards.

3. John Dernbach, *U.S. Adherence to Its Agenda 21 Commitments: A Five Year Review*, 27 ENVTL. L. REP. 10504 (1997).

4. Gregg Marland, Tom Boden, Antoinette Brenkert, Bob Andres, and Cathy Johnston, *Global CO_2 Emissions from Fossil-Fuel Burning, Cement Manufacture, and Gas Flaring: 1751–1996* (Oak Ridge, TN: Carbon Dioxide Information Analysis Center, March 5, 1999); Gregg Marland, Tom Boden, Antoinette Brenkert, Bob Andres, and Cathy Johnston, *National CO_2 Emissions from Fossil-Fuel Burning, Cement Manufacture, and Gas Flaring: 1751–1996* (Oak Ridge, TN: Carbon Dioxide Information Analysis Center, January 15, 1999); U.S. Department of Commerce, Bureau of the Census, International Database, *Total Midyear Population for the World: 1950–2050* (Washington, DC: Department of Commerce, December 28, 1998); U.S. Department of Commerce, Bureau of the Census, *Current Population Reports*, Series P-25, Nos. 311, 917, 1095, and Population Paper Listing PPL-91 (Washington, DC: Department of Commerce, April 2, 1998).

5. Daniel Esty, *Greening the GATT: Trade, Environment, and the Future* (Washington, DC: Institute for International Economics, 1994), p. 78.

6. United Nations, *Everyone's United Nations*, 9th ed. (New York: United Nations Department of Public Information, 1978), p. 168.

7. Economic Commission for Europe, *Convention on Public Participation in Decisionmaking and Access to Justice in Environmental Matters*, UN Doc. ECE/CEP/43 (adopted at Aarhus, Denmark, June 25, 1998).

ENVIRONMENT AND SECURITY POLICY

Stacy VanDeever

DURING JANUARY 28, 1998 TESTIMONY BEFORE THE SENATE Select Committee on Intelligence, U.S. intelligence officials asserted that military threats to U.S. interests are declining in magnitude while other types of threats, including environmental, have grown. General Patrick Hughes, director of the Defense Intelligence Agency, testified that environmental degradation, including pollution and shortages of fresh water and arable land, are among the post–cold war threats that are bringing "great stress to the international order." Despite this, environmental issues have not been integrated well into U.S. foreign and security policymaking. Recent efforts—many of them spearheaded by Vice President Al Gore—to foster interest within foreign policymaking organizations have raised awareness of environmental issues. So far, however, these have resulted in few changes in policy or resource allocation.

Small, newly established environment-related programs exist in various foreign policy–related government agencies, including within the State Department, Department of Defense (DOD), Department of Energy (DOE), and Central Intelligence Agency (CIA). But the information and analyses produced in these programs have neither a large audience nor a significant impact within policymaking circles. Nor have the programs embarked on education campaigns aimed at convincing skeptics, in the executive branch, in Congress, and among the American public, of the importance of integrating environment and security issues. Instead, program administrators tend to avoid congressional scrutiny in fear of being defunded by a Congress hostile to most international and environmental programs.

The office of the Undersecretary of Defense for Environmental Security is charged with bringing DOD into compliance with many U.S. environmental standards. It is not tasked, however, with assessing the environmental impacts of DOD spending and activities. As such, these are unknown. Nearly its entire budget (over $4 billion annually) is spent domestically for environmental cleanup operations and personnel safety at military installations. U.S. overseas military bases are not required by law to meet U.S. environmental standards (or environmental impact statement requirements), and DOD is not required to clean up these installations when Americans leave them. Because detailed information regarding U.S. military activities is often classified, it remains impossible for those outside DOD to discern overall environmental impacts.

Existing environment-related programs within the State Department, CIA, and DOE remain small, underfunded, and without clear organizational authority and responsibility. The same is true of the EPA's Office of International Affairs and its environmental security initiatives as well as of DOD's international cooperation programs. All remain understaffed, some languishing for months with personnel vacancies. Their programs and information generally remain peripheral to the central missions of their larger organizations. Individual environmental programs, such as international environmental policy workshops and training programs or individual cleanup operations, are organized on ad hoc bases and grafted to existing institutions. Even their narrowly defined missions remain underfunded, often authorized less money than executive branch officials have promised to international partners.

For instance, the State Department's environmental initiative organized by the Bureau of Oceans and International Environmental and Scientific Affairs (OES) and the new post of Under Secretary for Global Affairs (created in 1993) are attempts to draw greater attention to such interrelated problems as environmental issues, population growth, scientific cooperation, and migration. Yet the State Department's first Environmental Diplomacy report, issued in 1997, addressed strictly environmental issues, not the connections of these issues to other areas of policy. While State Department touts a related system of "regional environmental hubs" located in U.S. embassies, these hubs are being constructed without the additional resources needed in the field offices and without new personnel practices designed to attract career-minded civil servants with the relevant environmental, scientific, and technical expertise.

To be effective, U.S. security policy cannot be formulated—nor its environmental components assessed—separately from U.S. foreign policies concerning international trade, economic development, foreign assistance, human rights, and the need for more sustainable development. Recent controversies over the effectiveness and adverse social and environmental effects of U.S.-backed IMF restructuring programs illustrate this point. Yet the institutional legacies of the cold war era have resulted in a kind of balkanization of foreign and security policymaking across the federal bureaucracy, leaving the U.S. State Department unable (or unwilling) to integrate security policy with contemporary concerns for sustainable development, democratization, and human rights protection.

Foreign and security policymakers continue to miss opportunities to build political and economic cooperation among antagonists in the Middle East and Central Asia regarding scarce resources such as fresh water. These policymakers offer only tiny, token aid programs to assist states and citizens of formerly communist countries in combating environmental threats to human health. Yet, they dedicate significant efforts to ensuring that U.S. energy corporations have access to resources in the same region. U.S. assistance that improves human health and citizen access to environmental information and decision-making could help to build state legitimacy and enhance stability in many fledgling democracies.

For environmental concern and assessment to be integrated effectively into U.S. foreign and security policy, greater resources must be allocated to the government's centers of environmental, technical, and foreign policy expertise: the EPA and the State Department. The EPA's international affairs programs and the State Department's OES initiatives must be better funded and given greater authority and assessment and policymaking capabilities if environmental issues are to impact traditional U.S. foreign policies. The EPA needs a greater voice in U.S. international activities and policies, and the State Department must take more advantage of outside expertise, in addition to expanding its own environmental and technical expert resources. State Department officials' current interest in improving their scientific and technical capacities should be explicitly linked to their need for more environmental expertise.

POPULATION AND ENVIRONMENT

Robert Engelman

GLOBALLY, WOMEN TODAY HAVE HALF THE NUMBER OF CHILDREN—roughly three over their lifetimes—that they had in 1960. This average fertility would be lower still if not for the fact that an estimated 38 percent of pregnancies worldwide are neither sought nor desired. The reality is that women in developing countries (as well as industrialized ones) are participating in a demographic revolution. They seek to have fewer children, and to have them later in life, than ever before in human history.

Although the global rate of population growth peaked 30 years ago, human population has grown by nearly two-thirds since then. The ratios of people to fresh water, forests, cropland, fish, and the atmosphere have grown in tandem. Despite slowing growth, world population still gains nearly 80 million people each year, parceling land, fresh water, and other finite resources among more and more people. A new Germany is added annually, a new Los Angeles monthly.

There is no doubt that trends such as the loss of half of the planet's forests, the depletion of most of its major fisheries, and the alteration of its atmosphere and climate are closely related to the fact that human population expanded from mere millions in prehistoric times to nearly six billion today. How this increase in population size affects specific environmental problems is impossible to say precisely and has, for years, been hotly debated.

The long debate over the impact of population growth on the environment is gradually converging on a middle ground where most scientists can agree. The need now is to prod U.S. policymakers—distracted by political battles over abortion—to a consensus on which they can act. The United States should model its population policies after the Program of Action agreed to in 1994 at the United Nations International Conference on Population and Development, held in Cairo.

With remarkable consensus, those at the Cairo meeting agreed that although governments need to be concerned about the stabilization of population, they should neither require nor induce their own citizens to make reproductive decisions based on this concern. Lasting demographic trends respond to the childbearing choices people make themselves, not to those imposed by the state, church, or other outside institutions. The conference reaffirmed that though decisions about the number, timing, and spacing of children belong exclusively to couples and individuals, all people should have access to both the information and the means they need to make reproductive decisions.

The education of girls through secondary school and improvements in economic opportunities for women are also essential components of population policy. It is this "win-win" strategy—slowing population growth by attending to the needs for health care, schooling, and economic opportunities—that should encourage policymakers to consider population-related policies when addressing environmental risks.

ENVIRONMENT AND CAPITAL FLOWS

Lyuba Zarsky

THE 1990S WITNESSED A SEA CHANGE IN THE PATTERN of international capital flows, thus generating one of the key environmental policy issues for the next decade. In 1990, more than half of international capital flowing to developing countries came from official sources; by 1995, over three-quarters came from private sources. Portfolio investment soared from $5 to $61 billion, and foreign direct investment (FDI) nearly quadrupled.

The FDI surge has been propelled by trends toward economic liberalization. Between 1991 and 1996, 95 percent of the 599 changes in laws and regulations governing FDI in developing countries were directed toward liberalization. While corporate investment has boomed, national regulatory capacities have not kept pace, and investment remains largely ungoverned at the international level. Given the stakes, the creation of global investment rules will be high on the political agenda in the next decade.

Environmentalists and free market proponents are engaged in a hot debate over the nature and content of these emerging rules. Environmentalists want to design investment rules to help channel the global economy toward sustainable development by explicitly embracing environmental and social regulation. Free marketeers want global rules based on neoliberalism—that is, the exclusive promotion of commerce—while leaving environmental and social regulation to nation-states. Both sides marshal evidence to show that their vision of global governance is socially optimal. Given the alarming rate of global ecological degradation, the central question is whether, and at what pace, neoliberal FDI will harmonize environmental standards upward or downward.

Environmentalists argue that the gravitational pull of neoliberal rules is decidedly downward. Gaps in standards either draw the dirtiest industries to developing countries or encourage foreign firms to pollute once they get there. In either case, the effect is the creation of pollution havens. Even more worrying is the intense competition among cities and countries to attract or retain FDI, especially by big multinational corporations (MNCs). Offering less onerous or more flexible environmental regulation is a common bargaining chip. The result is that standards race to the bottom.

Proponents of neoliberalism counter that FDI is good for the environment, because it diffuses cleaner technology and best management practices, creating "pollution halos" in developing countries. Moreover, "green consumers" in rich countries use market power to demand better environmental performance. And rising incomes in developing countries, helped by FDI, mean more money and citizen pressure for better environmental protection. The net effect of all these trends is that free markets propel global standards in a race to the top.

The evidence shows mixed effects. Differences in standards apparently have little influence on where firms locate, probably because costs of environmental compliance are low. In addition, the environmental performance of industry seems to be incrementally improving in developing countries. However, except for particular sectors in particular countries, such as energy in China, the main drivers are not foreign companies but effective national regulation and/or local community pressure. Finally, there is evidence that green consumers in Europe and North America are using ecolabels to positive effect, especially in sensitive resource-based products such as timber and bananas.

On the other hand, there are many cases—the Amazon, Nigeria, Bhopal—in which MNCs perform like environmental renegades. Moreover, the impacts of ecolabels may be marginal: bananas may be less toxic but are still grown in unsustainable, monocultural cropping patterns. Case study evidence also shows that policymakers are indeed highly sensitive to competition for FDI. They may not lower standards but may not enforce them either, and they certainly hesitate about raising them much. Indeed, the depressing effect of competition for investment is felt even within the United States, where states offer "flexibility" of environmental oversight to attract high-employment industries such as high-tech firms.

As a whole, the evidence points to two conclusions. First, environmental standards are not "racing" either up or down. Rather, they are pulled in both directions and are probably improving incrementally, at least at a microlevel. The problem is that the rate of change is slow, too slow to keep pace with environmental degradation, especially in terms of macroimpacts such as biodiversity loss, the bioaccumulation of toxic wastes, resource depletion, and atmospheric degradation. Environmental standards are "stuck in the mud," with policymakers and corporate managers alike looking over their shoulders at competitors. Second, to increase the pace of environmental improvement, governments need to collectively establish common global minimum performance and process standards for industries.

U.S. policy, which rests squarely on neoliberalism, is based on two tenets: (1) liberalization is, on average, good for the environment; and (2) the best way to increase global industrial environmental performance is through voluntary corporate self-regulation. In the process of the Multilateral Agreement on Investment (MAI), initiated and led by the United States, environmental and social concerns were not initially even on the radar screen. Even after a storm of public criticism, they made only a minor appearance. In the end, the MAI was defeated, in part by the opposition of labor, environmental, and other social activists.

Washington will play a decisive role in shaping the regulatory architecture for international investment. To shoulder its global role responsibly, the United States must first clearly define its policy goals—via a process of wide public debate and consultation—and then weave them together into a coherent policy framework. Under the right set of rules, international capital flows, both direct and portfolio, could act to promote ecological sustainability, which should be (and has been stated to be) a strategic U.S. foreign policy goal. Such rules would collectively define investor responsibilities, as well as those of both home and host countries, and would address both the micro- and macro-ecological impacts of investment. Moreover, to promote sustainable development, U.S. policy should aim to increase the flow of economically and environmentally beneficial foreign investment to developing countries, especially the poorest. And Washington must undertake policy innovations that enhance the social and environmental accountability of U.S. multinational corporations, both at home and overseas.

INTELLECTUAL PROPERTY RIGHTS
AND THE PRIVATIZATION OF LIFE

Kristin Dawkins

INTELLECTUAL PROPERTY RIGHTS (IPR) GRANT INVENTORS monopolies in ex-change for their socially valuable innovations, a privilege that the United States interprets as a corporate right to privatize plants, animals, and other forms of life. The U.S. government has made the rigorous enforcement of IPR a top priority of its foreign policy, using interna-tional trade negotiations as the means of continually ratcheting up the terms.

IPRs assign to inventors and artists (or, more often, their corporate sponsors) the op-tion to monopolize novel forms of commercially valuable knowledge—such as a new drug, software, graphic design, or musical recording—for extended periods of time, usually 20 years. They generally take the form of patents, trademarks, or copyrights.

Agrochemical and pharmaceutical companies, calling themselves the "life industry," assert that IPR are essential for research and development. Without royalties guaranteed through IPR, they say, they could not afford to invest in the search for plants whose active ingredients may be the source of new life-saving drugs. Nor could they conduct research in genetic engineering, with which they will "feed the world." These industries successfully crafted global IPR regulations through the 1994 Uruguay Round of General Agreement on Tariffs and Trade (GATT) trade negotiations.

Washington has made it clear to other governments that the global agreement on Trade-Related Aspects of Intellectual Property Rights (TRIPS)—one part of the Uruguay Round of GATT—is not sufficient. In every ongoing trade negotiation, the United States is seeking stronger "TRIPS-plus" terms.

Most developing countries find current TRIPS to be onerous enough—facilitating transnational corporations' access to their internal markets and resources and limiting their own capacity to develop. Public health advocates point out that patented drugs are far more expensive than their generic counterparts, generating windfall profits well beyond the ac-tual costs of development. Critics point out that investments in genetic research to date have yielded little agronomic value but instead have resulted in crops that tolerate high doses of herbicides—in effect, creating superweeds and superbugs that in turn lead to new blights of damaging insects and the demand for ever more chemicals.

In conjunction with other trade and investment policies, the global marketing of ex-pensive patented medicines and seeds limits many communities' access to food and health. Furthermore, there are profound ethical and moral questions about trade policies that con-vert seeds, plants, and other forms of life into private property. Monopoly control of plants is contributing to the destruction of food security and public interest research as well as to the loss of biological diversity and ecological health. Thus, the debate over what constitutes appropriate public policy governing IPR will continue to be of concern well into the next century.

U.S. officials say trade rules are the supreme international law, despite numerous inter-national agreements establishing the rights of farmers, indigenous peoples, and local com-munities to their natural resources. Every six months, under the infamous Super 301 clause, the U.S. Trade Representative (USTR) issues a list of countries against which the United

States might impose trade sanctions if they do not improve their IPR enforcement. According to the WTO, such unilateral exercise of trade sanctions is illegal, but no serious challenge has worked its way through the WTO process as yet.

Occasionally, threats of trade sanctions—which are almost always effective, due to their potential economic impact—are made on behalf of the auto, steel, or other manufacturing industries. With the advent of the "information age," this effort has been directed toward the computer and entertainment industries. In 1997, for instance, the United States unilaterally reimposed import duties on $260 million of Argentine exports in retaliation for Argentina's refusal to rewrite its patent legislation to the satisfaction of the USTR Office.

A number of nations, including Bolivia, India, Pakistan, and Thailand, have contested patents granted by the U.S. Patent and Trademarks Office (PTO) for biological materials, especially plants, taken from their peoples. This biopiracy, as it is often called, yields new profits for U.S. companies, which take the raw material, alter it in the laboratory to claim an invention, and win the patent. For source countries, this represents double trouble for their economies. First, their natural resource has been appropriated by a foreign corporation, and they are prohibited from further developing the resource domestically. Second, there will be a net outflow of foreign exchange, as licensing fees and royalties are paid on any commercial products eventually exported back to their domestic markets.

A third major problem resulting from the patenting of plants is genetic pollution and the loss of biodiversity. Vast monocultures are planted with genetically identical seed, which in turn leads to thriving blights and the disappearance of local plant varieties. This genetic pollution becomes part of the gene pool and can never be remediated. Extinction is forever.

But many nations—including Thailand, India, and much of Africa—are developing their own systems that recognize the rights of farmers to save seed and of traditional peoples to regulate outsider access to their knowledge of medicinal plants. This recognition of human rights is fully consistent with TRIPS as well as a number of international conventions. Indeed, The Netherlands and Italy have filed suit with the European Court of Justice arguing that a recent European directive allowing patents on plants and animals is a violation of human rights.

The United States should cease its campaign to outlaw the *a priori* rights of communities to the resources that sustain them. It also should cease utilizing Super 301 and other bullying tactics and instead join the world community of nations in finding multilateral solutions to the struggle over valuable natural resources. High on the agenda of any credible multilateral regime must be the regulation of transnational corporations to enable local and regional resource management and governance systems to evolve. In fact, the Convention on Biological Diversity provides a framework for the development of such systems, if the United States would choose to respect—and ratify—this otherwise universally adopted body of international law.

U.S. TRADE POLICY BACKS AN ECONOMIC LOSER: WEAPONS OVER ENVIRONMENTAL TECHNOLOGY EXPORTS

Miriam Pemberton

THE MORAL AND STRATEGIC ARGUMENTS AGAINST THE CURRENT U.S. policy of massive taxpayer-financed subsidies for the arms trade are clear. As if these arguments were not enough, this policy turns out to be bad economics as well. In a comparison of the world markets for arms versus environmental technologies (commonly referred to as "envirotechs"), the arms trade ends up the loser. Yet the U.S. currently devotes far more time, energy, and money to seeding the world with American-made weapons than with environmental technology to improve human health and productivity. In addition to its other defects, this policy of peddling technologies that sink all boats instead of those that lift them contradicts U.S. economic self-interest.

Environmental technology includes public infrastructure (water and sewer systems, e.g.) as well as spending by the private sector both to clean up pollution and to prevent it. Estimates of the size of the market for these technologies consistently set worldwide demand well above $400 billion a year. By 1995 this market was already twice the size of the world market for all types of military hardware. In recent years the international market for U.S. envirotechs has been outstripping the domestic market and is forecasted to remain strong, matching or exceeding its current growth, and outperforming the global economy as a whole.

By contrast, while congressional leaders and the Clinton administration appear bent on further increases to the U.S. military budget (despite the lack of a strategic rationale for doing so), no forecasts predict the international arms market to rebound from its current slump.

Despite this clear advantage for envirotechs over weapons as trade opportunities, in 1995 (the most recent year for which comparative statistics are available) Washington spent $12 promoting arms exports for every dollar it spent promoting envirotech exports. As worldwide military spending has fallen in the post–cold war period, federal subsidies underwriting American arms exports have come to constitute more and more of the industry's profits. While the take for U.S. industry from the international arms market in 1995 was about $16 billion, government subsidies amounted to nearly $7 billion. Thus nearly one dollar of every two in arms export revenues is coming from U.S. taxpayers. This is poor bang for the buck indeed. For the envirotech market, by contrast, about the same export revenues—$15 billion—have been generated from about $600 million in promotional expenditures, or about one public dollar to produce $25 in revenue.

Funding for research and development, procurement spending, regulation, and technology verification are the principal tools that government can use to help develop a technology for export. With the exception of regulation, far more federal muscle has been applied behind each of these tools in the promotion of weapons than of environmental technologies. By reversing these funding priorities, the United States would be doing well by doing good and getting better economic returns by serving more compelling needs.

LATIN AMERICA and the CARIBBEAN

Atlantic Ocean

Caribbean Sea

CUBA
DOMINICAN REPUBLIC
JAMAICA   HAITI
PUERTO RICO (U.S.)

MEXICO   BELIZE
GUATEMALA   HONDURAS
EL SALVADOR   NICARAGUA
COSTA RICA
PANAMA

VENEZUELA
FRENCH GUIANA
GUYANA
SURINAME

COLOMBIA

ECUADOR

PERU

Pacific Ocean

BRAZIL

BOLIVIA

CHILE   PARAGUAY

URUGUAY

ARGENTINA

U.S. POLICY IN LATIN AMERICA AND THE CARIBBEAN: PROBLEMS, OPPORTUNITIES, AND RECOMMENDATIONS

Coletta Youngers

COMPARING CONDITIONS IN THE WESTERN HEMISPHERE today with the situation 15 years ago, there appears to be much room for optimism. The armed conflicts in Central America, which were at the center of policy debates in the United States, have all ended with negotiated solutions, and the authoritarian dictators that ravaged South America were one by one replaced by elected civilian officials. Massive, government-sponsored human rights abuses have declined dramatically as a result, and economic growth has resumed after a lost decade.

Upon taking office, senior Clinton administration officials painted this rosy assessment of regional trends and proposed a foreign policy agenda for Latin America centered around the concept of "enlargement and engagement," based on the now-familiar arguments that open economies foster growth and allow greater political freedoms and that democracies make more reliable allies. With the exception of Cuba, they point out, every country in the hemisphere is on the same economic and political track, headed toward the completion of a free trade alliance from Alaska to Tierra del Fuego to be established by the year 2005. Waving the free trade banner, the Clinton administration has made promoting U.S. economic interests its number-one priority in U.S. policy toward the region. In an interview with the *New York Times* just prior to beginning his second term in office, President Clinton boldly proclaimed that pursuing free trade agreements with Latin American countries would be among his highest priorities during his second term.

Clinton, however, did not live up to his word, and shortly into his second term Latin America faded from the administration's agenda (with the important exception of the "war on drugs"). More important, the Clinton administration's message rings hollow for the vast majority in Latin America and the Caribbean who have failed to benefit either from democracy or economic growth, which has not trickled down as promised. Elected civilian governments remain fragile and are threatened by continued military impunity and weak institutional guarantees of fundamental civil, political, and individual rights. Today there is mounting evidence that the obstacles to democratic consolidation are growing and that the neoliberal economic model is simply not capable of addressing such fundamental problems as the lack of employment opportunities and the inequitable distribution of income and resources. Moreover, it fails to take into account the very real danger of sharp reversals in the positive regional trends of democratization, demilitarization, and greater respect for human rights.

OBSTACLES TO DEMOCRATIC CONSOLIDATION

A visible example of this shortsightedness is the tendency of U.S. policymakers to equate elections with democracy. Elections are, of course, a necessary and important component of democratic systems. But elections alone do not ensure that citizens have effective input and influence over important decisions and policies that affect their lives. In many Latin American countries, authoritarian traditions, corrupt and elite-dominated political parties, and nascent electoral systems combine to limit both the content and consequence of electoral choice. Weak or nonexistent mechanisms for civil society to debate policies and to engage with elected officials in an ongoing fashion exacerbate the problem. International financial institutions (IFIs) send a conflicting message about democracy when, while promoting electoral reforms to ensure broader political participation and hence the legitimacy of elected leaders, they insist that the economic policies of developing countries adhere to a uniform model not subject to domestic debate.

To date, Latin American governments have proven unable to confront the unprecedented levels of crime across the region and the corresponding rise in fear for personal safety, often resulting in popular support for militarized solutions to the public security crisis. (In fact, the Latin America/Caribbean area has the dubious distinction of being the most violent region in the world.) High unemployment, massive poverty, and growing inequality are all contributing to the crime wave, and local police forces are often perceived as part of the problem—through their participation in organized crime, gangs, and routine bribery—rather than part of the solution. More often than not, judiciaries function only for those with money to grease the wheels of the bureaucracy. Public opinion surveys suggest that only a tiny minority of Latin Americans have any confidence that their police and judicial systems are adequate to the challenge.

Although the overall record regarding human rights has improved remarkably in much of Latin America, the patterns of behavior that lead to abuses are far from eradicated. Throughout the region, impunity remains the norm for those who continue to commit human rights violations, and those seeking truth and justice often face political obstacles and personal threats. This was vividly illustrated in the murder on April 26, 1998, of Monsignor Juan Gerardi, Auxiliary Bishop of Guatemala and director of the *Guatemala Nunca Más* (Guatemala No More) project, an effort initiated by the Guatemalan bishops to document abuses by all sides in the Guatemalan conflict. Monsignor Gerardi was killed just two days after the release of the final report. Violence over land rights and natural resources continues to erupt in countries such as Brazil and Ecuador. Civil conflict rages in Colombia, where guerrillas battle government forces and powerful right-wing paramilitary groups, resulting in levels of political violence and human rights abuses comparable to (if not worse than) those that ravaged the region in previous decades. In 1997 alone in Colombia, there were at least 185 politically motivated massacres (defined as the killing of four or more individuals), taking the lives of 1,042 people. Over the decade of the 1990s, between 3,000 to 4,000 Colombians have lost their lives each year as a result of political violence.

In Mexico, the brutal massacre of 45 indigenous peasants in the town of Acteal in the Chiapas region in December 1997 brought international attention to the ongoing human rights violations stemming from efforts to suppress the Zapatista National Liberation Army. The conflict in Mexico starkly reveals the failings of a political system where state largess can no longer buy political loyalty and stability. As was the case in the Central American conflicts of the previous decades, at the root of the struggles taking place in Colombia and Mexico are undemocratic political systems that have failed to allow for meaningful political participation or to remedy the imbalances between the haves and the have-nots.

Poverty, lack of access to land and resources, and tremendous income disparities remain fundamental problems that have yet to be addressed adequately throughout the region. According to the UN Economic Commission for Latin America and the Caribbean (CEPAL), during the 1990s the proportion of the population living in poverty has decreased slightly; however, the number of people living in poverty has increased significantly due to population growth. Some 75 million more people live in poverty today in the region than in 1980. The Latin American region continues to have the highest level of income inequality in the world, a situation that has seen virtually no improvement in most countries and has deteriorated even further in some. (In Colombia, according to CEPAL, the richest 10 percent increased its share of the income pie by a whopping 7 percent in just four years between 1990 and 1994.) Despite average annual growth rates of 3.2 percent since 1990, the richest 10 percent of households maintained or increased income levels, while the poorest 40 percent held steady or experienced decreased income. In other words, the modest and even, in some cases, exceptional economic growth rates of the 1990s have not led either to fewer people living in poverty or to a more equitable distribution of income.

Nor has economic growth resulted in stability, as evident in the economic crises in Mexico in 1994 and Brazil in 1998, both leading to billion-dollar bailout packages. In both cases, investor flight led to near-economic collapse as nervous investors, able to move millions with a click on the keyboard, pulled out capital overnight, thereby revealing the fragility of economies built on short-term, high-yield investments rather than long-term investments in infrastructure and industry. The tendency toward speculative investment means that more jobs are lost than created in countries like Mexico, where nearly 2 million jobs have been lost (even taking into account employment in the maquiladora sector) since the North American Free Trade Agreement (NAFTA) went into effect in 1993. Despite decades of free market and structural adjustment policies, high unemployment and widespread underemployment—and hence pervasive poverty—remain rampant in the region.

Even World Bank and other IFI officials now recognize that the focus on market-driven economic growth alone is unlikely to reduce poverty and lead to greater equality. Both the World Bank and the Inter-American Development Bank are engaged in a range of projects designed to strengthen local institutions, build human capital, and improve education. Yet as a result of the mandatory fiscal restraint required by the IFIs, local governments have vastly fewer resources to invest in development programs than in the past, and U.S. development assistance has dropped to an all-time low. IFI-supported safety net programs may be too little too late, because they ignore the structural causes of poverty and underdevelopment. Economic power remains in the hands of traditional and new elites, who have been the main beneficiaries of reforms. For them, "globalization" has meant the opportunity to invest capital wherever in the world it can bring the greatest return at the least risk.

Although direct foreign investment and IFI loans have replaced the United States as the main suppliers of development capital to Latin America and the Caribbean, Washington remains the most important external actor because of the markets and investment that the United States represents and also in part because of the influence its wields within the IFIs. In addition to the traditional U.S. hegemony in the region, U.S. economic interests have expanded as "globalization" trends have taken hold. U.S. exports to Latin America and the Caribbean have tripled in the last ten years to the point where almost half of all U.S. exports to developing countries go to the Latin American region; within ten years Latin America is expected to be the primary market for U.S. products and services. Mexico now rivals Japan as the second largest U.S. trading partner. Goods purchased from the United States represent more than 40 percent of all imports by countries in Latin America and the Caribbean and nearly 60 percent of all foreign investment in the region comes from the United States. (see figure 6–1.) The hemisphere is well on its way toward economic integration, with or without "fast track."

FAST TRACK DERAILED

The debate over NAFTA provided potent premonitions of what was to come in the "fast-track" debate during 1997 and 1998. The centerpiece of U.S. trade policy toward Latin America at the time, NAFTA set guidelines for eliminating most trade and investment barriers between Canada, Mexico, and the United States.

Figure 6.1 U.S. Trade Balance with Latin America and Selected Countries ($U.S. millions)

Country/Region	1991	1992	1993	1994	1995	1996	1997	1998
Latin America	501	6,648	3,401	4,034	−9,143	−15,141	−6,119	−3,454
Mexico	2,148	5,381	1,664	1,350	−15,809	−17,506	−14,549	−15,857
Caribbean	932	621	874	702	1,538	932	1,774	2,797
Central America	1,023	1,422	1,419	1,502	1,243	622	210	591
South America	−3,602	−776	−556	480	3,885	811	6,446	9,015
Brazil	−569	−1,858	−1,421	−581	2,607	1,944	6,289	5,035
Chile	537	1,078	1,137	963	1,684	1,877	2,075	1,532

Source: Department of Commerce, "Total Trade Balances with Individual Countries, 1991–1998," *Foreign Trade Highlights*, March 15, 1999.

Approved by the U.S. Congress in November 1993, NAFTA sparked bitter debate pitting U.S. corporations with overseas interests against a broad coalition of social groups, including unions and small business groups, concerned about the potential loss of U.S. jobs and downward pressures on wages, the potential detriment to the environment, and the economic impact in Mexico. NAFTA opened a schism in the Democratic party over these issues that is still felt at the turn of the century.

Both NAFTA and its labor and environment side agreements were negotiated with fast-track authority, under which negotiated trade pacts are voted on without amendments by the U.S. Congress. This facilitates negotiations by preventing Congress from altering trade agreements when voting on them. But in late 1997 and again in September 1998, the Clinton administration failed to win fast-track authority to negotiate trade agreements in order to advance its hemispheric free trade agenda in the wake of the December 1994 Miami Summit. No sooner had the hemisphere's heads of state signed off on the economic integration project—a Free Trade Area of the Americas (FTAA) by the year 2005—than it began to unravel. Within days of the summit, Mexico plunged headlong into a financial crisis that required a major U.S. financial bailout. Although NAFTA was not the cause of Mexico's economic crisis, it compounded and accelerated the problems created by structural adjustment and trade policies in place for over a decade.

From that point on, both NAFTA and the FTAA became domestic political liabilities for President Clinton. In the midst of the Mexico crisis and in the heat of his 1996 reelection campaign, he was unwilling to request further negotiating authority from Congress. When he finally did request fast-track authority in late 1997 to continue the integration agenda, Congress, at the urging of the majority of Democrats, promptly refused to comply. Clinton became the first president since Gerald Ford to be denied such authority. Not surprisingly, a subsequent congressional effort led by Republicans in September 1998 fared no better. With Congress in turmoil over the release of the Starr report and debating possible impeachment of the president, Clinton decided not to support the measure, fearing that he would further alienate fellow Democrats and would ignite a firestorm over a divisive issue within the Democratic party just weeks before crucial midterm elections.

At every stage, Latin American governments and economic elites hoping to negotiate free trade deals with Washington, and thereby gain greater access to lucrative U.S. markets, were increasingly discouraged and disappointed. Following the first defeat of fast-track authority, *Foreign Policy* editor Moises Naim commented that the "Washington consensus" on key economic tenets had taken hold throughout the region—with the apparent exception of Washington itself. The Clinton administration mantra of "trade, not aid" was ridiculed by many in the region as "neither trade nor aid."

In Washington, discouragement set in as well. Latin America slipped lower and lower on the U.S. foreign policy agenda. A leadership vacuum became more pronounced, as high-level officials in Latin America–related posts failed to speak out forcefully to bring attention to the region and failed to win bureaucratic battles for scarce foreign aid resources. Key ambassadorships went unfilled for prolonged periods, including posts to Mexico and Argentina. The special presidential adviser on Latin America, Clinton's boyhood friend Thomas "Mack" McLarty, announced his resignation and left the administration in mid-1998; the position re-mained vacant for nearly a year. Only the near-economic collapse in Brazil in the fall of 1998 refocused attention temporarily on Latin America, as U.S. officials again pulled together a multibillion-dollar bailout package to rescue the region's largest economy and prevent spillover effects that could provoke a regional economic collapse. (See figure 6–2.)

The fast-track debacle appears to have derailed U.S. policy toward Latin America. Efforts to promote free trade and economic integration continue, but U.S. policy toward the hemisphere increasingly lacks focus and leadership. (Perhaps the only important exception is the role the United States has played in supporting multilateral mediation efforts to resolve the Peru-Ecuador border conflict, which received sustained attention and resources from the administration and ultimately led to a brokered settlement.) As is often the case in Washington, issues are dealt with individually, and policies and programs often work at cross-purposes. Moreover, U.S. policy toward Latin America is increasingly driven by domestic agendas and by perceived threats emanating from the hemisphere: immigration, illicit drugs, and communist Cuba.

THE LOOMING "THREATS" TO U.S. NATIONAL SECURITY

In the absence of a deeper vision of more durable democracy and sustainable development in Latin America, what remains are policies driven by domestic political considerations and perceived "threats." The most visible U.S. actor in much of the

Figure 6.2

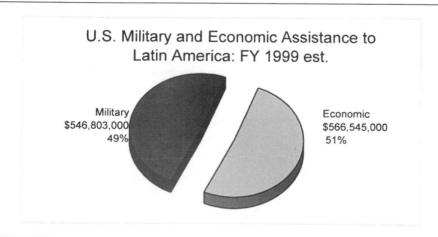

U.S. Military and Economic Assistance to Latin America: FY 1999 est.

Military $546,803,000 49%

Economic $566,545,000 51%

Source: Secretary of State, *Congressional Presentation for Foreign Operations, Fiscal Year 2000* (Washington, DC: Department of State, 1999): pp. 1324–5.

region is the U.S. drug czar, General Barry McCaffrey. Debates on Capitol Hill related to Latin America center almost exclusively on the issues of immigration, drug trafficking, and Cuba. The only new addition to the list is Colombia, where cold war and drug war villains are conveniently combined. As succinctly stated by Representative Dan Burton (R-IN) in an International Relations Committee hearing on March 31, 1998: "I've been told by our sources . . . that the entire country is in jeopardy of being lost. The entire northern tier of South America could be lost to narco-guerrillas and traffickers, and that would be horrible for the United States . . . [and] the entire Western Hemisphere." As is the case in Colombia, the policies driving the U.S. role in the region repeat many of the errors made during the cold war and often ignore the views and concerns of Washington's Latin American allies.

The latter is particularly true with regard to immigration policy, which repeatedly emerges as a sticking point in bilateral relations with Mexico as well as Central American and Caribbean countries. The backlash in the region from the deportation of record numbers of Latin American immigrants is notably absent from the U.S. debate on immigration policy. Yet sharp decreases in remittances from family members in the United States can wreak havoc on the economies of small countries as well as on individual families. Moreover, large numbers of deportees with criminal records—many of whom have not even lived in the countries they are being "returned" to—often go on to foster gang or other criminal activities in Latin America, contributing to significant increases in violent crime. Relaxations in the harsh 1996 anti-immigration legislation came about not as a result of pressure from Latin American countries but rather out of growing interest on the part of the Republican party in winning the voting support of the Latin American population, soon destined to be the largest minority in the United States.

International Drug Control

Likewise, U.S. international drug control policy is driven largely by domestic politics. The vast majority of U.S. politicians perceive that they have little to gain by questioning the U.S. "war on drugs" in Latin America but much to lose if they do not look "tough on drugs." As a result, each election year produces a myriad of legislation toughening U.S. drug laws and pouring more taxpayer dollars into costly eradication and interdiction efforts abroad, despite the fact that to date these programs have failed, by any measure, to diminish the flow of illicit drugs into the United States.

Drug production and trafficking do present a serious threat to Latin American countries, eroding local governments and institutions by stimulating corruption, fueling political violence and common crime, and skewing local economies. But current U.S. international drug control policies are, in fact, doing more harm than good. Militarized antidrug efforts undermine regional trends toward democratization and demilitarization and put U.S. assistance into the hands of human rights violators. Rather than taking advantage of the end of the cold war to redefine and limit local military roles, the U.S. government is expanding those roles. Insisting that militaries become involved in internal counternarcotics programs endorses local militaries in maintaining internal public order—precisely when Latin American governments are trying to keep local forces in the barracks—and strengthens the military at the expense of civilian institutions. U.S. insistence on the adoption of draconian antidrug legislation erodes the very civil liberties that fledgling Latin American governments have sought to construct to keep restless militaries and intelligence services in check.

Ironically, while elected civilian governments became the norm throughout the region, support for Latin American military and police forces actually increased as the drug war replaced the cold war as the primary vehicle for the U.S. military to maintain and strengthen ties with its Latin American and Caribbean counterparts. (See figure 6–3.) A 1998 study, *Just the Facts*, undertaken by the Latin America Working Group and the Center for International Policy reveals a plethora of Defense Department channels for providing military aid and training to regional forces, all in the name of fighting drugs. These programs lack adequate congressional oversight mechanisms and are therefore extremely difficult to track.

In addition, the foreign aid budget assigned to international drug control efforts nearly tripled over the course of the 1990s. In contrast, U.S. economic assistance to the region was cut by two-thirds. For fiscal year 1999, the U.S. Congress appropriated $321 million for development assistance for all of Latin America and the Caribbean, as compared to $469 million for international narcotics control programs, 97 percent of which are carried out in Latin America and the Caribbean and a mere 3 percent in the rest of the world. (See figure 6–4.) Over and above this amount is the funding allocated by U.S. intelligence agencies for counternarcotics operations; the Central Intelligence Agency (CIA) has also utilized the drug issue as its meal ticket for maintaining large operations in the Latin American region.

Counternarcotics aid is provided to forces responsible for some of the worst human rights violations in the hemisphere today. In Peru, the nefarious National Intelligence Service (SIN)—responsible for death squad activity; ongoing harassment of opposition politicians, journalists, and human rights activists; and continuous

Figure 6.3   U.S. Military Aid to Latin America and Caribbean

- Foreign Military Sales (FMS) (1998): $176 million
- Direct Commercial Sales (DCS) (1997): $1.05 billion
- Emergency Drawdown (1998): $75 million
- Excess Defense Articles (EDA) (1997): $26 million (originally valued at $87 million)
- International Military Education and Training (1998): $10.25 million
- Counternarcotics
    International Narcotics Control (INC) (1999 est.): $261 million
    Supplemental drug control spending (approved 1998): $51 million for Latin
        America and U.S. security forces over the three years 1999–2001
    Pentagon Counternarcotics (section 1004) (1998): $163 million
- Training
    School of the Americas Training (1998): 816 attendees
    Military Training Teams and Joint Exercises: Each year over 50,000 U.S. military
        personnel are sent to Latin America and Caribbean on more than 3,000
        deployments.

Sources: Adam Isacson and Joy Olson, "Just the Facts: A Quick Tour of U.S. Defense and Security Assistance to Latin America and the Caribbean," Center for International Policy, *International Policy Report*, December 1998; Secretary of State, *Congressional Presentation for Foreign Operations FY 2000* (Washington, DC: Department of State, 1999).

Figure 6.4   International Narcotics and Law Engorcement Affairs: 1999 est.

Total Narcotics	$U.S. Thousands	Percent of Total Narcotic Request
Total narcotics	468,600	100
Law enforcement assistance and institution development	301,390	64.3
Alternative development/eradication	126,775	27.1
International organizations	8,00	1.7
Drug awareness/demand reduction	6,090	1.3
Law enforcement training	6,200	1.3
Program development and support	20,145	4.3
Anticrime programs	25,000	
Total program plan	493,600	

Source: Secretary of State, *Congressional Presentation for Foreign Operations FY 2000* (Washington, DC: Department of State, 1999).

setbacks to democracy—receives economic as well as political support from U.S. officials who publicly praise SIN's counternarcotics efforts. In Mexico, Washington helped set up, finance, and train an elite army special forces unit in counternarcotics tactics. Not surprisingly, that unit was subsequently involved in counterinsurgency campaigns and is widely implicated in drug trafficking–related corruption. Moreover, the General Accounting Office (GAO), the investigative arm of the U.S. Congress, has documented how some U.S. counternarcotics assistance was diverted to counterinsurgency efforts in Chiapas.

In Mexico, the line between counternarcotics and counterinsurgency may be blurry; in Colombia, that line has been obliterated. In Colombia, the so-called narco-guerrilla threat is used to justify increased counternarcotics aid and an expanding role for U.S. military and intelligence forces. In a throwback to the cold war, the country with the worst human rights situation in the hemisphere today, Colombia, receives more U.S. security assistance than all of the other countries in the region put together. The Pentagon is engaged in a range of activities in Colombia, including the provision of military equipment and hardware, training, and intelligence-gathering. It has trained and equipped a 900-man army "counternarcotics" battalion, with two more in the works, and has set up intelligence-gathering centers within the military high command and in Tres Esquinas, Putumayo in the southern coca growing region. On any given day, there are nearly 300 U.S. military and intelligence personnel on the ground in Colombia. While Colombian security forces were slated to receive roughly $300 million in U.S. assistance in fiscal year 1999, both the Administration and Congress are proposing an additional one to two billion dollar aid package over the next three years. The Clinton administration has slid down the slippery slope of greater involvement in the hemisphere's most brutal counterinsurgency campaign.

As concern for the regional security threat posed by Colombia grows in the minds of U.S. military officials, the U.S. government is conveniently establishing "forward operating locations" (FOLs)—a euphemism for U.S. military bases—in four locations circling Colombia. With the closure of Howard Air Force base as part of the U.S. military withdrawal from Panama, Washington has sought to establish other locations where it can land sophisticated spy aircraft that provide blanket coverage of key drug trafficking areas. FOLs are now established in Manta, Ecuador, on the Dutch islands of Aruba and Curaçao, and yet another is to be located in Central America, possibly in Costa Rica. The planned investment in these bases guarantees a long-term U.S. military presence in those countries.

The U.S. war on drugs is characterized by yet another cold war relic: the big-stick approach. Mandated by Congress in 1986, the annual "certification" process provides Congress with the opportunity to criticize both the administration and countries such as Colombia and Mexico for failing to do enough to keep drugs out of the hands of U.S. children. (See figure 6–5.) Each year the administration must produce a list of major drug-producing or drug-transit countries, which are then rated for their antinarcotics efforts. Unless granted a "national security waiver," countries that are not certified face mandatory sanctions, including suspension of all U.S. assistance (with the exception of humanitarian aid and antinarcotics assistance), "no" votes on IFI loans, and possible trade sanctions. This unilateral, score-card approach by the world's largest consumer of illicit drugs angers Latin Americans across the political spectrum and strains bilateral relations, undermining cooperation and, ironically, other U.S. government interests.

Cuba

Another throwback to the cold war, U.S. policy toward Cuba also continues to be conducted via the big stick. Originally rooted in cold war politics and in the U.S.

Figure 6.5   Latin American Countries Subjected to Certification

Country	Years	Number	Certified	Denied	Waiver
Bahamas	87–99	13	13	0	0
Belize	all but 95	12	11	0	1
Bolivia	87–99	13	11	0	2
Brazil	87–99	13	13	0	0
Colombia	87–99	13	9	2	2
Dominican Republic	95–99	5	5	0	0
Ecuador	87–99	13	13	0	0
Guatemala	91–99	9	9	0	0
Haiti	95–99	5	4	0	1
Jamaica	87–99	13	13	0	0
Mexico	87–99	13	13	0	0
Panama	87–99	13	10	2	1
Paraguay	87–99	13	8	0	5
Peru	87–99	13	11	0	2
Venezuela	92–99	8	8	0	0

Source: Drug Strategies and University of California Annenburg School of Communications, "Passing Judgement: The U.S. Drug Certification Process" (Washington, DC: Drug Strategies, 1998).

desire to contain Soviet expansionism in the hemisphere, U.S.-Cuba policy is increasingly driven by the electoral strength of conservative Cuban groups in Florida and New Jersey, two states important to winning presidential primaries and elections. Considered a swing state, Florida, for example, has 25 electoral votes (the fourth largest in the country) and a Cuban American population of over 800,000. In addition, it has become an important source of funding for both Republican and Democratic electoral campaigns. New Jersey, which also has a large Cuban American population, is a must-win for any presidential contender: No candidate has ever won the presidency without taking that state.

Cuban American political clout became evident two weeks before the November 1992 elections, when the Bush administration reversed its long-standing opposition to the Cuba Democracy Act, championed by then-Representative Robert Torricelli, a New Jersey Democrat. (Now a senator, Torricelli has received significant campaign contributions from conservative Cuban American groups, led by the Cuban American National Foundation, CANF.) At the time, the electoral outcome in Florida was uncertain, and Democrats were touting their support of the measure to gain votes in both Florida and New Jersey.

Several years later, when the Clinton administration took some hesitant steps to relax tensions with Cuba, conservative forces on Capitol Hill responded by introducing the Helms-Burton legislation, tightening the U.S. embargo on Cuba. The downing by Cuban fighter jets in 1996 of two private U.S. planes flown by anti-Castro militants—on an announced mission intended to violate Cuban air space—assured the passage of Helms-Burton by the U.S. Congress. With the 1996 presidential elections looming, President Clinton reversed his previous position and signed the bill into law. U.S. policy has been frozen in place ever since. Following the visit by Pope John Paul II to Cuba in January 1998, the Clinton administration did relax restrictions on remittances to Cuba, family travel, and the sale of medicines, but such tinkering at the margins of U.S. policy occurs periodically and does not fundamentally alter the U.S. position that only a Cuba without Castro offers the opportunity for improved relations.

The Helms-Burton legislation takes the unprecedented step of attempting to force other countries to enforce the U.S. embargo by punishing foreign corporations for doing business with Cuba, provoking outrage by U.S. allies and foes alike. It also allows U.S. nationals (including Cubans who have become citizens) to sue foreign entities for properties nationalized by the Castro government in the early 1960s. Of particular concern to the international business elite, the law bars entry into the United States of executives of foreign companies (along with their wives and children) who have "trafficked" in these properties. The member nations of the European Union retaliated by filing a complaint with the World Trade Organization, agreeing to suspend it only after the Clinton administration pledged, in principle, to pressure the U.S. Congress for reform of the Helms-Burton legislation.

U.S. efforts to internationalize its economic embargo of Cuba have also met with firm opposition throughout Latin America and have deeply antagonized one of the U.S. government's closest allies, Canada. In its annual General Assembly meeting in June 1996, the Organization of American States (OAS) voted unanimously to reject the Helms-Burton legislation. Subsequently, the OAS Inter-

American Juridical Committee ruled that Helms-Burton violates international law on at least eight counts. In clear defiance of U.S.-Cuba policy, Canada and Mexico (as well as the European Union) enacted retaliatory legislation that makes it illegal for their citizens to comply with Helms-Burton. Although other countries in the hemisphere have moved to normalize relations with Cuba while encouraging political openings within that country, the U.S. government remains locked in a cold war mentality that will be satisfied only with the ouster of Fidel Castro.

Opposition to U.S.-Cuba policy from within the United States is also growing, while the influence of the Cuban exile community and of the Cuban American right has begun to diminish. With the death in November 1997 of its powerful and effective founder, Jorge Mas Canosa, the CANF lost prestige and is no longer the hegemonic force in the Cuban American community. Moderate Cuban American voices are becoming more vocal, especially after the Pope's visit, when more than 200 Cuban Americans went to Washington in March 1998 to participate in a day of Congressional Advocacy and Education. The U.S. business community remains deeply concerned about Helms-Burton–style sanctions and their impact on U.S. business interests worldwide. The Chamber of Commerce, USA Engage (a broad business coalition heavily funded by oil companies), and other business sectors support an end to the trade embargo. Finally, the religious and activist communities are increasingly engaged in advocacy work on Cuba policy, as illustrated in the letter signed during the Pope's visit by more than 150 religious leaders calling for a rethinking of U.S. policy toward Cuba. Growing domestic pressure on the administration will not alter U.S. policy in the near future, but it does lay the groundwork for eventual change.

The only other country in the Caribbean to receive significant U.S. attention is Haiti, the poorest country in the Western Hemisphere. Responding to three years of ruthless military rule from 1991 to 1994, the Clinton administration sent 21,000 troops and a multilateral contingent of international police monitors to restore deposed President Jean-Bertrand Aristide to power. In March 1995, a United Nations peacekeeping mission took over, and a UN police mission remains in Haiti. While the United States phrased out of the UN operation, it maintained a permanent bilateral mission scheduled to end in late 1999, with U.S. troops and police rotating into Haiti to provide training programs.

U.S. engagement has proven to be a double-edged sword. While Washington was restoring Aristide to power and working to establish a new civilian police force to replace the abusive security forces of the past, the CIA was undermining democracy-building efforts by supporting those corrupt and abusive forces. The Clinton administration has also been hampered by the hostility of Republican leaders who opposed the intervention and have sought to prove Haiti policies a failure ever since.

The initial euphoria of the return of Aristide quickly wore off, however, as the political and economic situation in Haiti steadily worsened. Many factors underlie this situation, including the lack of a political tradition of participatory democracy, the disintegration of the democratic movement known as "Lavalas" into politically warring factions, a grueling electoral calendar, and the chronic weakness of state institutions. Moreover, more often than not, international donors have failed to tailor aid programs to Haitian realities, often providing little support to agriculture in a country where 70 percent of the population depends on subsistence agriculture for survival.

OPENING THE FLOODGATES FOR HIGH-TECH ARMS

In Haiti and many other countries throughout the region, U.S. efforts to promote democracy often fall short and are sidelined when other U.S. objectives—such as combating drug trafficking or promoting U.S. economic interests—prevail. Another policy shift taken in response to domestic political pressures could have far-reaching and disastrous consequences for democratization and demilitarization efforts in Latin America: the Clinton administration's decision to lift a two-decade ban on sales of advanced weapons to Latin America. The lifting of the ban opens the floodgates for high-tech weapons and could ignite an arms race in the region. Like U.S. drug policy, the administration's action flies in the face of its own stated policy objectives to promote regional demilitarization and democratization trends.

The 20-year ban did not prevent sales of other weapons. According to the Congressional Research Service, between 1988 and 1995 the United States sold or gave approximately $2.2 billion worth of arms and military equipment to its southern neighbors. Even before the ban was lifted, the United States was supplying three times as many weapons to the region as any other arms exporter.

With the ending of the cold war, domestic demand for high-tech military equipment dropped dramatically, as did purchases by traditional allies. As a result, U.S. arms manufacturers (which also happen to be major campaign contributors through industry political action committee funds) sought new customers abroad, often looking to previously neglected markets, such as Latin America. In calling for the policy shift, they argued that foreign companies were gaining the upper hand in Latin America, which was obtaining the weapons anyway. Why not let U.S. companies reap the benefits instead of foreign competitors? Some Clinton administration officials also argued that the ban was obsolete, given the democratic transition throughout the region.

The administration's decision to lift the ban paved the way for the sale of F-16 fighter aircraft to Chile. Given the ongoing border disputes throughout the hemisphere and other rivalries, critics fear that Chile's acquisition of sophisticated planes could lead other countries to follow suit. Former U.S. President Jimmy Carter, who along with former Costa Rican President Oscar Arias led the fight against the lifting of the ban, noted that selling F-16s to Chile would "open up a Pandora's box," provoking further sales. Argentina, another regional heavyweight, was among the most disgruntled when the decision was announced. Three weeks later, the U.S. government announced that it would consider Argentina a non-NATO ally in recognition of its close collaboration with the United States and its participation in peacekeeping operations. This move added fuel to the fire, further aggravating anxieties about U.S. intentions and reigniting long-standing suspicions between Southern Cone countries. The calls by Jimmy Carter and others for the Clinton administration to at least implement a two-year moratorium on sales to allow for the implementation of confidence-building and transparency mechanisms, such as the publication of defense budgets, have gone unheeded.

TOWARD A NEW POLICY

From United Fruit to Lockheed-Martin and McDonnell-Douglas, U.S. companies have helped shape—and sometimes have dictated—U.S. actions in Latin America and the Caribbean. U.S. domestic interests have historically played a preponderant role in U.S. policy toward Latin America and the Caribbean, and its importance has only grown in the post–cold war environment. If U.S. policymakers were willing to stand up to narrow political and economic interests and to play a leadership role in unmasking the "threats" from abroad, they could reshape U.S. policy toward the hemisphere in fundamental ways. Washington must address the asymmetrical power relations between Latin American countries and the United States by integrating Latin American viewpoints into U.S. foreign policy, allowing countries to determine their own national development paths, and providing both the resources and the preferential trade and investment policies needed to overcome the vast differences in wealth and power between North and South.

Three concrete steps could be taken to move in a new direction. First, the U.S. government should make poverty elimination the centerpiece of its policy toward Latin America and should redirect economic resources toward that end—even if that means cuts in the virtually untouchable defense budget. Second, Washington should recognize that it will never be able to solve the very real problems of illicit drug abuse and drug-related violence through military action overseas. Although the United States can and should provide resources both for judicial and police reform and for alternative development efforts in Latin America, illicit drug control efforts should prioritize treatment and education efforts in the United States. Likewise, Washington should resist the temptation to support militarized solutions to the very real problem of crime sweeping Latin America and should instead focus instead on the difficult task of promoting long-term institutional reform and the strengthening of civilian institutions, such as the judiciary. Such reform processes must be participatory to be successful, incorporating civil society and citizen involvement.

Finally, Washington should act more forcefully to promote democratization trends in Latin America by eliminating U.S. security assistance to military forces, strengthening the capacity of local elected civilian governments and citizens to define the role of those forces, and speaking out more forcefully to defend democracy when transgressions occur. A range of other initiatives should be adopted as well, including an end to the Cuban trade embargo; the initiation of a policy of constructive engagement toward Cuba; closure of the notorious U.S. Army School of the Americas (SOA), which has been dubbed the School of the Assassins because it has trained some of Latin America's most brutal human rights violators; and a halt to the sale of sophisticated weapons to Latin American governments.

In this post–cold war era, with democratically elected governments in place throughout most of the region, there is a historic opportunity to transform Latin America policy beyond mere calculations of opportunities and threats to an outlook of engaging the region's citizens and leaders in constructing a common vision of the hemisphere's promise—a promise of durable and inclusive democracy, respect for human rights, and sustainable and shared prosperity.

WESTERN EUROPE

North Sea

SWEDEN

FINLAND

NORWAY

DENMARK

IRELAND

UNITED KINGDOM

NETHERLANDS

GERMANY

BELGIUM

LUXEMBOURG

LIECHTENSTEIN

AUSTRIA

SWITZERLAND

FRANCE

ANDORRA

ITALY

CORSICA

BALEARIC ISLANDS

SARDINIA

PORTUGAL

SPAIN

GREECE

Mediterranean Sea

SICILY

MALTA

U.S.-Western European Relations: The Transatlantic Partnership in the Shadow of Globalization

Jonathan P. G. Bach

Disagreements between the United States and its close allies in Western Europe seldom cause anxiety about the viability of the Atlantic alliance. Recently, however, concern about a "coming clash of Europe with America" has escalated.[1] Although alarmist sentiments by their very nature exaggerate potential rifts, the counterclaims that United States–Western European disputes are minor deviations in an otherwise stable relationship overlook the significance of the end of the cold war for Western democracies.

What we see emerging in U.S.–Western European relations at the end of the twentieth century is much more than a succession of family feuds. We are witnessing a struggle among those countries that benefit most from globalization over the character of the norms and rules that will regulate the world economy's infamously erratic disposition. Both the U.S. state apparatus and the American public are being forced to confront a loss of U.S. global influence, while the European Union (EU) perches on the cusp of a potentially new era of unprecedented economic power and political integration. Partially in response, the United States has sought a larger and more assertive NATO as the centerpiece of a new, controversial security relationship. The juxtaposition of these conditions makes U.S.–Western European relations particularly volatile.

Trade, politics, and the military form the enduring constellation of U.S.–Western European relations, although the implications and meaning of this policy mix shift over time. From the days of the American Revolution through

World War II, bilateral relations between the United States and individual European nations dominated transatlantic affairs. Today, however, U.S.–Western European relations are defined largely with respect to the EU and NATO. The current constellation of trade, political, and military relations examined here reflects the larger policy issues at stake in the transatlantic partnership: the shape of globalization, the future of international law, and the definition of international security.

A CRISIS OF HEGEMONY AND AN EMERGING EUROPE

After the cataclysm of World War II, a shattered Western Europe had good practical reasons for accepting American dominance: fear of the Soviet Union, the need for economic recovery, and hope for political reconciliation. Hegemony, in the Gramscian sense, rests on consent, and consent to U.S. leadership—from genuine to grudging—was in abundance during the cold war. In part this relationship resembled the idealized Freudian-tinged tale of the United States in cold war Western Europe as the young, free-world leader guiding its spiritual and cultural progenitors to prosperity after rescuing them from internal collapse. For all the truths, half-truths, and pure fictions in this narrative, the United States exerted an unparalleled influence in every sector of postwar European statecraft and society. This influence, while never absolute, was pervasive and tended to relegate European dissension on vital matters to the level of public rhetoric. There were insignificant exceptions—notably France's refusal to integrate its military into the U.S.-led NATO command—yet by and large Washington's closest allies showed deference, if not full-fledged support, to its will.

More than a decade after the cold war, the United States can no longer assume that the common goals of security and prosperity suffice for resolving most differences toward a favorable U.S. outcome. The habits of half a century of being *primus inter pares*, however, makes this difficult for Americans to accept. Partly in reaction to this power shift, U.S. foreign policy is becoming increasingly unilateral, as Charles William Maynes details in chapter 4. In its dealings with Western Europe, the United States relies heavily on the multilateral framework established with its European allies, ranging from trade forums to NATO. Yet even within these settings, the United States is often perceived as pursuing its interests with a newfound vigor bordering on the bellicose. Although the pursuit of self-interest is neither novel nor one-sided, Washington is increasingly relying more on unsubtle measures than on the persuasive power of its preeminence. More forceful assertions of U.S. interests, combined with an increasingly dismissive attitude toward international obligations and opinion, engender growing resentment from even the best of friends.

Three post–cold war developments undergird this shift in emphasis from cooperation toward confrontation with Western Europe. First are the changes in the EU itself, which has increased its political and economic power while gaining greater maneuvering room since the end of the East-West conflict. Second, both the deterioration of the Japanese economy and an inflated sense of U.S. economic invincibility (vis-à-vis both Japan and the EU) have contributed to a perception that a strategic U.S.-EU effort to constrain the Japanese model of trade is no longer pressing.[2] Third, in the wake of the European Monetary Union (EMU), there is an increased sense of the EU as a competitor, especially regarding emerging markets. Added to this is the Republican-controlled U.S. Congress, which views cooperative ventures with suspicion.

The European Monetary Union, unless spectacularly unsuccessful, will create a European trading bloc of which dreams (or nightmares, for skeptics of all shades) are made. (See figure 7–1.) For the first time since industrialization catapulted the United States into becoming the largest economy in the world, there will be another unit rivaling America in nearly every indicator. The EU has a bigger "domestic" market (374 million people vs. 268 million in the United States), a higher aggregate GDP, and—perhaps most important—a higher percentage of world trade.[3] For the first time since the dollar replaced gold as the world's most stable currency, the European Currency Unit (ECU) has the potential to challenge the dollar's supremacy. If the seemingly viable plans of European Monetary Union proceed apace, the United States faces a truly novel situation vis-à-vis its largest trading partner.[4]

More than merely a big, new trade competitor, the EU seeks to increase its role in setting the global economic agenda and, increasingly, the political agenda as well. This is part of a historical reordering of the international system. In 1944, the United States and Europe agreed at Bretton Woods on the fundamentals of an international economic order with the United States at the hub of two new institutions: the International Monetary Fund and the European (later International) Bank for Reconstruction and Development, better known as the World Bank. By lending massive amounts of dollars while increasing imports, Washington made states around the globe dependent on the United States (and to a lesser extent, Europe) for their trade, foreign investment, and technology.[5] Although the United States was the single greatest benefactor of the new international system, the diversified economies of Europe thrived too, while less developed economies in Latin America and Africa found themselves driven into spirals of debt and dependency.

In creating the rules that govern international trade and investment, the United States and Western Europe have been indispensable partners. As Acting Assistant Secretary of Commerce Franklin J. Vargo points out, "no trade round or other major multilateral initiative has been achieved without the joint leadership of the United States and Europe. . . . Experience has shown that, large as we are, we

Figure 7.1   European Union (EU) Members

Austria[a]	Germany[a]	Netherlands[a]
Belgium[a]	Greece	Portugal[a]
Denmark	Ireland[a]	Spain[a]
Finland[a]	Italy[a]	Sweden
France[a]	Luxembourg[a]	United Kingdom

[a]Members of Economic and Monetary Union (EMU).

cannot open the global marketplace on our own."[6] Before countries can "open the global marketplace," however, they must agree on the rules, an increasingly divisive task made more difficult by the confluence of economic globalization and the end of the cold war.

Globalization as we know it was born with the end of the gold standard in 1971 and the ensuing introduction of free-floating currencies, allowing capital to become mobile in ways heretofore scarcely imaginable.[7] The potential detrimental effects of this shift on U.S. economic predominance were tempered by America's continued position at the heart of the international political system, secure in its cold war position as global leader.[8] With the end of the cold war, however, the U.S. role at the center has become more precarious. Although the increased mobility of financial markets in the 1990s has brought the United States continuous economic growth, the world economy from Asia to Latin America to Russia seems to spin ever faster out of control. With no gold standard and no cold war, the United States is left searching for new ways to anchor itself at the nerve center of the global international and political system.

Yet the end of the cold war also brought a (painfully) slow realization in the United States and Europe that the demands of mobile capital undermine the social promise of the welfare state, and that volatile currency markets are playing havoc with the economies of otherwise stable countries. The EU is generally more cautious than the United States about dismantling trade barriers, which could be considered fundaments of the postwar social market economy.[9] With European prosperity and stability rooted even more strongly in the postwar compact among labor, business, and government than is the case in the United States, Europe feels the pinch more acutely and in different ways. For example, the EU has been preoccupied with bringing down high unemployment—22 percent in Spain, 15 percent in Finland, and over 12 percent in France, Belgium, and Italy—while the United States' prosperity has been dependent on low-wage jobs.

One might expect a more spirited reaction to the vagaries of globalization, yet the EU is less actively resisting the neoliberal logic of global free trade than tortuously coming to terms with its limits. Ironically, Washington's resort to trade wars drives the EU into a corner and strengthens those elements within the ruling social democratic parties that favor market-driven policies. Critics such as French writer Ignatio Ramonet see this trend as nothing less than the betrayal of social democracy in Europe by the very politicians entrusted with its resurgence.[10]

Both the United States and Europe also wish to pursue the maximum share of emerging markets in light of their unprecedented ability to reach new consumers throughout Latin America, Asia, and Africa, but this frames a paradox: seeking to take advantage of new markets calls for less regulation of the global economy (at least less for each country's businesses), whereas concern over the domestic impact of globalization has led to calls for more regulation. Combined with the crisis of U.S. hegemony and the rise in European unity described above, the post–cold war era appears less as a ready-born system of neoliberal economics and democratic politics moving seamlessly into place than as a time of renegotiating the basic structure of the international system. Here the United States, Western Europe, and Japan still play the leading roles. It is at the nexus of these developments that the significance of U.S.–Western European relations resides.

BANANAS, BEEF, AND
THE SHAPE OF GLOBALIZATION

The U.S.-EU disputes over fruit or meat, although often banal sounding, belie more fundamental international shifts in trade and politics. The common denominator in the issues at stake between the United States and the EU is not free trade per se but the authority of the World Trade Organization (WTO) both to determine what counts as free trade, or barriers to trade, and to compel member states to comply with its rulings. The World Trade Organization, birthed in January 1995, is developing a functioning arbitration system that will enable its decisions to have even greater impact on domestic economies. The trade disputes of today are setting the rules and forging the parameters of tomorrow's international economic system.

Trade barriers have expanded to include a panoply of environmental, health and safety, and liability legislation, often negotiated at great political cost.[11] A country's health and labor laws risk being construed as some corporation's nontariff trade barrier, and member states of the WTO can sometimes find themselves having to enforce domestically deleterious rulings. If a corporation has the legal backing of the WTO, a democratic state's ability to influence the outcome of the ruling is limited. Behind the concerns about specific products lies this more fundamental paradox, which links the difficulties of "opening the global marketplace" to an expanding definition of trade extending to "the workings of a large portion of each nation's economic and *political* structures."[12]

Exemplifying this development are the high-profile disputes over bananas and beef that have erupted periodically between the EU and the United States since the mid-1990s. Beef figured twice in this regard. The first stage of the battle concerned the colloquially termed "mad cow disease," or BSE (bovine spongiform encephalopathy), the rare, fatal brain disease passed on to humans from infected cattle. The EU banned the import of any product—from animal feed to pharmaceuticals made with beef tallow—that included those parts of the cow deemed at risk to the disease. This threatened $14 billion of U.S. exports,[13] and Washington, in turn, took the dispute to the WTO. In July 1999 the WTO, in an opinion that favored the United States, ruled that the EU beef import ban damages U.S. trade. In response, the United States imposed 100 percent duties on EU products by suspending tariff concessions covering EU trade in an amount of $116.8 million per year.

The second stage of the battle involved the EU banning the importation of hormone-treated beef, originally slated to take effect January 1, 1998. The Europeans claim the health risks are not adequately known to justify its consumption. The United States claims that protectionist sentiments for the European beef market, not health concerns, are the real reason behind the ban. The WTO has decided in America's favor, ruling that the EU's ban was based on "faulty science."[14]

The issue at stake for beef was whether a national (or in this case EU) law based on its enactors' perceptions of health risks can be subordinated to decisions about free trade made by an international trade organization. The case of bananas is different, but it also concerns the ability to prioritize issues in the national (or EU) interest due to considerations other than trade. Europe's former colonies in the Caribbean receive preference in exporting bananas to Europe. Chiquita Brands and Dole, the major U.S. corporations with banana plantations in Central America, contend Europe's preference for its former colonies constitutes an unfair barrier to selling U.S.-marketed bananas in Europe. Allowing these firms to compete freely in Europe, however, while making bananas cheaper for consumers, would hurt seriously, perhaps fatally, the Caribbean farmers who benefit from the current arrangement.

The ironies of the colonial legacy are rife. The same European countries that imposed their rule and turned their colonies into single-product, export-led economies now take on the role of protectors of their former subjects' livelihoods with little recognition of the vestiges of the colonial mentality still at play. On the other side of the dispute, decrying the lack of free trade, are the infamous Chiquita and Dole conglomerates, whose Central American practices helped coin the term "banana republic." The debate about banana prices and farms gave little voice to the banana growers themselves.

The significance of both the banana and beef disputes lies in their role as test cases for the WTO to enforce its rulings. At a purely economic level, Europe is interfering in free trade by banning hormone-treated beef and maintaining quotas for bananas from former colonies. The WTO has ruled in both cases that Europe must give up these policies. Europeans have resisted on both accounts, seeking to appeal or circumvent the rulings. For the Clinton administration, these two issues became a test of the WTO's ability to "mandate that nations change their trading practices."[15] As a sign of its seriousness, in 1999 the administration imposed extremely punishing retaliatory tariffs on European imports: 100 percent tariffs on $191 million worth of European luxury goods to counter European quotas on Caribbean bananas, and the threat of tariffs on a "target list" of $900 million in European goods in potential requital against EU beef policies.[16] The WTO's authorization of U.S. retaliatory tariffs against the EU for its banana policy is a landmark: the first such permission given to a member state for action against another member in the 50 year history of the WTO and its predecessor organization, the General Agreement on Tariffs and Trade (GATT).[17]

The punishment of thousands of European companies over bananas and beef has transformed negotiations between the United States and the EU into a hostile standoff.[18] With WTO rulings in its favor, Washington claimed that EU defiance of the international arbitrator would scuttle the norms that officials on both sides of the Atlantic had worked so hard to institute. Thus, with WTO permission, the United States moved swiftly to retaliate. The EU, stung by the magnitude and speed of Washington's retribution, maintained that the appeals process had not been allowed to run its course, unfairly forcing the issue. The EU trade commissioner, Leon Brittan, likened the U.S. reprisals to entering a courtroom "pointing a pistol at the other side."[19] In both cases, however, the amount of trade is smaller than the rhetoric: together the tariffs on bananas and beef amount to less than 0.2 percent of all EU trade.

The United States has been quick to threaten retaliation on other issues as well, including banning the Concorde jet from flying to the country, unless the EU changes its stance disallowing noise-reducing mufflers for its airplanes—dubbed "hush kits"—to meet stringent, new U.S. standards on airplane noise. Again, Washington interprets the EU stand as a threat to, and a test of, multilateral institutions. Complicating the picture is the fact that hush kits are a U.S. product used mostly on U.S.-produced planes, while Airbus, the European-produced competition for commercial airliners, meets the EU's own noise requirements. That both sides have vested interests in seeing their opinion prevail is hardly novel. What is new is how this issue will test the WTO provision that "unilateral standards" are allowable on grounds of health or environmental protection concerns.[20] In all of the above cases, the extent to which claims about health, safety, environmental protection, and even a country's sense of responsibility to the past (as with Europe's bananas) can be considered barriers to free trade is being assessed.

The political nature of trade issues appears even clearer in another big dispute between the United States and the EU over the privacy of personal data, from credit ratings to medical histories to airplane meal preferences. Under the global definition of barriers to trade, international standards on personal information are entering new and uncertain terrain. The United States has traditionally adopted a laissez-faire approach to regulating data, allowing private actions from clothes purchases to website visits to be bought and sold in the world's largest information economy. Influenced partly by historical memory of the totalitarian appropriation of records by the Nazis in pursuit of policies of exclusion and extermination and partly by an approach to privacy as an explicit, rather than inferred, right, the EU enacted a 1998 regulation known as the European Union Data Protection Directive.[21] It requires a number of potentially time-consuming and expensive actions, from notifying individuals when information is gathered to giving individuals the right to sue "data controllers" in national courts.[22] Most important for U.S. companies, however, is the requirement that data cannot flow freely out of the EU to countries that lack similar standards, most notably the United States, nor can the provision be circumvented by rerouting through a third country.

Washington sought a compromise by creating a voluntary system of compliance called "safe harbors." This was scoffed at by the EU negotiating team: "We would not accept a situation where the only way to deal with a problem is to sort it out with the company that is the root of the problem in the first place. Our member states would think we have gone mad."[23] The immense dependence of modern commerce on electronic data and the burgeoning neophyte world of electronic commerce make the stakes in this battle tremendous. Yet again the crux of the matter lies less in dollar figures than in the underlying difference between U.S. and EU approaches to globalization. Self-regulation is the preferred U.S. mode of operation, while the EU is far more willing to regulate industry in the name of the public good. The dominant neoliberal logic views regulation with hostility and as antithetical to the brave new world where, ideally, free trade seeks a frictionless environment. The U.S. Congress is also hostile to regulation, though often for different reasons.[24] Against this trend, the election in Western

Europe of left-of-center governments in every major country has reinforced the rhetoric, if seldom the reality, of restoring the public good to a prominent place in national and EU agendas.

Seen from the Washington's neoliberal vantage point, Europe's positions on all the major free trade disputes are most likely insupportable. This is the preferred discourse, especially in the United States, where the implications for trade render the issue black and white. Switch to a political discourse, however, and a different picture emerges. The EU certainly has self-serving reasons for wanting to ban U.S. beef or for disallowing hush kits for airplanes. EU bureaucracy is admittedly an oft-maligned sloth of a beast. Yet the EU's hesitation to embrace the free-for-all approach of the WTO, which it helped create, demonstrates an uneasiness with this approach that Washington would be well advised to heed. There is a difference between protectionism of key areas of one's economy and the desire to preserve key areas of one's legislative ability, especially in a democracy.[25] Trade under conditions of globalization blurs the line more than any international economic development before it, and this tension lies at the political heart of U.S.-EU economic relations today. This is far from a trivial issue, for, as Robert Kuttner, editor of *The American Prospect*, points out, even educational and training systems in the United States and Europe "can be seen as forms of trade-distorting subsidy, just as surely as Pentagon R&D [research and development] contracts and agricultural research appropriations. So should we renounce research and education because they distort trade?"[26]

OPENING THE GLOBAL MARKETPLACE

A major reason why so much political capital is invested in these trade showdowns beyond the relative dollar figure of the goods in question is because U.S.-EU agreement on the ground rules will, as Acting Assistant Secretary of Commerce Vargo put it earlier, allow the pursuit of "opening the global marketplace." The global marketplace, almost in a throwback to neocolonial rhetoric, appears ready and waiting to be opened by the United States and Europe once their feuds over the best way to do so are resolved. Yet it is hardly being cast as a joint venture.

The EU's volume of global trade is larger than that of the United States, and it commands a greater share of markets in the Middle East, China, and Southeast Asia's "emerging economies."[27] (See figure 7–2.) As the U.S. economy becomes more export-driven than at any time in its history (exports currently account for nearly 30 percent of U.S. GDP), new markets are the key to both continued economic health and new heights of growth. The U.S. Trade Representative predicts, perhaps overoptimistically, that by 2010, Asia and Latin America, in that order, will become America's largest export markets, bumping the EU to third place.[28] If the EU is seen as posing barriers to U.S. trade in these markets, it becomes more an opponent than a partner. (See figure 7–3.) Anything that interferes with what may become 55 percent of the U.S. export market in 2010 can easily be construed as a threat to U.S. national interests, and invoking national interest enables exemption from WTO rules.

Figure 7.2   Global Trade: U.S. and EU Exports and Imports: 1998, excluding EU intratrade

Rank	Exporter	$U.S. billions	Global Share (%)	% Change from 1997
1	European Union	813.8	20.3	0
2	United States	683.0	17.0	−1

Rank	Importer	$U.S. billions	Global Share (%)	% Change from 1997
1	United States	944.6	22.5	5
2	European Union	801.4	19.1	6

Source: World Trade Organization, press release, "World Trade Growth Slower in 1998 after Unusually Strong Growth in 1997," Appendix Table 2, April 16, 1999. Available on the Internet at: http://www.wto.org/intltrad/998app2.htm.

Figure 7.3

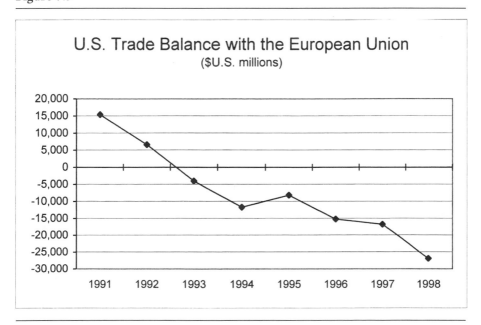

U.S. Trade Balance with the European Union
($U.S. millions)

Source: U.S. Total Trade Balances with Individual Countries, 1991–1998 (Washington, DC: Dept. of Commerce, 1999).

When the EU pursues "strategic trade policies" and "preferential trade arrangements [read: bananas]" warns U.S. Trade Representative Charlene Barshefsky, it "will open up markets for their exporters, their products, their workers and their farmers."[29] Free trade seems to work best for those whose national interests are most served by the particular arrangement. Hence we see an almost comical battle of contending "free trade" agreements, where the EU is pursuing a free trade pact with the southern cone or MERCOSUR countries of Argentina, Brazil, Paraguay, and Uruguay and a separate one with Chile. Washington considers these encroachments as counterproductive, if not outright threatening, to its efforts to extend the North American Free Trade Agreement (NAFTA) into a Free Trade Area of the Americas (FTAA). Likewise in Asia, the United States seeks to work through the forum known as Asia Pacific Economic Cooperation (APEC), while the EU has formed the Asia-Europe Meeting (ASEM) with ten key nations in Asia, including China and Japan.[30]

United States or EU exporters stand to gain or lose in these regions according to how current U.S.-EU disputes are settled. Yet persistent trade wars with the EU are not in Washington's best interests, which might explain why the Clinton administration seeks to provoke such confrontations now (a dubious strategy) in an attempt to wring concessions and ground rules before more free trade agreements are negotiated covering Latin America and Asia.

WHEN IS FOREIGN POLICY NOT FOREIGN POLICY?

As U.S. domestic politics unsettles the paradigmatic internationalism of the post–World War II era, the resulting impetus for unilateral action raises the specter in Europe of a United States increasingly unwilling or unable to distinguish between its interests and the interests, or concerns, of others. This is most marked in foreign policy concerning close allies, where cooperation—not confrontation—is the preferred modus operandi. The impression is that Washington is unwilling to play by the rules of the game itself, while demanding that others tow the line when doing so enhances U.S. interests. This harkens back to the older issue of the Soviet gas pipeline to Western Europe during the early 1980s, which pitted an adamantly opposed Reagan administration against irritated European governments.

The most prominent example concerns high-profile U.S. economic sanctions against Cuba, Iran, and Libya, with far-reaching implications for European companies. Compared to the banana/beef contentions, the issues here are almost reversed: in the case of Cuba, the 1996 Helms-Burton law mandates sanctions against any foreign corporation whose business involves expropriated U.S. property.[31] The EU complained to the WTO that this constituted an unfair barrier to trade, but Washington refuses to acknowledge the legitimacy of the complaint, claiming this is a foreign policy affair, not a trade issue. Even more worrisome to an already skeptical EU, the United States openly warned that it would not abide by any eventual WTO ruling on the matter. Is this less disruptive to the organization than the EU refusal to comply with the WTO's ruling on beef or bananas? Washington realizes the irony of this, which is why the Clinton administration has consistently waived the most controversial parts of the Helms-Burton law punishing companies based in other countries, thereby avoiding a showdown within the European Union. Yet these issues carry implications that reach far beyond mere trade disputes.

The critical issue about sanctions is whether any one country can make a law that binds a third country without its consent. Although Washington prefers international endorsement of—if not active participation in—its sanctions, there are cases, especially concerning Cuba, where world public opinion is simply not aligned with U.S. policy. The need to unilaterally impose sanctions indicates a lack of support, but recent developments have turned questions of support into fundamental questions of international law. Can one state's legislation have extraterritorial jurisdiction? If this is a matter of foreign policy, as the Clinton administration claims, then is it not an unacceptable infringement of sovereignty? If this is a matter of trade, is it not an attempt by one country to diminish, by coercion, the losses it would incur if others continued to trade with the sanctioned state? Can sanctions, then, be allowed only by consensus?

Speaking explicitly about Western Europe, Ellen Frost, a senior fellow at the Institute for International Economics, maintains that "the corrosive effect of U.S. unilateral economic sanctions goes well beyond business interests. Such sanctions violate transatlantic norms and expectations, thus undercutting the encouraging trend toward a widely accepted, rules-based, market-oriented trade and investment system."[32] Thus the United States attempts to build a rules-based system in its divisive confrontation with the EU over trade while undermining this system through its extraterritorial sanctions. Sir Leon Brittan, former vice president of the EU, puts it more bluntly: "What on earth is the point, when you are trying to deal with a country like Iran or Libya or Burma, of passing a law which creates a confrontation with precisely those partners who are your closest allies in dealing with countries of that sort, even if they do not always agree 100 percent with your policy prescription?"[33]

The Helms-Burton Act is an exemplary sore point in Europe, but EU support of France's investment in Iran's South Pars oil fields is perhaps more significant. France was prepared to risk U.S. penalties and, backed by an EU able to retaliate against U.S. firms, got Clinton to waive the mandated penalties in the name of national interest.[34] This immediately set a precedent for waivers, and as Iran opens more oil pipeline routes for bidding, U.S. and EU interests in the Near East are becoming more discordant. Washington favors certain oil pipeline routes from the Caspian Sea to Turkey, rather than through Iran (among other options), both in support of Turkish desires for regional hegemony and out of concern that oil flows would be dependent on an ideologically hostile Iran. The EU is more willing to do business with Iran, despite its own set of serious political disagreements, and is increasingly interested in seeing its own best interests served in the region rather than those of the United States. "Although some foreign governments may be happy to have a U.S. security umbrella," writes the *Crossborder Monitor,* "few of them are likely to be sympathetic to laws which benefit U.S. politicians at the expense of major domestic companies."[35]

THE POLITICS BEHIND ECONOMICS

The vociferousness of European opposition to the sanctions came as a surprise and an irritant for the United States, for it underscored divergence on issues that represent political, rather than economic, ideals. In 1998, Washington also endured sharp criticism for human rights, a censure that domestic U.S. discourse normally reserves for foreigners. The U.S. human rights violations fall into three main categories, according to Amnesty International: police brutality, violence against people in detention (especially asylum seekers and noncitizens, but also women prisoners), and the death penalty. Especially irksome to European sensibilities has been the relatively vigorous reimposition of capital punishment in most U.S. states, the number of executions (over 380 since 1990), and the killing of minors, the mentally ill, and noncitizens. The European Council will not admit members that do not prohibit—or at least call a moratorium on—the death penalty, and in 1999 the EU submitted an anti–death penalty resolution to the UN's Human Rights Commission, which passed 30 to 11 in April 1999, further isolating the United States in European public opinion.[36]

The United States has also already garnered significant negative sentiment by its refusal to join 134 other countries in signing the international treaty to ban land mines (forbidding their production, stockpiling, and use), which achieved the force of international law on March 1, 1999.[37] Likewise, Washington is seen as preventing the conclusion of an international treaty on biodiversity and is in embarrassing arrears regarding its UN dues.[38] The United States also lobbied hard for Michael Moore of New Zealand, instead of Thai commerce minister Suphachai Panichpakdi, to succeed WTO chief Renato Ruggiero. The relative merits of the two candidates aside, the EU was unhappy with Washington's attempt to exercise a de facto veto, sabotaging a theoretically equitable selection process. Not all European countries opposed Moore, but EU commissioner Brittan complained to the WTO that "unnamed countries" threatened a veto and that "anonymous vetoes are plainly inconsistent with the kind of transparency within the WTO that we have been seeking."[39]

FISSURES IN THE BEDROCK

Not all is quiet on the military front either. The North Atlantic Treaty Organization is regarded as the bedrock of U.S.-European relations. A primary reason for its perseverance after the demise of its raison d'être, the Warsaw Pact, is that NATO's rationale extended beyond deterring the Soviet Union. NATO institutionalized U.S. military relations with Europe in a way that interwar internationalists could only have dream of. The original impulse rested most immediately, of course, on the Soviet Union as a threat. But there was also a perception that a lack of American military commitment to Europe per se was threatening, allowing instability and its consequences, whether fascist or communist. Decades later, NATO capitalized on this perception by recasting itself as a political/military organization whose existence was justified by this original concern. NATO was billed as tantamount to U.S. commitment, and hence stability, in Europe.

The decision to retool NATO for a post–cold war role essentially meant abandoning alternative European security constellations such as: Organization for Security and Cooperation in Europe (OSCE), a wide-ranging, informal consultative body that includes both the United States and Russia; an approach drawing on nonoffensive defense; or a collective security model.[40] (See figure 9–2.) As NATO increasingly became the only game in town, those critical of the alliance hoped it was truly capable of metamorphosing from a collective defense system into some form of collective security for Europe. The principal concern among critical voices was that Washington would seek to develop NATO as a U.S.-led police force to enhance its interests around the world. This prompted the out-of-area debate about whether NATO forces could be used outside its members' territory for reasons other than self-defense, a question answered by NATO's de facto military action first in Bosnia and then in Kosovo.

Although European member states support "upgrading" NATO, they are not as sanguine about continued U.S. dominance within the organization. France, historically suspicious of Washington's perception of European defense, postponed reintegrating its forces with the NATO military command, insisting that a French admiral should command the Southern Fleet. Washington's hypocritical position—refusing to subordinate U.S. troops to any other command while expecting and insisting that other troops defer to U.S. commanders—is becoming more of an issue. In this context, recent U.S. proposals to give NATO a more explicit role in the maintenance of global stability—including combating nuclear, biological, and chemical weapons—were met with a decidedly cool reaction in Europe. Combined with NATO enlargement and military action in Yugoslavia, Washington's attitude has fueled critics' and skeptics' worst fears of NATO evolving from a defensive alliance into a semiautonomous regional actor drawing new partitions in a Europe still unhealed from cold war rifts.

Both European hawks and doves take issue with the U.S. role in NATO. Critics fear that Washington will use NATO as a military extension of its own global activities, subordinating Europe's interests and dragging the alliance into unwanted wars. Even supporters of more aggressive military engagements within Europe criticize Europe's military dependence on the United States, citing the lack of a European capacity for air transport of troops, strategic reconnaissance, and military technologies such as laser-guided bombs.[41] (See figure 7–4.) Thus even among more traditionally inclined officials there is growing sentiment for a more autonomous voice in European military affairs, even if this means working outside of NATO.

Here is where divisions within NATO between the United States and the EU could become explosive. The oft-maligned Common Foreign and Security Policy of the European Union, while still a pale version of its economic and social counterparts, remains a pivotal feature of continued European integration.[42] European foreign ministers have now replaced the moribund West European Union, until now the military coordination arm of the EU, with a common defense policy that would allow independent military action. The new entity consists of an EU military committee headed by a new High Representative for the Common Foreign and Security Policy. Javier Solana, NATO Secretary General since 1995, assumed the new position in December 1999.[43] The EU will now develop its own satellites, intelligence sources, and military staff and would have the option to lead operations with or without NATO assets.[44] At the same time, the 1997 Amsterdam Treaty, which sets forth the most complete guidelines to date on a Common

Figure 7.4

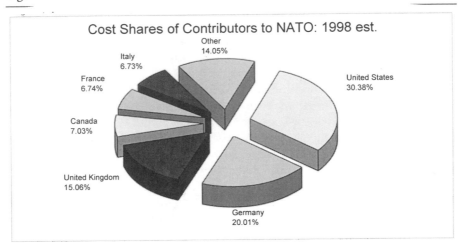

Cost Shares of Contributors to NATO: 1998 est.

- Other 14.05%
- Italy 6.73%
- France 6.74%
- Canada 7.03%
- United Kingdom 15.06%
- United States 30.38%
- Germany 20.01%

Source: Compiled from *NATO Handbook: 50th Anniversary Edition* (Brussels: NATO Information Service, 1998). Available on the Internet at: http://www.nato.int.

Foreign and Security Policy, allows an "opt-out" option for EU member states that, for reasons of neutrality or history, feel they cannot participate in a military mission. This procedure is known in Euro-lingo as "constructive abstention," reflecting a desire to dilute the need for unanimity required by the Maastricht Treaty, the 1990 landmark agreement on European political integration.

European gestures toward new defense institutions first achieved a new level of significance during NATO's fiftieth anniversary in April 1999, which wore a beleaguered look of gnawing self-doubt illuminated by the failure of air strikes intended to prevent a humanitarian catastrophe in Kosovo. The war over Kosovo injected an air of near panic about the future of the alliance: "If we do not achieve our goals in Kosovo," warned Senator Joseph Biden, Jr. (D-DE), ominously in the midst of the anniversary celebration, "NATO is finished as an alliance."[45] The Europeans are generally more sanguine about NATO's future, regarding U.S. supremacy—rather than the alliance itself—as being at stake, but the Kosovo crisis clearly highlights the contradictory impulses of NATO's attempt to redefine itself.

The war over Kosovo began as a call to maintain NATO's solidarity in the face of seemingly shameful inaction. It became the most serious test yet of NATO's unity in the face of unclear political aims and ineffective military force, which precipitated the very humanitarian catastrophe it was supposed to prevent. As loops of argumentation for and against military action in Kosovo devolved into infinite regress, two consequences resonate: NATO can no longer shroud itself in the mantle of pan-European security where Russia is concerned, and Russian concerns are European concerns.

For all the soothing rhetoric in selling NATO enlargement to the Russians, Russia has now gained the ammunition it needs to credibly present NATO as an aggressor and NATO enlargement as a threat. For U.S.-European relations, this reality harbors long-term consequences. At first glance, Washington could exploit the image of a bellicose, if impoverished, Russia to strengthen the alliance. But given the European desire to jettison the U.S. foreign policy umbrella, if not the Pentagon's security umbrella, Washington will not find a replay of the hegemonic aspects of the cold war possible. For Western Europe, and especially Germany, good relations with Russia are of paramount importance, and official support for a renewed enemy image is likely to be lukewarm at best.

Beyond the problems unleashed by excluding Russia from meaningful participation in the original decision to use NATO forces in Kosovo, the Balkan war opened rifts both between NATO allies and within them. Greece and Italy grudgingly accepted the air war, more out of fear of reproach than any enthusiasm. Hungary became a front-line state two weeks after joining NATO, tempering its show of support after its hard-won NATO acceptance with its concern over the war. In Germany, the historic Social Democratic/Green Party coalition government struggled with the once seamless, now contradictory, sentiments of "never again war" and "never again Auschwitz."

Having failed miserably in preventing the violent implosion of former Yugoslavia, Europe uneasily participated in the U.S.-led effort. After so much inaction, the European allies were in a weak position to criticize the NATO intervention, especially when President Clinton made it the centerpiece of his foreign policy. However, major changes in NATO are likely to arise in the aftermath of the war in Kosovo. European politicians are preparing the public for higher military expenditures, viewing a modernized military as enabling more options. "We Europeans," states the otherwise pro-American British Prime Minister Tony Blair, "should not expect the United States to play a role in every disorder in our back yard."[46]

For the United States this does not mean the end of NATO but rather the politically palatable possibility that NATO could henceforth undertake missions using U.S. military equipment but not U.S. troops.[47] NATO is still too important to the new Europe's sense of self and too central to America's role as the purveyor of global security to be discarded rather than modified. Thus, to satisfy both European desires for more autonomy and U.S. desires for less troop risk, the future NATO may look increasingly to ad hoc operations (premised on the idea of "Combined Joint Task Forces") collaborating with Europe's nascent independent military capacity. Washington could then assemble "coalitions of the willing"—those European allies inclined to participate—rather than seeking unanimity within NATO. Should this become the trend, the criticism that selective military action serves geopolitical rather than humanitarian reasons stands to gain more credibility.

ENDGAMES AND NEW BEGINNINGS

Whether in NATO or in trade negotiations, the United States is seeking to maintain its role as the center of the core. However, the center becomes harder to hold as the domestic impacts of globalization and the elusiveness of military solutions intensify. On one hand, America seeks to maintain its position by creating international institutions in its own image. On the other hand, it attempts to use its sheer weight in support of its interests. When it emphasizes the latter, it privileges unilateral over multilateral action. Yet even when emphasizing the former, Washington is increasingly succumbing to a narrow view of the possibilities of multilateralism. The result, ironically, is not disengagement from international events but quicker recourse to unilateral or uncompromising actions. We see this trend today both in military undertakings marked by growing disregard for international consensus and in economic posturing to control the shape of globalization.

President Clinton spoke frankly early in his administration when he announced that the United States would act "multilaterally when possible but unilaterally when necessary."[48] As time passed, the necessity for unilateral action (or its threat) grew relative to the perception of multilateral possibilities. Multilateral action became increasingly acceptable only if it offered clear advancement of U.S. national interests.[49] The potential impact on relations with Western Europe is revealed in criticism from EU trade ambassador Roderick Abbott who, referring to the tariffs leveled in the banana dispute, claims that "the U.S. is declaring war on any or all WTO members whose compliance it decides is inadequate and—to judge from our recent experience—on the basis that it will enforce its rights but will not necessarily respect its obligations."[50] Although the larger significance regarding the bananas case may ultimately lie with the broad definition of "barriers to trade" in the WTO, Abbott echoes a common sentiment about America promoting its rights while sidestepping its obligations under the very rules it helps create.

Supporting multilateralism while reserving the right for unilateral action is a form of having one's cake and eating it too. The problem is that the latter interferes with the former.[51] Yet it is ironic that the United States needs to work *through* multilateral organizations even to act unilaterally. This situation provides new opportunities for influencing policy. It also requires greater critical attention to the formative forces in the disputes dominating U.S.–Western European relations. As the world's two largest economies seek to forge the emerging global order after their own fashion, they define their positions increasingly against each other. In this situation, the United States turns to the advantage of its recent hegemonic past to define the possible futures for multilateral forums. Behind the banality of bananas and the bravado of the new NATO, we can begin to discern the trajectories of America's next incarnation in world affairs.

NOTES

1. William Pfaff warns of the "Coming Clash of Europe with America," *World Policy Journal* XV:4, Winter 1998/99; Fred Bergsten worries about a "Clash of Titans," *Foreign Affairs* 78:2, March/April 1999; Walter Russel Mead writes of ominous signs between the "former cold war allies in Western Europe" in "Friendly Fire: As Far as Europe Is Concerned, Nothing the U.S. Does—Economically, Culturally or Politically—Is Right," *Los Angeles Times*, March 14, 1999; while Peter Grier in the *Christian Science Monitor* of March 9, 1999, opines the United States and Europe are "alienated allies" in "From Kosovo to Banana Trade, Disputes Pull Apart the Transatlantic Alliance as Europe Challenges America More."

2. Thanks to John Nagle for this point.
3. Population and GDP figures are from Eurostat, EU GDP for 1997 (in billions of Euro) was 7,078 compared with 6,022 in the United States, although the United States remained higher for per capita GDP: 22,470 compared to 18,925 (Euro, 1997). Organization for Economic Cooperation and Development figures put the EU's aggregate GDP at $8.1 trillion and the U.S. GDP at $7.8 trillion for 1998 (cited in Pfaff, "Coming Clash," p. 4). In external trade, the 1996 EU volume totaled $1.9 trillion compared with $1.7 trillion for the United States. In C. Fred Bergsten, "The Dollar and the Euro," *Foreign Affairs*, 76:4, 1997, p. 87. Also see discussion of this point in Robert D. Blackwill and Kristin Archick, *U.S.-European Economic Relations and World Trade*, paper presented at the Council on Foreign Relations conference entitled "The Asia Crisis: Economic and Political Implications," April 15, 1998.
4. The Euro could seriously challenge the dollar's role as the world's reserve currency. If major investors shift their money into Euros, exchange rates could become even more wildly unstable. (See Bergsten, "The Dollar and the Euro," 1997 and Blackwill and Archick, *U.S.-European Economic Relations*.) Politically, a successful Euro really means increased autonomy for a Europe suddenly less dependent on exports, with stronger bond markets, and capable of far greater coordinated competitiveness on the world stage, creating a potential U.S. rival. (See Pfaff, "Coming Clash," and David P. Calleo, "Strategic Implications of the Euro," *Survival* 41:1, 1999). Of course, the EMU will also cause widespread dislocation within Europe, with unpredictable political consequences that may mitigate its benefits.
5. See Ethan B. Kaptstein, "A Global Third Way: Social Justice and the World Economy," *World Policy Journal* 15:4, Winter 1998/99, p. 29.
6. Franklin J. Vargo, quoted in Blackwill and Archick, *U.S.-European Economic Relations*, p. 4.
7. Ibid.
8. Although the energy crisis of 1973 called unprecedented attention to U.S. economic vulnerability.
9. The United States is more concerned about maintaining recourse to the "national security" exception of the WTO to justify otherwise contestable trade actions.
10. Ignacio Ramonet, "Social Democracy Betrayed," *Le Monde Diplomatique*, April 1999.
11. The expanding nature of "barriers to trade" includes the WTO's designation of a government's "objectives" as possible barriers, which compels national legislative procedures to follow WTO rules.
12. Ralph Nader and Lori Wallach "GATT, NAFTA, and the Subversion of the Democratic Process," in Jerry Mander and Edward Goldsmith, eds., *The Case Against the Global Economy* (San Francisco: Sierra Club, 1996), p. 95.
13. See Neil Buckley, "U.S. Threatens EU Over Meat Safety Rules," *Financial Times*, November 6, 1997, p. 4.
14. David E. Sanger, "Imports Face Higher Tariffs on Beef Issue," *New York Times*, March 23, 1999, p. 1.
15. David E. Sanger, "Ruling Allows Tariffs by U.S. over Bananas," *New York Times*, April 3, 1999. He attempts to soften the appearance of forcing Europe to change for the benefit of U.S. companies by arguing that the ability to convince Congress to do the same in a reverse situation would thus be enhanced.
16. The eventual amount, according to analysts in 1999, is closer to $300 million. Sanger, "Imports Face Higher Tariffs on Beef Issue."
17. Frances Williams, "U.S. Wins Permission for Sanctions on EU," *Financial Times*, April 13, 1999. For the dueling claims of the United States and the EU as to the

nature of barriers to trade and investment, see, respectively, *Report on United States Barriers to Trade and Investment* (Brussels: European Commission, 1998) and the *Report on Barriers to Trade* (Washington, DC: U.S. Department of Commerce, 1998).

18. See Brigitte Granville, "International Trade: Bananas, Beef and Biotechnology," *The World Today*, April 1999.

19. John-Thor Dahlburg, "U.S., Europe Edging to the Brink of a Trade War," *Los Angeles Times*, March 15, 1999.

20. Brandon Mitchner, "Airplane Noise Added to Clash over Free Trade," *Wall Street Journal*, March 15, 1999.

21. EU Directive 95/46/EC.

22. "EU Privacy Rule Threatens Bilateral Commerce," *Journal of Commerce*, February 10, 1999.

23. Gerard de Graaf, member of the EU negotiating team, quoted in ibid.

24. Of course neoliberal theory is often employed more rhetorically than literally, for protectionism is very much alive in the U.S. Congress. Yet despite some outright criticism from both the populist right and from the left, neoliberalism remains the underlying governmental premise and shapes official attitudes toward other country's attempts to protect their markets.

25. The nondemocratic nature of the EU, however, poses a serious impediment to their claiming the high ground on democratic legitimacy of economic policy. These issues are even graver for the South, where political systems are still struggling with institutionalizing the democratic procedures that globalization is busy dismantling.

26. Robert Kuttner, "Why the U.S. Banana War? Slippery Claims About Free Trade," *Boston Globe*, March 7, 1999, p. C6.

27. EU external trade for 1996 was $1.9 trillion vs. a U.S. volume of $1.7 trillion. In the Middle East, the EU had 40 percent of the market compared to 13 percent for the U.S., 16 percent of the Chinese market compared to America's 12 percent (all figures for 1995), and 15.7 percent of total exports to East Asia compared to America's 12.3 percent in 1996. These figures are from Blackwill and Archick, *U.S.–European Economic Relations*, p. 7.

28. Ibid.

29. Quoted in ibid., 1998, p. 7.

30. Of course the United States and the EU are also seeking to free trade among themselves. The idea from 1995 of a "Transatlantic Free Trade Area" (TFTA), however, never progressed far, and the 1998 idea of a "New Transatlantic Marketplace" put forth by the European Commission died under French protests the same year. The next version of the search for a U.S.-EU free trade agreement is the emerging EU-supported "Transatlantic Economic Partnership" whose future, within both the EU and the United States, is still uncertain. See Brian Hindley, "New Institutions for Transatlantic Trade?" *International Affairs*, January 1999.

31. These include denying visas to the executives (and their families) of the sanctioned company.

32. In Blackwill and Archick, *U.S.–European Economic Relations*, p. 22, fn. 104.

33. In *Report on United States Barriers to Trade and Investment* (Brussels: European Commission, 1998).

34. Michael S. Lelyveld, "New Showdown Looms Over Iranian Pipeline," *Journal of Commerce*, June 3, 1998.

35. "Global Firms Watch as Cost of Sanctions Mount," *Crossborder Monitor*, November 14, 1997.

36. Elizabeth Olson, "Good Friends Join Enemies to Criticize U.S. on Rights," *New York Times*, March 28, 1999; "UN Panel Votes for Ban on Death Penalty," *New York Times*, April 29, 1999.

37. Jerry White, "U.S. Must Sign Treaty to Ban Land Mines," *Christian Science Monitor*, March 8, 1999.

38. The United States owes the UN $1.69 billion as of December 1998, according to a 1999 *UN Financial Crisis* report.

39. Elizabeth Olson, "U.S. and Europe at Impasse on New World Trade Chief," *New York Times*, April 1, 1999. Similarly, the United States opposes including representatives of the Euro–11 group (the coordinating group of ministers from the eleven countries participating in the European Monetary Union) in G-7 meetings if they are not currently members. The EU feels that the Euro-zone should have representation of its own, while the United States, Japan, and Canada fear both overrepresentation and formalization of a traditionally informal forum. "U.S. Blocks Bigger Euro-zone Role in G-7 Forum," *European Voice*, March 4, 1999.

40. See, for example, such proposals as the collective security system envisioned in *From the Law of the Strongest to the Strength of the Law: A European Security System* (Hamburg, Germany: Institute for Peace Research and Security Policy at the University of Hamburg, April 1993).

41. Roger Cohen, "Dependent on U.S. Now, Europe Vows Defense Push," *New York Times*, May 12, 1999.

42. See Philip H. Gordon, "Europe's Uncommon Foreign Policy," *International Security*, Winter 1997/98.

43. Craig R. Whitney, "NATO Leader Is Moving to New Security Post," *New York Times*, June 5, 1999.

44. Craig R. Whitney, "European Union Vows to Become Military Power," *New York Times*, June 4, 1999; Richard Norton-Taylor, "Cook Supports an EU Military Force: Ministers Seek a Defence Role Independent of NATO," *Guardian*, March 18, 1999.

45. Quoted in Jane Perlez, "NATO Confronts a New Role: Regional Policeman," *New York Times*, April 22, 1999.

46. Quoted in Cohen, "Dependent on U.S. Now," 1999.

47. See Cohen, 1999.

48. President Clinton, "Confronting the Challenges of a Wider World." Speech before the UN General Assembly, September 27, 1993.

49. This increased willingness to act unilaterally within multilateral frameworks also reflects public sentiment, reinforced by political rhetoric and policy. The 1999 survey on American Public Opinion and Foreign Policy shows support for "guarded engagement," noting that a "preference for engagement through multilateral institutions and alliances suggests that Americans would rather share risks and build consensus. However, this inclination does not necessarily translate into support for engagement that would primarily benefit others." See John E. Reilly, "Americans and the World: A Survey at Century's End," *Foreign Policy*, Spring 1999. Also see Garry Wills, "Bully of the Free World," *Foreign Affairs*, 78:2, March/April 1999.

50. Naomi Koppel, "Europeans Accuse U.S. of Waging Unfair Trade War," *Detroit News*, March 9, 1999.

51. This reflects the historical tension between isolationists and internationalism, which in today's undeniably interdependent world metamorphoses into unilateral internationalism versus multilateralism. See chapter 4 in this volume. See also the first section of Jonathan P. G. Bach, *The Partnership and the Pendulum: The Foreign Policy Debate in the United States and Implications for European Security* (Hamburg, Germany: Institute for Peace Research and Security Policy at the University of Hamburg, 1995).

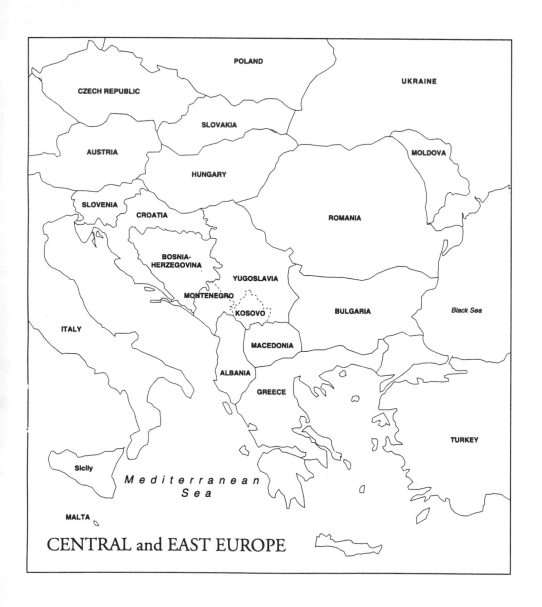

POLAND

CZECH REPUBLIC

UKRAINE

SLOVAKIA

AUSTRIA

MOLDOVA

HUNGARY

SLOVENIA

CROATIA

ROMANIA

BOSNIA-
HERZEGOVINA

YUGOSLAVIA

MONTENEGRO

KOSOVO

ITALY

BULGARIA

Black Sea

MACEDONIA

ALBANIA

GREECE

TURKEY

Sicily

*Mediterranean
Sea*

MALTA

CENTRAL and EAST EUROPE

CHAPTER 8

CENTRAL AND EAST EUROPE IN TRANSITION: A MIXED RECORD

Richard F. Kaufman and Janine R. Wedel

THE DEMOCRATIC UPHEAVALS OF 1989, the collapse of the Soviet Union, and the demise of the Warsaw Pact were widely interpreted as cold war victories for free market capitalism. Throughout the 12 countries of Central and East Europe—Albania, Bosnia-Herzegovina, Bulgaria, Croatia, the Czech Republic, Hungary, Macedonia, Poland, Romania, Slovakia, Slovenia, and Yugoslavia—there was a sense of liberation from politically repressive and economically restrictive systems and a widespread desire to "return to the West." Washington viewed its task as assisting with reforms in order to rapidly establish democracy and capitalism in these former communist countries. After the breakup of Yugoslavia, several of the newly independent countries of the former Yugoslav federation were assisted by the West as well. On the military front, Washington quickly pushed NATO expansion to include former communist countries under the Western security blanket. (See essay 8–1: NATO Expands East.)

The conventional view among Washington policymakers is that their reforms have mostly succeeded. As a March 1999 State Department report put it, "A region that was once the tinderbox of European conflict has become an area of increasing stability, security, and prosperity."[1] This unfortunately timed statement was contained in a document issued just days before NATO began bombing Yugoslavia. In reality, the record of the transitions to democracy and capitalism in Central and East Europe is mixed: there have been successes, and there have also been failures and lost opportunities.

Beginning in the early 1990s, there were voices who cautioned that there could be social and political backlashes if swift transitions to market economies caused severe economic disruptions, high unemployment, and increased poverty. Today, those who believe that the reforms worked argue that those fears were exaggerated. On the political side, conditions in the region are vastly improved over the communist period. One-party rule is over. Nearly all the countries have held free, multiparty elections, and civil liberties have been largely restored. On the economic side, however, sweeping claims of victory are premature and obscure the mistakes committed, the continuing turmoil, the regional disparities, and the serious problems that remain. With regard to security and NATO expansion, the 1999 war in Yugoslavia demonstrates the persistence of internal instabilities and regional tensions.

THE WASHINGTON CONSENSUS AND U.S. POLICY

During the 1990s, both U.S. bilateral and multilateral aid policies toward Central and East Europe (and elsewhere) were largely shaped by a doctrine prescribed by the multilateral banks—dubbed the Washington Consensus—and by the supply-side economics school of thought. Elements of the Washington Consensus had existed for years, but they gelled into a rigid framework during the presidency of Ronald Reagan. At that time, U.S. officials, the International Monetary Fund (IMF), and the World Bank formalized an approach to economic growth and development that emphasized reducing the role of governments and allowing private markets to flourish. Under the mantra of liberalization, stabilization, and privatization the Washington Consensus promotes curbing the state's role in the economy, reducing government spending for health and social programs, and consigning to the private sector as many public activities as possible. The multilateral lending institutions—in particular the IMF and the World Bank—began insisting that countries receiving assistance comply with structural adjustment policies (SAPs). These policies included reduced government spending, balanced budgets, elimination of price controls, privatization, and the lifting of restrictions on foreign trade and investment.

The Washington Consensus resembles the policies championed by advocates of supply-side economics. This school of thought, which came into vogue in the United States with the election of Ronald Reagan, believes that government is too intrusive in the U.S. economy. The supply-siders prescribe a "cold-turkey" withdrawal from dependency on government through drastic cuts in spending programs. They are also strong advocates of deregulation and privatization, convinced that the economy will blossom and grow if only government will "get out of its way." They are willing to risk a short-term recession and high unemployment to attain lower inflation and higher productivity.

Yugoslavia was among the first countries in East and Central Europe where economic reforms were attempted following the 1989 revolutions. In late 1989, Prime Minister Ante Markovic announced a program aimed at stabilizing the economy through rapid convertibility of the local currency (the dinar), cuts in government expenditures, and continuation of a privatization program enacted by the federal parliament a few months earlier. These "shock therapy" measures aimed at radical transformation of the economy were foisted upon the government by the IMF and the World Bank and were promoted by Harvard economist Jeffrey Sachs. Almost simultaneously, the Polish government adopted a similar reform package, also recommended by the multilateral banks and promoted by Sachs. In 1990, the Czech Republic announced its own shock therapy reforms after the World Bank and the IMF conditioned loans to adoption of these reforms.[2]

This pattern of financial assistance provided by the international banks, tied to conditions that attempted to predetermine reforms, was repeated throughout the region. Some governments were more aggressive than others in the implementation of the changes, some adopted more gradualist measures. In all countries, however, the immediate consequences of the reforms were steep declines in production and sharp increases in inflation and unemployment.

With the fall of communism, there was also some discussion of a less theoretical type of economic assistance: a post-cold war "Marshall Plan." Just as the United States had provided large amounts of capital to rebuild Western Europe's infrastructure and industrial capacity after World War II, there were expectations in the region that the United States and the West would generously aid in upgrading and modernizing, along Western capitalist lines, the "other Europe" after the "other war." Soon after the Berlin Wall was demolished, donor nations and agencies expressed their commitment to help the nations of Central and East Europe.

In the last days of November 1989, the U.S. Congress rushed through the so-called SEED (Support for East European Democracy) legislative package. Championing the two nations that spearheaded the region's revolutions, SEED initially authorized nearly $1 billion "to promote political democracy and economic pluralism in Poland and Hungary by assisting those nations during a critical period of transition." Between 1990 and 1999, SEED funding increased from $291 million to $430 million.[3] (See figure 8–1.) As part of this effort, President George Bush established "Enterprise Funds" to promote the development of the private sector and launched other initiatives to offer American know-how to the region.

In addition, the United States provided modest levels of assistance to the region through a variety of mechanisms, including food assistance via the Agriculture Department, business development training through the Peace Corps, and loan guarantees and insurance services for U.S. exports and investments through the Export-Import Bank and the Overseas Private Investment Corporation (OPIC). Washington also extended Most Favored Nation status to most of the countries of the region and announced a policy of promoting trade and investment.

At the beginning of the reform period, there was much optimism in Washington and in the former communist capitals that these changes would lead to an increase in trade with the United States and greater investment by American business. The results, however, have been disappointing. From 1991 through 1998, U.S. imports from the region increased from $1.7 billion to $4.4 billion, and U.S. exports rose from $1.6 billion to $2.9 billion. Although the United States has a trade deficit with the region, it is modest, and the amounts of the trade flows are

188   RICHARD F. KAUFMAN AND JANINE R. WEDEL

Figure 8.1   Support for Eastern European Democracy (SEED): 1990–1999
             ($U.S. thousands)

Year	Amount	Year	Amount
1990	290,778	1995	424,813
1991	331,580	1996	509,872
1992	415,626	1997	473,144
1993	258,174	1998	537,692
1994	480,923	1999 (est.)	430,000

Sources: Department of Eastern European Assistance, "U.S. Assistance to Central and Eastern Europe, Obligations by Country," Department of State, September 30, 1998; Secretary of State, "Congressional Presentation for Foreign Operations, Fiscal Year 2000" (Washington, DC: Department of State, 1999).

lower than expected. By comparison, U.S. imports from the Dominican Republic were $4.4 billion in 1998, as much as all of Central and East Europe. In the same period (1991 to 1998), U.S. imports from France increased by $10.7 billion and from Germany by $23.7 billion. Of course, America's trade with Central and East Europe is a tiny fraction of its trade with Western Europe. (See figure 8–2.)

U.S. foreign direct investment (FDI) in Central and East Europe, while increasing, is also small, totaling about $1.5 billion in 1998—less than 1 percent of

Figure 8.2   U.S. Imports-Exports with Central and Eastern Europe
             ($U.S. millions)

Country	U.S. Imports		U.S. Exports	
	1991	1998	1991	1998
Albania	3	12	18	15
Bulgaria	56	219	142	112
Czechoslovakia (former)	145	839	123	680
Czech Republic	(NA)	(673)	(NA)	(569)
Slovakia	(NA)	(166)	(NA)	(111)
Hungary	367	1,567	256	483
Poland	357	784	459	882
Romania	69	393	209	337
Yugoslavia (former)	674	555	371	349
Bosnia-Herzegovina	(NA)	(7)	(NA)	(40)
Croatia	(NA)	(73)	(NA)	(97)
Macedonia	(NA)	(175)	(NA)	(15)
Serbia and Montenegro	(NA)	(13)	(NA)	(74)
Slovenia	(NA)	(287)	(NA)	(123)
Totals	1,671	4,369	1,578	2,858

Source: Compiled from data from U.S. Department of Commerce, International Trade Administration, May 1999.

U.S. FDI overseas. The UN's World Investment Report for 1998 finds it surprising that FDI is not higher in the region and that foreign investors have not taken advantage of new opportunities there, as they have done in China. The report concludes that the reluctance of foreign investors is probably due to such factors as legal and regulatory problems, a deep and protracted transition-related recession, and the prolonged privatization processes.[4]

Within a few years, the promises of a new era of cooperation between the West and the former communist countries had soured. Despite talk of a new Marshall Plan for reviving the economies of the eastern bloc, few Western policymakers were prepared to commit tens of billions of dollars in capital assistance, and such levels of aid would not have been supported by the Bush administration. Thus, although the post–World War II program was displayed as a shining model of what could be and served as a rhetorical and ideological reference in both East and West, aid to the region bore little resemblance to it. Whereas the Marshall Plan consisted largely of capital assistance, U.S. aid to Central and East Europe emphasized technical assistance. Whereas the Marshall Plan was funded and directed by the U.S, after the fall of communism, a number of Western nations stepped forward to provide assistance to the former Soviet bloc countries. Whereas the Marshall Plan was implemented at the top-level of the U.S. government, the aid programs to Central and East Europe were dispersed within the Washington bureaucracy and among many other governments and multilateral institutions.

Polish press reports during 1989–90 that the West was sending billions of dollars to the region failed to explain that the aid included export credits and loans that would have to be repaid, and that most of the grant aid consisted of "technical assistance" rather than cash. In 1992, Polish President Lech Walesa articulated his country's growing resentment when he spoke at the European Parliamentary Forum in Strasbourg, charging that "it is you, the West, who have made good business on the Polish revolution. . . . The West was supposed to help us in arranging the economy on new principles, but in fact it largely confined its efforts to draining our domestic markets."[5] A Marshall Plan–style program for Central and East Europe—implying strategic planning, commitment of high-level officials, and above all, massive capital assistance—never happened.

For other reasons as well, Central and East Europeans began to doubt the idea of foreign aid as "help." Much of it was in the form of technical, not capital, assistance, and frequently the technical assistance was of dubious value. Western experts arrived on short-term contracts with prepackaged ideas and "solutions" and scant understanding of the nature and legacies of communism. Although some aid officials contend there was a division of labor between the technical assistance provided by the United States and other bilateral donors on one hand and the capital assistance provided by the international financial institutions on the other, there was little coordination between the loans and the technical assistance.

The ready solutions that the consultants offered—liberalization, stabilization, and privatization—did not adequately consider the logical starting point for reform: the planned economies and state socialism of East Europe. Under the Soviet umbrella, properties throughout the region had been nationalized, and, at least officially, most private enterprise had been eliminated. Entire communities of workers had been created around state-run enterprises. These "company towns" guaranteed not only lifetime employment but also housing, social security, healthcare, and child care. Despite the pretense that Central and East European countries were second-world candidates for first world status—meaning that they already had significant industrial and agricultural capacities—many short-term Western consultants applied inappropriate assumptions and drew upon experience they had gleaned from work in third-world countries, which lacked physical infrastructure, skilled labor, and productive capabilities. This misjudgment of the economic realities of the region insulted people who considered themselves exemplars of European culture and civilization and reinforced their perception that many Western consultants were unfamiliar with the specific institutions of postcommunist economies.

Joseph Stiglitz, senior vice president and chief economist of the World Bank, became an outspoken critic of the Washington Consensus, observed that the consultants frequently applied an overly simplistic doctrine based on only a few economic indicators: inflation, money supply, interest rates, and budget and trade deficits. Stiglitz has been critical as well of the fact that foreign economic and technical consultants would arrive in a country, assess the data, and make policy recommendations in the space of a couple of weeks.[6] The Polish press quickly coined a phrase—the Marriott Brigade—for these "fly-in, fly-out" consultants who stayed at Warsaw's pricey new Marriott Hotel and hurtled among five-star hotels across Central Europe.[7]

At first, Central and East European officials welcomed the consultants, but after hundreds of "first meetings" with an endless array of World Bank, IMF, Agency for International Development (AID), and other experts, the honeymoon ended. By January 1992, many Polish and Hungarian officials concluded that their countries were "technically over-assisted," as Marek Kozak, a Polish official who monitored foreign aid, put it, and that the assistance was doing more harm than good. Overburdened top-level officials complained that they could not do their jobs, because they had to spend so much time meeting with fact-finders and consultants. Kozak suggested that the main benefit derived from the Marriott Brigades was not the expertise or loan packages they provided but the hard currency their lifestyles pumped into the local economy.[8]

Gradually, however, relations began to improve somewhat. After early frustration and resentment about the inadequacies of foreign consultants and the aid they offered, officials in the Czech Republic, Hungary, and Poland became better at identifying their needs and more selective about the foreign (and local) advisors whose advice they accepted. In some cases, these governments concluded that the time required to work with a foreign aid program outweighed the benefits, and they chose to forgo the program. In addition, as officials in these three "northern tier" countries developed their own technical capacities, the need for foreign aid–sponsored consultants diminished.

Tensions eased with the growth of a new stratum of government bureaucrats whose careers and economic well-being were tied to their relations with foreign technicians and aid. By 1994, many Western consulting groups were hiring more local citizens and expatriates who spoke Polish, Hungarian, Czech, and Slovak. Donors also recruited some former high-level Central European officials who had served in the first postcommunist governments.

Even if both sides initially came away from the aid table disappointed, person-to-person contact has helped to reduce the isolation stemming from the cold war. Despite its mixed legacy, aid to these countries has been part of a broader process of establishing "normal" relationships between West and East, and aid programs have contributed to the interchange of people and ideas. This is not to say that all potential for antagonism toward "the West" has dissipated, especially in countries and regions where large segments of the population perceive themselves as doing poorly.

THE REFORMS: SUCCESSES AND FAILURES

In Washington's haste to replace communism with capitalism, privatization and private business development were high on its list of priorities. The United States allocated more of its regional aid to privatization, private-sector development, and "economic restructuring" than to any other programs, at least initially. An AID official based in Central Europe remarked that "privatization is our first, second, and third priority."[9] Viewing privatization as a symbol of capitalism, Western donors initially competed to finance the privatization of a few large "model" and "demonstration" projects, believing, as a General Accounting Office report put it, that this "would have a ripple effect on the economy." The United States supported highly visible projects, notably the privatization of huge Polish enterprises employing thousands of people such as the Huta Warszawa steel mill, the Sandomierz glass factory, and the national airline, LOT.[10] Although Washington later expanded its priorities to focus more on supporting new private enterprises, creating stock exchanges, and establishing security and exchange commissions, many early efforts focused on privatization of company towns, along with their social amenities such as healthcare, child care, and employee retreat centers. By transforming these "white elephants," donors aimed to drive a free enterprise stake through the heart of socialism.

Officials in the recipient states largely embraced these measures, although, as Hungarian intellectual and former member of parliament G. M. Tamas argues, East Europeans did so more out of antipathy toward communism than from any yearning for capitalism and liberal democracy. Thus, with the collapse of communism, states Tamas, "what happened to us in the absence of a new social idea of our own was capitalism." Most people, he contends, were glad to be rid of the repressive features of communism, but the new regimes continued many of the problems of the old one: poverty, corruption, abuse of power, and lack of sympathy for the unfortunate. Tamas argues that these countries "suffered" rather than embraced liberal democracy.[11]

The rise of new elites who have profited from the Western reforms, the demon of high unemployment, galloping inflation, and the other economic and social afflictions imposed on much of the population have kindled a rude awakening among many Central and East Europeans. Even ardent supporters of the reforms acknowledge that some of them, such as the privatization of state-owned enterprises, have been abused by public officials and others to plunder public resources. In Poland, the term "Post-Solidarity Style Corruption" has been coined to designate the new forms of improper behavior accepted at the highest levels of government. For instance, a Polish deputy minister in charge of joint ventures owned a consulting firm that specialized in joint ventures. When, in 1990, the prime minister issued a decree forbidding government officials from owning consulting firms, the deputy minister simply transferred ownership of his firm to his wife.[12] In 1997, the World Bank reported that in many transition countries, insiders have used privatization for their own gain and that this "has deepened public cynicism about reform and undermined the legitimacy of the post-reform economic system."[13] The World Bank concluded that there will be a reaction if the reforms benefit only a few, if economic growth is too long postponed, and if corruption is seen as endemic.

Those who maintain that the reforms were largely successful assert that most of the countries have managed to transform their economies to market systems, that they have reversed the pattern of decline and inflation, and that several, including Poland, Hungary, and Slovakia, have achieved—or soon will—sustained growth. Supposedly, the northern tier countries, which undertook to transform themselves first, have gone the farthest in establishing both democracy and market economies. But some egregious examples of corruption occurred in these countries—for example, the privatization scandals in the Czech Republic and Poland. Moreover, a steep price was—and continues to be—paid for the imposition of market reforms in the northern tier countries. The economic downturns went much deeper and lasted much longer than most reformers anticipated, and neither the governments nor their Western advisors were prepared for the increases in unemployment and poverty that followed in their wake.

Officials in Washington predicted at the outset that the reform process would take only a few years to complete. Such predictions were later revised. In 1993, the official report on the progress of the U.S. assistance program stated that the initial projections of a three- to five-year turnaround for the recipient countries were "naively optimistic" and that the economic downturn was "both deeper and of longer duration than first predicted."[14] Robert L. Hutchings, special advisor to the secretary of state and responsible for U.S. assistance programs for Central and East Europe in 1992 and 1993, has also acknowledged the official overoptimism: "The common assumption during the heady days of 1989 was that a three- to five-year burst of external assistance—balance of payments and structural adjustment support from the international financial institutions, bilateral technical assistance programs coordinated through the Group of 24 industrialized nations (G-24), and facilitation of foreign trade and investment—would propel these countries toward integration into the global economy."[15] The record of what actually happened in the 1990s tells a sobering story.

Through the early 1990s, gross domestic product (GDP) declined by double digits for most countries, with comparable increases in unemployment. Depression-level downturns were so deep, partly because of the disruption of traditional trade patterns among the former communist countries, the fighting beginning in

1991 in Yugoslavia (See essay 8–2: U.S. Policy in the Balkans.), interruptions of supplies, and hyperinflation. Some bounce-back should have occurred once the widespread political unrest ended and trade was resumed. But the recoveries have been modest to weak in most countries and in some cases short-lived. With regard to the size of the economies of the region as measured by GDP, by 1998, only 3 (Poland, Slovakia, and Slovenia) of the 12 countries had regained or were slightly above their 1989 levels. In several countries, including those in the northern tier, growth has subsided in recent years, and in some countries, recession or stagnation has returned.

Of course, measures of national economic performance, such as GDP and unemployment, conceal the regional disparities within countries. In the Czech Republic and Poland, for example, private investment tends to be concentrated in the large urban centers, and unemployment tends to be lower in those areas. In the rural regions and in places where factories are outmoded and industrial pollution is high, the macroeconomic statistics often do not reveal patterns of low living standards and poor quality of life.

Even in the northern tier countries—including eastern Germany—which were more industrialized and economically advanced than the other communist countries, the record is spotty. For the most part, growth has stagnated or subsided in recent years. The economy of eastern Germany is still limping along nearly ten years after unification with its western counterpart. The growth of GDP there was under 2 percent and unemployment averaged 18 percent in 1997 and 1998. Meanwhile, only in 1995 did the Czech Republic register an impressive GDP growth rate of 6.9 percent; it subsequently slipped back into recession in the late 1990s, expanding by only 1 percent in 1997 and declining by 1 percent in 1998. Hungary's growth was sluggish until 1997, when it reached a respectable 4.4 percent. Growth expanded in 1998, largely because of heavy deficit spending, an activity that the reforms were supposed to curb. Of the northern tier countries, Poland has enjoyed the most sustained growth, with GDP expanding 6–7 percent in the mid-1990s and waning somewhat to 5 percent in 1998. Inflation has eased substantially in these countries, but it remains close to or above 10 percent. By the late 1990s, unemployment stood at double-digit rates in all the northern tier countries.

The trends are worse in most of the other countries, with sluggish growth and a weakening of economic prospects in 1998.[16] Recently there have been deep recessions in Bulgaria and Romania, the two largest countries in the southern tier. Bulgaria's economy tumbled 18 percent in 1996–1997, rebounded briefly in early 1998, and then weakened again. Bulgaria has had only two years of positive growth in the past decade, and both were in the feeble 2 percent range. Romania, shaken by a new round of social unrest, strikes, and protests, saw its GDP fall by 11 percent in 1997 and 1998. Slovakia's economy expanded at respectable rates for several years but was again slipping by the late 1990s, with GDP forecasted to grow by only about 2 percent in 1999.

Although the economies of the former Yugoslav republics—Bosnia-Herzegovina, Croatia, Macedonia, Slovenia, and Albania—expanded at modest to rapid rates in the late 1990s, the NATO bombing campaign, Serbian military operations in Kosovo, and the outpouring of Kosovar refugees quickly obliterated most, if not all, of these economic advances. Between 1994 and 1999, Slovenia's GDP expanded by about 4 percent annually. However, its unemployment rate has been averaging 14 percent, and there is little evidence that it will improve. Croatia's growth rate was averaging about 6 percent until 1998, when growth slowed to 4.2 percent. Unemployment there has been in double digits and rose to 17.5 percent in 1998. Macedonia's economy expanded by 5 percent in 1998, the first year of significant growth since it became independent. Serbia had modest growth for several years, prior to the NATO air war. Both Macedonia and Serbia suffer from hyperunemployment rates: 40 percent in Macedonia, 25 percent in Serbia. Impoverished Albania can boast the fastest growth in the region—except for 1997, when there was a deep decline—but it battles with high unemployment, and the refugee flows and other fallout from the Kosovo conflict will only worsen conditions.

It is easy to overlook other measures of economic health when examining the standard macroeconomic indicators of overall growth, inflation, and unemployment. All these countries are poor in comparison with the West, and a few are close to the level of developing countries. This precarious status is apparent in the figures for per capita gross national product (GNP), which provides a measure of average levels of economic output. In 1997, Slovenia's per capita GNP of $9,680 was the highest in the entire Central and East European region. The Czech Republic's per capita GNP was $5,200, Hungary's was $4,430, and Poland's was $3,590. The per capita GNPs of the other countries that year ranged from $1,420 for Romania, to $1,140 for Bulgaria, to $750 for Albania, the poorest country in the region. By way of comparison, Germany's per capita GNP in 1997 was $28,260; the U.S. figure was $28,740.[17] The countries of this region will have to grow at rapid rates over a sustained period of years in order for them to close the gap with the industrialized West.

PRIVATIZATION AND ITS PROBLEMS

The privatization of state-controlled enterprises—many of which were notoriously inefficient—has been a centerpiece in the strategy for transforming the economies of the former communist countries. U.S. officials considered rapid privatization and restructuring as the key to starting sustained economic recoveries, and state-enterprise sell-offs were often linked to IMF loans. According to a 1991 report by the Central Intelligence Agency (CIA), which was monitoring the reforms, "IMF programs call for tight budgets that leave little room to subsidize bankrupt firms left over from the Communist era."[18] Unfortunately, privatization became almost an end in itself for both the givers and receivers of Western assistance. In the name of privatization, corruption flourished and there was widespread failure to develop the institutional frameworks necessary for markets to function properly.

Both insiders and outsiders benefited from corruption in the privatization process in several ways. Often former members of the *nomenklatura*—the ruling elite under communism, who still held important posts—and other officials used their influence for personal gain. In the rush to privatize, state enterprises were sometimes priced below their market value. This enabled insiders, including the managers of the enterprises, to buy shares of a newly formed private company at bargain prices. In some instances, government officials formed or joined business entities that took over government enterprises even before outsiders had a chance to bid for them. In other cases, insiders milked the assets of a state enterprise by forming a private company that entered into sweetheart deals with the enterprise. Using freewheeling tactics reminiscent of the era of American corporate robber barons, outside "reformers" sometimes operated without corporate governance and accountability mechanisms such as regulated capital markets, financial disclosure requirements, and enforceable antifraud laws—all vital to protect shareholders against insider trading and other management wrongdoings. Absent such protections, privatization scandals have proliferated.[19]

In Poland there were instances where officials in the Ministry of Privatization took paid positions with companies they were privatizing, both as consultants and as members of the boards of directors. When the companies were sold to foreign investors, these bureaucrats would resign from government to become directors of the foreign-owned company or would join the foreign consulting firm that helped negotiate the sale. In some cases, officials stayed in government but continued to serve on boards of directors of the privatized or partially privatized companies. Thus, during the first wave of privatizations, *nomenklatura* members in both Poland and Hungary were able to become owners of companies they had previously managed as state functionaries. Although such practices were not always illegal, they compromised the legitimacy of the government's role, since officials often made privatization decisions based on personal gain instead of the public interest.[20]

Particularly acute privatization scandals resulted in political upheavals in the Czech Republic and Albania. The Czech Republic was thought to be a model of transition until 1997, when it was overwhelmed by revelations of wrongdoing. Under Prime Minister Vaclav Klaus, a devotee of the unbridled capitalism of conservative U.S. economist Milton Friedman and British Prime Minister Margaret Thatcher, the Czech government, after some delay, rushed to privatize numerous government-owned businesses—whether they were managed efficiently or not—without providing full disclosure or adequate accounting information. The CIA praised the Czech leaders in 1994 for their successful mass privatization program and announced that the tasks of economic transformation would be completed in a few years.[21] But in 1997, the government fell when Prime Minister Klaus was forced to resign by members of his own party, largely because of privatization-related scandals.

The Klaus government's mass privatization program was a decision to virtually give away state enterprises. Vouchers, which were like shares of stock, were handed out to millions of Czech citizens at nominal or zero cost, but the public knew little about the management of the companies or how they had performed under communism. As a consequence, most Czechs were ignorant of the real value of the firms, did not understand the economic advantages or disadvantages of privatizing them, and were unclear about the concept of owning vouchers. In these circumstances, it was only a matter of time before insiders—usually well-placed government officials—gained control of many of the companies. One mechanism of control occurred through the formation of Investment Privatization Funds, which accumulated vouchers from individual shareholders. Although, in the view of one participant in the reform process, "the privatized Czech economy was a free market riddled with insider dealing," Klaus resisted regulation of the burgeoning stock market.[22] The Czech parliament finally approved legislation creating a Securities and Exchange Commission to regulate the market, but the exchange lacked enforcement authority and was considered toothless.[23]

Among the Klaus government's worst mistakes was the decision to allow the privatized banks, which collaborated with the Investment Privatization Funds, to gain control of certain industrial companies. The inevitable outcomes of such combinations were lax loan policies toward the industries controlled by the banks, industrial inefficiency, and embezzlement. The final blow to the government came from disclosures by the finance minister that there was a Swiss bank account with money allegedly given to Klaus's political party for privatization deals. In 1999, new allegations emerged of bribes paid to the Klaus government by a Dutch telecommunications firm in return for an interest in a Czech company. The Czech and Dutch governments announced they would investigate these charges, and the Czech government began investigating past privatizations as well. Disillusioned by such scandals, the Czech Republic and other governments have considered renationalizing some businesses. For example, the Czechs, in an effort to control soaring natural gas prices, began trying to buy back controlling interest in the gas distribution industry. Privatization of Czech banks slowed as well.[24]

In Albania, the government also attempted a mass privatization program through the distribution of vouchers to the general public. Over one million citizens received privatization vouchers, but they were induced to sell them at a fraction of their presumed value in order to invest in what turned out to be a pyramid scheme. When the pyramid scheme collapsed in 1997, three-fourths of all Albanians lost their entire savings. The social unrest that followed brought the country close to anarchy, and the government fell. A 1998 survey conducted by the World Bank and an Albanian research center ranked Albania among the world's most corrupt nations. Ironically, before the pyramid scandal broke, Albania had been considered one of the most promising transition countries because of its rapid economic growth.[25]

COLLAPSE OF THE SAFETY NETS: POVERTY AND THE CHILDREN OF THE TRANSITIONS

Regional policymakers and their foreign advisors and donors failed to provide mechanisms to cushion the social and economic tempest unleashed by the rapid dismantling of existing institutions such as occurred under the privatization schemes. Former Polish Prime Minister Jan Krzysztof Bielecki recalls that when the IMF and other foreign advisors discussed reforms with Polish officials, "nobody raised the issue of the social safety net."[26] With the sales and giveaways of state assets, many of the communist-era social welfare programs in health, child care, education, housing, and employment were dismantled. From the outset, U.S. officials recognized that the transition from state-run to market systems would cause rising unemployment, falling standards of living, and potential social and political turmoil. In 1990, CIA officials told the Joint Economic Committee of Congress that moving rapidly "risks severe economic disruptions and political instability." However, despite early warnings of the social costs, the U.S. government, the IMF, and others proceeded with their reform agendas.[27]

The fact that the economic downturns and disruptions were greater and lasted longer than was anticipated has left scars and continuing wounds. Recently, international agencies have begun to study and document the social damage that has occurred in the region since 1989. The studies show that the transition depressions of the early 1990s triggered surges in poverty and health problems. The partial economic recoveries ameliorated, but have not solved, these problems, and some will linger for years.

The erosion of family incomes and savings during the downturns boosted poverty throughout the region. In some countries—including Bulgaria, the Czech Republic, Slovakia, Poland, and Romania—poverty rates soared. Because real wages and employment continue to lag behind the recovery of overall economic output, household welfare remains depressed.[28]

Medical services and health conditions have deteriorated in most of these countries. Although the reasons are not entirely understood, poor diet and nutrition, stress brought on by unemployment and insecurity, and increased consumption of alcohol, drugs, and tobacco are contributing factors. The control of infectious diseases has become more difficult. For example, the incidence of tuberculosis in the region declined in the 1970s and 1980s but has been rising since 1990. The recent severe outbreak of poliomyelitis in Albania concerns health authorities, because it was believed that that disease had been eradicated in Europe and the eastern Mediterranean. Mental health has also been affected. The rate of suicide in the region increased substantially after 1990, although by the end of the decade it appeared to be subsiding. The environmental degradation that occurred during the communist era—due to antiquated equipment, poor environmental codes, and ineffective enforcement procedures—has also contributed to health problems. Improvements in this area, especially with regard to water and air quality, have been slow in coming.[29]

The economic reforms contributed both directly and indirectly to health care problems. In some countries, the health sector has been privatized in ways that make medical services both expensive and inaccessible to poorer sectors of the population. Health privatization has not been accompanied by regulatory mechanisms to assure that patients receive quality care. In the Czech Republic, the rapid privatization of pharmacies has inflated the cost of drugs. Since free markets were introduced in the early 1990s, the importation and sale of cigarettes and tobacco have risen, as have the incidences of alcohol-related and smoking-related diseases.[30]

Children have been seriously affected by the rupturing of the social fabric and the social safety net. A United Nations Children's Fund report found that since 1989: children in Central and East Europe have been hurt more by the spreading poverty than other groups; in several countries, the poverty rates for children have risen much faster than the overall poverty rates; economic pressures on parents are reducing the amount of child supervision; there is evidence of increasing child maltreatment, including the use of harmful child labor; the number of children living in broken families has swelled; and there are greater numbers of children living in orphanages and other children's institutions. Not surprisingly, the report found that the decline in living standards has disproportionately affected poorer families, causing rises in late fetal deaths and infant mortality rates.[31]

In addition, rates of pre–primary school enrollment fell after 1989 in a number of countries including Bulgaria, the Czech Republic, Hungary, Poland, Romania, and Slovakia. Rates of primary school enrollment have also declined in several counties. Families are forced to pay for textbooks, extracurricular activities, and other primary and secondary school services that the government used to provide for free, and this has created additional difficulties for the children of poor families. There has also been an increase in alcohol and drug abuse among youths, and teen suicides have increased in some countries.

One postcommunist horror story that captured international headlines described the plight of children in Romanian orphanages. The UN Children's Fund found that in Romania and elsewhere in the region, children living in institutional care had become "a forgotten underclass, whose voice to the outside world was never heard."[32] They lived in facilities housing 150 to 600 children, often staffed by unqualified elderly or very young persons, cut off from families and friends, and without recourse when subjected to cruelty, abuse, and sometimes subhuman conditions. These conditions, while extreme, reflect a more generalized trend toward frequent institutionalization of children in orphanages and other children's homes. From 1989 through 1995, the percentage of children in public care increased in five of the six countries for which data were available—the Czech Republic, Slovakia, Poland, Bulgaria, and Romania. Only in Hungary did the percentage decline. According to the UN Children's Fund, "The stagnant or increasing pool of children in public care is a bitter pill and a clear disappointment for all those who had hoped the reform movement would bring beneficial results."[33]

The sexual exploitation of children is another disturbing development. Child pornography and prostitution gained a strong foothold in several countries as a result of the poverty, abandonment, and surge in homelessness. Although there are no definitive statistics, the prostitution of teenagers is reportedly flourishing in Bulgaria, Hungary, Poland, and Romania, where thousands of children live on the streets, and organized gangs recruit both boys and girls. In addition, there has been an expansion of illegal trafficking—particularly of young women—from Central and East Europe to the West for prostitution and work in sweatshops. These trafficking networks are often linked to organized crime and other illegal activities such as drug smuggling.

CRACKS IN THE WASHINGTON CONSENSUS

By the end of the 1990s, it was obvious that the economic reforms had not achieved many of their stated objectives. Market systems had been introduced, but in many cases they were hollow replicas of the more vibrant economies in the West. Rapid, sustained economic growth had not occurred in any of the countries, and there was little likelihood that performance beyond slow to moderate growth—coupled with high unemployment and poverty rates—would occur in the foreseeable future. By 1999, most of the Central and East European countries had not yet regained the level of total output that they had reached in 1989. This has led some economists, especially World Bank official Joseph Stiglitz, to openly reconsider the premises of the Washington Consensus and the assumptions of the architects of the "reforms."

Stiglitz, and a few other World Bank and IMF officials, began conceding that their programs failed to include the institutional framework, the implementing measures, and the goals that could have assured greater success of the programs and better protection for the people affected. Stiglitz asserts that the approach of the Washington Consensus neglects many of the requirements of well-functioning markets, such as sound financial regulation and competition policy. He states that rapid privatization in the transition economies led to unregulated monopolies— which are also inefficient—and that trade liberalization alone does not always create competition.[34]

The worst errors committed under the Washington Consensus concern the economic, social, and political turmoil set in motion by the reforms. A certain amount of inconvenience and pain may be inevitable when such vast systemic changes take place. But the mistakes made went beyond the lapse in providing "safety nets," as narrowly conceived for the purpose of providing emergency relief and temporary support. There was no sound reason to allow contractions of output and expansions of unemployment to proceed virtually unchecked. It was callous and counterproductive not to have included countercyclical programs that would prevent the sharp economic downturns or at least provide softer landings for the falling economies.

In addition, the "reformers" misunderstood the requirements of a well-functioning market economy. As Stiglitz observes, it is easy to give away state property to one's friends and cronies. The difficult task is to create a private, competitive market economy. To achieve that "requires an institutional framework, a set of credible and enforced laws and regulations." Stiglitz concludes that when privatization is widely viewed as illegitimate, the state is weakened and the social order is undermined. He argues that it was both costly and inefficient to move workers from low-productivity employment in state companies to unemployment without vigorous programs of job creation, adding that the advice of the swarms of Western advisors "sometimes contributed as much to the problem as [to] the solution."[35]

More than anywhere else in this region, Yugoslavia defies facile assertions that Central and East Europe have made smooth transitions to Western-style democracy and capitalism, or that fears of a backlash to "reforms" were exaggerated. In Yugoslavia, the inappropriately harsh reforms prescribed by the international financial institutions and foreign advisors were among many factors that contributed to the disintegration of political and civil order and the collapse of the state into nationalist regimes. As mentioned earlier, Yugoslavia, in an effort to cope with its foreign debt, was among the first to try the kind of economic "shock therapy" medicine later prescribed for the other former communist countries. As Susan Woodward (who served as a UN special representative in the former Yugoslavia in 1994) wrote in her history, *Balkan Tragedy*, the post–cold war period was a time "when the economic austerity and reforms required by a foreign debt crisis triggered a slide toward political disintegration."[36]

Yugoslavia was among the many countries whose economy was affected by the increase in energy prices in the early 1970s, followed by a recession in the West and the decline of world trade. At that time, international commercial banks were eager to recycle "petrodollars" by lending money to poorer countries at low interest rates, and Yugoslavia borrowed heavily in order to maintain the growth of its economy. But in the late 1970s another sharp rise in oil prices inflated bank interest rates—which were pegged to the U.S. dollar—to double-digit figures. Meanwhile, the commercial banks cut back on loans to East Europe, including Yugoslavia.

Belgrade sought to counter its debt crisis by adopting measures to restrict imports of consumer goods and encourage greater exports. These efforts to improve the trade balance failed; domestic production fell and imports continued to exceed exports. The results were aggravated balance-of-payments and foreign debt problems. In the 1980s, Yugoslavia borrowed even more from the International Monetary Fund, the Organization for Economic Cooperation and Development, other governments, and commercial banks in order to stabilize its foreign debt. Initially there was improvement in the external accounts, but the economy stagnated and debt payments had to be repeatedly rescheduled. Toward the end of the 1980s, only the IMF would provide additional loans. These loans always came with conditions attached, requiring more belt tightening measures from Belgrade.[37] In 1987, the IMF's conditions also included overtly political demands for increased federal authority over Slovenia, Croatia, and the other autonomous republics in order to facilitate implementation of the austerity measures and economic reforms. In the republics, these recommendations were viewed with deep suspicion. By 1988, Yugoslavia's economy had deteriorated badly, with inflation close to 200 percent and unemployment at 15 percent. The IMF advanced another loan with conditions that included limits on wages, government spending, and the money supply; the removal of price and import controls; and the beginning of a privatization program.

The government's efforts to enforce those conditions led to further difficulties, including food shortages and pay cuts. In reaction, there was a series of strikes and protests and a wider split between the federal government and the republics, where there was rising opposition to Belgrade's efforts to broaden the powers of the federal government. Complicating the situation were the heightened tensions among the various ethnic groups. These included Serbs, Croats, Slovenes, Macedonians, and Montenegrins—who were each the majority within their respective republics but were minorities in one another's republics—along with other minority groups such as Albanians and Muslims.

Beginning in 1990, there were protests in Slovenia, where a Serbian domination plot was suspected. These were met by an explosion of Serbian nationalism led by then-communist party boss Slobodan Milosevic, a neo-Stalinist who supported moves for greater control by the federal government over the various regions. This included Kosovo, which had been granted status as an autonomous province rather than a republic. Milosevic manipulated public opposition to the economic austerity measures to gain support for his brand of Serbian nationalism. Those in Serbia who supported the economic reforms and the federal arrangement as it had existed became politically isolated. Slovenia and Croatia, both exhibiting broad support in principle for the liberal economic system that the reforms were attempting to achieve, became increasingly wary of Serbian nationalism and the threat to the republics.[38]

With the economy worse than ever, Prime Minister Branko Mikulic resigned at the end of 1988 and was replaced by Ante Markovic, who proceeded to implement the reforms set in motion by the IMF and the government's Western advisors. But the economic decline persisted, and at the end of 1989, Markovic unveiled a "shock therapy" stabilization program requiring additional cuts in spending. In 1990, a new privatization scheme was announced in which shares in firms would be given to workers and managers.

As late as 1990, Washington still believed things were going well in Yugoslavia. The Central Intelligence Agency reported that the economic stabilization program adopted the year before "makes bringing down inflation its first priority and has currency reform and a tight monetary policy as its centerpieces." The CIA stated in a report submitted to the Joint Economic Committee that the initial results were favorable but that tougher measures needed to be implemented.[39] However, U.S. policy toward Yugoslavia was shifting. Once communism collapsed in Central and East Europe, the special relationship Washington had maintained with Yugoslavia seemed less important than it had been during the cold war. In the early 1980s, the State Department had helped organize a consortium of banks, called "The Friends of Yugoslavia," to assist that country with its foreign debt problem. However, later in the decade, the Bush administration rejected a request by Markovic's government for economic assistance with the reform process.[40]

Fighting broke out in 1991 in Slovenia and Croatia, which had been the first republics to gain their independence. Eventually an extremely bloody civil war and an "ethnic cleansing" campaign were waged in Bosnia-Herzegovina. By 1994, an estimated 200,000 people had been killed, and 3.4 million more were made refugees or displaced persons before that republic achieved independence.[41] In 1999, a decade of violence was capped with a new war in Kosovo, when the NATO alliance attacked Serbia in response to the intensified persecution of Kosovar Albanians.

It will never be known whether the train of political and military events that began in 1989 could have been prevented or ameliorated. Although a multitude of factors were involved, a better outcome may have resulted if the West had adopted a more flexible approach to Yugoslavia's financial and economic needs before the state broke apart. The United States and the West lost whatever chances there were to deal with Yugoslavia's economic problems before they grew to crisis proportions, helping to ignite extreme ethnonationalism.

RECOMMENDATIONS

U.S. and Western economic policies toward the countries of Central and East Europe following the collapse of communism were a patchwork of grants, loans, and technical assistance. The policies were generally not well conceived, adequately coordinated, or wisely implemented. No one should be surprised that such a mixed bag has netted mixed results. It was most unfortunate that a critical (if not the leading) role was given to the international financial institutions and especially the IMF. Their ideas for transforming the economies of the region were poorly designed and contributed to the deep and prolonged economic downturns and disruptions that spread throughout the region. The repercussions of the unemployment, poverty, corruption, and other social ills and injustices that ensued are still being felt, and large segments of the population are still suffering. A successful assistance program must include the following reforms.

First, there is a need to change the approach to assisting countries in transition. "Shock therapy" and other rapid or radical changes should not be employed unless accompanied by countercyclical programs to prevent or soften the effects of economic downturns. Such ameliorating measures must protect children, the elderly, and other vulnerable parts of the population.

Second, in assessing the results of assistance, there should be less reliance on traditional macroeconomic indicators—such as gross domestic product, inflation rates, foreign direct investment, and budget and trade deficits—and greater emphasis on (1) the presence of an institutional framework, such as a legal and regulatory infrastructure for a market economy; (2) democratic governance; and (3) social indicators such as education, health, poverty, and the environment. Often policies that respect local opinion and democratic practices will help produce sustainable change.

Third, programs—such as the privatization of state-owned enterprises and the removal of trade barriers and price controls—should not be undertaken as ends in themselves but should be matched by actions that assure greater accountability, competition, legal justice, and fairness.

Fourth, substantial amounts of targeted grant assistance—not just technical advice—should be extended to countries in transition in order to improve social and environmental conditions. Preservation and improvement of the social safety net should be considered as important as any other part of a reform proposal.

NOTES

1. U.S. Department of State, *SEED Act Implementation Report*, Fiscal Year 1999 (Washington, DC: U.S. Department of State, March 1999), p. 1.
2. Susan L. Woodward, *Balkan Tragedy: Chaos and Dissolution After the Cold War* (Washington, DC: Brookings Institution, 1995), pp. 114, 126–27; The WEFA Group, *Centrally Planned Economies Outlook* (Washington, DC: WEFA, October 1990), pp. 9.3–9.6.
3. Public Law 101–179, *Support for East European Democracy (SEED) Act of 1989*, November 28, 1989; Department of Eastern European Assistance, "U.S. Assistance to Central and Eastern Europe, Obligations by Country," Department of State, Sep-

tember 30, 1998. For authorization and allocation amounts, see U.S. General Accounting Office, *Eastern Europe: Donor Assistance and Reform Efforts* (Washington, DC: U.S. GAO, November 1990), pp. 14–15.

4. United Nations, *World Investment Report 1998, Trends and Determinants* (New York: United Nations, 1998), p. 283. The UN includes in its definition of Central and East Europe: Russia, Estonia, Latvia, Lithuania, Ukraine, Belarus, and Moldova in addition to the countries discussed in this chapter.

5. Blaine Harden, "Poles Sour on Capitalism," *Washington Post*, February 5, 1992, p. A1.

6. Joseph E. Stiglitz, "More Instruments and Broader Goals: Moving Toward the Post-Washington Consensus," WIDER Annual Lectures 2 (Helsinki, Finland: UNU World Institute for Development Economic Research, 1998), p. 6.

7. See, for example, Jacek Kalabinski, "The Marriott Brigade in Action," *Gazeta Wyborcza*, June 21, 1991, and "The Misfortune of the Marriott Brigade," *Gazeta Wyborcza*, October 18, 1991.

8. Marek Kozak cited in Janine R. Wedel, "The Unintended Consequences of Western Aid to Post-Communist Europe," *Telos*, No. 92, Summer 1992, p. 133.

9. Quoted in Janine R. Wedel, *Collision and Collusion: The Strange Case of Western Aid to Eastern Europe, 1989–1998* (New York: St. Martin's Press, 1998), p. 50.

10. United States General Accounting Office, *Poland: Economic Restructuring and Donor Assistance* (Washington, DC: GAO, August 1995), p. 57.

11. G. M. Tamas, "Victory Defeated," *Journal of Democracy*, January 1999, pp. 63–68.

12. Antoni Z. Kaminski, "The New Polish Regime and the Specter of Economic Corruption," (Washington, DC: Woodrow Wilson International Center for Scholars, April 1996).

13. World Bank, *World Development Report, 1996* (New York: Oxford University Press, 1997), p. 12.

14. Department of State, *SEED Act Implementation Report* (Washington, DC: U.S. Department of State, 1993), p. 1.

15. Robert L. Hutchings, "Five Years After: Reflections on the Post-Communist Transitions and Western Assistance Strategies," in John P. Hardt and Richard F. Kaufman, *East-Central European Economies in Transition* (New York: M. E. Sharpe, 1995), p. 184.

16. UN Economic Commission for Europe, *Economic Survey of Europe, 1988; PlanEcon Review and Outlook for Eastern Europe* (Geneva: United Nations, December 1988).

17. World Bank, *World Development Report: Knowledge for Development 1998/99* (New York: Oxford University Press, 1999), pp. 190–91. The World Bank's figures measured at purchasing power parity show somewhat higher results.

18. Central Intelligence Agency, "Eastern Europe: Coming Around the First Turn," in United States, Congress, Joint Economic Committee, Subcommittee on Technology and National Security, *Global Economic and Technological Change: Hearings Before the Subcommittee on Technology and National Security of the Joint Economic Committee, Congress of the United States, One Hundred Second Congress, First Session, May 16 and June 28, 1991* (Washington, DC: U.S. Government Publishing Office, 1991).

19. Miriam Z. Klipper, "The Governance of Privatized Firms: Authority, Responsibility and Disclosure," *Economics of Transition*, Vol. 6, No. 1, 1998, pp. 101–11.

20. Kaminski, "New Polish Regime"; Marie Lavigne, *The Economics of Transition: From Socialist Economy to Market Economy* (New York: St. Martin's Press, 1995), pp. 158–59.

21. Central Intelligence Agency, "Eastern Europe: Reforms Spur Recovery," prepared for the Joint Economic Committee, Subcommittee on Technology and National Security, U.S. Congress, July 1994, p. 5.

22. Klipper, "Governance of Privatized Firms," p. 103.
23. Jane Perlez, "Czech Premier Steps Down After Havel Seeks Ouster," *New York Times*, November 30, 1997.
24. Tony Weslowsky, "Czech Scams," *In These Times*, April 11, 1999, pp. 13–14; Jane Perlez, "For the Czechs, The Fairy Tale Is All Over Now," *New York Times*, December 1, 1997; Jan Stojaspal, "Nothing to Toast About: Czechs Struggle to Mend the Tattered Remnants of Their 'Velvet Revolution,'" " *Time International*, March 15, 1999; *PlanEcon Monthly Report*, Vol. 15, No. 1, January 1999, p. 23.
25. *PlanEcon Review and Outlook for Eastern Europe*, 1998, pp. 15, 18.
26. Wedel, *Collision and Collusion*, p. 75.
27. United States Congress, Joint Economic Committee, Subcommittee on Technology and National Security, "Allocation of Resources in the Soviet Union and China, Part 15, [Executive Sessions]," *April 20, May 16, June 28, 1990: Hearings Before the Subcommittee on Technology and National Security of the Joint Economic Committee, Congress of the United States, One Hundred First Congress, Second Session* (Washington, DC: U.S. Government Printing Office, 1991), p. 246.
28. United Nations Children's Fund, *Children At Risk in Central and Eastern Europe: Perils and Promises* (Florence, Italy: UNICEF, 1997), pp. 5, 22–26.
29. World Health Organization, *Health in Europe 1997* (Copenhagen: WHO, 1998), pp. 10–11, 24–25, 27, 34–36.
30. Richard B. Saltman and Josep Figueras, World Health Organization, *European Health Care Reform: Analysis of Current Strategies V* (Copenhagen: WHO, 1997), pp. 49–50, 45–49.
31. United Nations Children's Fund, *Children At Risk*, pp. 39–44.
32. Ibid., p. 64.
33. Ibid., p. 66–67.
34. Stiglitz, "More Instruments," p. 6; summarized in *WIDER Angle*, December 1997/January 1998, No. 1/97.
35. Joseph E. Stiglitz, "Whither Reform? Ten Years of the Transition," Address to the World Bank Conference on Development Economics, Washington, April 28–30, 1999.
36. Woodward, *Balkan Tragedy*, p. 4.
37. The WEFA Group, *Centrally Planned Economies Outlook for Foreign Trade*, January 1990, pp. 10.3–10.4.
38. The International Institute for Strategic Studies, *Strategic Survey 1988–1989* (London: Brassey's, 1989), pp. 95–97; Woodward, *Balkan Tragedy*, pp. 96–97.
39. U.S. Congress, "Allocation of Resources in the Soviet Union and China," pp. 250–51.
40. John R. Lampe, *Yugoslavia as History* (New York: Cambridge University Press, 1996), p. 320; Woodward, *Balkan Tragedy*, p. 154.
41. International Institute for Strategic Studies, *Strategic Survey, 1993–1994* (London: Brassey's, May 1994), p. 104.

NATO EXPANDS EAST

William D. Hartung and Richard F. Kaufman

WHILE WESTERN ADVISORS AND FINANCIAL MANAGERS were working to reshape the economies of Central and East Europe along capitalist lines, Clinton administration officials, military experts, and weapons salesmen set their sights on realigning the region under the umbrella of an expanded and redefined NATO alliance. Bolstered by support from strongly anticommunist ethnic communities living in the United States and by top political and military leaders in the region, and backed by generous government subsidies and media campaigns, NATO expansion moved from the drawing board in 1992 to reality in March 1999, just two weeks before the alliance itself launched its first ever armed conflict.

Official and popular support for NATO expansion within the region suggested "their almost reflexive fear of Russia, and a desire to be enveloped in a Western security blanket," the *New York Times* reported in June 1997. In Poland, the *Times* reported, political leaders pushed the idea of joining NATO "as a panacea to all kinds of problems, a golden bridge to the West." NATO membership was also widely viewed as a stepping stone to membership in the European Union. However, the EU, preoccupied in the late 1990s with a myriad of difficult issues causing divides among its Western European members, was unwilling to consider admitting the economically weaker, largely agricultural former communist countries.

Among Poland, Hungary, and the Czech Republic, public opinion surveys revealed that support for joining NATO was not uniform. It ran highest—between 79 and 88 percent—in Poland, a country historically on the fault line between Russia and Germany, where the military has long been held in high esteem and where pro-American sentiment is strong because many Poles have relatives in the United States. In contrast, both the Czech Republic and Hungary feel secure following the demise of the Warsaw Pact, perceive no real external threat, and hold their own armed forces in low esteem. Popular support in the Czech Republic, where there has been strong concern about NATO's economic and social costs, ranged from 28 to 42 percent, depending on how the question was phrased. In Hungary as well, support was subdued—under 50 percent—with people concerned about the costs of updating their armed forces and resistant to the possibility of foreign troops being stationed on their soil.

The Clinton administration and arms manufacturers worked to counter this somewhat lackluster support for NATO through media campaigns and financial enticements. In 1994, several major U.S. military manufacturers set up offices in the region to promote their products, and in 1996, defense giant Lockheed Martin organized a series of "defense planning seminars" for officials in Poland, Hungary, and the Czech Republic, a soft-sell, relationship-building approach intended to demonstrate the benefits of buying American. In 1997, in the months leading up to public referendums, the Czech, Hungarian, and Polish governments, as well as U.S. arms manufacturers, launched aggressive media campaigns to win public support. On Hungarian television, a popular sitcom suddenly had a new character, a military commander who spouted the virtues of NATO, while school libraries gave away slick pro-NATO CD-ROM games supplied by McDonnell Douglas.

After years of reducing their defense budgets and converting military facilities to peacetime uses, the three countries began allocating more economic resources for military purposes. A 1998 report by the Congressional Research Service found that Hungary planned to double the share of defense spending going for modernization, while Poland announced a 15-year program in which modernization and procurement will grow at constant annual rates of 3 and 2 percent respectively. The Czech Republic also stated its plans to use 20 percent of its increased defense spending for arms modernization. However, these increases will not be sufficient. According to an estimate in a March 1996 Congressional Budget Office (CBO) study, to bring these three countries (plus Slovakia) up to NATO standards, funding for procurement of new weapons needs to increase *six times* above current levels. This, the CBO study concluded, "might be difficult for those nations to afford."

Beginning in the mid-1990s, a majority of U.S. government subsidized loan programs for weapons exporters were being used to underwrite sales of U.S. military equipment to potential new members of NATO. Two-thirds of the countries receiving support from the Pentagon's Foreign Military Financing (FMF) fund, the largest direct subsidy program, were in Central and East Europe or the former Soviet republics. Between 1996 and 1998, 19 of these countries were slated to receive over $150 million in FMF financing via the Clinton administration's Partnership for Peace (PfP) program. PfP funds were specifically intended, according to the State Department's fiscal year 1998 congressional presentation, to "'prepare countries for NATO membership' by supporting 'acquisition of NATO compatible equipment.'" These funding levels are likely to grow as new states prepare to join NATO. In addition to the bountiful PfP funds, additional monies totaling $157,053 were slated for the countries of Central and East Europe in 1999. (See figure 8–3.)

One new program, the Central European Defense Loan Fund (CEDL), provides creditworthy countries in Central Europe and the Balkans with loans to purchase NATO-compatible equipment. Under another program, the Defense Export Loan Guarantee (DELG), the U.S. government guarantees up to $15 billion in loans for the export of U.S. military hardware. Created after years of lobbying by the major military contractors, DELG covers 39 countries, including 10 in Central and East Europe. The first DELG loan went to Romania for $16.7 million for the purchase of unmanned military planes.

In addition to grants and loans, the Pentagon is also giving new and prospective NATO members massive amounts of "surplus" U.S. military equipment. Under the Excess Defense Articles program, a dozen East and Central European countries are slated to receive free weapons including military cargo trucks, patrol boats, and cargo aircraft. The Pentagon has also stepped up weapons exports via no-cost and low-cost leases, including offers of F-16 and F/A-18 fighter planes to Poland, Hungary, and the Czech Republic. As a further enticement, the Defense Department arranges test flights of U.S. fighter aircraft for potential Central and East European customers and holds foreign air shows and military exhibitions. In 1996 to 1997 alone, the Pentagon sponsored at least six major weapons shows attended by Central and East European officials, plus a number of smaller shows directly in Hungary, Poland, and the Czech Republic.

Other U.S. government agencies, including the State and Commerce departments, have arms promotional programs that are being used in NATO-aspirant countries. The largest source of indirect financing for arms exports is the United States Agency for International Development's Economic Support Funds (ESF), which provides over $2 billion a year in balance-of-payments and commodity imports support to important U.S. security partners. Historically most ESF funds have gone to Israel, Egypt, and Turkey, while Central and East Europe have received development funding through the SEED (Support for East European Democracy) program. But as SEED funding declined, the State Department signaled in its 1998 presentation to Congress the administration's determination to find "enhanced support for those countries seeking NATO membership," and ESF funds may be tapped. Already being tapped to support NATO expansion are Export-Import Bank (ExIm) loan guarantees, which, thanks to successful arms industry lobbying, can now be used for "dual-use" equipment—that is, equipment that can be used for both civilian and military purposes. In 1997, for instance, ExIm gave a $90 million loan to finance Romania's purchase of five radar systems from Lockheed Martin.

While lulled by propaganda, lured by the illusion of imminent EU membership, and lavished with new subsidized military hardware, the people of Poland, Hungary, and the Czech Republic were given little concrete explanation of the potential costs or obligations of NATO membership. Majorities in both Hungary and the Czech Republic, however, correctly discerned that increased government spending on the military would come at the expense of education and health. In all three countries, the *Washington Post* reported in June 1997, support was low for allowing routine NATO exercises on their soil or sending troops to defend NATO allies.

These concerns were set aside when, just 12 days after the formal induction of Hungary, Poland and the Czech Republic, NATO began bombing Yugoslavia, marking the first time in its 50-year history that the alliance had gone to war. In the weeks that followed, the three new members offered various degrees of modest military and civilian support for the war. Polish leaders repeatedly stressed Warsaw's support for NATO's war. Hungary, the only NATO country directly bordering Yugoslavia, agreed to allow NATO planes to use the Taszar airfield and the country's airspace for bombing and supply missions. The Czech Republic also approved fly-overs of NATO military aircraft engaged in the Kosovo war and donated a field hospital, unarmed transport planes, and relief supplies to assist refugees in Albania. In addition, the Czech Republic accepted several thousand refugees from Kosovo. Following the June cease-fire, the three countries announced plans to send token forces of less than 1,000 soldiers each, to be part of the NATO peacekeeping operation.

However, all three governments indicated certain unease with the NATO military operation. After the bombing began, there were demonstrations by the communist and other left-leaning parties, Slav ethnic organizations, and human rights activists in each country. The Hungarian government's decision to allow combat missions to be launched from its territory came despite weak public support and continued resistance from the Socialists, the largest opposition party. The Czech government was most lukewarm about the NATO operation, declaring its opposition to sending in ground troops; in May 1999, it even joined with Greece to set forth a peace proposal. After the war ended, Hungary, estimating that it had lost millions of dollars in trade because of the conflict, called on the international community to guarantee compensation in the form of contracts for rebuilding Kosovo. Worried particularly about the fate of the 350,000 Hungarians living in the northern Serb province of Vojvodina, the Budapest government stressed the importance of reaching a comprehensive settlement for the entire Balkans, rather than one narrowly confined to Kosovo.

NATO's war against Yugoslavia heightened unease about further expansion of the Alliance, its long term role and mission, and the precedent for international law and practice of military intervention without a threat of foreign aggression without UN approval. The was also heightened tensions with Russia, increasing rather than decreasing fears among Central and East Europeans. Moscow's initial reactions to the war were to denounce the bombing and threaten to train its nuclear weapons on any NATO state supporting the war. After Belgrade agreed to remove its forces from Kosovo, Russia unilaterally moved a small military unit into the airport at Pristina, the Kosovo capital, creating a temporary impasse with NATO. Almost simultaneously, the Russian armed forces began its largest military maneuvers in recent years. Although the military denied the exercises were linked to the war, the *Moscow Times* reported that they were "a sign that Russia remains deeply suspicious of NATO." In addition, the war triggered new demands within Russia for increased military spending.

The Kosovo war also raised the possibility that the European NATO members will increase their military spending. A number of these countries expressed unease about the military gap within NATO, their inability to match U.S. military capabilities, and their continued dependence on the United States. There have been renewed discussions about the establishment of a European military force under EU auspices, as well as proposals from Germany and some other countries for increased military spending. As NATO Secretary General Javier Solana stated in a June 1999 *Washington Post* interview, reshaping defense forces requires political will and harmonizing Europe's military industries, "but most of all it's a matter of money." Defense budgets will have to rise, he said, although "it's hard to say how much is enough."

Parallel with these pressures for increased military spending in Russia and Western Europe, a number of Central and East European countries, including the trio already admitted to NATO, had by mid-1999 begun scaling back or substantially delaying their ambitious plans to buy big ticket Western equipment like fighter planes. The Clinton administration had also decided to go a bit slower on new rounds of expansion, in large part due to concerns raised in Congress over the costs of expansion. And at least one subsidy program, the DELG, was targeted for elimination both by Pentagon bureaucrats and by key members of Congress. Despite the Clinton administration's efforts to claim Kosovo as a military success, sobering economic and political realities were casting doubts on the wisdom of NATO's new, more expansionist role.

U.S. POLICY IN THE BALKANS

Robert Greenberg

DURING THE COLD WAR, THE GEOPOLITICAL MAP OF THE BALKANS was relatively simple. Bulgaria and Romania were in the Soviet orbit; Albania was isolated and allied only with the People's Republic of China; while Greece leaned westward, first as part of NATO and later when it joined the European Economic Community as well. Yugoslavia under President Josip Broz Tito, occupied the greatest section of the Balkan Peninsula, and was officially nonaligned.

The United States interpreted Tito's stance as being staunchly anti-Soviet. Yugoslavia accepted Western overtures while at the same time maintaining its distance from NATO and the Western democracies. The stated U.S. policy remained to develop friendly relations with Yugoslavia, despite its communist ideology, in order to prop up an anti-Soviet regime bordering on three Warsaw Pact states.

After Tito's death in 1980, the United States largely ignored the rising tensions that were tearing the Yugoslav Federation apart. The Socialist Federal Republic of Yugoslavia consisted of six republics (Bosnia-Herzegovina, Croatia, Macedonia, Montenegro, Serbia, and Slovenia) and two autonomous provinces within Serbia (Kosovo and Vojvodina). The dominant ethnic groups in the republics were considered to be the Slavic "nations" of Yugoslavia; other non-Slavic ethnic groups—for example, Albanians, Turks, Hungarians—had the status of "nationalities" or "national minorities."

Already in 1981, the first serious challenge to Yugoslav stability was the outbreak of mass demonstrations in Kosovo, an autonomous province of Serbia where the Albanian majority demanded that Kosovo become a constituent republic of Yugoslavia. Fearing an upsurge in Albanian nationalism, the central authorities used violence to suppress the demonstrations. The Reagan administration, intent on prevailing over the Soviets, continued to support the central government in Belgrade despite its apparent human rights violations in Kosovo.

During the 1980s, Yugoslavia experienced a serious economic crisis, with rising inflation, increasing budget deficits, and a significant rise in foreign debt. Increased pressures from the IMF intensified the problems. The specter of Albanian nationalism and economic decline provided ideal conditions for Slobodan Milosevic to rise in the communist hierarchy of Serbia. In 1987, Milosevic rallied the Serbian people by using nationalist rhetoric, evoking the threat to Serbian sovereignty over Kosovo.

Milosevic used mass demonstrations as a tool for gaining power on the local level. Such demonstrations brought down governments in the Republic of Montenegro and then in the Serbian Autonomous Province of Vojvodina, both in 1988. After his election as the president of Serbia in 1989, Milosevic rescinded Kosovo's autonomous status and enacted direct Serbian rule in that province. The Croats, Slovenes, and Bosnian Muslims feared that Milosevic would seek to take over the entire country. In 1989, the Slovene parliament approved amendments to the republican constitution that provided for the right of Slovenia to secede from Yugoslavia. Serbia reacted harshly by imposing economic sanctions on Slovenia.

The rise of ethnic nationalism in Serbia sparked the revival of nationalist sentiments in Croatia, and in 1990 the Croats elected the nationalist Croatian Democratic Union to power, headed by Franjo Tudjman. Given these sharp nationalist internal divisions and the West's reluctance to support the integrity of the unified Yugoslav state, Yugoslavia's disintegration was now inevitable.

The Reagan and Bush administrations failed to respond to the rise of ethnic nationalism in the Balkans. As late as 1991, on the eve of Croatian and Slovene declarations of independence, Secretary of State James Baker reiterated U.S. support for the territorial integrity of a unified Yugoslavia. However, with the demise of the Soviet Union and the American government's preoccupations with the Persian Gulf, the Bush administration entrusted the West European powers to deal with the turmoil in Yugoslavia.

Western powers appeared to be ill-prepared for the outbreak of hostilities when Slovenia and Croatia declared their independence on June 25, 1991. The Europeans, following Germany's lead, pushed for early recognition of Slovenia and Croatia. This action, rather than preventing further bloodshed, resulted in the intensification of the war in Croatia. The Serbian population in Croatia, which the 1981 Yugoslav census estimated at 11.6 percent of the population, declared its independence from Croatia and set up the Republic of Serbian Krajina. Former U.S. Secretary of State Cyrus Vance helped to broker a cease-fire in Croatia, to be monitored by the UN. In the meantime, Bosnia-Herzegovina was inching closer and closer to the brink of civil war.

The winners of the 1990 elections in Bosnia were the three ethnic parties—the Serbian Democratic Party, the Croatian Democratic Union, and the Muslim-dominated Party for Democratic Action. The Serbs boycotted a referendum on Bosnian secession from Yugoslavia, and in early 1992, only several months after the recognition of Slovenia and Croatia, the United States and the members of the European Union recognized the Muslim-led government in Sarajevo.

Once again, early recognition precipitated ethnic conflict. The three sides had been on the verge of an agreement to divide Bosnia into three cantons, one for each of the ethnic groups. President Alija Izatbegovic of Bosnia, however, rejected this plan in his hope of preserving his power in a multiethnic Bosnia. As in Croatia, the Serbian minority sought to secede from Bosnia and link up with Serbia. Already in his presidential campaign in 1992, Bill Clinton declared his support for the Muslims in Bosnia. He advocated lifting this embargo (which the United Nations had imposed in 1991 on all sides in the Yugoslav conflicts) in order to arm the Muslims, who had the least access to Yugoslav heavy military equipment.

After Clinton took office, however, the war became much more complicated; the Serbs declared an independent Serb Republic in eastern and northwestern Bosnia, and the Croats declared an independent state in Herzegovina. The war now involved all three ethnic groups, and atrocities and civilian casualties mounted on all sides. Upon taking office, Clinton did not follow through on his promise to lift the arms embargo, and from the outset he continued the Bush administration's policy of refusing direct intervention. The Europeans took the lead in trying to negotiate a settlement. Their efforts included the Vance-Owen peace plan that would have divided Bosnia into ten, rather than three, cantons.

With Sarajevo under siege and news reports of concentration camps and ethnic cleansing spreading, U.S. and European policymakers realized the need for more active intervention. As in Croatia, the Western powers and the United States turned to the United Nations, which authorized humanitarian assistance for Sarajevo and set up safe havens to protect the Bosnian Muslim population. However, the Security Council, led by the United States, refused to expand the peacekeepers' mandate and numbers sufficiently to provide real safety. In 1995, two of the safe havens were overrun by Bosnian Serbs; the most notorious was the safe haven of Srebrenica, where the Serbs massacred thousands of Muslims. The Dutch contingent stationed at Srebrenica was only lightly armed and incapable of stopping the Serb onslaught or carrying out its mission to protect the civilian population. The UN's failure in maintaining the safe havens was used to justify the Clinton administration's decision to circumvent the UN and European security organizations, such as the Organization for Security and Cooperation in Europe (OSCE), in favor of NATO.

The Clinton administration blamed the Serbs and Milosevic for the wars in the former Yugoslavia and allied itself with the Croatian and Bosnian governments. The administration exerted pressure on Tudjman and Izatbegovic to halt the brutal Croat-Muslim conflict. American efforts resulted in the establishment of a Croat-Muslim Federation. American support for the federation strengthened perceptions among the Serbs that the United States was pursuing an anti-Serbian policy, and increased their resolve to continue the armed struggle.

Meanwhile, NATO became more actively involved through its enforcement of a no-fly zone in Bosnia. In 1995, with U.S. assistance, the Croatian military mounted a decisive military campaign against the Serbs of the Krajina region. Approximately 200,000 Serbs fled from the area around Knin and Western Slavonia. This defeat had significant implications for the Bosnian war, since having retaken Krajina, the Croats were in a position to attack the Bosnian Serbs in Bosnia from the north, and under combined Muslim-Croat pressure, the Bosnian Serbs began losing territory. In reaction to a Bosnian Serb rocket attack that killed scores of civilians in a Sarajevo marketplace, NATO carried out its threat to bomb the Bosnian Serbs. Faced with military defeats on the ground and NATO bombing from above, the Bosnian Serbs were brought to the negotiating table at Dayton, Ohio in November 1995.

The U.S. desire to intervene in Bosnia was motivated by political pressure caused by increased public alarm at the evolving humanitarian disaster. Throughout the period, Serbian claims were largely ignored, and Serb atrocities were widely condemned, while Muslim and Croat killings and ethnic cleansing were often minimized or overlooked. The Dayton Accords did not differ significantly from the original European plan to divide Bosnia into three cantons. A more even-handed approach would have taken into account legitimate concerns of all of Yugoslavia's ethnic groups and could have prevented the violent disintegration of the country.

NATO's involvement in the Bosnian war represented the alliance's first-ever offensive action. Perhaps even more significantly, this action was taken outside of NATO's area of operations and did not directly serve to protect a NATO country from an aggressor. This signaled an undeclared shift in NATO's mission in a post-Soviet Europe, which NATO chief Javier Solana officially outlined in April 1999, as NATO prepared its fiftieth-year celebration in Washington and its second offensive action in its history, in Yugoslavia. Such a strategic policy implies that NATO alone—not the UN, the OSCE, or the EU—could secure the peace of Europe.

During the Bosnian war, the Western powers imposed economic sanctions against the Federal Republic of Yugoslavia, with the aim of weakening the Milosevic regime in Serbia and punishing Serbia for its support of the Bosnian Serbs and Croatian Serbs. Yet the United States was negotiating directly with Milosevic to reach a solution for the Bosnian war and authorized him to negotiate on behalf of the Bosnian Serbs at Dayton. In return for his cooperation, the United States lifted the economic sanctions against Yugoslavia and relied on Milosevic as a guarantor of the Dayton peace agreement. But the sanctions had resulted in a dramatic worsening of living standards for all citizens of Yugoslavia, regardless of ethnicity. Sanctions helped criminal and antidemocratic elements prosper, and certainly did not create a positive backdrop for ethnic reconciliation between Serbs and Albanians.

In the early 1990s, the Kosovo Albanians set up a shadow government under the leadership of Ibrahim Rugova, who promoted nonviolent means for attaining eventual independence. Having made little progress toward these goals, the Albanians became increasingly frustrated. Tension in Kosovo rose dramatically when the Kosovo Liberation Army (KLA) emerged in 1997 with its declared aim of achieving the Kosovo Albanians' political aspirations for independence through armed struggle. Violence broke out in early 1998, initially between Serbian police units and the KLA forces. According to unofficial reports, by October 1998 approximately 2,000 Albanians and Serbs had been killed and some 200,000 people, mainly Albanians, had been displaced.

In the summer of 1998, the United States and European Union reimposed sanctions on Yugoslavia and threatened to bomb Serbian positions if the violence persisted. Once again they blamed the Serbs for the deteriorating situation and singled out Milosevic as the main culprit. In October 1998, U.S. special envoy Richard Holbrooke negotiated a cease-fire and a Serbian pullback from Kosovo. The truce was to be guaranteed by up to 2,000 unarmed monitors under the auspices of the OSCE. In the vacuum of the Serbian military withdraw, the KLA took over many of their positions. During the first few months the OSCE monitors successfully managed to contain violence between the KLA and Serbian paramilitary forces. However, by January there were some serious skirmishes, leading to some calls for sending in greater numbers of OSCE monitors.

In February, the United States brought both sides to the negotiating table at Rambouillet, France, and worked hard to impose a settlement on the two reluctant sides. The U.S.-orchestrated plan sidelined both the United Nations and the OSCE and placed NATO in a new role outside both its traditional strategic mandate and its territory of operation. Under the terms of the agreement, a NATO-led international force was to be given access to operate in all of Yugoslavia, not only in Kosovo. It also included a provision for a referendum to be held in Kosovo after three years to determine the province's future political status. After much arm twisting the Albanians signed the agreement. The Serbs were presented with an ultimatum: sign an agreement that would have brought about the end of Serbian control over Kosovo or be bombed. When the Serbs refused to sign, NATO followed through on its threats to bomb Yugoslavia. On March 24, 1999, President Clinton declared that he had ordered the bombing in order to save the Kosovo Albanians from Serbian aggression and to prevent the Kosovo conflict from spreading to Macedonia. Such a development could have potentially resulted in a wider regional war involving two NATO countries—Greece and Turkey.

The bombing campaign lasted 79 days. It devastated the Yugoslav economy, destroyed bridges, factories, oil refineries, government buildings, the environment, and Yugoslav military equipment. It also accelerated, rather than prevented, ethnic killing of Albanians in Kosovo and caused unnecessary civilian deaths and destruction in Serbia and Montenegro. The casualty figures are staggering; unofficial reports suggest that some 850,000 Albanians fled or were expelled from Kosovo, around 10,000 Albanian civilians were killed, and thousands of Yugoslav soldiers and civilians lost their lives.

In June, through the efforts of Finnish and Russian intermediaries, Milosevic finally agreed to withdraw the Yugoslav army and Serbian police units from Kosovo. The agreement provided for 50,000 international troops, with "significant" NATO participation and, different from Rambouillet, under UN mandate, to occupy Kosovo and guarantee a safe return of Albanian refugees. Unlike Rambouillet, the terms for peace did not include a referendum to determine the future of Kosovo, but instead guaranteed that Kosovo would have broad autonomy within Yugoslavia.

In the days following the agreement, the balance of power between NATO and the UN for ultimate authority over the peacekeeping forces became a point of contention. Russia, China, and Yugoslavia, among others, insisted that the UN should take command; the United States remained adamant that NATO be at the core. Ultimately NATO assumed command of the multinational force, under a mandate from the UN Security Council.

Overall, the United States chose to intervene in the Balkans more out of frustration with Milosevic rather than after careful planning. However, the Clinton administration's initial disregard for the UN Security Council, despite unequivocal requirements in the UN Charter specifying that only the council can authorize the use of force against a sovereign state, serves as a dangerous precedent. The choice of a military alliance such as NATO, rather than a political/diplomatic one, as the instrument to both legitimate and implement the U.S.-led air war encourages military solutions to future conflicts, while threatening the primacy of the UN in peace and security issues.

While Dayton and the Kosovo agreement have stopped the fighting, they have not included frameworks for ethnic reconciliation or multiethnic societies. At the end of the twentieth century, the challenges in the Balkans remain daunting. Tensions remain high in both Albania and Macedonia. Nationalism continues to fester in Croatia, Bosnia-Herzegovina, Serbia, Albania, and Macedonia. Montenegro has threatened to secede from Yugoslavia, and the Muslims of the Sandzak feel threatened in Serbia. Policy should be directed toward finding a regional solution to these problems. The Western powers need to take an unequivocal stand against nationalist leaders and movements on all sides and provide real incentives for the peoples of the Balkans to embark on the path of reconciliation and civil societies.

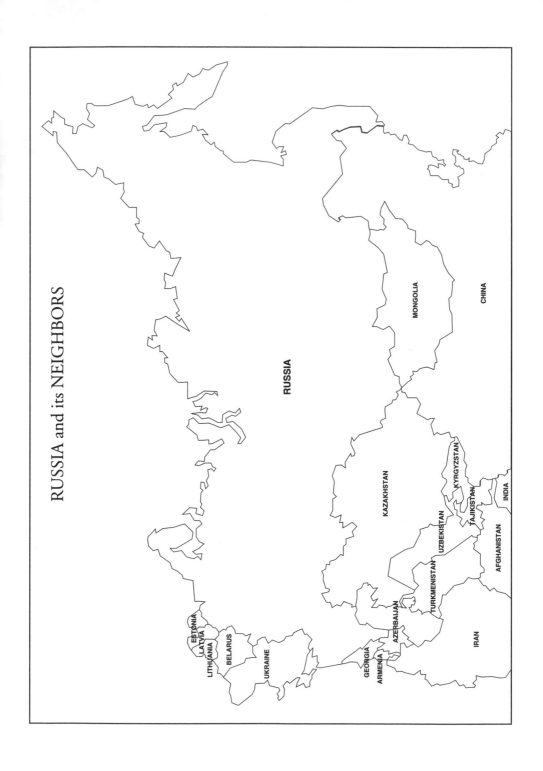

RUSSIA and its NEIGHBORS

CHAPTER 9

CONTAINMENT LITE: U.S. POLICY TOWARD RUSSIA AND ITS NEIGHBORS

John Feffer

IF THE U.S. GOVERNMENT HAD WANTED TO DESTROY RUSSIA from the inside out, it could not have devised a more effective policy than its so-called strategic partnership. From aggressive foreign policy, to misguided economic advice, to undemocratic influence-peddling, the United States has ushered in a cold peace on the heels of the cold war. Containment remains the centerpiece of U.S. policy toward Russia. But it is a "soft" containment. It is Containment Lite.

On the foreign policy front, for instance, Containment Lite has consisted of a three-tiered effort to isolate Russia from: its neighbors, Europe, and the international community more generally. The Clinton administration's policy of "geopolitical pluralism," designed to strengthen key neighbors such as Ukraine and Kazakhstan, has driven wedges into the loose confederation of post-Soviet states. By pushing ahead recklessly with expansion of the North Atlantic Treaty Organization (NATO), the U.S. government is deepening the divide that separates Russia from Europe, effectively building a new iron curtain down the middle of Eurasia. Instead of consulting with Russia over key foreign policy issues such as the Iraq bombings and allied policy toward the former Yugoslavia, Washington has attempted to steer Moscow into a diplomatic backwater where it can exert little global influence.

Part of this three-tiered foreign policy of "soft" containment has been to eliminate Russia's last claim to superpower status—its nuclear arsenal—without providing sufficient funds for mothballing the weapons and without pursuing commensurate reductions in U.S. stockpiles. By implementing a missile defense system, the United States has put several arms control treaties in jeopardy; by opposing key sales of Russian military technology, arguing that these sales would lead to arms proliferation, while itself continuing to export weapons technology, the United States has applied a double standard. By announcing the largest increase in the military budget since the end of the cold war, the Clinton administration began 1999 with a clear signal that Russia's decline would have little effect on the Pentagon's appetite.

Although Russia's geopolitical fortunes have been grim, its economic position is even grimmer. In 1992, while implementing Russia's first market reforms, President Boris Yeltsin predicted that good times were just around the corner. This corner has retreated further and further into the distance (particularly after the crisis of August 1998, when the ruble went into free fall and Moscow defaulted on its treasury debt). Today, Russia's gross domestic product (GDP) is half what it was ten years ago. The government is suffocating under $150 billion in foreign debt, some $100 billion of which was inherited from the Soviet Union. Between 1996 and 1998, Russia's foreign debt grew approximately $20 billion. Barter has reemerged as a dominant mode of economic transaction.[1] Workers are paid in kind when they are paid at all. Poverty is rampant. Life expectancy is dipping, the population is declining, and Russia is flirting with third world status.

Economic reform in Russia has not only been unsuccessful, it has been profoundly undemocratic. By collaborating almost exclusively with Boris Yeltsin and his handpicked "reformers"—and circumventing Russia's popularly elected legislature, the Duma—the Clinton administration placed expediency over accountability, transparency, and the checks and balances of a truly democratic system. The international community poured billions of dollars into Russia, money that did not trickle down but was instead diverted into the pockets of a select few. The result was a crony capitalism far more pronounced than anything on show in Asia: all the corruption with none of the growth.

Under its cold war containment policy, the United States relied on aggressive rhetoric and military might to confront a powerful Soviet Union. By contrast, today's Containment Lite takes advantage of Russia's economic and military weakness and, at first glance, has relied more on carrots than sticks. In reality, however, the United States has wielded these carrots much like cudgels. Washington's aid and investments, expert advice, and high-profile workshops are designed to reduce the military and diplomatic reach of its erstwhile superpower rival and to remake the Russian economy in the neoliberal image regardless of the social costs. Prodded by these carrots, Russia is moving along a path that has led to economic chaos and escalating resentment.

The Clinton administration is acutely aware of the dangers of a Russian implosion. Yet the administration has crafted policies that are inexorably leading to the realization of its own worst fears.

ROOTS OF U.S. POLICY

For the better part of the twentieth century, U.S. policy toward the Soviet Union fluctuated between aggressive confrontation and brief attempts at détente. During their respective eras, Harry Truman and Ronald Reagan were bent on containing the Soviet Union and, when possible, rolling back its influence in East Europe and the third world. Richard Nixon, without compromising his anticommunism, managed in the 1970s to ease tensions between East and West with a mixture of arms control measures and modest openings in the East for Western business. In the cold war period, confrontation and engagement often followed one another with little breathing room, as in John Kennedy's near-apocalyptic showdown with Nikita Khrushchev over Cuba in 1962 followed by the negotiation of the first major arms control treaty with the Soviet Union in 1963. Whether in confrontation or détente mode, however, successive U.S. administrations sought (often unsuccessfully) to limit Soviet influence in the world and blunt the impact of communism.

Beginning in 1985, when the Soviet Union began a complex dance of reform and decline, the Reagan and Bush administrations did little to encourage the former and much to hasten the latter. True, Washington slowly came around to supporting glasnost and perestroika rhetorically. But during this period, the United States largely withheld economic support for perestroika while continuing to maintain high levels of military spending and provocative rhetoric. From 1989 to 1991, the Soviet Union's terminal stage, Washington switched to damage-control mode in order to preserve the newly independent countries of East Europe, pressure the Soviet Union to back German unification, and prevent conflict from flaring up over the secession of the Baltic states.

In 1992, after the official collapse of the Soviet Union, the new Russian president, Boris Yeltsin, ushered in a "honeymoon" period with the United States. Yeltsin and his pro-Western foreign minister, Andrei Kozyrev, proceeded to follow the U.S. lead on arms control, economic reform, and global politics. The other leaders of the Commonwealth of Independent States (CIS)—notably Ukraine's Leonid Kravchuk, Georgia's Eduard Shevardnadze, and Kazakhstan's Nursultan Nazarbaev—largely followed suit, each competing for the affections and favors of the United States. In return, the United States promised to help Russia and the other CIS nations integrate into the global economy and later, through the Partnership for Peace, into European security structures. (See figure 9–1.)

The honeymoon did not last long. Russia never received the Marshall Plan it had hoped for. Nor did the U.S. government make room at the world's table for the new Russian entity. (The seven largest economic powers, the Group of Seven [G-7], extended membership to Russia, but this was largely a symbolic gesture.) As a result, the pro-Western faction in the Russian foreign policy establishment lost influence and Russian national interest became the new organizing principle for the Yeltsin team. The bloody and inconclusive 1994 to 1996 war in Chechnya, followed by the Russian army's autumn 1999 reinvasion of the separatist province; the refusal to atify the Start II strategic arms reduction treaty; and the elevating of relations with Serbia, Iran, and Iraq signified a change in Russian policy. For its part, the United States maintained support for Yeltsin personally but gradually withdrew from close bilateral relations. Washington strengthened relations with the other CIS nations to cover its bets and to balance Russian power in the region.

As Sergei Rogov, the head of Moscow's U.S. and Canada Institute, has remarked, the U.S. government's rhetoric toward Russia has changed from "strategic partnership," to "pragmatic partnership," to "realistic partnership," to just

Figure 9.1

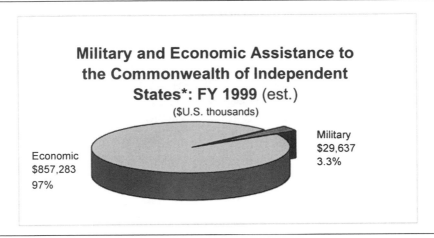

Source: Secretary of State, *Congressional Presentation for Foreign Operations, Fiscal Year 2000* (Washington, DC: Department of State, 1999).
*Lithuania, Latvia, and Estonia never joined the CIS and comprise the remainder of the former Soviet Union countries known collectively as the New Independent States (NIS).

plain realism—a realism that aims to minimize the impact of Russia's economic and military collapse on the world at large.[2] The partnership is gone, and this change in rhetoric is mirrored very concretely in a range of issues from security to economics to politics.

SECURITY ISSUES

At one time, Russia was the preoccupation of U.S. foreign policy analysts and intelligence agencies. Beginning in the 1950s, the Soviet Union underwrote anti-colonial revolts throughout the third world and provided significant aid to countries ranging from Cuba and Angola to Syria and India. Today, Russia's importance has dwindled considerably. It no longer plays a role in the developing world. It has scant influence in East Europe. Closer to home, it has retained certain ambitions—to maintain the integrity of its own territory (as in Chechnya) and to maintain influence in its "near abroad" (i.e., Belarus, Ukraine, Georgia, and Moldova). But its ambitions outstrip its capacity, as the losses in Chechnya and peacekeeping failures in the "near abroad" suggest.

The truth is, the Russian military is in dire condition—the size of its armed forces cut by a quarter in 1998, its weapons systems in deteriorating condition, and few funds available for new acquisitions. (By 2005, according to current trends, only 5 to 7 percent of Russia's military equipment will be new.)[3] The U.S. State Department acknowledges that the Russian army's combat readiness is in "rapid decay."[4] The morale of the army is even lower now than at the time of the Chechen campaign. As for Russia's ability (or desire) to project force beyond its borders, little Estonia recently declared that its giant neighbor was no longer a military threat.[5] Even its nuclear arsenal, the one card that keeps Russia in the game, is deteriorating rapidly. Russia is contained, quite literally, by its own weakness.

The United States, particularly through the vehicle of NATO expansion, is taking advantage of this weakness. NATO was designed to deter Soviet expansion into Europe. The Soviet Union is no more, and Russia desperately wants to join Europe, not invade it. Yet without an enemy in sight, NATO is marching right up to Russia's door. In April 1999, Poland, the Czech Republic, and Hungary became NATO's first new members since Spain in 1982. Fifteen countries now belong to the Partnership for Peace (PfP) program, a halfway entry house for NATO candidates that need help in modernizing their militaries. Virtually every country in the former Soviet bloc supports NATO expansion, partly because of NATO's own aggressive public relations campaign and partly as a first step toward joining the European Union. Lacking NATO's high profile are two institutions formed at the 1990 Paris Summit to reduce cold war tensions: the Treaty on Conventional Armed Forces in Europe (CFE), which includes NATO and former Warsaw Pact member states, and the Organization of Security and Cooperation in Europe (OSCE), a far more inclusive institution committed to conflict prevention and the protection of human rights. Both the CFE and OSCE have been sidelined, largely through U.S. maneuvers to restrict its scope and funding. (See figures 9–2 and 9–3.)

Throughout the ups and downs of U.S.-Russian relations in the 1990s, Russia has considered NATO expansion a deliberate provocation, particularly when expansion has potentially included Ukraine and the Baltic states. The United States has responded to Russia's concerns with two initiatives. First, it extended membership to Russia in the PfP program. Then, promising a "special relationship," NATO concluded an accord with Moscow in May 1997 that established various mechanisms of consultation. The accord does not give either party the right to veto the actions of the other, but through the Permanent Joint Council (PJC), the two sides are supposed to meet regularly.

The PJC has been largely window dressing. The Russians have not taken it particularly seriously, and the United States has not used the mechanism to involve Russia in key foreign policy discussions. Russia has a long list of grievances on this score (some that predate the PJC), for the United States did not consult the Russians regarding air strikes against Libya (1993), Serbs in Bosnia (1994), Iraq (1995, 1996, 1998), and suspected terrorist facilities in Sudan and Afghanistan (1998). Most recently, the United States and NATO ignored Russia's attempts to prevent the conflict from escalating in Kosovo. NATO's bombing campaign failed to prevent the ethnic cleansing of Albanians; it killed many Serbian and Albanian civilians; it hobbled the democratic opposition in Serbia. With several NATO countries desperate for a diplomatic solution, Russia reentered the picture as a credible mediator, but still the United States was reluctant to take its proposals seriously.

Consultation is not Russia's only concern. The expansion of both NATO and the Partnership for Peace means a remilitarization along Russia's borders. The new NATO members will be modernizing their militaries substantially. PfP members,

Figure 9.2   Countries Participating in European Military Organizations

State	CFE[1]	NATO[2]	OSCE[1]	PfP[2]
Albania	✓		✓	✓
Andorra			✓	
Armenia			✓	✓
Austria			✓	✓
Azerbaijan			✓	✓
Belarus			✓	✓
Belgium	✓	✓	✓	
Bosnia and Herzegovina			✓	
Bulgaria	✓		✓	✓
Canada	✓	✓	✓	
Croatia			✓	
Cyprus			✓	
Czech Republic[a]	✓	✓[a]	✓	
Denmark	✓	✓	✓	
Estonia			✓	✓
Finland			✓	✓
France	✓	✓	✓	
Georgia			✓	✓
Germany	✓	✓	✓	
Greece	✓	✓	✓	
Holy See			✓	
Hungary[a]	✓	✓[a]	✓	
Iceland	✓	✓	✓	
Ireland			✓	
Italy	✓	✓	✓	
Kazakstan			✓	✓
Kyrgyzstan			✓	✓
Latvia			✓	✓
Liechtenstein			✓	
Lithuania			✓	✓
Luxembourg	✓	✓	✓	
Malta			✓	
Moldova			✓	✓
Monaco			✓	
Netherlands	✓	✓	✓	
Norway	✓	✓	✓	
Poland[a]	✓	✓[a]	✓	
Portugal	✓	✓	✓	
Romania	✓		✓	✓
Russian Federation	✓		✓	✓
San Marino			✓	
Slovakia	✓		✓	✓
Slovenia			✓	✓
Spain	✓	✓	✓	
Sweden			✓	✓

(continues)

Figure 9.2 Countries Participating in European Military Organizations

State	CFE[1]	NATO[2]	OSCE[1]	PfP[2]
Switzerland			✓	✓
Tajikistan			✓	✓
The Former Yugoslav Republic of Macedonia			✓	
Turkey	✓	✓	✓	
Turkmenistan			✓	✓
Ukraine			✓	✓
United Kingdom	✓	✓	✓	
United States of America	✓	✓	✓	
Uzbekistan			✓	✓
Yugoslavia (suspended from participation since 7/8/1992)			✓	

Source: Compiled from *The NATO Handbook 50th Anniversary Edition* (Brussels: NATO Information Service, 1998). Available on the Internet at: http://www.nato.int.

[a]Three former Warsaw Pact nations—Hungary, Poland, and the Czech Republic—were formally admitted to NATO in March 1999. Sen. William Roth (R-Del), president of the North Atlantic Assembly, made up of lawmakers from NATO countries, urged NATO to invite Slovenia as the next member and suggested Lithuania and Slovakia as the other most qualified countries to join NATO. Since Lithuania would be the first Baltic state that was part of the former Soviet Union to join NATO, some NATO members strongly objected, suggesting that its geographic location would preclude defense by conventional forces and would aggravate relations with Russia. Other countries applying for NATO membership are Romania, Albania, Bulgaria, Estonia, Latvia, and the former Yugoslav republic of Macedonia.

which include strife-torn Georgia and Moldova, have access to free U.S. "hand-me-downs" that substantially increase the threat of conflict in the region.[6] From Russia's perspective, NATO is expanding not just territorially but conceptually as well. Secretary of State Madeleine Albright has called for NATO to "move beyond a narrow definition of mutual defense" and take action without Security Council mandates.[7] She intends to enlarge NATO's sphere of potential action to include the Middle East and central Africa.[8] By encroaching even more on UN functions, NATO, in its new role, would enable the United States to act without concern for Russia's veto in the Security Council.

On the arms control front, meanwhile, the Clinton administration is doing little to balance NATO expansion with a commitment to mutual disarmament. Russian ratification of the START II treaty, for instance, was one of the many victims of U.S. military strikes on Iraq in December 1998. The U.S. government did not notify Russia or the UN Security Council before launching the attacks. In retaliation, the Russian Duma suspended debate just hours before the treaty was expected to be ratified. Arms control aside, Russia's nuclear force is declining daily. It is estimated that the Russian arsenal will fall below 1,000 warheads simply as systems are retired. Without START II, which puts a cap of 3,000 to 3,500

Figure 9.3   Description of European Military Treaties and Organizations

NATO	The North Atlantic Treaty was signed in Washington on April 4, 1949, creating an alliance of 12 independent nations committed to each other's defense. Four more European nations later acceded to the treaty between 1952 and 1982. On March 12, 1999, the Czech Republic, Hungary, and Poland were introduced in the North Atlantic Treaty Organization (NATO), which now has 19 members.
CFE	Treaty on Conventional Armed Forces in Europe (CFE), was signed at the Paris Summit on November 19, 1990, by NATO member states and the former Warsaw Pact states.[a] The treaty was intended to reduce tensions between the two rival organizations by placing a ceiling on conventional arms levels in Europe for both sides. Specifically, the CFE provides for a three-year deadline on troop reduction and defines inspection and verification procedures.
OSCE	The Charter of Paris for a New Europe, signed at the Paris Summit (November 19–21, 1990), began the institutionalization of the Conference on Security and Cooperation in Europe (CSCE) and was hailed as the official end to the cold war. The CSCE became a formal organization at the beginning of 1995. It has 55 members, including all European states, the United States, and Canada.[b]
PfP	In January 1994, the states participating in the then North Atlantic Cooperation Council (NACC) and other member countries of OSCE were invited to develop cooperative military relations with NATO, under the Partnership for Peace (PfP) program, for the purpose of joint planning, training, and exercises, in order to undertake missions in the field of peacekeeping, seach and rescue, humanitarian operations, and others as may subsequently be agreed.[c]

Sources: The NATO Handbook: 50th Anniversary Edition (Brussels: NATO Information Service, 1998). Available on the Internet at: http://www.nato.int.
[a]Original Warsaw Pact: Between the People's Republic of Albania, the People's Republic of Bulgaria, the Hungarian People's Republic, the German Democratic Republic, the Polish People's Republic, the Romanian People's Republic, the Union of Soviet Socialist Republics, and the Czechoslovak Republic, May 1, 1955. Following the dissolution of the Soviet Union (with the eight states with territory in the CFE zone succeeding from the Soviet Union), the unification of Germany, and the separation between the Czech and Slovak Republics, the number of CFE states parties changed from 22 to 30.
[b]"OSCE Participating States." Available on the Internet at: http://www.osce.org/e/partstat.htm.
[c]The Framework Document also states that a country's active participation in the Partnership for Peace will play an important role in gaining membership to NATO.

warheads on each side, the United States could remain at 6,000 warheads.[9] With the treaty, the United States will destroy warheads and Russia will destroy missiles, an asymmetry that puts Russia at a strategic disadvantage.[10] Although START II is in this sense a double bind for Russia, many Russian politicians still hope to ratify the treaty in order to salvage good relations with the United States, keep the aid flowing, and prepare for more significant disarmament initiatives such as START III. (See figure 9–4.)

Figure 9.4   Russian[a] and U.S. Nulear Arsenals

	Russia	U.S.
Strategic Warheads	5,972	7,200
Total Nuclear Weapons	22,500	12,070

Sources: William M. Arkin, Robert S. Norris, and Joshua Handler, *Taking Stock: Worldwide Nuclear Deployments 1998* (Washington, DC: Natural Resources Defense Council, 1998); Robert S. Norris and William M. Arkin, "U.S. Strategic Nuclear Forces, End of 1998," *Nuclear Notebook*, January/February 1999; Robert S. Norris and William M. Arkin, "Russian Strategic Nuclear Forces, End of 1998," *Nuclear Notebook*, March/April 1999.
[a]Russia has also received deliveries of all nuclear weapons stationed in the former Soviet republics of Kazakhstan, Ukraine, and Belarus.

Another challenge to current and future reductions in strategic arms is the Clinton administration's desire to modify—or perhaps even scuttle—the Anti-Ballistic Missile (ABM) treaty in order to pave the way for a new national missile defense system. Many Russian experts have declared the ABM treaty linked to START II—if the first dies, so will the second.[11] The Clinton administration favors "modification," but opponents such as powerful Republican Senator Jesse Helms of North Carolina have called for scrapping the treaty.[12] The Pentagon reportedly offered Moscow a disturbing quid pro quo on the ABM issue: If Russia looks the other way while the United States develops a missile defense system, Washington will allow Russia to deploy new strategic missiles with three warheads.[13] Although at peace with one another, paradoxically the two countries are moving away from arms control and toward arms augmentation.

Meanwhile, the lion's share of U.S. aid to Russia is directed toward the containment and dismantling of its weapons, much of it through the Cooperative Threat Reduction (CTR) program. In his 1999 State of the Union address, Clinton called for a 70 percent increase in funds to help Russia dismantle nuclear warheads and enhance control of its fissionable material.[14] The U.S. government is understandably concerned about the potential for Russia's nuclear weapons to circulate on the world's black market. For FY 2000 Congress appropriated $460.5 million for the CTR program, but eliminated $130 million, thereby zeroing out all funding for destruction of Russian stocks of chemical weapons. Disarmament communities in both countries are justifiably delighted to witness the destruction (and not the mere limitation) of nuclear weapons. But the funds provided by the Clinton administration are not sufficient even to pay for the implementation of START II, much less to cover the full range of arms control measures that the United States and Russia are—or should be—considering. This means that a cash-strapped Russia must pay for its own humbling, and the disarmament process is regrettably slowed.

ECONOMIC COLLAPSE

The economic system bequeathed by the Soviet Union to Russia was more a burden than a benefit. Although the Soviet Union had achieved remarkable growth rates in the immediate postwar era, the economy entered a long period of stagnation in the 1970s that lasted into the Gorbachev era. Mikhail Gorbachev unshackled Soviet culture and injected new life into the Soviet political system, but he was not successful in reviving the Soviet economy, which had deteriorated into barter, corruption, inefficiency, and mismanagement.

With the collapse of the Soviet Union and the rise of Russia came the promise of a new direction. In 1992, after introducing market reforms virtually overnight, Boris Yeltsin predicted results in less than a year. The U.S. government joined in the chorus of support. Despite rosy predictions, however, the Russian economy has only gone downhill since. Industrial production has plummeted, as has the standard of living for most Russians. A sharp divide between rich and poor has opened up, with 70 to 80 percent of Russians at or below subsistence level. Homelessness, particularly of children, is widespread in the large cities, and pensioners have grave problems making ends meet. And if it is bad in the big cities, it is even worse in most regions where public services have fallen apart and conditions have reverted to the nineteenth century.

In August 1998, with oil prices plummeting, the Asian financial crisis dealt yet another blow to the Russian economy. Real GDP fell by nearly 5 percent in 1998, with a similar drop expected in 1999.[15] Annual inflation is expected to go into triple digits in 1999.[16] Even nature has not cooperated: in 1998, Russia suffered its worst harvest in over 40 years.[17] In the wake of the August crisis, the International Monetary Fund (IMF) suspended its latest package of aid, and in February 1999, Standard and Poor's gave Russia a de facto default rating because the country did not meet its interest payments.[18] (See figure 9–5.) By early 1999, conditions had deteriorated so much that many Russians viewed the Brezhnev period, a notorious era of stagnation, as a "golden age."[19]

In September 1998, former Foreign Minister Yevgeny Primakov took over the reins of power as prime minister. Considered a consummate politician with a preference for state intervention in the economy, Primakov was hard-pressed to use the mechanisms of the central government to solve Russia's problems. With a huge foreign debt, a good portion inherited from the Soviet days, Russia is caught in the third world development trap of constantly falling behind in servicing its debt. The international community, led by the United States, is dictating fiscal conservatism, which makes Keynesian deficit spending impossible. Meanwhile, Russia's federal government cannot collect the taxes necessary to keep it afloat. (The major players are the worst offenders—the huge energy company Gazprom, for instance, owed the federal government approximately $1.9 billion as of July 1998.)[20] Although criticized in the West for its creeping statism, the government under Primakov's direction often tilted in the supply-side direction: its economic plan called for reducing the profit tax from 35 percent to 30 percent and cutting the value added tax (VAT).

The U.S. government is not doing much to help Russia rebuild its industries. For instance, the Clinton administration has threatened to restrict imports of cheap Russian steel, which would cost the Russian steel industry an estimated $1 billion in sales.[21] The United States has threatened to undercut the Russian space industry, one of the few world-class showpieces it has left, and has sought to con-

Figure 9.5

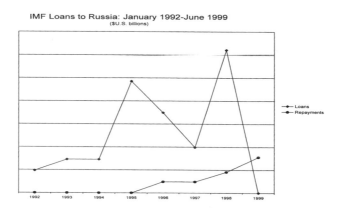

IMF Loans to Russia: January 1992-June 1999
($U.S. billions)

Loans
Repayments

1992 1993 1994 1995 1996 1997 1998 1999

Source: Constructed from IMF data. Available on the Internet at: http://www.imf.org/external/np/tre/tad/expurch1.cfm.

tain the expansion of Russia's energy interests in the Caspian region. Although U.S. sanctions against Russia for selling military technology to Iran are laudable from the nonproliferation point of view, Washington has simply not provided enough in conversion assistance so that Russia's military-industrial complex can redirect its production toward domestic needs. (Currently, with an arms export strategy based on selling sophisticated weaponry at low prices, Russia has climbed back to become the second largest supplier in the world and is challenging the United States for the top spot.)[22]

Whenever the Russian government has made noises about reining in the more destructive aspects of markets, Washington has provided stern lectures.[23] Secretary of State Madeleine Albright, for instance, wondered aloud to a business group in October 1998 whether the Primakov team, in "turning back the clock," truly understood "the basic arithmetic of the global economy."[24] The "basic arithmetic" in this case applied not only to the laws of supply and demand but also to the sheer amount of money the United States could withhold if Primakov and company departed from the IMF recipe.

In urging remedial economics courses and praising the IMF's role in the Russian reform process, Albright and company seem to have forgotten that they had already identified a group of radical market enthusiasts willing to abide by the international community's guidelines. Indeed, with their intimate knowledge of the basic arithmetic of the global economy, these Russian reformers robbed the international lenders blind.

This clique of Russian economists and bureaucrats came to the fore in 1992 when the West applied the policies of "shock therapy" developed in East Europe to the already shaky post-Soviet economy. Shock therapy involved a rapid destruction of the old system and the substitution of neoliberalism (also known as the Washington Consensus). Price controls were lifted practically overnight. Because the state did not simultaneously disband the monopolized production and distribution system, the result was hyperinflation and the destruction of personal savings. Incomes fell. Russian industry had its feet knocked out from under it. Agricultural production dropped. In came a flood of imports that few could afford.

The shock therapists, who administered all shock and very little therapy, were a select crew. On the American side were Jeffrey Sachs, director of the Harvard Institute for International Development (HIID), and his contacts in the Clinton administration, such as Lawrence Summers and David Lipton, both in the Treasury Department. (Summers replaced Robert Rubin as Treasury Secretary in July 1999.)[25] Chief among the Russian "reformers" was Anatoly Chubais. The Harvard Project wrote the new Russian laws; Chubais and his cronies happily bilked the Russian public. Political analyst Boris Kagarlitsky, in testimony before the U.S. Congress after the August 1998 crisis, cited many examples of this misuse of international funds, including the Russian Central Bank's "bacchanalia of waste" and the $5 billion from the World Bank (intended to restructure the coal industry) that "simply disappeared."[26] In February 1999, Moscow was abuzz with news of up to $50 billion that the Russian Central Bank had secreted overseas in a shell company on the island of Jersey.[27] Estimates of capital flight over the last seven years range from $50 billion to as high as $230 billion.[28]

The newly emerging business sector also participated in the "bacchanalia." One mechanism for this monumental theft was the handover of thousands of enterprises to insiders rather than to the public at large. In 1995, Chubais presided over this loans-for-shares privatization, which distributed Russia's best and brightest enterprises to its worst and most corrupt "red capitalists." Oil companies such as Surgutneftegaz and Sidanko went for bargain-basement prices. Many privatized companies fell under the control of organized crime syndicates. Chubais's attitude toward the diversion of aid to shadowy business types was to "let them steal," for money would transform the crooks into legitimate capitalists.[29]

The shell game continues today. As political scientist Michael McFaul writes, "Through complex arbitrage schemes, the withholding of wages, and the use of parasitic 'offshore' companies . . . directors can amass individual wealth while their companies continue to operate in the red."[30] No wonder the average Russian thinks that capitalism is by definition *dikii*, or savage. And the culprits? The U.S. General Accounting Office, investigating HIID's activities in Russia, determined that at least two directors—Andre Shleifer and Jonathan Hay—had used their inside connections for personal profit. (Both were fired.) Chubais, meanwhile, became head of Russia's electricity monopoly, United Energy Systems of Russia.

The motives for Washington's insistence on Russia's swift, monetarist transition to capitalism are complex. U.S. economists and politicians, in cooperation with the IMF, focused on a single method for untangling from communism, a model developed and applied in Poland with mixed success. The Bush and Clinton administrations were also suspicious of allowing the Russian state to play a stronger role in economic recovery because of their residual antipathy toward any state authority emanating from the Kremlin. By acting quickly, the Western advisors expected to get the worst of the transition over before the public could vote the "reformers" out of office. (Economic pain is rarely popular at the polls.) And the U.S. government, pressured by business interests, wanted to establish a playing field in Russia that benefited U.S. commercial interests, particularly in the energy and mining sectors.

U.S. businesses are interested in Russia for very good reasons. Russia has an educated workforce, a strategic location straddling two continents, and a generous supply of natural resources, including gold and timber. But energy is the true jewel in the Russian crown. Oil and natural gas currently represent 60 percent of Russian exports and 25 percent of federal revenues. Even with the fall in energy prices, Russia can parlay its resources into hard currency—if the profits do not accrue principally to foreign companies, and if the U.S. government stops trying to undercut the future expansion of Russian energy interests in the Caspian Sea.

A good deal of oil lies beneath the Caspian Sea. The problems in getting that oil to market are manifold, not the least being the countries surrounding the potential oil fields—Azerbaijan, Iran, Kazakhstan, and Turkmenistan. Russia wants to work with the latter three countries to build a pipeline that (at least in part) runs through Russia. In that way, it can maintain an interest in the region. The United States, meanwhile, has exerted heavy pressure on a consortium of 11 major oil companies to build a 1,400-mile pipeline from Baku in Azerbaijan to Ceyhan in southern Turkey, skirting Russia altogether.

The U.S. plan suffers from numerous problems. The original estimates of 178 billion barrels are now thought by independent experts to be closer to 17.8 billion (a problem compounded by the current buyers' market). The estimated cost of the pipeline has recently risen by another $1 billion. The pipeline would pass through a very unstable Georgia, home to major insurgencies in Abkhazia and South Ossetia. The U.S. project also necessitates paying off Turkey, a strategic ally, and continuing to overlook this NATO member's continuing human rights abuses.[31]

But the plan's most important failing is that it denies Russia any piece of the pie. Russia believes it has natural interests in this region that the United States, halfway around the world, does not.

THE CIS

To counterbalance Russia's residual tendencies toward imperialism, the United States has attempted to strengthen the other countries of the CIS. On the face of it, this is an even-handed, sensible policy. However, "geopolitical pluralism" has forced the Clinton administration to support some of the most authoritarian leaders in the region.

As noted above, oil dictates the U.S. position in the Caucasus. To strengthen its relationship with Georgia and Azerbaijan, Washington has lavished aid and assistance on these countries, where human rights situations are dire. The United States has especially sought to include Azerbaijan in such major international organizations as the World Trade Organization (WTO) and NATO's Partnership for Peace. These overtures reflect the sheer amount of money pouring into the country for oil exploration ($40 billion from contracts with multinationals).[32] Azerbaijan has also announced that it would like to host U.S. and Turkish military bases to counter Russia and Armenia's warming relations. Washington has fortunately decided to treat the invitation as a joke.[33]

The U.S. State Department has routinely criticized the authoritarian Central Asian governments on paper, but the Clinton administration has increased government aid to them in order to consolidate U.S. influence at the expense of Moscow.[34] In Kyrgyzstan, for instance, U.S. aid increased from $24 million to $28.5 million from 1998 to 1999, despite a worsening human rights situation that included government involvement in the trafficking of women.[35] A similar increase in U.S. aid for Uzbekistan occurred over the same period, although the government of Islam Karimov engaged in systematic human rights violations.[36] U.S. appropriations for Turkmenistan nearly tripled from 1998 to 1999, because of potential cooperation in the energy sector. Indeed, after Washington provided credits to Exxon for pipeline exploration in Turkmenistan, the White House announced that Turkmenistan was "committed to strengthening the rule of law and political pluralism"—this in a country with no political opposition, no freedom of assembly, and considerable repression of the few dissidents who have stood up to the dictatorial President Saparmurat Niyazov.[37]

Ukraine represents the most likely counterbalance to Russian power. The problem, from the Clinton administration's point of view, is that a large number of Ukrainian leaders and a substantial portion of the population still hope for some sort of union with Russia. The recently ratified Friendship and Cooperation Treaty between Russia and Ukraine is a positive sign that Russia recognizes Ukrainian sovereignty; as relations improve, leaders on both sides hope that the treaty marks closer rapprochement rather than a more marked divide.

The United States, meanwhile, has tried to woo Ukraine on the cheap, through some loans and good press (even though President Leonid Kuchma's administration suffers the same problems of corruption and lack of transparency as its neighbors). Ukraine has grumbled at the meagerness of U.S. overtures. For instance, Kuchma's administration has supported—and thereby greatly facilitated—NATO expansion but has not received much in the way of actual commitments. Instead, Washington has pressured Ukraine to shun the Russian-Iranian nuclear deal. Meanwhile, Ukraine's market is flooded with imports, but its major exports still cannot break into foreign markets, particularly food into Europe and clothes into the United States.[38]

The CIS as an entity is in trouble. The collective security treaty at the heart of the commonwealth is under criticism from Uzbekistan, Azerbaijan, and Ukraine. Most members grumble at Russia's hegemonic economic policies. A likely result of the ongoing negotiations between Moscow and the 12 CIS countries will be a weakening of security provisions (diminishing Russia's influence in the affairs of its neighbors) but an enhancement of economic cooperation (for Russia is still both a major market and supplier).[39]

From Central Asia to Eastern Europe, the U.S. policy of "geopolitical pluralism" has done little to promote human rights, democracy, or economic progress in the countries surrounding Russia. Nor has U.S. policy helped to make the CIS an effective commonwealth of equals. As with NATO expansion, clumsy U.S. overtures have alienated Russia and gained few true allies.

POLITICS

From Washington's perspective, Boris Yeltsin was the leader who could do no wrong. He concentrated power in his own hands through the 1993 constitution, ruled by decree, bombed his own parliament, effectively stole the 1996 presidential election, brutalized the entire republic of Chechnya, presided over a monumental and largely opaque transfer of public wealth into private hands, and still the United States has stood by him. For, despite his liabilities and chronic illnesses, Yeltsin was actually quite compliant. He could, for example, be influenced on personnel decisions. (Clinton pressured him to retain the corrupt Chubais.)[40] More critically, as Dimitri Simes, president of The Nixon Center in Washington, DC, argued, Yeltsin "was prepared to subordinate Russian foreign policy interests to Western, and especially American, preferences to a much greater extent than the parliament or the Russian public at large."[41] Only in late 1999—with Yeltsin's mind wandering, his grip on politics weakening, his critics pushing for impeachment—did the Clinton administration finally step back to consider political alternatives for president of Russia. But Yeltsin's dramatic resignation on the last day of the millennium caught Washington off guard, as did the rapid ascension to power of prime minister Vladimir Putin, who won popular domestic support but Washington's ire as architect of the brutal military campaign in Chechnya.

Yeltsin's antidemocratic tendencies had taken a heavy toll on the Russian body politic. Weak political parties, a weak civil society, and a weak judiciary all characterize the Russian political scene. The press, while nominally free, is increasingly controlled by business interests. Assassination of public figures and journalists is an all-too-frequent expression of political opposition. On the bright side, Yeltsin's poor health and Russia's financial crisis both heralded a shift of power away from the presidency and toward the parliament, the government, and the regions.[42]

One reason for both the Yeltsin and Clinton administrations' lack of enthusiasm for democracy in Russia today was the enduring strength of the Russian Communist Party. In 1999, the frontrunner in several polls identifying the most popular parties, and party leader Gennady Zyuganov is a strong candidate to succeed Yeltsin as president.[43] Public dissatisfaction both with market reforms and with Yeltsin's leadership was high for many years, although it has not found a viable political outlet. Entire sectors of the workforce were out on strike, including miners and teachers. Although the Communist Party expected a larger turnout for its anti-Yeltsin crusade in October 1998, a million people did take to the streets.[44]

In the wake of the August 1998 financial crisis, the new prime minister, Yevgeny Primakov, managed within a short period to secure a rough political consensus. He appointed a communist deputy, Yuri Maslyukov, to be chief deputy minister for economics and thus received the Communist Party's support for an austere economic recovery plan. Primakov was well positioned to maintain a middle ground between pro-Western and nationalist voices as well as between statist and radical reform positions on the economy.

However, Primakov's success was also his greatest liability. His popularity with the Duma and with the Russian public prompted Yeltsin, whose own approval rating fell to single digits, to sack his prime minister in May 1999. Primakov's short-lived replacement, Sergei Stepashin, had a background in internal security, an anti-Left reputation, and an unswerving loyalty to Yeltsin. Yet Stepashin, who exhibited neither political nor economic skills, was replaced in August 1999 by yet another prime minister, Vladmir Putin, a former K. G. B. spy and law-and-order nationalist who quickly won popular support by relaunching the war against Chechnya. Four months later, when Yeltsin resigned, Putin was named acting president and was considered the leading candidate in the presidential elections expected to be held in March 2000.[46]

These leadership upheavals, Yeltsin's autocratic style, and Putin's nationalist populism masked the central challenge of how to forge a political consensus required to both enlist the support of Russia's regions, and to pull the Russian economy out of its hold.

Russia is a country of 89 regions. At present, Moscow has power-sharing arrangements with more than half of those regions. Only ten of the 89 regions are net contributors to Moscow's coffers; the rest are dependent on subsidies.[45] The federal government has an informal arrangement with the regions: the center will ignore human rights violations and corruption on the periphery if the periphery promises not to secede and acknowledges, if only rhetorically, the validity of federal policy.[47] One of the prime minister's tasks will be to figure out how to persuade (rather than force) Russians and non-Russians outside the center to contribute to the federal strategy of reconstruction.

Belying the notion of a harmonious, multiethnic Russia has been a profusion of extreme nationalist, racist, and anti-Semitic organizations. Quasi-fascist groups such as the Russian National Unity movement (RNE) have thrived in an atmosphere of lawlessness and antigovernment sentiment. Not only did the Yeltsin administration generally neglect this worrisome phenomenon, but the Ministry of Internal Affairs, local authorities, and military units occasionally acted in concert with the RNE.[48] The influence of these extremist groups is difficult to measure— they receive a good deal of attention in the Russian press, but the actual number of followers remains low. Because of the recent rise in anti-Semitism (as well as the general economic crisis), Jewish emigration has increased. Meanwhile, in Moscow, the level of racist violence, both by skinheads and by the police, has increased. The U.S. government spoke out on this issue only when a U.S. Marine was the victim of assault.[49]

RECOMMENDATIONS

The Clinton administration has responded to the prolonged Russian crisis with some good initiatives: it has provided a measure of humanitarian assistance, has helped support the free press, and has devoted a considerable amount of money to help Russia decommission its nuclear weapons. It has also developed useful projects such as the Congressional Research Service program to train library and research staff for newly created legislatures. But these are small points of light in an otherwise dismal picture.

NATO remains a key sticking point in U.S.-Russian relations at the moment. Particularly destabilizing from Moscow's viewpoint is NATO's interest in preparing the Baltic states for admission as well as efforts to absorb Ukraine into the alliance. Russia has drawn its version of a line in the sand—a "red line"—which it warns NATO not to cross or risk "destruction of the existing world order."[50] Given Russia's consistent opposition as well as the sheer number of actual and potential crises on Russia's border, the United States must consider whether admission to NATO will render the petitioning states more secure or less secure. Meanwhile, the United States must make a commitment to use the Permanent Joint Council to actively engage Russia on the broadest range of security issues, including arms limitation. NATO, for all its efforts to redefine its mission, has not spent much time on arms control. Indeed, the 1999 Washington Summit focused on the Defense Capabilities Initiative, a modernization effort.[51] For conventional arms control to proceed, NATO must concentrate more on the contraction of its forces than on the expansion of its influence.

To address Russian concerns about the asymmetry of nuclear arms control, the Clinton administration should consider the proposal by Jonathan Dean of the Union of Concerned Scientists to add a protocol to the current START II treaty that would limit total deployed warheads to 1,000 and then proceed with START III negotiations (concerning data exchange, warhead dismantling, tactical warheads, and sea-launched cruise missiles).[52] This disarmament process will cost money, of course, but every dollar spent neutralizing nuclear weapons on both sides is money well spent.

Although the Clinton administration must challenge Russia's residual hegemonic impulses, it must also be careful to recognize Russia's interests in Central Asia, Ukraine, and the Caucasus. This is not an easy balancing act. On the issue of Caspian Sea oil, for instance, the United States should work *with* Russia rather than *against* it in developing a sustainable approach to oil extraction and delivery to foreign markets. Through its largely rhetorical support for Russians in the "near abroad" and by maintaining influence in the CIS, Russia has retained a weak "imperial" identity. As Russia specialist Anatol Lieven warns, if the United States tries to destroy this weak imperialism by completely isolating Russia, virulent nationalism of the fascist and anti-Semitic variety is likely to fill the vacuum.[53]

On economic issues, Washington must start with humanitarian aid and debt forgiveness. In 1999, the Clinton administration offered 1.5 million tons of wheat plus a $600 million credit to finance imports. This is a good basis to build on. Where possible, the aid program should buy within Russia (or the CIS or East Europe) and distribute to the neediest regions in order not to undercut local agricultural production.[54] The United States should also lead the way in calling for debt forgiveness, particularly of the $100 billion debt that was inherited from the Soviet Union. In other words, the international community should apply the same standard to Russia that it did to Poland. Grzegorz Kolodko, former Polish minister of economics, recommends that the West forgive 80 percent of the inherited debt and 50 percent of the post-Soviet debt—a sensible proposal coming from a border country very concerned with the future viability of the Russian economy.[55]

Once these emergency situations are addressed, the United States should support a mixed economy in Russia (and the rest of the CIS). This option should permit the Russian government to pursue an "infant industries" approach to remaking the economy—picking likely economic winners and nurturing their growth. Even free market champion *Business Week* magazine has criticized the Clinton administration for undercutting Russia's capacity to rebuild itself.[56] Foreign direct investment can play a modest role, but the revival of Russian industry and agriculture must benefit Russians, not the owners and stockholders of multinational corporations.[57]

Meanwhile, the United States and Russia should take advantage of the environmental opportunity that the collapse of industrial production has inadvertently provided—Russian industry now generates 35 percent less air pollution than in 1991 and 15 to 18 percent less water and other pollution.[58] The Clinton administration should consider a large environmental package for Russia that would ensure that new production facilities and sewage treatment plants meet international standards. The administration should also come through with sufficient funds to clean up Russia's decommissioned nuclear submarines, an ecological disaster in the making.[59] The United States and the West must not simply call for environmental protection in Russia; they must pay for it. Otherwise, economic need will continue to induce Russia to undertake disastrous policies, such as the Atomic Energy Ministry's recent attempts to import nuclear waste from around the world—including the United States.[60]

On the political front, the Clinton administration should stop interfering in Russia's elite politics in a vain attempt to find the right mix of pliant reformers. Instead, the United States should concentrate on strengthening popular institutions—the judiciary, research institutes, and grass-roots organizations. For economic reform to proceed fairly and openly, Russia will need stronger watchdog agencies and citizen monitoring groups.

Russia, economically weak and militarily weakening, has not put up much of a fight against the U.S. policy of Containment Lite. It recalled its ambassador from Washington after the December 1998 bombings of Iraq; it has tried to outmaneuver the United States and its allies for the prize of Caspian oil; it has courted Iran and has largely repaired its relationship with North Korea. After the June 1999 NATO bombing cease-fire in Yugoslavia, Russian troops made a daring dash into the Kosovo capital in order to stake out a peacekeeping role denied it by NATO. In an attempt to form an "Asian triangle," Russia has even sought common cause with India and China.[61] These are perhaps improbable bedfellows given their historic tensions, yet aggressive U.S. policies are practically forcing them into a *menage à trois*.

But Russian challenges to U.S. containment policy are cautious. For the time being, Russia is treading very tentatively, careful not to antagonize its chief economic patron, the United States. But Russia will not always be so dependent on

U.S. aid or on money from multilateral institutions largely controlled by the United States. Russia is rich in history, in resources, in resourcefulness. It is rich, too, in strains of intolerance and anti-Western sentiment that are only strengthened by adversity and isolation. The Clinton administration (as well as its more anti-Russian critics on the right) should think twice about capitalizing on Russia's current dependency, for short-term gain may lead to negative consequences in the long term. It is time, finally, for the United States to restore partnership to the "strategic partnership" and to consign containment, Lite or otherwise, to the cold war past.

NOTES

1. Marshall Goldman, "The Cashless Society," *Current History*, October 1998, p. 319.
2. James Meek, "Russia Feels Sea Change in U.S. Policy," *The Guardian*, January 26, 1999.
3. Dale Herspring, "Russia's Crumbling Military," *Current History*, October 1998, p. 325; Business Information Service for the Newly Independent States, *Commercial Overview of Russia* (Washington, DC: Dept. of Commerce, June 1999). Available on the Internet at: http://www.mac.doc.gov/bisnis/country/9906russia1.htm.
4. Cited in the U.S. State Department's report delivered to the U.S. Congress on February 19, 1999; *Jamestown Monitor*, February 26, 1999.
5. Meek, "Russia Feels Sea Change."
6. This section relies on information from British-American Security Information Council (BASIC) "Preparing for the Next 50 Years: A Risk Reduction Strategy for NATO," February 1, 1999.
7. Madeleine Albright, speech to annual foreign ministers meeting at NATO HQ, December 10, 1998.
8. BASIC, "Preparing for the Next 50 Years."
9. "Russian Parliament Delays Work on START II Treaty," *Washington Post*, December 23, 1998.
10. Laura Payne, "U.S.-Russia Security Relations," *Foreign Policy In Focus*, September 1998.
11. "Russia Says START II Is Imperiled," *Washington Post*, January 22, 1999.
12. According to Helms, "We do not need to renegotiate the ABM Treaty to build and deploy national missile defense. We can do it today. The ABM Treaty is dead. It died when our treaty partner, the Soviet Union, ceased to exist." Jesse Helms, "Amend the ABM Treaty? No, Scrap It," *Wall Street Journal*, January 22, 1999.
13. *Washington Post*, January 22, 1999.
14. Steve Goldstein, "New Aid Sought to Battle Threat of Russian Nuclear Material," *Philadelphia Inquirer*, January 20, 1999.
15. Economic Intelligence Unit (EIU) *Country Report*, fourth quarter, 1998, p. 3.
16. Ibid.
17. Ibid.
18. *Agence France Presse*, February 2, 1999.
19. *Agence France Presse*, January 29, 1999.
20. David Treisman, "Russia's Taxing Problem," *Foreign Policy*, Fall 1998.
21. Fritz Kaegi, "Dumping U.S. Jobs: U.S. Steelmakers' Success in Charging Russia with Dumping Also Hurts the U.S.," *The Russian Business Review*, February 1999.

22. Frank Umbach, "Financial Crisis Slows but Fails To Halt East Asian Arms Race," *Jane's Intelligence Review*, September 1998, p. 36.

23. "Clinton Urges Russia to Extend Reforms," *Washington Post*, September 2, 1998.

24. Address by Secretary of State Madeleine K. Albright to the U.S.-Russia Business Council, October 2, 1998.

25. For a more detailed account, see Janine Wedel, *Collision and Collusion: The Strange Case of Western Aid to Eastern Europe 1989–1998* (New York: St. Martin's Press, 1998). By 1999, Sachs had broken substantially from this position. He became a leading advocate of substantial debt forgiveness delinked from IMF conditions, a position that put him directly at odds with the U.S. Treasury Department. See Jeffrey Sachs et al., "Implementing Debt Relief for the HIPC's," Harvard Center for International Development, August 1999.

26. Boris Kagarlitsky, Testimony before the Committee on Banking and Financial Services, United States House of Representatives, Hearing to Examine the Russian Economic Crisis and the International Monetary Fund, September 10, 1998.

27. Phil Reeves, "Russian Leaders Accused of Scam," *The Independent*, February 12, 1999.

28. Interior Ministry estimate from Interfax, March 11, 1999. Deputy Prime Minister Yuri Maslyukov has estimated $200 billion in capital flight since the beginning of the market reforms. *Itar-TASS*, March 16, 1999.

29. Quoted in Anatol Lieven, *Chechnya: Tombstone of a Russian Power* (New Haven, CT: Yale University Press, 1998), p. 176.

30. Michael McFaul, "Russia's Summer of Discontent," *Current History*, October 1998, p. 309.

31. "U.S.-Caspian Oil Pipeline Deal Near, *Associated Press*, January 21, 1999.

32. Human Rights Watch, *World Report 1999* (New York: HRW, December 1998), p. 242.

33. Ron Laurenzo, "U.S. Base in Azerbaijan Not in Cards," *Defense Week*, February 8, 1999. Some, however, take the invitation very seriously: John Ellis, "U.S. Should Build a Military Base in Azerbaijan," *Boston Globe*, February 6, 1999.

34. Rajan Menon, "American Interests in Central Asia," *U.S. Relations with the Former Soviet States*, Aspen Institute, 23rd Conference, August 17–21, 1998.

35. Human Rights Watch, *World Report 1999*, p. 275.

36. Ibid., p. 309.

37. Ibid., p. 301.

38. Alexander Motyl, "Ukraine: Politics, Economy, and Relations with the West," *U.S. Relations with the Former Soviet States*, Aspen Institute, 23rd Conference, August 17–21, 1998, p. 16.

39. Paul Goble, "The East: Analysis from Washington—Looking Beyond the CIS," Radio Free Europe/Radio Liberty, February 12, 1999.

40. Dimitri Simes, "Russia's Crisis, America's Complicity," *The National Interest*, Winter 1998/1999, p. 19.

41. Ibid.

42. See, for instance, Michael McFaul, "The Demon Within," *Moscow Times*, March 2, 1999.

43. "Russian Opinion Poll Puts Communists Ahead," *Bloomberg*, February 3, 1999, based on an opinion poll conducted by the independent Russian Social-Economic Agency from January 19–26, 1999.

44. While the *New York Times* downplayed the turnout, calling the protests "tepid," a million marchers is still a sizable number. "Communists and Workers March to Denounce Yeltsin," *New York Times*, October 8, 1998.

45. Peter Rutland, "A Flawed Democracy," *Current History*, October 1998, p. 318.
46. David Remnick, "Russia gets a new strongman," The Talk of the Town, *The New Yorker*, December 20, 1999, pp. 33–34; Daniel Williams, "The Successor: Need for Authority Figure Fuels Putin's Rise to Power," *Washington Post*, January 1, 2000, p. A31; Michael Wines, "What Putin's Rule Portends for Russia," *New York Times*, January 2, 2000, p. 4.
47. Human Rights Watch, *World Report 1999*, p. 281.
48. William Jackson, "Fascism, Vigilantism, and the State," *Problems of Post-Communism*, January/February 1999, p. 40.
49. Human Rights Watch, *World Report 1999*, p. 287.
50. Yevgeny Gusarov, the deputy foreign minister of Russia, quoted in Robert Burns, "Russian Opposes More NATO Expansion," Associated Press, February 7, 1999.
51. BASIC, "Preparing for the Next 50 Years."
52. Jonathan Dean, "Relaunching START II," *Moscow Times*, February 9, 1999.
53. Lieven, *Chechnya*, p. 383.
54. On whether Russia indeed has food supplies to draw upon, see Andrew Jack, "Critics Find Food Package to Russia Hard to Stomach," *Financial Times*, February 5, 1999.
55. See Grzegorz Kolodko, "Plan for Russia," talk delivered at the Institute for International Economic and Political Studies, Moscow, November 25, 1998.
56. "Washington Is Making It Hard for Russia to Help Itself," *Business Week*, February 8, 1999.
57. For a more detailed proposal, see Alice Amsden et al., "Strategies for a Viable Transition: Lessons from the Political Economy of Renewal," a report for the Institute for Policy Studies, June 13, 1995.
58. "Russian Crisis Has Helped Environment," Reuters, January 18, 1999.
59. The Clinton administration has announced its intention to help dispose of the subs and for FY 2000 Congress appropriated $25 million for the dismantling and disposal of nuclear submarine reactors in the Russian Far East. This is part of a total package of $460.5 million to help dismantle the Russian military—far short of the total cost for cleanup which is estimated at $2.6 billion. The United States has shown a preference, for strategic reasons, to focus on later-generation subs—the older models, however, pose an equal risk. See Simon Saradzhyan, "Russia Cheers U.S. Aid for Sub Disposal," *Moscow Times*, February 26, 1999; also James Meek, "Cook Visits Icy Nuclear Nightmare," *The Guardian*, March 4, 1999.
60. Lyuba Pronina, "Nuclear Waste Row Erupts," *Moscow Tribune*, February 19, 1999.
61. Pavel Felgenhauer, "Asian Triangle Shapes Up," *Moscow Times*, February 25, 1999. Also "Yeltsin, Zhu Discuss Strategic Partnership," *Daily Yomiuri*, February 27, 1999, and Stephen Blank, "Which Way for Sino-Soviet Relations?" *Orbis*, Summer 1998.

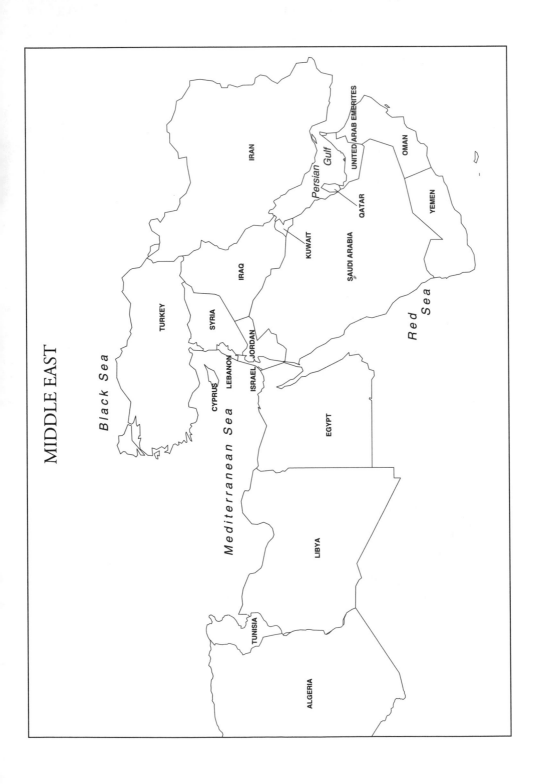

MIDDLE EAST

Black Sea

Mediterranean Sea

Red Sea

Persian Gulf

TURKEY

CYPRUS

SYRIA

LEBANON

ISRAEL

JORDAN

IRAQ

IRAN

KUWAIT

SAUDI ARABIA

QATAR

UNITED ARAB EMERITES

OMAN

YEMEN

EGYPT

LIBYA

TUNISIA

ALGERIA

CHAPTER 10

CONTINUING STORM:
THE U.S. ROLE IN THE MIDDLE EAST

Stephen Zunes

THROUGHOUT THE CENTURIES, WESTERN NATIONS HAVE TRIED to impose their order on the region now commonly known as the Middle East. For certain periods of time they have succeeded, only to find themselves at the receiving end of a popular and oftentimes violent backlash. Now, with the collapse of the Soviet Union and the triumph in the Gulf War, the United States stands—at least for a time—as the region's dominant outside power.

Washington has traditionally argued that because the United States has entered the region eschewing colonial ambitions, championing the rule of law and the authority of the United Nations, and seeking economic growth and political stability, America stands out as a singular and responsible overseer. Most of those in the Middle East and most independent Western observers, however, see the United States role as far less benign, citing U.S. support for repressive and corrupt monarchies, the exploitative practices by American oil companies and other multinational corporations, the promotion of a secular and materialistic lifestyle, the highly prejudicial use of the UN Security Council, the arming and bankrolling of a militaristic and expansionist Israel, destabilization efforts against internationally recognized governments, and periodic military interventions.

Whatever the nature of U.S. policy, however, there is no question that the United States recognizes the region's significance. At the intersection of three continents and the source of most of the world's petroleum reserves, the Middle East has been described by leading American officials as the most strategically important area in the world. No longer concerned that the region might fall to Soviet influence, the United States is still apprehensive about the influence of homegrown movements that could also challenge American interests. There is a widely perceived, ongoing threat from radical secular or radical Islamic forces, as well as concern over the instability that could result from any major challenges to the rule of pro-Western regimes, even if led by potentially democratic movements. The most crucial part of the Middle East, according to most U.S. policymakers, is the Persian Gulf region, where conservative, pro-Western monarchies feel under threat from the radical regimes in Iraq and Iran and look to the United States for protection.

THE GULF

The six Arab monarchies of the Persian Gulf are guardians of valuable oil reserves for which the United States seeks access, not just to supplement American reserves (currently around 18 percent of U.S. consumption) but as a means of maintaining a degree of leverage over the import-dependent European and Japanese markets. (See figure 10–1.) During the war between Iran and Iraq in the 1980s, the United States played the combatants off against each other to insure that neither of these militant regimes would become too influential. With oil, water resources, and a sizable population, both had the potential to become regional powers that could conceivably challenge American interests. Since 1993, the United States has articulated a policy of "dual containment" toward these governments, guarding against potential expansionist ambitions by either against the pro-Western sheikdoms, though the extreme hostility toward Iran may be lessening as a result of the election of a more moderate Islamic government in 1997.

The British had been the dominant power in the Persian Gulf for most of the 20th century, but—in recognition of their decline as a major world power—they announced their military withdrawal from the region in 1969. The United States, which had been increasing its presence in the Middle East since the end of World War II, was determined to fill the void. President Richard Nixon, facing growing opposition to the Vietnam War, knew that sending U.S. combat troops into this volatile region would not be politically feasible. By the early 1970s, antiwar sentiment had lessened, due in part to Nixon's "Vietnamization" program, whereby the reliance on South Vietnamese conscripts and a dramatically increased air war had minimized American casualties. As a result, the Nixon Doctrine (also known as the Guam Doctrine or "surrogate strategy") came into being, wherein Vietnamization evolved into a global policy of arming and training third world allies to become regional gendarmes for American interests.

The Persian Gulf was the primary testing ground, with Iran's shah—who owed his throne to CIA intervention in the 1950s and had long dreamed of rebuilding the Persian Empire—playing the part of a willing participant. Throughout the 1970s, the United States sold tens of billions of dollars worth of highly sophisticated arms to the shah, sending thousands of U.S. advisors to turn the Iranian armed forces into a sophisticated fighting unit capable of counterinsurgency operations. Such a strategy proved successful when Iranian forces helped crush a leftist insurgency in the southeastern Arabian sultanate of Oman in the mid-1970s.

Figure 10.1 Major Oil-Producing Nations

Major Oil-Producing Nations

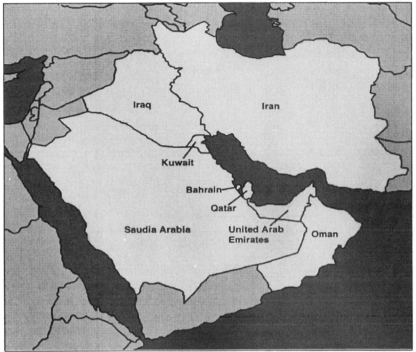

Saudi Arabia, Kuwait, Oman, Qatar, United Arab Emirates, Bahrain, Iraq, and Iran possess 64 percent of the world's proven oil reserves.

Source: Phyllis Bennis, "Middle East Oil," *Foreign Policy in Focus*, January 1997.

This strategy came crashing down in 1979, however, with Iran's Islamic revolution, which resulted from the popular reaction against the highly visible American presence in the country, the shah's penchant for military procurement over internal economic development, and his brutal repression against any and all dissent. The vast American-supplied arsenal fell into the hands of a radical anti-American regime. It was then that the Carter Doctrine came into being with the establishment of the Rapid Deployment Force (later known as the Central Command), which would enable the United States to strike with massive force in a relatively short period of time. This extremely costly effort would enable the United States to fight a war that would rely so heavily on air power, be over so quickly, and enjoy such a favorable casualty ratio that popular domestic opposition would not have time to mobilize.

This was precisely the scenario for Operation Desert Storm. Though the circumstances that would lead to such a war were not known, the military response had in effect been planned for more than a dozen years prior to the Gulf War and was designed in part for domestic political impact. For better or worse, it worked well. The massive international mobilization led by the United States forced Iraqi occupation forces out of Kuwait and severely damaged Iraq's military and civilian infrastructure in less than six weeks and with only several dozen American casualties. The war was a dramatic reassertion of U.S. global power, just as its former superpower rival was collapsing, and it consolidated the U.S. position as the region's most important outside power.

Ironically, the United States had been quietly supporting Iraq's brutal totalitarian regime and its leader, Saddam Hussein, through financial credits and even limited military assistance during its war against Iran in the 1980s. This included, as Alan Friedman documented in his book *Spider's Web*, offering Iraq technical support and supplying raw materials for the chemical and biological weapons programs and $1 billion worth of components necessary for the development of missiles and nuclear weapons. Washington downplayed and even covered up the use of chemical weapons by Saddam's armed forces against the Iranian military and Kurdish civilians during this period, and the United States opposed UN sanctions against Iraq for its acts of aggression toward both Iran and its own population. It was only after Iraq's invasion of the oil-rich, pro-Western emirate of Kuwait in August 1990 that Saddam Hussein's regime suddenly became demonized in the eyes of U.S. policymakers and the American public at large.

SINCE THE GULF WAR

Even prior to the Gulf War, the United States had thrown its immense military, diplomatic, and economic weight behind the monarchies of the Persian Gulf. Though they rule over less than 10 percent of the Arab world's total population, these regimes control most of its wealth. Prior to the war, it was difficult for the United States to engage in military exercises or even arrange a port call without asking for permission months in advance. Not any more.

There is now an effective, permanent U.S. military presence in the Persian Gulf. The financial costs are extraordinary—running between $30 and $60 billion annually, according to conservative estimates—and are shared by the United States and the gulf monarchies. Though there appears to be a bipartisan consensus in Washington that there is a clear strategic imperative to maintaining such an American presence, there are critics—even among conservatives—who argue that such a presence is too costly for the American taxpayer and creates a situation where American military personnel are effectively serving as a mercenary force for autocratic sheikdoms.

Most Persian Gulf Arabs and their leaders felt threatened after Iraq's seizure of Kuwait and were grateful for the strong U.S. leadership in the 1991 war against Saddam Hussein's regime. At the same time, there is an enormous amount of cynicism regarding U.S. motives in waging that war. Gulf Arabs, and even some of their rulers, cannot shake the sense that the war was not fought for international law, self-determination, and human rights, as the Bush administration claimed, but rather to protect U.S. access to oil and to enable the United States to gain a strategic toehold in the region. It is apparent that a continued U.S. presence is welcome only as long as Arabs feel they need a foreign military presence to protect them.

Iraq still has not recovered from the 1991 war, during which it was on the receiving end of the heaviest bombing in world history. The United States has insisted on maintaining strict sanctions against Iraq to force compliance with international demands to dismantle any capability of producing weapons of mass destruction. In addition, the United States hopes that such sanctions will lead to the downfall of Saddam Hussein's regime. However, Washington's policy of enforcing strict sanctions against Iraq appears to have had the ironic effect of strengthening Saddam's regime. With as many as 5,000 people, mostly children, dying from malnutrition and preventable diseases every month as a result of the sanctions, the humanitarian crisis has led to worldwide demands—even from some of Iraq's historic enemies—to relax the sanctions. Furthermore, as they are now more dependent than ever on the government for their survival, the Iraqi people are even less likely to risk open defiance. Unlike the reaction to sanctions imposed prior to the war, Iraqi popular resentment over their suffering lays the blame squarely on the United States, not the totalitarian regime, whose ill-fated conquest of Kuwait led to the economic collapse of this once-prosperous country. In addition, Iraq's middle class, which would have most likely formed the political force capable of overthrowing Saddam's regime, has been reduced to penury. It is not surprising that most of Iraq's opposition movements oppose the U.S. policy of ongoing punitive sanctions and air strikes.

In addition, U.S. officials have stated that sanctions would remain even if Iraq complied with United Nations inspectors, giving the Iraqi regime virtually no incentive to comply. For sanctions to work, there needs to be a promise of relief to counterbalance the suffering; that is, a carrot as well as a stick. Indeed, it was the failure of both the United States and the United Nations to explicitly spell out what was needed in order for sanctions to be lifted that led to Iraq suspending its cooperation with UN inspectors in December 1998.

The use of U.S. air strikes against Iraq subsequent to the inspectors' departure has not garnered much support from the international community, including Iraq's neighbors, who would presumably be most threatened by an Iraqi biological weapons capability. Nor have U.S. air strikes eliminated that capability. In light of Washington's tolerance—and even quiet support—of Iraq's powerful military machine in the 1980s, the Clinton administration's exaggerated claims of an imminent Iraqi military threat in 1998, after Iraq's military infrastructure was largely destroyed in the Gulf War, simply lack credibility. Nor have such air strikes eliminated or reduced the country's biological weapons capability. Furthermore, only the United Nations Security Council has the prerogative to authorize military responses to violations of its resolutions; no single member state can do so unilaterally without explicit permission.

KURDISTAN

The United States also usurped UN Security Council authority with a series of air strikes against Iraq in September 1996, justifying them on the grounds that Iraqi forces had illegally moved into Kurdish-populated areas of the country that had been under UN protection since Saddam's brutal repression of the Kurds at the end of the Gulf War. There is reason to believe, however, that these air strikes were not so much for the defense of the Kurds as simply another futile attempt by a frustrated administration to strike back at an upstart dictator who continues to challenge the United States.

The Kurds are a nation of more than 20 million people divided among six countries and containing nationalist movements rife with factionalism. (See figure 10–2.) The worst repression against the Kurds in recent years has come from Turkey, a NATO ally, which the United States considers part of Europe. Turkey receives large-scale military, economic, and diplomatic support from the United States; during the 1990s, U.S. military aid and arms sales totaled about $10.5 billion. On several occasions in recent years, thousands of Turkish troops have crossed into Iraqi territory to attack the Kurds. Though these incursions also took place in the UN safe zone and have been far greater in scope than Saddam's 1996 forays, President Bill Clinton supported the Turkish attacks, making his harsh response to Iraq's incursion appear to be motivated by other than humanitarian or legal concerns.

Although the United States clearly wants Saddam Hussein removed from power, the United States and other countries may not want to risk Iraq's total disintegration. Washington wants neither a victory by a radical Kurdish movement in the north nor a successful rebellion in the south of the country, where an Iranian-backed Shiite Muslim movement has challenged the authority of the Sunni Muslim-dominated government in Baghdad. At the same time, the totalitarian nature of the Iraqi regime renders prospects for internal change unlikely, at least as long as the population is suffering so much economic hardship from the sanctions.

In 1998, the United States successfully pressured Syria to expel Abdullah Ocalan, the leader of the Kurdistan Workers Party (PKK), a radical Kurdish nationalist guerrilla group fighting Turkey for greater autonomy. In February 1999, the United States assisted Turkish intelligence agents in locating Ocalan in Kenya, where he was kidnapped and brought to Turkey to face what virtually all outside observers (the Clinton State Department being an exception) see as unfair judicial treatment.

Figure 10.2   Kurdish Population Estimates: 1997

Country	Total Population (in millions)	Kurd Population (in millions)	% Kurds
Iran	65.0	6.5	10
Iraq	19.3	4.4	23
Syria	13.4	1.1	8
Turkey	65.0	14.3	22
Elsewhere		2.3	
Total		28.5	

Source: David McDowall, "The Kurds," Minority Rights Group Report, Washington Kurdish Institute, 1996. Excerpts available on the Internet at: http://www.clark.net/kurd/kurdname.html.

The U.S.-backed Turkish regime has used the PKK's sometimes brutal tactics as an excuse to crush even nonviolent expressions of Kurdish nationalism; for example, speaking the Kurdish language or celebrating Kurdish cultural life has been severely repressed. Kurdish civilians have been the primary targets of Turkey's counterinsurgency campaign. The United States has been largely silent against the Turkish government's repression but active in condemning what is sees as Kurdish terrorism.

Washington's military and diplomatic support of Turkey's repression of the Kurds is quite consistent with U.S. acquiescence to other controversial policies by this NATO ally. The United States has blocked enforcement of UN Security Council resolutions 353 and 354 calling for Turkey to withdraw its occupation forces from northern Cyprus. The United States has also failed to condemn the Turkish government for widespread human rights violations against its own population. And Washington has refused to even acknowledge the Turkish genocide against the Armenians earlier this century, in which well over one million people were slaughtered. This double standard, which rejects adherence to international law or basic standards of human rights, further undermines U.S. credibility in the region

ISLAMIC RADICALISM

The United States has been greatly concerned over the rise of radical Islamic movements in the Middle East. Islam, like other religions, can be quite diverse regarding its interpretation of the faith's teachings as they apply to contemporary political issues. There are a number of Islamic-identified parties and movements that seek peaceful coexistence and cooperation with the West and are moderate on economic and social policy. There are also some Islamic movements in the Middle East today that are indeed reactionary, violent, misogynist, and include a virulently anti-American perspective that is antithetical to perceived American interests. Still others may be more amenable to traditional U.S. interests but reactionary in their approach to social and economic policies, or vice versa.

Radical Islamic movements have risen to the forefront primarily in countries where there has been a dramatic physical dislocation of the population as a result of war or uneven economic development. Ironically, the United States has often supported policies that have helped spawn such movements, including giving military, diplomatic, and economic aid to augment decades of Israeli attacks and occupation policies, which have torn apart Palestinian and Lebanese society, and provoked extremist movements that were unheard of as recently as 20 years ago. Similarly, the United States has taken the lead in encouraging the adoption of neoliberal economic policies by a number of Middle Eastern governments. Such policies have destroyed traditional economies and turned millions of rural peasants into a new urban underclass populating the teeming slums of such cities as Cairo, Tunis, Casablanca, and Teheran. Though policies of free trade and privatization have resulted in increased prosperity for some, far more people feel left behind, providing easy recruits for Islamic activists rallying against corruption, materialism and economic injustice.

It is also noteworthy that in countries that have allowed Islamic groups to participate more fully in the democratic process—such as Jordan, Yemen, and, for a time, Turkey—Islamists have played a largely responsible role in parliamentary politics. It has only been in countries where democratic rights are seriously curtailed that Islamists have adopted the more radical, militaristic, and antidemocratic forms that the United States finds so disturbing. Many Islamic movements, such as those in Egypt, Palestine, and Algeria, include diverse elements that would span the ideological spectrum if they were allowed to function in an open, democratic system.

In a response that bears striking similarity to the perceived communist threat during the cold war, however, the standard U.S. reaction to radical Islamic movements appears to be to support authoritarian regimes in imposing military solutions to what are essentially political, economic, and social problems. The result of such a policy may be to encourage the very extremist forces Washington seeks to curtail.

What has made such policies particularly difficult to challenge is the role of influential elements in the American intelligentsia and foreign policy establishment, as well as certain Christian fundamentalist leaders, who have played upon the widespread prejudice many Americans have regarding Islam to create a popular antipathy toward Muslims that justifies hard-line policies towards Muslim countries, peoples, and organizations. Given the size and importance of the world's Islamic population, however, the development of a more enlightened policy is crucial.

TERRORISM

The United States has highlighted the threat of terrorism from the Middle East, billing it as America's major national security concern in the post-cold war world. Washington considers Iran, Iraq, Sudan, and Libya to be the primary sources of state-sponsored terrorism and has embarked on an ambitious policy to isolate these regimes in the international community. Syria's status as a supporter of terrorism has ebbed and flowed not so much from an objective measure of its links to terrorist groups as from an assessment of their willingness to cooperate with U.S. policy interests, indicating just how politicized "terrorist" designations can be.

The U.S. war against terrorism has been hampered by double standards. During the 1980s, for example, the Nicaraguan contras—armed, trained, and effectively created by Washington—were responsible for far more civilian deaths than all terrorist groups supported by all Middle Eastern countries combined. In addition, the most serious single bombing attack against a civilian target in the history of the Middle East was the March 1985 blast in a suburban Beirut neighborhood that killed 80 people and wounded 200 others. The attack was ordered by CIA director William Casey and approved by President Ronald Reagan as part of an unsuccessful effort to assassinate an anti-American Lebanese cleric. The U.S. role in the bombing, which was widely reported throughout the Middle East and elsewhere, has lent Washington's crusade against Middle Eastern terrorism little credibility in much of the world. (Although the initial report of U.S. involvement made the leading front-page headline of the *New York Times* and was described in detail in Bob Woodward's book *Veil*, it is rarely ever mentioned by so-called experts on Middle Eastern terrorism in the United States.) The perpetrators have never been brought to justice.

Libya has long been a major target of the United States regarding international terrorism. Between 1992 and 1999, the United States successfully pushed through a series of sanctions by the United Nations Security Council against the government of Libya for its failure to extradite two of its citizens to Great Britain or the United States, where they face criminal charges in the bombing of Pan Am Flight 103 over Lockerbie, Scotland in 1988. Libya cited both the absence of any extradition treaty with the United States or Great Britain and concerns over the likelihood of an unfair trial. When, in 1999, Libya and the United States reached a compromise agreement to extradite the suspects to the Netherlands for trial before a Scottish judge, UN sanctions were suspended but unilateral U.S. sanctions against Libya continue.

What apparently provoked the terrorists who destroyed the airliner was the 1986 American bombings of two Libyan cities, in which scores of civilians were killed. The United States justified the air strikes on the grounds that they would prevent future Libyan-sponsored terrorism, an ironic justification given the subsequent event. What is less well-known is the fact that the United States has similarly refused to extradite several American citizens charged with acts of terrorism. Both Venezuela and Costa Rica, for example, have outstanding warrants for CIA-connected individuals linked to a series of terrorist attacks in Latin America, including the 1976 bombing of a Cuban airliner, in which several dozen passengers were killed.

More recently, the United States has focused attention on the activities of Osama Bin Laden, the exiled Saudi millionaire orchestrating a number of terrorist cells operating out of the Middle East. Ironically, many of the key players in these terrorist networks originally received their training and support from the U.S. Central Intelligence Agency when they were mobilized to fight the Soviet-backed communist regime that ruled Afghanistan in the 1980s. In August 1998, the United States bombed suspected terrorist bases in Afghanistan—originally built by the CIA—in an effort to cripple Bin Laden's movement. The United States simultaneously bombed a civilian pharmaceutical plant in Sudan under the apparently mistaken belief that it was developing chemical weapons that could be used by these terrorist networks. Given the highly questionable strategic value of such air strikes, these responses seem to be little more than foreign policy by catharsis. Though strong intelligence and interdiction efforts are important in the fight against terrorism, such impulsive military responses are likely to merely continue the cycle of violence.

Another source of concern for the Clinton administration is the use of terrorism by Palestinian extremists determined to disrupt the peace process. Although both suicide and the taking of civilian life are explicitly proscribed in the Islamic faith, such prohibitions have not stopped underground movements from organizing several deadly suicide bombings against civilian targets in Israel. The United

States has pressured Palestinian authorities to crack down still harder on Islamic dissidents, including those not directly involved in acts of violence. Repression alone, however, will not work. Such desperate acts of terror erupt not from any outside conspiracy or from any inherent cultural or religious base, but from a people frustrated that the economic prosperity and national independence promised by Palestinian leader Yasir Arafat as a reward for Palestinian nonviolence and moderation has not been forthcoming. Some Palestinians have committed acts of terrorism for the same reasons as did some Kenyans, Algerians, and Zimbabweans: they feel that they are prevented from attaining their national freedom nonviolently. Indeed, the Zionist movement produced its share of terrorist groups during the Israeli independence struggle against Britain in the 1940s, with two prominent terrorist leaders—Menachem Begin and Yitzhak Shamir—later becoming prime ministers. As long as the United States and Israel oppose Palestinian statehood, such attacks will not end.

In addition, historically—and even since the Oslo Accords in 1993—far more Palestinian civilians have been killed by Israelis than the reverse. Extremist Jewish settlers—who are much like Islamic extremists in their zealotry, intolerance, and propensity toward violence—routinely conduct vigilante actions against the local Palestinian population. The difference is that these extremist Jewish groups are officially sanctioned, are issued arms by the Israeli government, and are often directly supported by elements of the Israeli military and private American contributors. A sizable number of these Jewish terrorists are American émigrés, openly recruited in the United States during the 1980s while the United States banned even moderate Palestinian leaders from coming into the country.

The Israelis use periodic acts of Islamic terrorism as an excuse to refuse to withdraw more of their occupation forces from the rest of the West Bank as promised under the Oslo Accords and subsequent agreements, even though the majority of the attackers have come from areas under Israeli control and the rate of terrorist attacks has actually declined since its peak in the 1970s. In addition, after largely destroying the indigenous Palestinian economy during almost thirty years of occupation—in order to create a cheap labor force—the Israelis have closed off Israel and Jerusalem to Palestinian workers, creating widespread unemployment and increasing the anger and frustration of the Palestinian population. The United States has refused to challenge these policies. Essentially, the Clinton administration, even more than its predecessors, sees Israeli security and Palestinian rights as mutually exclusive. In reality, however, they are mutually dependent.

ISRAEL AND ITS NEIGHBORS

One area where the Clinton administration has received high praises in the mainstream media is in its pursuit of peace between Israel and its Arab neighbors. Yet the United States has, in large part, hampered rather than promoted the peace process. For over two decades, the international consensus for peace in the Middle East has involved the withdrawal of Israeli forces to within its internationally recognized boundaries in return for security guarantees from Israel's neighbors, the establishment of a Palestinian state in the West Bank and Gaza, and some special status for a shared Jerusalem. Over the past thirty years, the Palestine Liberation Organization, under the leadership of Yasir Arafat, has evolved from frequent acts of terrorism and the open call for Israel's destruction to supporting the international consensus for a two-state solution. Most Arab states have made a similar evolution toward favoring just such a peace settlement.

However, the United States has traditionally rejected the international consensus and currently takes a position more closely resembling that of Israel's right-wing governments: supporting a Jerusalem under exclusive Israeli sovereignty, encouraging only partial withdrawal from the occupied territories, allowing continuation of the illegal policies of confiscation of Palestinian land and the construction of Jewish-only settlements, and rejecting an independent Palestine. As a result, there are serious questions as to whether the United States can actually serve as a fair mediator in the conflict. A more neutral arbiter, such the United Nations, might better serve the peace process in the Middle East.

Although successive U.S. administrations have—on occasion—criticized certain Israeli policies and actions, Washington is more likely to come to Israel's support. For example, the United States has blocked enforcement of UN Security Council resolutions calling for Israeli withdrawal from southern Lebanon and has defended Israeli attacks on Lebanese villages—in retaliation against Muslim guerrillas fighting Israeli occupation forces—even when such attacks have resulted in large-scale civilian casualties. Washington also refuses to insist upon Israeli withdrawal from the Golan region of Syria, even after the once-intransigent Syrian regime finally agreed to international demands for strict security guarantees and eventually normalized relations with Israel in the early 1990s. Regarding the Palestinians, the interpretation of autonomy by Israel and the United States has thus far led to only limited Palestinian control of a bare one-tenth of the West Bank in a patchwork arrangement that more resembles American Indian reservations or the infamous Bantustans of apartheid-era South Africa than anything like statehood.

Most observers recognize that one of the major obstacles to Israeli-Palestinian peace is the expansion of Israeli settlements in the occupied territories. However, the United States has blocked enforcement of UN Security Council resolutions calling for Israel to withdraw its settlements from Palestinian land. These settlements were established in violation of international law, which forbids the colonization of territories seized by military force. In addition, the Clinton White House—in a reversal of the policies of previous administrations—has not opposed the expansion of existing settlements and has shown ambivalence regarding the large-scale construction of exclusively Jewish housing developments in Israeli-occupied East Jerusalem. Furthermore, Clinton has secured additional aid for Israel to construct highways connecting these settlements and to provide additional security, thereby reinforcing their permanence. This places the United States in direct violation of UN Security Council resolution 465, which "calls upon all states not to provide Israel with any assistance to be used specifically in connection with settlements in the occupied territories."

Meanwhile, the Clinton administration has launched a vigorous campaign to rescind all previous UN resolutions critical of Israel. Washington has labeled them "anachronistic," even though many of the issues addressed in these resolutions—human rights violations, illegal settlements, expulsion of dissidents, development of nuclear weapons, the status of Jerusalem, and ongoing military occupation—are still germane. The White House contends that the Oslo Accords render these earlier UN resolutions obsolete. However, such resolutions cannot be reversed without the approval of the UN body in question; the United States cannot unilaterally discount their relevance. Furthermore, no bilateral agreement (like Oslo) can supersede the authority of the UN Security Council, particularly if one of the two parties (the Palestinians) believe that these resolutions are still binding. As a result, given U.S. efforts to undermine UN authority vis-à-vis Israel, even pro-Western Arab states take issue with Washington's insistence on the strict enforcement of UN resolutions against Afghanistan, Sudan and Iraq.

The U.S. relationship with Israel is singular. Israel represents only one one-thousandth of the world's population and has the 16th highest per capita income in the world, yet it receives 40 percent of all U.S. foreign aid. In terms of U.S. aid to the Middle East, Israel received 54 percent in 1999, Egypt 38 percent and all other Middle East countries only 8 percent. Direct aid to Israel in recent years has exceeded $3.5 billion annually and has been supported almost unanimously in Congress, even by liberal Democrats who normally insist on linking aid to human rights and international law. Although the American public appears to strongly support Israel's right to exist and wants the United States to be a guarantor of that right, there is growing skepticism regarding the excessive level and unconditional nature of U.S. aid to Israel. Among elected officials, there are virtually no calls for a reduction of current aid levels in the foreseeable future, particularly as virtually all U.S. aid to Israel returns to the United States either via purchases of American armaments or as interest payments to U.S. banks for previous loans.

Despite closer American strategic cooperation with the Persian Gulf monarchies since the Gulf War, these governments clearly lack Israel's advantages in terms of political stability, well-trained military, technological sophistication, and the ability to quickly mobilize human and material resources and thereby they can never substitute for the U.S. relationship with Israel. In addition, given that Washington's continued support of Israel has not interfered in recent years with an unprecedented degree of cooperation from Egypt and the Gulf monarchies or with rapprochement with Syria, there appear to be few risks involved with the United States continuing such an Israeli alliance, even as Washington cultivates closer strategic relationships with authoritarian Arab regimes.

Despite serious reservations about Israel's treatment of the Palestinians, most individual Americans have a longstanding moral commitment to Israel's survival. Official U.S. government policy supporting successive Israeli governments in recent years, however, appears to be crafted more from a recognition of how Israel supports American strategic interests in the Middle East and beyond. Indeed, 99 percent of all U.S. aid to Israel has been granted since the 1967 war, when Israel proved itself more powerful than any combination of its neighbors and occupied the territories of hundreds of thousands of Palestinians and other Arabs. Why, then, is U.S. aid to Israel higher now—in light of peace treaties with Jordan,

Egypt, and the Palestinians, the destruction of Iraq's military capability, and a severely weakened Syria—than it was when these nations were threatening Israel's survival?

Israel has helped suppress victories by radical nationalist movements in Lebanon, Jordan, and Yemen, as well as in Palestine. The Israeli military has kept Syria, for many years an ally of the Soviet Union, in check, and its air force is predominant throughout the region. Israel's frequent wars have provided battlefield testing for American arms. Israel has also served as a conduit for U.S. arms to regimes and movements—such as apartheid-era South Africa, Iran, Guatemala, and the Nicaraguan contras—too unpopular in the United States for overt and direct military assistance. Israel's military advisors have assisted the contras, the Salvadoran junta, and other governments allied with the United States; its secret service has assisted the United States in intelligence gathering and covert operations. Israel has hundreds of intermediate-range ballistic missiles and has cooperated with the U.S. military-industrial complex regarding research and development for new jet fighters, antimissile defense systems, and even the Strategic Defense Initiative. No U.S. administration wants to jeopardize such an important relationship.

The end of the cold war has not lessened the military relationship between the United States and Israel, inspired in large part by the strong economic imperatives of their joint military-industrial complexes and the policy objectives of government officials in both countries. Indeed, though Israel has never been more secure strategically in its history, U.S. military support is at an all-time high. Another reason for the continued high levels of strategic cooperation may be related to the belief that there are still potential threats to the two countries' interests—unrelated to international communism—that require them to maintain an overwhelming military superiority.

Some Israelis, however, are disturbed that this close strategic cooperation enables their government to resist necessary compromises for peace. "Palestinian weakness and American callousness have together brought expansionism once again to the center of the Israeli political arena," wrote Israeli journalist Haim Baram, in a March 1996 piece in *Middle East International.* Baram noted, "This development is doubly distressing, because the Israeli public is more prepared for real territorial concessions than ever before." Some Israelis feel like they are being used to advance the policy goals of a foreign country. Others, noting that many Arabs have often blamed "Zionism" for their problems rather than Western powers or their own leaders, draw the analogy with the Jews of medieval Europe who served as moneylenders and tax collectors for the ruling elites, only to be abandoned later by their overlords and become convenient scapegoats.

As long as U.S. military, diplomatic, and economic support of the Israeli government remains unconditional despite Israel's ongoing violation of human rights, international law, and previous agreements with the Palestinians, there is no incentive for the Israeli government to change its policies. The growing Arab resentment that results can only threaten the long-term security interests of both Israel and the United States.

THE STRUGGLE FOR DEMOCRACY

The growing movement favoring democracy and human rights in the Middle East has not shared the remarkable successes of its counterparts in Eastern Europe, Latin America, Africa, and parts of Asia. Most Middle Eastern governments remain autocratic. Despite occasional rhetorical support for greater individual freedoms, the United States has generally not supported tentative Middle Eastern steps toward democratization. Indeed, the United States has reduced—or maintained at low levels—its economic, military, and diplomatic support to Arab countries that have experienced substantial political liberalization in recent years while increasing support for autocratic regimes such a Saudi Arabia, Kuwait, Egypt, and Morocco. Jordan, for example, received large-scale U.S. support in the 1970s and 1980s despite widespread repression and authoritarian rule; when it opened up its political system in the early 1990s, the United States substantially reduced—and, for a time, suspended—foreign aid. Aid to Yemen was cut off within months of the newly unified country's first democratic election in 1990.

Despite its laudable rhetoric, Washington's real policy regarding human rights in the Middle East is not difficult to infer. U.S. aid to Israel increased during the 1980s, when the Israeli government's repression in the occupied territories reached record levels. In addition, American occupation forces failed to stop widespread repression—even lynchings—of Palestinian residents in Kuwait immediately after liberation from Iraq. Aid to Morocco grew as that country's repression in occupied Western Sahara (and even within Morocco itself) continued unabated. The United States largely welcomed the 1992 military coup in Algeria that nullified that country's first democratic elections. Washington has pressed Syria, an authoritarian government undergoing some gradual liberalization, to crack down even harder on left-wing Palestinian groups based in Damascus who were critical of the U.S.-led peace process. The Clinton administration has also pressured the Palestinian authorities to engage in active suppression against both Islamic and secular opposition groups within areas of their administrative jurisdiction. Whatever the actual intentions of the United States, the message to Middle Eastern countries appears to be that democracy is not important.

The Middle East is the destination of the majority of American arms exports, creating enormous profits for politically influential weapons manufacturers. (See figure 10–3.) Despite promises of restraint, U.S. arms transfers to the region have topped $50 billion since the Gulf War. Joe Stork, in a survey for the Middle East Research and Information Project, argues that the ongoing Middle Eastern arms race continues for three reasons: 1) arms sales are an important component of building political alliances, particularly with the military leadership of recipient countries, 2) there is a strategic benefit arising from interoperability—having U.S.-manufactured systems on the ground in the event of a direct U.S. military intervention, and 3) arms sales are a means of supporting military industries faced with declining demand in Western countries. One episode revealing the facade of the security argument justifying increased weapons sales occurred during a 1993 off-the-record seminar involving assistant Secretary of State Richard Murphy, top Saudi officials, and the vice-chairman of the board of Morgan Guaranty (the bank that organized the financing of Saudi Arabia's 1991 war effort), where it was acknowledged that arms transfers had little to do with the objective security needs for the Saudi kingdom.

To link arms transfers with human rights records would lead to the probable loss of tens of billions of dollars in annual sales for American weapons manufacturers, who are among the most powerful special interest groups in Washington. This may help explain why the United States has ignored the fact that UN Security Council resolution 687, which the United States has cited as justification for its military responses to Iraq's possible rearmament, also calls for region-wide disarmament efforts, something the United States has rejected.

With the exception of Israel, which has provided an exemplary democratic system for its Jewish citizens, none of America's allies in the region could really be considered democracies. Yet none require democratic institutions in order to fulfill American strategic objectives. Indeed, the opposite may be true: the Middle Eastern countries that most vigorously opposed the U.S. war against Iraq in 1991—Jordan and Yemen—were the two Arab states with the most open political systems. Most observers acknowledge that close strategic cooperation with the United States tends to be unpopular in Arab countries, as are government policies that devote large sums toward the acquisition of weapons, most of which are of U.S. origin. Were these leaders subjected to the will of the majority, they would likely be forced to greatly reduce arms purchases from and strategic cooperation with the United States. As the British-based Middle East specialist Dilip Hiro explained in a February 1993 article in *New Statesman and Society*, the United States does not actually support democracy in the Middle East because "it is much simpler to manipulate a few ruling families (and to secure fat orders for arms and ensure that oil prices remain low) than a wide variety of personalities and policies bound to be thrown up by a democratic system." Elected governments might reflect the popular sentiment for "self-reliance and Islamic fellowship."

It is undeniable that democracy and universally recognized human rights have never been common in the Arab-Islamic world. Yet the tendency in the United States to emphasize cultural or religious explanations for this fact serves to minimize other factors that are arguably more salient—including the legacy of colonialism,

Figure 10.3   Major Middle East Arms Importers: 1994–1996

Country	$U.S. billions	% of World	% from U.S.
Saudi Arabia	26.6	22.2	44
Egypt	5.7	4.7	67
Turkey	5.0	4.2	64
Kuwait	3.4	2.8	56
Israel	2.9	2.4	91
United Arab Emirates	2.2	1.9	35

Source: U.S. Arms Control and Disarmament Agency, *World Military Expenditures and Arms Transfers 1997* (Washington, DC: U.S. Arms Control and Disarmament Agency, February 1, 1999).

high levels of militarization, and uneven economic development—most of which can be linked in part to the policies of Western governments, including the United States. There is a circuitous irony in a U.S. policy that sells arms, and often sends direct military aid, to repressive Middle Eastern regimes that suppress their own people and crush incipient human rights movements, only to then claim that the resulting lack of democracy and human rights is evidence that the people do not want such rights. In reality, these arms transfers and diplomatic and economic support systems play an important role in keeping autocratic Arab regimes in power by strengthening the hand of the state and supporting internal repression. (See figure 10–4.)

Indeed, Clinton's view of the Middle East is not unlike Reagan's view of Central America: discount the authoritarianism, poverty, and social injustice within allied countries and blame their internal unrest on outside forces; insist that military solutions are required to resolve what are essentially political and economic problems; define terrorism and extremist movements as the primary problem rather than the gross injustices that spawn these movements; apply strict interpretations of international law and United Nations resolutions to governments the United States opposes and ignore these laws and resolutions when they target governments the United States supports; and position the United States as the primary economic, military, and diplomatic force in the region, even to the exclusion of Washington's European allies.

So far, U.S. policy has largely been successful in extending American strategic, economic, and diplomatic interests in the region. However, as the Romans,

Figure 10.4

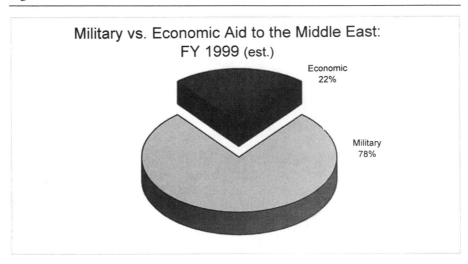

Source: The Secretary of State, *Congressional Appropriations for Foreign Operations 2000* (Washington, DC: Department of State, 1999).

Crusaders, Mongols, Ottomans, French, and British all learned, such hegemonic relationships with the Middle East can be short-lived and even disastrous for the once-hegemonic power. Given the growing resentment over America's role by much of the Middle Eastern population, there will likely be continued conflict between the United States and the peoples and governments of the region unless there are some dramatic changes in U.S. Middle East policy.

AFRICA

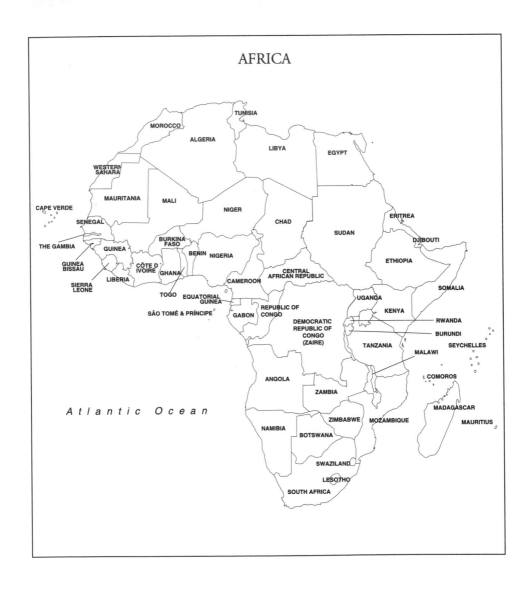

CHAPTER 11

THE UNITED STATES AND AFRICA: STARTING POINTS FOR A NEW POLICY FRAMEWORK

William Minter

PRESIDENT CLINTON'S 12-DAY TRIP TO AFRICA in spring 1998 was the most extensive ever by an American president. Boosters of the trip inside the administration hoped that it would dramatically signal a constructive U.S. engagement with the continent—a new policy for a new Africa. In the months before the trip, Assistant Secretary of State for Africa Susan Rice laid out a "new vision for Africa" and called for a "new partnership" with partners who "listen to one another, learn from one another, and compromise with one another."[1]

Many critical observers, probably exaggerating the level of U.S. interest in Africa that the trip represented, viewed Clinton's tour as an aggressive assertion of rivalry with Europe for economic predominance in the continent. Cynics saw it as driven by White House concerns to throw a symbolic bone to the African American electorate and to divert attention from the then-infant Monica Lewinsky scandal.

U.S. policy toward Africa has long been plagued by marginalization and pervasive negative stereotypes. To President Clinton's credit, the trip was shaped in large part by the need to address this crippling policy context. Selection of five of the six countries on the tour—Ghana, Uganda, South Africa, Botswana, and Senegal—was intended to highlight the continent's success stories. Rwanda was added at the insistence of officials who recognized that it would be unconscionable to ignore the failure of the international response to the 1994 genocide in that country.

In speeches during the trip, President Clinton acknowledged the damage to Africa from the slave trade, colonialism, and the cold war, and he even apologized for the failure of his own administration to respond to the Rwandan genocide, in which more than half a million people were slaughtered. A symbolic visit to the slave depot at Goree Island in Senegal underscored the roots of the U.S. connection to Africa, and the presidential entourage was reported to be the most racially diverse ever for a presidential trip.

Despite these encouraging signals, Clinton's tour also reflected fundamental problems with the administration's policy. In keeping with the dominant policy climate in Washington, the trip was characterized by pervasive promotion of free market fundamentalism as the solution to Africa's economic woes. The message of U.S. support for democracy was ambivalent and muffled by clear disarray within the administration about what stance to take toward the military dictatorship of Sani Abacha in Nigeria. The apology for international failure to respond to the Rwandan genocide was accompanied by no coherent policy or commitment for responding to ongoing violent conflicts in Zaire (later the Democratic Republic of the Congo), Algeria, Burundi, Sudan, Liberia, and elsewhere. And the acknowledgment of historical responsibility both for the slave trade and for cold war destruction was a momentary blip rather than the beginning of a serious debate. In reaction to the flurry of U.S. commentators who argued that the United States had nothing to apologize for, the theme vanished from administration statements for the rest of the trip.

Events in the months following Clinton's tour made it clear that the "new start" would be slow to take off. Despite the efforts of Africa-focused officials within the administration, Africa quickly resumed its place near the bottom of the agendas of the highest officials—and not only because of the president's growing domestic problems. The outbreak of the border war between Eritrea and Ethiopia, the eruption of a new war in the Democratic Republic of the Congo, and the resumption of fighting in Angola had profound regional implications but apparently caught the administration without contingency plans. None led to more than a minute fraction of the high-level attention given to the crises in the former Yugoslavia.

Meanwhile, Washington's response to the terrorist attack in August 1998 on U.S. embassies in Dar es Salaam and Nairobi exposed the "partnership" theme as empty rhetoric. The instinctive focus by U.S. officials on U.S. casualties, although they were far less numerous than Kenyan and Tanzanian victims, provoked immediate resentment. And the U.S. retaliatory strike on a pharmaceutical factory in Sudan as well as on a guerrilla training camp in Afghanistan was not only unilateral but also almost certainly counterproductive to its stated aims of reducing the terrorist threat. For instance, it undermined opponents of the abusive fundamentalist regime in Sudan by allowing that regime to present itself as a victim and thus gain international sympathy. And the Clinton administration was eventually forced to concede that the Khartoum factory had no tie to terrorists.

Those within the administration who were trying to get top cabinet members and their staff to focus on Africa did persist, and their efforts bore fruit in the Conference on U.S.-Africa Partnership in the 21st Century held in Washington in March 1999. Although some early plans had projected a meeting confined to Washington's favorite "reformers," the invitation list was broadened at African insistence: cabinet-level representatives from 50 African countries participated in the meeting with their U.S. counterparts. At the conference, one could see the beginnings of more substantive dialogue between U.S. and African officials.

In practice, however, Washington's legacies of neglect and of inappropriate policies toward Africa have remained largely in place with the same overall guidelines. On one hand, there is promotion of doctrinaire free market prescriptions—including foreign trade and investment, production for export, elimination of trade barriers, and privatization of state enterprises—as a panacea. On the other hand, we see endorsement of democracy, human rights, and conflict resolution, although implementation of this policy is primarily by ad hoc response to crises without sustained high-level attention.

This harsh judgment is admittedly a caricature of a far more complex policy picture regarding specific issues and countries. Those in the government dealing with Africa on a day-to-day basis, many of whom are struggling to implement programs and policies that do respond to specific African needs, will most likely see it as unfair. As an overall assessment of results rather than intentions, however, it is unfortunately more accurate than the lofty rhetoric accompanying the president's trip.

The failure, however, is not unique to the Clinton administration's Africa policymakers. Although the "Africa advocacy" and "progressive" foreign policy communities have been vocal on selected issues, and at times effective, they have failed to build consensus around convincing and coherent policy frameworks, have not adequately addressed the complex issues at stake, and have emphasized criticism rather than offering alternative perspectives to guide what should be done. Unlike the period of clear-focused campaigns against colonialism and apartheid, there is no clear overall framework being advanced collectively by African states and non-state movements.

This chapter, which attempts to cover 54 countries of the African continent and a host of issues, does not claim to fill that gap. It is also stronger on critique than on charting out a comprehensive alternative policy framework. It does, however, offer starting points for such a framework as well as suggested prerequisites for moving toward greater clarity. Such a framework, if it is to be authentic and convincing, must emerge from a sustained and systematic dialogue with a range of diverse voices in the distinct regional contexts of the continent. Such a dialogue is just beginning. As state-to-state and business-to-business contacts accelerate, progressives must also ensure that their contributions to the debate reflect real encounters with diverse African voices and not just the assumptions we bring from other periods and political arenas.

In the post–cold war world, the stated general goals of U.S. foreign policy are, in fact, congruent with those of African peoples. Salih Booker, a longtime African activist and leading spokesperson on Africa at the Council on Foreign Relations, argues that "it is in the U.S. interest that, within each African region, as elsewhere in the world, countries and peoples should be able to advance the common goals of achieving security, democracy and development."[2] When one asks how best to achieve those widely endorsed goals, however, there is a veritable chasm between perspectives crafted purely in the U.S. foreign policy arena and those rooted in African realities.

AFRICA'S "SECOND INDEPENDENCE"

Like the rest of the world, African countries are struggling to find direction in the post–cold war era. Yet debates about the structure of African societies and states are related less fundamentally to the aftermath of that East-West conflict than to the legacies of the colonial era and the failures of the first postcolonial generation. Africa is, of course, caught up in the worldwide trend toward globalization, but its niche is still largely shaped by its particular history of slavery, colonialism, and racism.

From the fifteenth into the nineteenth century, Africa's primary link with the world was through the export of slaves. In the nineteenth and twentieth centuries, export of raw materials became the dominant link. This role as commodity supplier—whether of high-valued ivory, gold, diamonds, and oil or of precariously priced crops such as coffee and cocoa—largely excluded Africa from the more dynamic sectors of manufacturing, financial services, and information technology.

Political independence beginning in the 1960s did not change this fundamental reality. Today Africa's primary exports remain unprocessed agricultural products and, for a handful of countries, minerals and oil. Even South Africa's relatively developed economy is extremely vulnerable to the fluctuating price of gold. And although Ghana, one of the World Bank's "success stories," increased its income from nontraditional commodities to 18 percent of total export earnings by 1996, most export revenue still came from cocoa (32 percent) and gold (45 percent). Countries that depend almost exclusively on agricultural exports, such as Rwanda and Burundi, are most vulnerable. Oil producers, such as Nigeria and Angola, may be better off in comparison, but they endure boom and bust cycles as the world oil price shifts.

Africa's first postindependence generation—broadly speaking, from the 1960s to the end of political apartheid in South Africa in 1994—made significant advances. Most notably, the newly independent states educated far more of their children than preceding colonial regimes, and many made impressive strides in delivery of basic healthcare and potable water, expansion of infrastructure, and industrial production for the domestic market. Africa's independence struggles also gave impetus to the civil rights movement in the United States, while African culture gained new prominence on the world scene. African states formed significant voting blocs in the United Nations and other international organizations, and African professionals excelled in their fields both at home and abroad.

This generation's failings were also considerable and painful—repressive, ineffective, and corrupt bureaucracies, military dictatorships, and one-party states; deep indebtedness to international institutions and banks; a stifling of grass-roots initiatives, public debate, and other civil liberties. These failings were compounded by an international system that fostered ill-conceived, nonfunctional, and costly development projects, heavy financial borrowing, and cold war–linked civil wars, which left newly independent countries with little economic cushion or political leeway for policy errors.

Kofi Annan of Ghana, the first United Nations Secretary General from sub-Saharan Africa, divides this era into two "waves": the first, during the 1960s and

1970s, was characterized by postcolonial enthusiasm and economic advance; the second, running from the 1980s to the early 1990s, was "too often marked by civil wars, the tyranny of military rule, and economic stagnation."[3] Autocratic leaders, whatever their proclaimed political ideology, turned to police state repression and cold war patrons to stay in power. The worst perpetrated enormous human rights abuses. Even the best failed to deliver on the hopes of independence regarding political liberties, social services, and economic improvement. Thus, much of the economic advance of the 1970s was rolled back in the 1980s and early 1990s as a result of both internal failure and a tougher world economic climate, including the oil crises in the 1970s, a steady fall in world prices for Africa's leading agricultural exports, and the linking of international assistance to draconian structural adjustment policies (SAPs).

Often not acknowledged is the central role the World Bank, the International Monetary Fund (IMF), and various Western bilateral aid agencies—including the United States Agency for International Development (USAID)—played in undermining efforts by the postindependence generation of Africans to improve basic social services. Beginning in the early to mid-1980s, the World Bank, the IMF, and the United States began preconditioning aid and loans to many African countries on acceptance of structural adjustment policies, which included slashing government spending. "If you ask governments to cut down expenditure, it's almost an authorization that they cut on health and education, and where education is not for everyone, it is left for the privileged," former Tanzanian President Julius Nyerere told the World Health Organization (WHO) in outlining the impact of structural adjustment policies.[4]

Yet at the millennium, Africa is clearly entering a new political phase, variously referred to as a "second independence struggle," a "third wave" of change, or, as popularized by South Africa's then deputy president (and in June 1999, president) Thabo Mbeki, an "African Renaissance." Whatever the terminology, a common theme throughout the continent today is that a critical mass of Africans—including government officials, professionals, business owners, academics, journalists, religious leaders, trade unionists, and small farmers as well as human rights, women's movement, and environmental activists—are organizing with new dynamism, new demands, and new expectations. The current generation, which has come of age in the post–cold war, postapartheid era, is determined to fulfill the promises of widely shared economic progress, democratic rights for all, and security that will enable ordinary people around the continent to pursue their own dreams in peace. Although enormous obstacles remain, Africa has entered a new stage of social transformation.

The primary dynamic in Africa is internal. It should be no surprise that the transformation of African national and state structures, still largely derived from colonial models, remains unfinished. To cite only one reason among many, it is little more than one generation since the first large wave of young children entered the school systems so rapidly expanded after independence. At Tanzania's independence in 1961, for example, 85 percent of adults were illiterate, and less than half the country's children were in school. Although some countries were better off—Nigeria and Ghana, in particular, had long histories of educational development at home and study abroad—others were even further behind. At Mozambique's independence in 1975, 93 percent were illiterate, and less than a third of primary-age children were in school. In their first decades of independence, almost all African countries rapidly expanded primary and secondary education and founded new universities. The sheer number of years it takes for a significant number of students to advance from primary school through professional education and experience partly explains why the 1990s began seeing so large a wave of people with the skills and contacts to speak out at home and abroad on the issues facing the African continent.

Another structural reason for this upsurge is that the capacity to suppress such internal forces decreased as states lost their cold war patronage. And there are other factors, some unique to particular countries or regions, others due to aspects of the changing international environment. What is certain is that there is a new dynamic. Its outcome—for good or evil—is not so certain. The transformation needed for new voices and social forces to make a real impact will not be easy, and it will be uneven. Its chances will depend, above all, on African initiatives, not only by African governments but by groups and individuals in African countries on both national and local levels.

But the chances of success also depend in large part on whether African realities and priorities are recognized in decision-making arenas in multinational and rich-country institutions. There are many initiatives, on and off the continent, to promote African demands for human rights, social justice, peace, and economic development leading to sustainable and equitable improvement in the quality of African life. These initiatives, however, are not yet coherent enough or powerful enough to break through the old patterns of how the outside world deals with Africa. Among the common obstacles they face is the pervasiveness of simplistic stereotypes and one-size-fits-all remedies from outside the continent. One indispensable requirement for constructive outside involvement is greater sensitivity to the diversity and complexity of African realities.

Misleading perceptions affect policymakers and shape public opinion. And they include not only long-established negative stereotypes about Africa but also simplistic presentations of new trends. The importance of leadership is undeniable, yet the desire to tout success stories—and to identify them with particular leaders, such as those visited by President Clinton in 1998—can easily mask wider issues. In Addis Ababa in December 1997, Secretary of State Madeleine Albright praised Africa's "new leaders" who, she said, "share a common vision of empowerment—for all their citizens, for their nations, and for their continent." The administration provided no comprehensive list of the "new leaders," and interactions by Secretary Albright and President Clinton grouped a very diverse array, from Nelson Mandela in South Africa, to Laurent Kabila in the Democratic Republic of the Congo, to the leaders of Senegal, Ghana, Rwanda, Uganda, Botswana, Ethiopia, Zimbabwe, and others. To place hope for the future—and to base policy projections—on a new set of rulers is to set oneself up for quick disappointment, when the new leaders also turn out to have feet of clay and prove to be less homogeneous than initially portrayed. The future depends on institutional change at many levels, not just on leaders.

Another dangerous half-truth pursuit is to enshrine open markets as a fundamentalist dogma and then to impose rigid formulas for open economies and macroeconomic adjustment to the neglect of fundamental requirements for development. U.S. policy statements commonly cite the principal goal of "integrating Africa into the world economy" and often praise nations that "adopt sound macroeconomic policies and make the transition to free market economies."[5] Rarely, if ever, do U.S. officials acknowledge that the policy package they advocate is sharply criticized by large sectors of African public opinion (and by many government leaders as well, when they feel free to speak back to their "donors"). Achieving economic growth is indeed indispensable for achieving other goals, and it does require greater competitiveness and freedom from inefficient or corrupt bureaucratic restrictions. But growth will be neither sustainable nor fair unless it: (1) is directed toward job creation and poverty reduction; (2) produces for domestic and regional consumers and not only for international markets; (3) is undergirded by public investment in health and education; and (4) is protected from abuse of worker rights and the environment. This is why both the World Bank and the United Nations Development Program now agree that poverty-reducing growth, not just "growth," must be clearly defined as an objective.[6]

Meanwhile, market integration—without other structural changes—leaves Africa still dependent on a small number of export commodities, deeply in debt, and capable of attracting only a small fraction of world investment capital. In 1997, excluding South Africa, the entire continent attracted only $4.7 billion in global capital, a mere 3 percent of that year's direct investment in developing countries.[7] If policy is based on the assumption that wide-open markets will automatically produce other desired results, the most likely outcome is that the promised benefits will accrue only to a favored few. Some countries and some sectors may advance, but at the price of continued growth of poverty along with greater inequality within and between African countries.

For its fortieth anniversary conference in April 1998, the Economic Commission for Africa chose the theme "African Women and Economic Development: Investing in Our Future."[8] The choice reflected the growing recognition that progress for Africa depends on the advance of women in all spheres of life. Africa's women face particularly great obstacles. Female adult literacy rates are 50 percent or less in 29 African countries; only the southern Africa region reaches the global developing country average of 61 percent. Maternal mortality rates for sub-Saharan Africa averaged 980 per 100,000 live births in 1990, as compared with 12 for the United States and 470 for all developing countries.[9]

According to WHO, female education levels are closely correlated with improved family health and reduced infant mortality. In addition, a WHO study found that "women with even a few years of schooling have more self confidence, are better able to assume responsibility, and often enjoy a higher status in the family and community, giving them a greater voice in making decisions."[10] Addressing gender disparities is thus not only an imperative in its own right, it is essential for Africa's economic and political advancement.

A prerequisite for Africa's advance on multiple fronts is participation from a wide range of sectors in developing goals and initiatives, implementing them, and monitoring results. A series of global, continent-wide, and regional conferences in the 1990s—sponsored by United Nations agencies, the Economic Commission for Africa, regional African organizations, and a variety of nongovernmental coalitions—made considerable progress in defining objectives: advances in health, education, sustainable economic development, security, democratic participation, and gender equality. Implementation of such goals will require maximizing collaboration both within and across national and continental boundaries.

FREE MARKET FUNDAMENTALISM
OR PARTNERSHIP FOR DEVELOPMENT?

During the cold war, U.S. policy toward Africa, including aid and economic relationships, was shaped overwhelmingly by competition with the Soviet Union. The leading African recipients of U.S. aid between 1962 and 1988 were Ethiopia, Kenya, Liberia, Somalia, Sudan, and Zaire—not at all the list one would choose on the basis of development goals or even in terms of prospects for trade and investment. In 1987, in an effort to define congressional goals for development assistance and in reaction to President Ronald Reagan's earlier efforts to divert money from African aid, Congress established the Development Fund for Africa (DFA) with the laudable goal of helping "the poor majority of men and women in sub-Saharan Africa to participate in a process of long-term development through economic growth that is equitable, participatory, environmentally sustainable, and self-reliant." The act also established a minimum level of funding for Africa each year. The DFA, administered as designated funds within AID, began by disbursing $562 million in 1988 and reached over $800 million annually in the early 1990s. However, for FY2000, AID requested only $513 million for the DFA—a rather paltry sum, given the level of need, DFA's objectives, and the Clinton administration's rhetoric on Africa.[11]

If implemented, the DFA's laudable objectives would have revolutionized U.S. development assistance programs. However, in practice, Washington's cold war allies in Africa, such as Kenya and Zaire, continued to receive much of the assistance.[12] During the 1990s, with no new strategic framework to replace the cold war mind-set, the case for aid lost its anti-Soviet rationale, and supporters of continued or reformed development assistance struggled to find new arguments in a generally skeptical political climate. Curiously, Clinton administration "reformers" within AID chose to drop poverty alleviation (as well as education) as a rationale or "pillar," arguing that it already underlaid what were articulated as the agency's six new central objectives: (1) economic growth and agricultural development; (2) democracy and good governance; (3) human capacity development (other than basic education); (4) health and population; (5) management of the environment; and (6) providing humanitarian assistance. The AID administrator declared that Washington's two foreign policy goals in Africa were "to accelerate Africa's integration into the global economy and to combat serious transnational security threats there, including HIV/AIDS and outbreaks of violence."[13]

Without a convincing overall framework justifying U.S. contributions to development either worldwide or in Africa, the case for investment in African development became difficult to make. U.S. development aid to Africa declined from $826 million in 1991 to $689 million in 1997. Since 1996, Congress has refused to earmark funds specifically for Africa, leaving the regional allocation of funds to decisions within AID. For 2000, AID requested a mere $305 million (for economic support funds and child survival and disease programs) on top of the $513 million for the DFA.[14]

During 1997 and 1998, the lion's share of the Washington debate about Africa centered on the congressional Africa Growth and Opportunity Act and the parallel presidential initiative for a Partnership for Economic Growth and Opportunity in Africa. The act initially emerged from initiatives by liberal Democratic Representative Jim McDermott from Seattle and members of the Congressional Black Caucus (CBC), who portrayed it as a way of getting Africa its share of U.S. trade and investment. It was then sold as a bipartisan plan and developed in conjunction with conservative Republican Representative Phil Crane of Illinois. Republicans were comfortable in signing on because of the strong emphasis on support for U.S. exports and corporate investment. Sponsors presented initial versions of the act as a "paradigm shift" from aid to trade. And despite endorsements of aid, debt relief, and human rights inserted into later versions of the legislation, the bill's principal backers continued to assert that their intention was to replace aid with trade and to bring Africa into the mainstream of the world economy by using private capital as the main engine of growth.

Although the act suggested the possibility of future "free trade" pacts with Africa, its operational provisions were in fact very limited: a regular forum for U.S. cabinet-level officials to meet with their counterparts from selected African countries; $650 million in investment funds allotted by the Overseas Private Investment Corporation (OPIC), which provides insurance for U.S. foreign investments; extending duty-free entry for many African products, including primarily minerals and agricultural products; and elimination of import quotas for African textiles entering the United States. Those African countries and companies already well placed to compete in a market economy would be given greater access to the U.S. market, and U.S. business with Africa would be facilitated by new contacts and subsidies. (See figure 11–1.)

During the 1998 legislative session, U.S. companies with interests in Africa joined with African ambassadors, the Clinton administration, and congressional backers in lobbying passionately for the bill. But resistance also grew both from critics who opposed the bill's simplistic promarket bias and from textile-state representatives who argued that import quota reductions would hurt U.S. manufacturers. Both the CBC and nongovernmental Africa advocacy groups were split roughly into three camps in response to the bill, with views ranging from passionate support, to adamant opposition, to more nuanced positions that offered several amendments. Many of those who supported the bill did so because they hoped it would help Africa get a larger slice of the global market by promoting "equal opportunity" among exporting nations. Opponents saw little benefit for ordinary

Figure 11.1

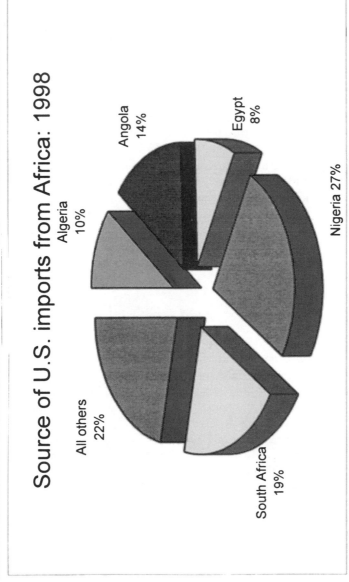

Source of U.S. imports from Africa: 1998

Algeria 10%

Angola 14%

Egypt 8%

Nigeria 27%

South Africa 19%

All others 22%

Source: U.S. Department of Commerce, *U.S. Total Exports-Imports to Individual Countries, 1998* (Washington, DC: Department of Commerce, 1999) (preliminary).

Africans in the bill and feared considerable damage from its emphasis on strict free market macroeconomic policies.

The vehemence of the debate can be understood only as contention related to broader symbolic issues. For many proponents, the main intent was to counter Africa's marginalization by rejecting the "aid seen as welfare" model and insisting on Africa's incorporation into the current economic mainstream through expanded trade and investment. But most opponents rejected that mainstream model as damaging to African grass-roots interests and long-term development prospects. "Structural adjustment" packages imposing similar policies have a mixed record at best in promoting economic growth, and they exact a high price from ordinary citizens in the form of cutbacks of government programs and a rising cost of living. Yet the critique, for the most part, failed to acknowledge that passage of this particular bill would add little to the pressures already felt by African countries from internationally imposed structural adjustment programs, the conditionality of bilateral aid programs, and Africa's lack of competitive clout in the world marketplace. As CBC Chairperson Maxine Waters commented in floor debate, both proponents and opponents should recognize that this bill is neither "the best thing" nor "the worst thing" that could happen to Africa.

In 1999, the level of debate advanced somewhat with the introduction of the alternate "HOPE for Africa Act" by Representative Jesse Jackson, Jr. of Illinois. This act calls on the United States to cancel all its bilateral debt with sub-Saharan African countries and to urge that the IMF and World Bank cancel Africa's multilateral debts without any linkage to structural adjustment programs. It therefore provides a positive vehicle behind which critics of the Growth and Opportunity Act can rally. Still, the fact that there continues to be division within the CBC and within the Africa advocacy community has left the fate of both bills in limbo. Neither bill provides a viable comprehensive framework for expansion of mutually beneficial U.S.-African economic relations. Thus, although congressional support for additional debt reduction is growing in response to public pressure, the chance of successful action even on this unifying issue has been reduced by the lack of coordination between different congressional initiatives.

Although Africa clearly does need more trade and investment, the real issues are what type of trade and what actions are needed to attract capital. The recipe prescribed by free market fundamentalism is simple: remove trade barriers, offer incentives to foreign investors, and greatly reduce the role of government in regulating the economy, and economic growth will follow. Critics, however, argue that sustainable and equitable economic growth requires that: (1) production be geared for local and regional consumption, not simply for overseas export markets; (2) locally owned industries and enterprises must be supported; and (3) substantial new investments are needed in both human and physical infrastructure. The reality is that private capital is not going to make the necessary investments in education, healthcare, clean and accessible water, electricity, roads, ports, airports, and the like; such infrastructure requires government planning and development cooperation from international agencies.

Instead of debating "trade versus aid," those concerned with building a prosperous and stable Africa should be debating what mix of public and private investment in which sectors can best build an economic environment for sustainable and equitable growth. In order to change its situation, Africa must be able to build physical and institutional infrastructure, invest in its human resources, and break out of dependence on unprocessed exports. International investments, hungry for the highest and quickest profit margins, are not well matched for such long-term objectives, but, if carefully scanned, they can help African governments raise revenue to finance some public efforts.

The urgent need for public investment in health, education, and the advancement of women in Africa—by international as well as by African institutions—is not a question of "aid/welfare." These are goals not only of development but also essential prerequisites for economic advance. Drastic cuts in African government budgets, such as cutbacks in free public health services, not only impose suffering but also delay the building of social capital, which is one of the requirements for a productive work force. HIV/AIDS alone, a December 1998 UN report estimated, affects more than 10 percent of the adult population in nine African countries. Malaria, WHO estimates, can retard income growth by as much as 12 percent in many African countries. Such issues, it is clear, will not be addressed by the economic marketplace. With a focus squarely on such substantive issues, one could debate whether the United States is contributing its fair share of investment; what policies are most appropriate to advance the goals of improved health, education, and gender equality; and what roles U.S. public and private institutions might play.

The United States does, through AID's six main objectives, address many of these issues not only with rhetoric but also in programs. But there are legitimate issues concerning the quality and size of American aid. (See figure 11–2.) Among developed countries, the United States provides the lowest percentage of its central government budget for development assistance (0.81 percent in 1996) and the lowest as a percentage of GNP (0.08 percent).[15] AID, for instance, provides over $200 million annually to assist with African health issues as well as additional sums through the Centers for Disease Control, WHO, and other agencies. The total, however, falls far short of what would constitute a contribution commensurate with U.S. resources and mutual interests. If Washington were serious about responding to the scale of Africa's various health crises and addressing the handicap that health problems impose for development, top U.S. officials would lobby for massive increases in funding and would broadly publicize that 67 percent of people worldwide living with HIV/AIDS are in Africa and 83 percent of global deaths from AIDS are in Africa. Not only is AIDS damaging the continent's prospects for development, but, as these statistics reveal, a disproportionate number of Africans are dying from AIDS—an indication that treatment remains woefully inadequate.

Many issues need to be considered in order to develop guidelines for U.S. economic relations with Africa that transcend private sector boosterism. The following three starting points illustrate how to shift the debate away from the pros and cons of private financing to the more substantive issues of investment (public and private): in what activities, on what terms, and for whose benefit.

First, Africa needs more diversified investment beyond the traditional concentration in the extractive industries. Moreover, investments in those sectors must become more environmentally sustainable. All investments need to be

Figure 11.2   U.S. Aid to Sub-Saharan Africa, 1999–2000 ($U.S. millions)

Program	FY 1999 (actual)	FY 2000 (requested)
Development Fund for Africa	460.1	512.6
Child Survival and Disease Programs	251.2	232.4
Economic Support Fund[a]	98.2	73.0
African Development Foundation	11.1	14.4
Peace Corps	54.6	56.0
Voluntary Peacekeeping Operations	19.0	28.0
International Military Education and Training	8.1	8.5
Foreign Military Financing	10.0	10.0
Contributions to International Peacekeeping	29.2	57.2
African Development Bank	0.0	5.1
African Development Fund	128.0	127.0
Non-food Aid Total	1,069.5	1,124.2
Food Aid	224.4	134.4
Total	1,293.9	1,258.6

Source: Raymond W. Copson, "Africa: U.S. Foreign Assistance Issues," CRS Issue Brief for Congress, August 19, 1999, available on the Internet at: http://www.cnie.org/nle/econ-51.html.
[a]ESF, a security assistance program, increased dramatically in 1999 (up from $26 million in 1998) because of a supplemental appropriation in response to bombings of U.S. embassies in Kenya and Tanzania.

managed/regulated by African institutions and governments accountable to their people.

Currently, with the exception of a more diversified relationship with South Africa, U.S. imports from Africa and U.S. investments are both heavily concentrated in the oil sector. In 1996, 71 percent of U.S. imports from sub-Saharan Africa were energy-related. That same year, oil producers Nigeria and Angola ranked twenty-sixth and thirty-fourth worldwide in the value of their total imports to the United States (ahead of South Africa, at thirty-eighth) while oil producers Algeria and Gabon ranked fortieth and forty-fourth, respectively. In certain cases, environmental groups and prodemocracy activists have succeeded in raising questions about the behavior of international oil corporations—for example, their support for the military dictatorship in Nigeria, their responsibility for environmental damage, and the proposed investment by a consortium including Exxon in the new Chad/Cameroon project. But neither the general issue of social responsibility in the oil industry nor the development implications of investment revenues accruing to unaccountable governments has been addressed systematically in any policy forum.

Second, the United States should promote telecommunications expansion (not simply privatization) and should support creative initiatives for serving disadvantaged communities.

The expansion of telecommunications and Internet connections in particular provides a significant opportunity for Africa to reduce its disadvantages in the world economy. At the simplest level, a telephone connection from a remote village to the national capital may enable a farmer to keep up with crop prices and improve her bargaining position with traders. Yet Africa still lags far behind in terms of telecommunications links. Outside South Africa, most countries in the continent have less than 1 main telephone line per 100 people, as compared to over 50 in most advanced industrial countries. Telephone connections and even Internet connectivity are growing very rapidly, however. Almost all African countries have some Internet e-mail connection, and the number of Internet host computers on the continent is growing at more than 85 percent a year.

It does not take a free market enthusiast to see that bureaucratic government monopolies with years-long waiting lists for access to phone service are one obstacle to faster growth in the telecommunications sector. Yet unregulated privatization would certainly lead to foreign companies serving only the most profitable markets and accelerating inequality of access. The upcountry peasant farmer still would not have a phone connection to the capital. The International Telecommunications Union (ITU), meeting at Africa Telecom 1998 in Johannesburg, cited the need to include universal access as a goal in the regulatory framework. Citing the South African experience, the ITU noted that companies can be required to provide public telephones and to serve disadvantaged communities and rural areas.[16]

Even with the limited investments to date, new electronic technologies are creating new opportunities for collaboration, both within Africa's regions and at a continental level, by lowering the cost of long-distance communication. This trend also facilitates more direct communication and collaboration between Africa and the rest of the world. With strategic thinking about the best ways to make such tools serve grass-roots African advancement, these new technologies may enable Africa to leapfrog some barriers to advancement.

Third, the United States should move toward acceptance of African demands for debt cancellation, including delinking of such cancellation programs from onerous structural adjustment programs.

After several years of the World Bank's Heavily Indebted Poor Countries (HIPC) Initiative, which includes 31 African countries, it is clear that the program is having only a marginal impact in reducing Africa's debt burden, which cripples the continent's chances for significant economic growth. Beginning shortly after World War II, the Allies lowered Germany's debt payments to less than 3.5 percent of export earnings, which was deemed to be the maximum "sustainable" level for that war-torn country. Yet even after Mozambique's debt relief plan went into effect in 1999, the country still pays more than 11 percent (or $100 million) of its annual export earnings to service its debt. Debt service-to-export ratios for Africa's regions range from a high of 30 percent in West Africa to 12.1 percent in southern Africa.[17]

Sub-Saharan Africa's debt includes about $4.5 billion in bilateral debt to the United States out of a total long-term debt of $179.1 billion; another $54.8 billion is owed to multilateral institutions such as the World Bank and the IMF. (See figure 11–3.) Yet only $8.2 billion is being spent on the entire HIPC debt reduction program, a figure dwarfed by the $50 billion in "bailout" packages given by the World Bank and the IMF in 1998 alone for Russia, Brazil, and several other countries.[18]

Figure 11.3

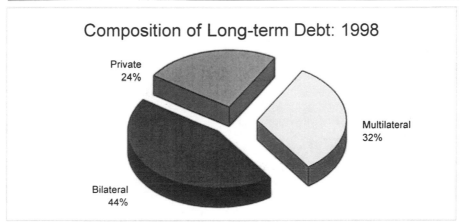

Composition of Long-term Debt: 1998

Private 24%

Multilateral 32%

Bilateral 44%

World Bank, *Global Development Finance 1999, Analysis and Summary Tables* (Washington, DC: The World Bank Group, March 30, 1999).

Source: World Bank, *Global Development Finance 1999, Analysis and Summary Tables* (Washington, DC: The World Bank Group, March 30, 1999).

More generally, over the last few years, voices both within and outside the African continent have begun to articulate alternatives to the "U.S. model" of free market fundamentalism. Rather than a single alternative perspective, there are now many proposals with different starting points than the vaunted "Washington Consensus." Some World Bank officials, for example, advocate "poverty-reduction" as a coequal goal with economic growth. Many grass-roots and other more radical critics call for an end to structural adjustment conditionalities, for debt cancellation for the poorest countries, and for "bottom-up" development projects. In a variety of international forums, there are active debates about what policies and what mix of private, state, and nongovernmental actions can best promote development. The United States should join these debates rather than assuming that it has all the answers.

WHAT ROAD TO DEMOCRACY?

In contrast to the serious gap between Washington discourse and African public opinion about the best road to economic progress, there is much more consensus on the desirability of fundamental political rights, including democracy, the rule of law, human rights, citizen participation, a free press, and accountable governments with minimal corruption. In the eloquent words of UN Secretary General Kofi Annan's 1997 address to the Organization of African Unity (OAU):

> The success of Africa's third wave depends on respect for fundamental human rights. I am aware of the fact that some view this concern as a luxury of the rich

countries for which Africa is not ready. I know that others treat it as an imposition, if not a plot, by the industrialized West. I find these thoughts truly demeaning, demeaning of the yearning for human dignity that resides in every African heart.

Do not African mothers weep when their sons or daughters are killed or maimed by agents of repressive rule? Are not African fathers saddened when their children are unjustly jailed or tortured? Is not Africa as a whole impoverished when even one of its brilliant voices is silenced? So I say this to you, my brothers and sisters, that human rights are African rights, and I call upon you to ensure that all Africans are able fully to enjoy them.

As Annan stressed, postcolonial governments in Africa, irrespective of ideology or proclaimed goals, have rarely lived up to these goals. Many of the worst offenders survived by serving their cold war patrons, paying lip service to one global ideology or another while pursuing their agendas of control and aggrandizement. As President Clinton cautiously acknowledged during his 1998 trip, much to the annoyance of officials of previous administrations who argued that the United States had no need to apologize, "very often we dealt with countries in Africa based more on how they stood in the struggle between the United States and the Soviet Union than how they stood in the struggle for their own people's aspirations."[19]

Remembering the decades-long support for military dictator Mobutu Sese Seko in Zaire, U.S. collaboration with the apartheid regime, and numerous other cases, most of those familiar with African history will find the "apology" enormously understated. But it did serve to indicate that the stated goals in Washington and those among African democracy advocates are much more compatible today than during the cold war period. Statements of desirable objectives have a high degree of overlap, whether they come from U.S. policymakers, international conferences, or prodemocracy groups in particular African countries. The congressionally mandated annual U.S. State Department human rights report, although not entirely free of bias in its approach to different countries, has become a valuable resource for holding governments accountable, complementing the efforts of local human rights groups and established multilateral organizations such as Amnesty International and Human Rights Watch.

The president's trip, however, highlighted abundant inconsistencies in Washington's advocacy of democratic political goals. The currents of opinion within the administration that saw "human rights" in practice as a dirty word to be avoided, whether out of traditional diplomatic expediency or in the belief that prioritizing economic advance would automatically bring progress in other areas, remained highly influential. Calls for Clinton to speak out and act clearly for democracy in Africa's most populous country—Nigeria—fell on deaf ears, for example, and the celebration of Africa's "new leaders" in South Africa, Uganda (where political parties are banned), and elsewhere eclipsed the need to advance democracy on multiple fronts.

Particularly troubling is the assumption that economic progress (as defined by market-friendly policies and macroeconomic growth) is automatically correlated with political freedom or that it should take priority when the two clash. In fact, imposition of strict structural adjustment policies is likely to undermine a democratic leader's popular base by imposing immediate burdens, while supposed benefits are often postponed indefinitely or awarded to a privileged elite. The road toward greater democracy is not always obvious and is certainly not the same in different countries. The degree of democracy, as measured by participation and open debate, is not necessarily matched with the number of political parties. But the tendency of many U.S. officials to downplay democratic failings among favorite governments and leaders as long as their economic policies please Washington repeatedly blurs the clarity of the prodemocracy message.

This double standard is particularly obvious, of course, in the case of countries with major resources of interest to Washington. Over the years since the military regime canceled Nigeria's 1993 election, the United States has joined others around the world in criticizing the lack of democracy in that country. But although the Clinton administration protested with a few concrete steps—stopping Nigerian airline flights and denying visas to top military leaders—the surging flow of money sent a different message: U.S. investments in Nigeria, predominantly in the oil sector, grew from around $4 billion to as much as $7 billion in the five years from 1992 to 1997, and bilateral trade increased from $4.9 billion in 1994 to $6.7 billion in 1996.[20]

While policy reviews within the Clinton administration dragged on, Washington officials were dispatched to oppose citizen campaigns to enact state and local sanctions against Nigeria. And when President Clinton signaled in Cape Town that it might be acceptable for the dictator Sani Abacha to run as a civilian candidate, administration officials scrambled to explain the contradiction with earlier State Department assertions that the United States would stand firm against military rule in civilian clothing.

Abacha's death in June 1998 and the subsequent death in prison of Moshood Abiola, winner of the 1993 presidential election and a focal point of prodemocracy proponents, altered the political situation in Nigeria. Opponents of the military regime differed regarding how much trust to place in Abacha's successor, General Abdusalam Abubakar, who released some political prisoners and promised a return to civilian rule in 1999. When President-elect Olusegun Obasanjo assumed authority in place of the military regime in June 1999, many predicted that the transition to "civilian rule" in Nigeria was now complete. But the basic issues related to promoting broad-based and lasting democracy in Nigeria continue to fester. Particularly explosive are the failures to address regional and ethnic inequalities, the division of powers between the federal government and other units, and the distribution of oil wealth, currently concentrated in the country's delta region. Both the Nigerian military government and international oil companies that exploit the region's wealth (Shell, Mobil, Chevron, and others) are being challenged as never before. Questions raised about the fairness of the election—as well as President Obasanjo's military background and his apparent initial assumption that input from prodemocracy, human rights, and other grass-roots groups is no longer necessary— suggest that durable solutions may be long in coming. The temptation to rely primarily on repression rather than dialogue is still a major threat.

Although the ambivalence of U.S. policy regarding Nigeria rests above all on the priority given to economic interests, Washington's rhetoric about "new leaders" derives partly from trying to find simple slogans to justify and orient policy and partly from focusing on the leadership level rather than on more fundamental institutional change. While the success story of Nelson Mandela's leadership in South Africa was matched by high-level attention to bilateral relations, U.S. policymakers at middle levels were and are divided on how precisely to deal with democratic issues in countries as diverse as Uganda, Ethiopia, and Eritrea, not to mention those with deep internal conflicts such as Rwanda and Congo (Kinshasa). One common policy element is Washington's priority on stability and economic cooperation; another is its "flexibility" regarding the compliance of African regimes with human rights and democratic standards.

Critics of this framework are convincing when they say that standards of human rights should be applied across the board. They are less convincing, however, in laying out strategies for ensuring that such rights are implemented in practice. Expedient diplomatic silence on major abuses is not justifiable. Public exposure of those abuses, by both domestic and international agencies, is needed. But it is insufficient. Regarding further action, no "one-size-fits-all" approach will work, whether it be sanctions, aid conditionality, high-profile diplomatic statements, financial support for prodemocracy groups, or "quiet diplomacy."

What might serve as an alternative to ad hoc expediency or generalized prescriptions? Clearly, policymakers and citizen groups need to develop guiding principles for when to impose sanctions, aid cutoffs, military embargoes, and other measures designed to strengthen democracy and equitable growth. The following is not a complete framework, but perhaps it can serve as a starting point.

- There should be no blanket endorsement of leaders, however admirable. The quick collapse of the "new-leader" paradigm, with Ethiopia and Eritrea at war and with different leaders taking sides in the complex conflict in the Democratic Republic of the Congo, should be a warning to both policymakers and analysts. It is also not advisable simply to widen the paradigm by including selected "civil society" leaders in addition to the political ones.
- Priority should be given to identifying the worst and most consistently abusive regimes (and rebel groups) and concentrating the most intense negative pressures on those cases.
- Freedoms of expression and organization for civil society as well as opposition political groups are prerequisites for democratic advance.
- Whatever the form of electoral system, participation, transparency of government operations, and the rule of law are just as important as, if not more significant than, the conduct of elections.
- Support for prodemocracy forces should take a regional perspective within Africa.[21] Priority should be given to networking across national boundaries within Africa's regions—west, east, central, southern, and north—and to developing contacts with a broad range of civil society and political groups in key countries in each region. Regional networks often can support each other and help maintain the momentum of prodemocracy campaigns even when conflict or repression in a particular country makes it impossible for democratic elements to operate openly there. Among many examples, one can point to the increasing contact among in-

dependent media in southern Africa in particular. Nongovernmental organizations (NGOs) have coordinated campaigns on land mines, debt cancellation, structural adjustment policies, and other issues, working most effectively when they have developed strong links among countries within particular regions of the continent.

- Judging what action to take in particular national contexts cannot possibly be done responsibly without regular consultation with a range of nongovernmental as well as political actors in each country. This is essential not just for U.S. diplomatic representatives but for NGOs and analysts critical of U.S. policy.

THE SECURITY GAP

From the 1960s to 1990, superpower competition dominated U.S. security interests in Africa, from interventions in the Zaire and Angola to shifting alliances in the Horn of Africa. The anti-apartheid struggle succeeded in imposing an additional dynamic, with international sanctions against South Africa in the last years of apartheid contributing to the successful transition to majority rule.

Some think they see a replacement framework emerging by defining the new goal as protecting the United States from African-derived threats such as "weapons proliferation, state-sponsored terrorism, narcotics flows, the growing influence of rogue states, international crime, environmental degradation, and disease."[22] In fact, such formulations of threats give policymakers little specific guidance (good or bad) for determining either friends and enemies or appropriate policies for dealing with conflict.

It is also too simplistic to interpret U.S. policies of support for particular clients—such as Uganda, Rwanda, or Ethiopia—as a coherent U.S. strategy for competing with Europe (particularly with France) or with South Africa, either in the security field or in regional geopolitical arenas. The different policies advocated and pursued in response to particular crises reveal widely divergent and shifting views within the U.S. government, the State Department, the White House, the Pentagon, and among ambassadors or special representatives in the field. To craft consistent policies in response to rapidly changing crises requires far greater attention from high-level officials than has so far been the case.

Media coverage of humanitarian crises compels such attention only momentarily, and Africa-focused officials within the U.S. government have little clout to persuade their superiors to expend political capital on issues regarded as marginal and remote. (See figure 11–4.) Crafting a consistent response to a complex crisis is difficult enough when it is high profile; it can be even more difficult when attention from the top is intermittent or when existing policy guidelines are quickly outpaced by events.

Thus the record shows a lurching from one approach to another: intervention (as in Somalia), indifference to looming genocide in Rwanda, a desire to "leave it to Mandela," and mixed signals in response to successive crises in the Democratic Republic of the Congo in 1997 and 1998. The global "antiterrorism" theme has

Figure 11.4

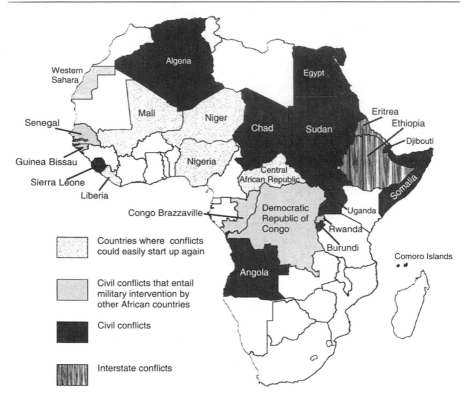

African Countries in Conflict

Interstate conflicts
Eritrea and Ethiopia

Civil conflicts
Algeria
Angola
Burundi
Chad
Comoro Islands
Djibouti
Egypt
Sierra Leone
Somalia
Sudan
Uganda

Civil conflicts that entail military intervention by other African Countries
Congo-Brazzaville
Democratic Republic of Congo
Guinea-Bissau
Rwanda
Senegal
Western Sahara

Countries where civil conflicts could easily start up again
Central African Republic
Liberia
Mali
Nigeria
Niger

Source: Adapted from Marina Ottaway, "Africa: Think Again," *Foreign Policy*, Spring 1999 (Updated Sept. 1999).

ensured a focus on Sudan, but the decision to bomb the commercial factory in Khartoum without a terrorist link was based on bad intelligence and was formulated without input from officials knowledgeable about Africa.[23]

In terms of military assistance, the United States has provided some $10 million to the Organization of African Unity (OAU) to support its conflict resolution capability, essentially to establish a management center and to supply equipment to enable the OAU to send military observers on short notice to crisis areas. Washington has also played key roles in supporting the UN peacekeeping mission in Angola and in encouraging regional conciliation efforts in Liberia and Sierra Leone. Yet the centerpiece of recent administration policy has been the Africa Crisis Response Initiative (ACRI), providing for training of battalions from selected African countries for participation in peacekeeping missions. The most concrete result of the initiative has been a series of short-term training exercises, each lasting about 60 days and costing about $3 million. The United States also provided financial support for a similar exercise in April 1999, sponsored by the Southern African Development Community, which brought 3,000 troops from 12 nations to South Africa.[24]

ACRI was slow to get started and is a scaled-down version of Washington's 1996 proposal for an African Crisis Response Force (ACRF), which would have involved a permanent force capable of intervention. Given the serious concerns raised by African and European governments as well as U.S. legislators about the ACRF proposal, the ACRI has focused only on training. Yet doubts remain about its impact and the use to which the training might be put. Two of the countries receiving training (Senegal and Uganda) are themselves involved in conflict. The scale of the program, in comparison either to the potential African needs for peacekeeping or to Washington's unpaid dues for UN peacekeeping operations, is not great.

Another obscure but substantial initiative is the Pentagon's Africa Center for Strategic Studies, for which Congress has appropriated $42 million. According to Pentagon planners, the center is not modeled after the notorious School of the Americas (which has trained many Latin American dictators and human rights abusers) but is rather one of a string of "Regional Centers for Security Studies," the first of which—the George C. Marshall European Center for Security Studies in Garmisch, Germany—was founded in 1993. Its curriculum, designed for executive-level military officers and civilian counterparts, stresses democratic civil-military relations, national security decision-making, and management tools. The center's mission statement says it will "encourage an appreciation of appropriate civil-military relationships and an understanding of effective defense resource management across African governments."[25]

Whatever the content of the curriculum, an important effect of these and other training programs will be to build closer ties between the U.S. military establishment and African military and civilian defense officials. The assumptions that these ties are purely "technical" and will automatically contribute to accountability and respect for human rights are highly dubious. It is a step forward that African as well as U.S. civilians have been invited to participate in early curriculum planning for the center, but this falls far short of the public scrutiny necessary for accountability.

Nevertheless, there is general agreement between official U.S. positions and African public opinion regarding peace and security goals, just as there is on issues related to democracy and civil rights. Although many Africans deplore the unilateral

U.S. response to terrorist bombings, there is little popular support for terrorist strategies even in countries where these armed groups are active in internal conflict, such as Algeria and Egypt. Despite the persistence of conflict in a score of countries, the overwhelming demand of civil society groups, when they are free to speak, is for peace. Women's groups, church groups, human rights organizations, and conflict resolution groups advocate negotiation, understanding, and compromise. Disgust with leaders who find ideological or ethnic excuses for continuing or reigniting conflicts is a powerful sentiment in almost all African countries.

The end of the cold war generated significant progress in negotiating the end to a series of African conflicts. The 30-year regional war associated with the apartheid regime's struggle to survive ended with the emergence of a democratic South Africa and the end of conflicts in Mozambique, Namibia, and, at least temporarily, Angola. The overthrow of the Mengistu dictatorship in Ethiopia in 1991 led to the successful conclusion of Eritrea's struggle for independence.

Yet the 1990s have also seen a bewildering profusion of old and new internal conflicts, most notably in Angola, Sudan, Somalia, Liberia, Sierra Leone, Algeria, Rwanda, Congo (Brazzaville), and Zaire, including not only the genocide of more than half a million people in the space of a few months in Rwanda but also massive abuses against civilians in each country mentioned. In 1998, the specter of more conventional interstate conflict emerged as well, with the border dispute between Ethiopia and Eritrea as well as the danger that the Democratic Republic of the Congo maelstrom would continue to suck its neighbors into deeper confrontation with each other.

This is one arena in which modesty is particularly appropriate for critics of administration policies, given the intractable, complex, and diverse causes of ongoing conflicts and the disagreement among international agencies, civil society groups, and progressive analysts about "what is to be done" in particular cases. Anyone who does not admit to being uncertain about analysis and prescription applying to the range of conflicts mentioned above is either dishonest or uninformed. In formulating conflict control policies, the following suggestions are, therefore, offered as starting points rather than conclusions.

- Arms control efforts, while important, are insufficient to halt Africa's conflicts.

  Measures such as the international treaty to ban land mines, new efforts to monitor and restrict the flow of small arms, and international bans on weapon sales to parties guilty of gross human rights abuses against civilians are important. The U.S. failure to sign the Ottawa land mine treaty is a blatant example of U.S. indifference to the emerging international consensus on this issue. Continued progress in these arenas is worth campaigning for, despite foot-dragging by the United States and other major global weapons suppliers. However, such international arms control efforts are likely to have little short-term effect on particular conflicts, unless they are vigorously and deliberately employed to weaken the military position of a particularly recalcitrant party to the conflict, such as UNITA (National Union for the Total Independence of Angola), the right-wing rebel army that has waged a 25-year war against the Angolan government.

- Economic problems both lead to and result from armed conflicts. They are also often closely tied to the absence of democratic institutions and processes for managing the distribution of national—and often scarce—resources.

  The "vicious circle" phenomenon applies with a vengeance to the two-way interaction between conflict and economic development. For example, competition for scarce land and vulnerability to dropping coffee prices in Rwanda and Burundi is one factor contributing to the escalation and intractability of conflict in those countries. Meanwhile in Angola, Sierra Leone, and Liberia, the supply of arms has often been dependent on smuggling in diamonds and other commodities. Conflict, moreover, is one of the major factors impeding African economic development not only by disrupting directly affected countries but by eroding general business confidence, given the tendency of outside observers to lump the entire continent south of the Sahara into one amalgam.

- Conflicts not only threaten the countries directly involved but also generate powerful ripple effects within African regions and for the continent as a whole.

  Individual country success stories, however significant, cannot be isolated from the impact of conflict in their region and even across regional boundaries. The U.S. strategy of countering Afro-pessimist stereotypes and promoting development by concentrating on a handful of "successful" countries is dangerously shortsighted and incomplete. Ongoing conflicts even within Senegal and Uganda, for example, tie into instability across their borders. Within a given region, the spillover impact of refugees and border insecurity even from conflicts in small countries can be significant. When a giant such as Zaire in central Africa dissolves into an arena of shifting battlefields, the divisive shock waves extend even to east and southern Africa. If the unresolved struggles for democracy in Nigeria or Kenya were to lead to a similar downward spiral, the impact on their regions and beyond would be similarly dramatic.

- In most current African conflicts, the United States should add its influence, whether by direct mediation or by supporting the efforts by others, to encouragement of all-party negotiations aimed at compromise solutions. However, there may be exceptions in which taking sides is appropriate. And inadequately planned diplomatic involvement sometimes may be worse than no involvement at all.

  There is no guarantee of success or any magical formula for international facilitation of peace accords, despite a burgeoning of the conflict resolution industry in the post–cold war period. Nevertheless, what influence the United States has should be directed toward seeking compromise solutions. It is important to avoid encouraging intransigence by supporting favored governments or leaders. In Africa's current conflicts, there are few plausible candidates for good-guy status deserving of unconditional diplomatic support, much less military aid or exemption from criticism for human rights abuses. And it sometimes may be necessary to include in negotiations even forces that are responsible for horrific abuses of human rights—if they retain significant capacity to cause military damage or enjoy the adherence (voluntary or involuntary) of major population groupings.

There are two major qualifications to this rule that need to be noted, however. Peace talks with a military leader with a demonstrated history of sabotaging peace agreements may create the illusion of progress toward peace while in reality serving as a recipe for repeated failure. In such cases, most prominently UNITA leader Jonas Savimbi in Angola, negotiations in bad faith—and international willingness to promote them—contribute to continuing war, not to peace. The other proviso is that negotiations encompassing only military leaders with questionable political legitimacy, without some mechanism for involving unarmed opposition political groups and civil society, are unlikely to promote sustainable solutions to conflict. Although predictions are perilous, this seems to be a fatal flaw in efforts to stem the fighting in Zaire.

- International involvement in major crises—exceeding diplomacy and including the delivery of humanitarian aid, provision of peacekeeping forces, or, in the worst instance, military intervention to block or limit genocidal assaults on civilians—is often necessary. But no intervention is "neutral," and the chances of prolonging a conflict or making it worse are significant. One case in point is the enormous humanitarian intervention to aid refugees after the Rwandan genocide, which served in large part to strengthen those forces with primary responsibility for the killings.

A blanket no external-intervention guideline with respect to internal conflicts should be recognized as de facto support for the strongest "internal" party. The Organization of African Unity's postindependence consensus on nonintervention in internal conflicts may have decreased the chances for interstate conflict, but it also reinforced existing regimes. This long-standing consensus is now eroding rapidly.

In recent years, there is increasing recognition, including at the OAU, that massive abuses of human rights in internal conflicts—most particularly those reaching the scale of genocide—may justify external intervention. But there seems to be no emerging consensus—and there is unlikely to be one—on who should intervene and who should decide when abuses are massive enough to justify intervention. As a result, countries and groups of countries are now likely to intervene in conflicts based on varying definitions of their own interests.

The concept of a purely "humanitarian" intervention, intending merely to aid innocent civilians and devoid of political or military implications, is a fraud. An intervention with limited mandate—for example, to protect corridors or relief supplies—may or may not be justified in a particular case. But it will have political consequences; it will weaken some forces and strengthen others. Armed parties who gain access to relief supplies because they control access to civilians, whether in Somalia, Sudan, or other conflicts, quite accurately regard this humanitarian relief as one of the factors affecting their military prospects.

It is therefore highly unlikely that any "formula" for determining a justifiable intervention will be adequate. There is also no avoiding "political" judgments about particular situations, which are linked to one's evaluation of: (1) the relative merits (and demerits) of the internal parties in conflict; (2) the relative merits (and demerits) of the potential "interveners"; and (3) the likely de facto, unintended, and long-term consequences of an intervention, as well as its announced goals and short-term, life-saving potential.

It does make sense to be very cautious in supporting external intervention in internal conflicts, whether by neighbors or by multilateral forces. Even if "innocents" can be saved or the "good guys" (or more likely, the "less-bad guys") can be aided to "win" by outside forces, the sustainability of such an outcome is questionable once the outside party's interest wanes. But the exceptions are numerous enough to make a blanket prohibition unwise—"interventions" can in fact save lives, tip a military balance toward one side, or enhance the possibility of negotiation. Decisive action to reinforce and expand the mandate of the UN force in Rwanda as the genocide was beginning in early 1994 might have saved hundreds of thousands of lives. Other examples are more ambiguous. Leading Congolese scholar and democracy activist Georges Nzongola-Ntalaja, for example, is a strong critic both of Laurent Kabila's government, which succeeded that of Mobutu, and of later Rwandan intervention in 1998 against Kabila. However, he argues that the original military intervention by other African countries to overthrow Mobutu in 1997 was justified.[26]

• The United States should contribute to peacemaking in Africa's conflicts, but successes are likely only if U.S. involvement is coordinated with engagement by African and international mediators. Support for peacekeeping by UN or regional organizations should take priority over bilateral U.S. military support.

The presence or absence of U.S. involvement—whether in the form of diplomatic pressures, financing to bolster peacekeeping and conflict resolution at the UN and regional organizations, or logistical support for relief operations—is a key factor in sustaining outside intervention. Although the Clinton administration has provided some such support for example, for UN forces in Angola and West African forces in Liberia and Sierra Leone—the glaring U.S. default in payment of UN dues undermines Washington's credibility as well as any effective international capacity to respond to crises.

Meanwhile, U.S. training missions for African armed forces are expanding without open accountability or civilian review. According to a *Washington Post* investigation, special forces have been engaged in training exercises in 31 of 54 African countries, including many currently engaged in conflict, such as Ethiopia, Guinea-Bissau, Rwanda, Senegal, and Uganda.[27] The scale of the operations, known as the Joint Combined Exchange and Training (J-CET) program, is probably not yet large enough to have much influence on military balances. Some activities carried out under J-CET or other Pentagon programs, such as training in demining, specific support for African peacekeeping, or humanitarian relief, are likely justified. But training programs can also send signals of partisan support or approval for military forces involved in conflict or human rights abuses. They build unexamined links between the U.S. military and African armies. There is little evidence that they contribute to their stated objectives of promoting the values of democracy among trainees, and their contribution to peace-keeping capability is unproven. Without full provision for transparency and monitoring by civilians outside the Pentagon—including African human rights groups—such bilateral programs should not continue.

The proliferation of bilateral U.S.-African military ties is disturbing not necessarily because of the weight of any one program or involvement or be-cause of the existence of a "grand plan" for U.S. engagement. Rather, the scale of the financial resources available to the Pentagon makes accounta-bility problematic even for the congressional oversight committees and for U.S. diplomats, and much more so for civil society either in the United States or in African countries. It is particularly disturbing that the standard J-CET mission includes instruction in FID (foreign internal defense), de-fined in training manuals as attempting "to organize, train, advise and as-sist" a foreign military so that it can "free and protect its society from subversion, lawlessness, and insurgency."[28] Not only are such internal func-tions more appropriately the responsibility of police, not militaries, but army and police units involved in similar U.S. training in Latin America, Indonesia, and elsewhere have been responsible for widespread human rights abuses.

Whether the issues are economic ties, democracy, or conflict resolution, the quest for a constructive policy framework for U.S. relations with Africa will be abortive unless it is built on an extensive and continuing dialogue. That dialogue must involve not only official government representatives and the private for-profit sector but also diverse political and nongovernmental sectors both in the United States and in Africa's different regions. This is the essential prerequisite for the emergence of a genuine "new partnership" with participants who "listen to one another, learn from one another, and compromise with one another."[29] Despite the fact that the Clinton administration has taken more steps toward dialogue with Africa than have previous administrations, neither the level of dialogue nor the substantive frameworks for policy resemble an Africa policy that is genuinely re-ciprocal and mutually beneficial.

NOTES

This chapter expresses the author's personal views and does not necessarily reflect the positions of APIC as an organization.

1. Susan Rice, "A New Vision for Africa: Remarks to Blacks in Government Lun-cheon" February 5, 1998. Available on the Internet at: http://www.state.gov/www/regions/africa.
2. Salih Booker, *Thinking Regionally: Priorities for U.S. Policy Toward Africa*, APIC Back-ground Paper, March 1996. Available on the Internet at http://www.africapolicy.org.
3. Kofi Annan, speech to Organization of African Unity, June 2, 1997.
4. Tafadzwa Mumba, "Tanzania: Unbridled Structural Adjustment a Sure Recipe for Ill Health and Female Illiteracy, Warns Nyerere," *InterPress Service*, September 9, 1995.

5. Rice, "New Vision for Africa."
6. For example, World Bank Report No. 15575-AFR, *Taking Action for Poverty Reduction in Sub-Saharan Africa*, May 1, 1996.
7. *Africa Recovery*, Department of Information, United Nations, November 1998, p. 32, based on *UNCTAD World Investment Report 1998*.
8. Available on the Internet at: http://www.un.org/depts/eca/eca40th.
9. UNICEF, *The State of the World's Children 1999* (New York: UNICEF, 1999). Available on the Internet at: http:www.unicef.org/sowc99/.
10. Mumba, "Tanzania."
11. Testimony of J. Brian Atwood, administrator, USAID, to House International Relations Committee, March 3, 1999.
12. Douglas Tilton, *USAID in South Africa*, APIC, 1996, p. 5. Also available on the Internet at: http://www.africapolicy.org.
13. Atwood testimony, March 3, 1999; Secretary of State, *Congressional Presentation for Foreign Operations, FY2000* (Washington, DC: Department of State, February 1999), pp. 1054–55; Martha Honey's interviews with AID officials.
14. Ibid.
15. Organization for Economic Cooperation and Development, Development Assistance Committee. Latest statistics can be found on the Internet at: http://www.oecd.org/dac.
16. Available at: http://www.itu.int/TELECOM/aft98.
17. APIC, *Africa's Debt*, APIC Background Paper, December 1998. Excerpts available on the Internet at: http://www.africapolicy.org/docs99/dbt9903b.htm.
18. Interview with IMF officials.
19. "Remarks by the President [Bill Clinton] to the Community of Kisowera School in Mukono, Uganda, March 23, 1998," released by the Office of the Press Secretary, The White House, Washington, DC.
20. Undersecretary of State Thomas Pickering, speech to Council on Foreign Relations, January 30, 1998.
21. Booker, *Thinking Regionally*, March 1996.
22. Susan Rice, Assistant Secretary of State for African Affairs, "U.S. Africa Policy," statement before the Subcommittee on Africa, House Foreign Relations Committee, March 17, 1998. Available on the Internet at: http://www.state.gov/www/regions/africa/rice_980317.html.
23. See, among other articles on the lack of evidence for administration charges of chemical weapons production at the factory, Tim Weiner and Steven Lee Myers, "Flaws in U.S. Account Raise Questions on Strike in Sudan," *New York Times*, August 29, 1998.
24. On the ACRI, available at: http://www.state.gov/www/regions/africa/fs_acri_980327.html; Africa Research Project, Africa Policy Report No. 8, March 31, 1998; see http://www.defenselink.mil/news for October 26, 1998 and additional stories available on the Internet at: http://www.eucom.mil.
25. Included in materials provided to January 20, 1999, Roundtable hosted by Office of African Affairs, Office of the Secretary of Defense.
26. Available at: http://www.africapolicy.org/docs98/con9811b.htm.
27. Dana Priest, "Special Alliances: The Pentagon's New Global Engagements," *Washington Post*, July 14, 1998.
28. *Field Manual 31–20, Doctrine for Special Forces Operations*, issued in April 1990, quoted in series by Dana Priest, "Free of Oversight, U.S. Military Trains Foreign Troops," *Washington Post*, July 12, 1998.
29. Rice, "New Vision for Africa."

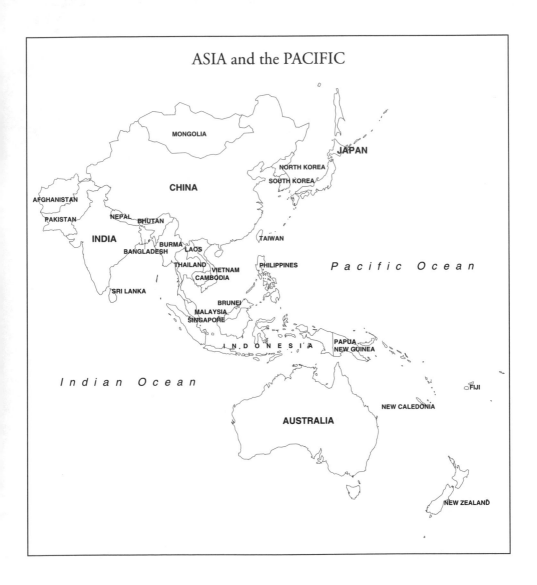

ASIA and the PACIFIC

MONGOLIA

JAPAN

NORTH KOREA

SOUTH KOREA

CHINA

AFGHANISTAN

PAKISTAN

NEPAL

BHUTAN

INDIA

BURMA

LAOS

BANGLADESH

TAIWAN

THAILAND

VIETNAM

CAMBODIA

PHILIPPINES

SRI LANKA

Pacific Ocean

BRUNEI

MALAYSIA

SINGAPORE

I N D O N E S I A

PAPUA
NEW GUINEA

FIJI

Indian Ocean

NEW CALEDONIA

AUSTRALIA

NEW ZEALAND

CHAPTER 12

STILL THE PACIFIC CENTURY?
U.S. POLICY IN ASIA AND THE PACIFIC

John Gershman

SOME ASIAN ECONOMIC ELITES AS WELL AS WESTERN OBSERVERS have
asserted that the region's spectacular economic growth would lead to a coming Pacific Century. However, the Asian economic crisis and the political turmoil it has
caused have called these assumptions into question. As the twentieth century ends,
Asia—home to 55 percent of the world's people—is a region in turmoil.[1]

The Asian economic crisis that began in July 1997 spread worldwide, expanding what was a depression in some Asian countries into the most serious international financial crisis in 50 years. Following the May 1998 nuclear tests in India
and Pakistan, the *Bulletin of the Atomic Scientists* moved the minute hand of the
"Doomsday Clock," its symbol of nuclear peril, five minutes closer to global destruction; it now stands at nine minutes to midnight. Relations between China and
the United States remain uneasy. The closer ties marked by the November 1999
trade agreement and the resumption of military-to-military contacts come against
the backdrop of the bombing of the Chinese embassy in Belgrade, allegations of
nuclear espionage by China, evidence of campaign finance contributions by the
Chinese military to Clinton's 1996 campaign, and continued tension over U.S
plans for a missile defense system. The 1994 Agreed Framework, under which
North Korea agreed to exchange development of its nuclear weapons program for
international inspections and resources to meet its energy needs, often appears to
be one step away from collapse.

And there are other reasons why Americans need to be concerned: Asia has
the highest rate of growth for greenhouse gases, the fastest rate of deforestation
among developing regions, and more than half of all new HIV/AIDS infections

worldwide. If present trends continue, China alone will account for one-third of the increase in the world's nuclear power over the next two decades.[2] Yet in terms of institutions for resolving economic, political, and military disputes and crises, the Asia-Pacific region is exceptionally weak. Of all the world regions, the Asia-Pacific region contains the smallest number of regional intergovernmental organizations, and those that do exist do not function effectively.

Close to 40 percent of total U.S. trade is now conducted with the East Asia and Pacific region. However, this dramatic expansion has been accompanied by the development of large, recurring trade deficits with some U.S. trading partners. In 1997, the United States amassed trade deficits with most economies in the region with the exception of South Korea, Brunei, Australia, and New Zealand. However, as the global financial crisis led to declining imports and increased exports throughout East and Southeast Asia, the overall U.S. trade deficit with Asia rose from $141 billion in 1997 to $180 billion in 1998—or 78 percent of the U.S. worldwide trade deficit.[3] (See figure 12–1.) The U.S. merchandise trade deficit with China in September 1999 was the highest for any single country in U.S. history.

Within the United States, the presence and prominence of Asians has also grown. There are currently 10 million citizens of Asian ethnic descent (up from just under 7 million in 1990) living in the United States, with one-third residing in California. The anti-Asian backlash in the wake of the Chinese "Donorgate," nuclear espionage, and other scandals seems to have played a role in spurring a more unified Asian American presence in U.S. politics, leading to the founding of the National Council of Asian-Pacific Americans in May 1998. This council coalesced 17 major Asian American associations, the first serious attempt by Asian Americans to mobilize at the national level. This consolidation has been spurred partly by the inability of the press and policymakers to distinguish between Asians and Asian Americans and partly by a growing sentiment that a glass ceiling exists for Asian Americans at top levels of the U.S. political system. For example, Clinton's cabinet, the most diverse in memory, has no Asian American.

Asia is home to more than 3.2 billion people, divided among East, Southeast, and South Asia, and Oceania.[4] China and India alone account for two-thirds of Asia's population. South Asia contains the largest absolute number of poor people in the world—more than half a billion—with India home to an estimated 340 million poor, up from 300 million in the late 1980s.[5] For all these reasons, the future of Asia is the future of the world.

FROM MIRACLES TO MELTDOWN

The Asian crisis—which began with the devaluation of the Thai currency, the baht, in July 1997—led to a severe depression in much of Asia and soon threatened global deflation as it spread via Russia and Latin America. In Southeast Asia, the impact of the economic crisis was exacerbated by environmental disasters: forest fires in Indonesia in 1997 harmed health, devastated tourism, and inflicted losses exceeding $4 billion, and the El Niño/La Niña weather patterns in 1998 hurt agri-

Figure 12.1   U.S. Trade Balance with Asia ($U.S. millions)

	1995	1996	1997	1998
Asia	–124,245	–119,282	–141,450	–180,282
China	–133,790	–39,520	–49,695	–56,898
Japan	–59,137	–47,580	–56,115	–64,094
East Asia NICs	–7,773	–7,002	–7,938	–22,663
Australia & Oceana	7,709	8,485	7,986	6,859

Source: U.S. Department of Commerce, The Office of Trade and Economic Analysis, "U.S. Foreign Trade Highlights," Table 8, "U.S. Total Trade Balances with Individual Countries," 1999. Available on the Internet at: http://www.ita.doc.gov.

cultural production. GDP figures for the latter part of 1998 and the first quarter of 1999 show a slowing or reversal of the decline in GDP growth in some of the countries (Philippines, Thailand, Malaysia, and South Korea) but continued problems for others (Indonesia and Hong Kong). By early 1999, some analysts were arguing that the upswing in Asian stock markets signaled that the worst had passed.[6]

There is, however, good reason to doubt the most optimistic forecasts, and mistaking capital market swings as indicators of the health of the real economy is dangerous. The 1999 first-quarter upswing in Asian stock markets was largely due to external factors, such as the continued highs in the U.S. stock market, low global interest rates, and a gradual return of Western institutional funds to investing in Asia. A number of events, singly or in combination, could turn the tables again: a currency devaluation by China, a significant fall in the U.S. stock market, or an increase in U.S. interest rates.[7] Overall, commercial banks and non-equity investors will continue to drain funds from the region, and foreign direct investment and foreign aid will still constitute the major sources of inflows.

The growth in Asian GDP is also tentative, driven by significant deficit spending and by looser fiscal and monetary policies in several of the crisis countries. Such deficits are not sustainable in the long-term and more substantial economic reforms loom ahead. Furthermore, given that three-fourths of the record 1998 U.S. trade deficit occurred in Asia, it is unclear how long America can afford to continue as the main destination for Asian exports.

Finally, even if growth does rebound, the fallout of the crisis remains massive in a region where public safety nets such as unemployment insurance are virtually nonexistent. Even in countries that have begun to turn the corner, the impact of 1997–1998 is staggering. (See figure 12–2.) In Indonesia, the most seriously affected country, the price of rice more than tripled in 1998, and the government estimates that 17 million households (89 million people) can afford only one meal per day.[8]

One final effect of the crisis was a significant increase in inequality, particularly in wealth. According to the *World Wealth Report 1999*, Asians with assets over $1 million increased their collective worth by 10 percent in 1998 to $4.4 trillion. This wealthy class escaped the worst of the crisis, in part because many of its assets are held abroad and were shifted quickly from local currencies to

Figure 12.2   Impact of the East Asian Crisis on Poverty Levels (using national poverty lines[a])

Urban Poverty Incidence	Indonesia[b]	Thailand	Korea
1997[c]	11.0	11.4	8.6
1998	19.9	12.9	19.2
Change in Average Standards of Living			
1997–98 (percent)	–24.4	–13.6	–21.6

Source: World Bank, World Bank Poverty Update: Trends in Poverty (Washington, DC: World Bank, 1999).
[a]National poverty lines are around $1/day in Indonesia, $2/day in Thailand, and $4/day in Korea.
[b]Survey evidence from selected areas.
[c]Poverty incidence for Thailand as of 1996.

dollars. In contrast, between 1997 and 1998, poverty increased from 11 percent to 20 percent in Indonesia and from 9 percent to 19 percent in South Korea.[9]

The Clinton administration, recognizing an opportunity to advance U.S. corporate interests, responded to the Asian crisis with a mad rush to pry open sectors of Asian economies previously sheltered from foreign participation. Whether as part of International Monetary Fund (IMF)–assisted austerity programs linked to financial "bailout" packages or through bilateral pressure by Washington, the U.S. approach is in accord with its use of trade warfare as a key element of its neomercantilist strategy in Asia. With the Commerce Department and the United States Trade Representative (USTR) controlled by strategic traders who view Asia from a geoeconomic perspective, the Clinton administration has been unrelenting in opening doors to U.S. trade and investment. As the USTR noted in arguing for "concerted U.S. trade policy engagement" despite the financial crisis, "the opportunities for more truly open markets in a number of Asian countries are indeed promising."[10]

At a time when Africa and Latin America were starved for capital during their debt crises, Southeast Asia was awash in foreign capital, with the Philippines an anemic latecomer to the party. Since the mid-1980s, Japanese capital has driven economic integration in East and Southeast Asia. The 1985 appreciation of the yen against the dollar made many Japanese exports uncompetitive, thereby contributing to an expansion of Japanese foreign direct investment in the United States and Southeast Asia. In the 1990s, although Japanese capital was still dominant, U.S. capital joined in through an expansion of bank lending and portfolio investments led by the expansion of mutual funds, hedge funds, and other forms of short-term capital holdings. The historically unprecedented growth that resulted from the varying combinations of these factors led to significant reductions in absolute poverty in Asia and to improvements in some basic health and education indicators. By the early 1990s, however, the high-growth model was already showing cracks, with mounting inequality (in what had been relatively equitable patterns of growth), high social and ecological costs, and increasingly restive labor, human rights, farmer, and prodemocracy activists.

Even without the economic crises, the ecological costs of high-speed growth in the region already posed serious challenges regarding, for example, overfishing, massive logging activities, and growing air pollution.[11] The forest fires in Indonesia in 1997 destroyed 5 million hectares (12 million acres) of forest and scrub and caused an estimated $4.4 billion worth of damage to tourism, air and shipping services, and public health. As a result of the Asian financial crisis, Indonesia now has fewer resources to combat or prevent such environmental disasters. Thus, the financial crisis has exacerbated the ecological crisis spawned by high-speed growth.

The Clinton administration overemphasized the lack of transparency and weak financial sector regulation as the key cause of the Asian crisis and underemphasized the impact of unruly international capital markets. Hence, the administration's proposals focused more upon liberalizing and restructuring Asian banking systems to meet international capital adequacy standards, shut down and consolidate firms and businesses, strengthen financial regulatory capacities, and restructure the relationship between the state, banks, and businesses that enabled high-speed growth.

But transparency itself is not a panacea. There was publicly available information dating back at least to the mid-1990s and the aftermath of the Mexico crisis regarding weaknesses in Asian (particularly Southeast Asian) economies. But (speculative foreign) investors, the IMF, and the World Bank chose to ignore it. And in cases where information was not available (or it was incorrect), investors chose to invest anyway.

The depth of the crisis has less to do with transparency than with the tendency of capital markets to fall victim to panics and manias, the inappropriate liberalization of the financial sectors in Asian countries, and flawed IMF policies. Unlike the U.S. economy, which relies on capital markets and corporate earnings, the Asian economy depends on high personal savings and corporate investment rates (driven by debt) with banks as the main financial intermediaries. The financial sector is the key link in the institutional structure that distinguishes Asian developmental capitalist states: close interlocking ties among the state, banks, and corporations form the framework of Asia's "network capitalism." These close government-bank-firm relationships enabled Japan, Korea, and Taiwan to "govern markets" and to emerge as the most successful developing countries in the post–World War II period.[12] But two of the key elements of their successes—restrictions on capital flows and the insulation of government-bank-firm collaboration from short-term political coalitions—were reduced in the 1990s: the former by financial sector liberalization and the expansion of stock markets, the latter by expansion of electoral competition among political elites driven by short-term interests and unaccountable to broad-based organizations in civil society.

Accompanied by aggressive domestic and international bank lending and large inflows of portfolio capital, newly deregulated capital markets met speculators looking to ride the "tiger" of rapid Asian growth. The inflows of foreign capital strengthened exchange rates, which—because those rates were pegged to the U.S. dollar—made borrowing in foreign currencies more attractive than in local ones. These overvalued exchange rates also made imports more attractive and depressed the values of exports. Increased pressure from China and Vietnam as new players

in such labor-intensive exports as electronics ratcheted competition to higher levels of intensity, leading to fresh demands for funds for investment and expansion of
capacity.[13] When the ride ended, IMF policies had the effect of screaming "fire" in
a crowded theater. Tight monetary policies and sky-high interest rates—combined
with advice simply to shut down banks and corporations in countries with no de-
positor's insurance or bankruptcy laws—spurred capital flight and heightened
volatility, as internal IMF documents later revealed.[14]

Japan remains the key to restarting growth in the region. The Clinton administration has chastised Japan for not doing enough to respond to the crisis, but
such criticism ignores the fact that Japan responded quickly, proposing the formation of a $100 billion Asian Monetary Fund in August 1997. Washington
squelched the initiative that it viewed as a competitor to the IMF. The Japanese
proposal would have enabled countries to gain access to funds without requiring
IMF-style conditions that would require rapid liberalization. Instead, the United
States pushed the IMF to be the lead agency in responding to the crisis. Japan
pumped $43 billion into the region in the year after July 1997, in contrast to $7
billion from the United States (See figure 12–3.)

As the crisis became global and as global deflation loomed, a spate of articles
appeared in the popular and business press critical of the IMF approach, including
one by Paul Krugman in *Fortune* that raised the previously taboo subject of capital
controls.[15] In September 1998, Malaysia established limited capital controls and
Hong Kong (which a year earlier had made a relatively peaceful political transition
from Great Britain to China) intervened directly in financial markets to support its
currency. China also placed new restrictions on foreign investors. Malaysia successfully returned to the bond markets in May 1999, proof that its capital controls
had not harmed its economy and had helped provide the breathing room for a restructuring of its financial system. Despite all this, the U.S. Treasury Department
continued to adamantly oppose capital controls.

To date, the effects of the East Asian crisis have not been felt in South Asia,
which is much less integrated into the global economy. The World Bank estimates
per capita GDP growth for the South Asia region at 2.7 percent. That reflects
wide variation between the three major countries: India, Bangladesh, and Pakistan.
U.S. economic and commercial interests are much smaller in South Asia; however,
U.S. ties to India have expanded since the early 1990s as a result of Indian economic reform policies and India's growth as an export market for U.S. goods, services, and investment, primarily in major infrastructure. U.S. foreign economic
policy in the region has focused on hastening the pace of economic liberalization,
including removing import barriers and encouraging patent protection, deregulation, and privatization.[16] Such policies are inappropriate, given the level of poverty
in South Asia, because they serve to widen the gap between rich and poor, weaken
the central government, and force cutbacks in spending on education, healthcare,
and other social services.

Countries elsewhere in Southeast Asia were less directly affected by the financial crisis. Cambodia, which by mid-1999 was effectively at peace for the first time
in three decades, has until recently largely been a political and economic pariah
like Burma (renamed Myanmar by the ruling military junta). In Vietnam, the Clin-

Figure 12.3 **Commitments of the International Community and Disbursements of the IMF in Response to the Asian Crisis ($U.S. billions)**

Country	IMF[a]	Multilateral[b]	Bilateral	Total	IMF Disbursements as of 8/28/98
Indonesia	11.2	10.0	21.1	42.3	6.0
Korea	20.9	14.0	23.3	58.2	18.0
Thailand	4.0	2.7	10.5	17.2	2.8
Total	36.1	26.7	54.9	117.7	26.8

Source: The IMF's Response to the Asian Crisis, January 17, 1999. Available on the Internet at: http://www.imf.org/External/np/exr/facts/asia.htm.
[a]IMF commitments to the Philippines are not included.
[b]World Bank and ADB.

ton administration initially took several positive steps, including normalizing relations. However, overall U.S. policy in Southeast Asia remains dominated by the shadow of the U.S. war a quarter of a century ago. Vietnam and Laos are two of just seven countries worldwide that do not enjoy normal trade relations (NTR) with the United States.[17] Although the United States and Vietnam agreed to a bilateral trade treaty "in principle" in July 1999, the treaty has yet to be completed and ratified by the legislatures of both countries—a key step in achieving NTR.

The crisis has hurt exporters across the region, including Vietnam and China, two countries that otherwise weathered the financial upheavals relatively well. For example, while export volumes increased, export earnings fell due to lower international prices. Thus foreign investors continue to shy away. In 1999, Vietnam appeared likely to receive only 20 to 30 percent of the $1 billion in foreign investment it received in 1998, and the country was beginning to feel the pinch in its balance of payments.[18] China, which is in the midst of a massive economic transformation, has also begun to feel the effects of its own financial sector crisis: it has allowed its first bank to fail since 1949 and is in the process of privatizing large sections of its economy, including enterprises previously managed by the military. The financial sector—both state banks and the provincial and municipal fund-raising and investments institutions known as ITICs (International Trust & Investment Corporations) are also in serious trouble. A restructuring of the nonbank financial institutions is under way. Managing these transformations, at a time when overall and export growth rates are slowing and inequality is growing, is a massive challenge.

The social and ecological costs of China's transformation, which began in 1979, have been immense. Growing inequality within urban areas and between urban and rural areas suggest that significant grievances and unrest lie just below the surface. At the national level, explicit challenges to the Communist Party's monopoly of power are met with repression and, overall, China's record on human rights is mixed and uneven. Yet in terms of the Asian-cum-global economic crisis, China has played a key role in preventing it from worsening because its economy does *not* resemble the open, liberalized model the United States has been trying to export elsewhere. China's lack of foreign exchange convertibility has prevented extensive speculative attacks on its currency.

FROM (IN)STABILITY TO (IN)SECURITY?

The Asian financial crisis exposed the dark undersides of the countries boasting so-called miracle economies by: (1) revealing the largely externally driven nature of their markets and their dependence, in particular, on Japan; (2) highlighting the weakness or absence of their safety nets; (3) illustrating the danger in their lack of transparent and accountable economic regulatory institutions, particularly in the financial sector; and (4) identifying the narrow interests represented in their political institutions, which shaped their basic development models. The crisis has also exposed the dark underside of U.S. policies toward the region: (1) a single-minded emphasis on liberalization and curbing government; (2) the subordination of human rights issues to short-term commercial gain; and (3) the lack of commitment to building regional economic institutions.

The Asian economic crisis and its associated political crises have continued the erosion of the basic bargain that existed between Washington and its Pacific Asian allies during the cold war. Within the U.S. government, the geopolitical/ military perspective, based in the Pentagon and the National Security Council, dominated U.S. policies in the Asia-Pacific region through the mid-1980s. They viewed the critical issue to be maintaining U.S. military supremacy and using it, via unilateral and bilateral action, to guarantee U.S. military hegemony in the region. Under this strategy, the United States provided the security umbrella and a guaranteed market for manufactured exports, allowing its allies to industrialize. This worked fine as long as growth in both the United States and Pacific Asia was sustained. By the 1980s, however, the bargain began to break down. The United States demanded that Korea and Japan increase their expenditures for the cost of basing U.S. troops in their countries, which they did. Japanese peacetime, host-nation support is the most generous of any U.S. ally, averaging about $5 billion each year.[19] A new multiyear agreement with South Korea for 1999 to 2001 calls for payments of $333 million for 1999 with future contributions linked to Korea's GDP growth and inflation.[20] In the 1980s, the United States also began to withdraw Pacific Asia's free access to the U.S. market, pressuring Korea, Taiwan, and Japan to strengthen their currencies, adopt a range of export restraints, and liberalize regulations on foreign investment.

The original bargain continues to unravel with the ongoing economic crisis, as disgruntled citizens challenge ruling elites, and as the lack of a common enemy shifts economic conflicts rather than military ones to the foreground. Ironically, under its current policy, the United States runs the risk of being cast as the new common enemy of the region. The Asian economic crisis has led to a crumbling of several pillars in the cold war arrangement in East Asia, and it may yet precipitate a security crisis. As in all crises, there are new opportunities and obstacles in the new insecurity.

Even before the Asian crisis, several factors—the economic transformations of the last two decades, the end of the cold war, and growing popular opposition to a permanent U.S. military presence in the region—were reshaping the "living museum" of cold war–era security institutions in the region, particularly in Pacific Asia. The economic crisis has deepened the challenges posed by these trends. It is now incumbent on Washington to realign U.S. security policy in a manner that both addresses the economic crisis and enhances the security of citizens of both Asia and the United States. But military spending in the region is bucking a global trend. While global military expenditures declined by around one-third from 1988 to 1997, military expenditures increased by 25 percent in South and East Asia over the same period.[21] In the Pacific, bilateral alliances with Japan, Korea, Australia, and some Southeast Asian states form the core of United States defense strategy. South Asia, on the other hand, has traditionally been a strategic backwater for United States security policy.

U.S. Military Power in the Unpacific Pacific

The Pacific Command is the oldest and geographically largest of America's nine unified military commands.[22] Long the dominant force in determining U.S. policy in the region, the Pentagon has advanced a heavily militarized approach to security issues in the region, relying on the forward deployment of 100,000 U.S. troops (37,000 in Korea and the remainder in Japan and Okinawa) at a cost to U.S. taxpayers of about $8 billion per year in base expenses alone, according to military sources.

Having transformed the Pacific into an "American Lake" during the cold war, the United States remains the hegemonic military power in the region.[23] Since the end of the cold war, however, commercial interests in both the neoliberal internationalist and more mercantilist forms have increasingly challenged Pentagon hegemony. For example, commercial interests often triumphed over weapons proliferation concerns in dealing with China from 1993 to 1998. Revelations in 1999 of espionage and illegal campaign finance contributions by the Chinese government, however, may reshift the balance.

Popular opposition to the U.S. military bases in the Philippines (combined with the eruption of Mt. Pinatubo) led to a historic vote in the Philippine Senate that forced U.S. forces to withdraw from their bases in 1991. Military exercises between the two countries have been suspended since 1996, although a Visiting Forces Agreement was ratified by the Philippine Senate in mid-1999, allowing exercises to resume and giving U.S. ships access to Philippine ports. In Okinawa, popular opposition has also led to a reduction in the land area of the military base on the island, due in part to revulsion over the rape of a schoolgirl in 1995 by three American GIs. The trajectory of these efforts, however, has been blunted by the inertia behind cold war–era bilateral military alliances that have traditionally linked U.S. policy and ruling elites in many of the Southeast and Northeast Asian countries.

Dismayed by these developments and uncomfortable with the Bush administration's policy of maintaining close ties with China, which many military analysts view as Washington's emerging strategic opponent, the Pentagon has successfully shifted policy under the Clinton administration. In 1995, the Department of Defense produced a document called *U.S. Security Strategy in the Asia Pacific Region*, which announced that U.S. troop levels in the Pacific would not fall below 100,000 troops and clarified that multilateral initiatives to resolve conflict—such as the ASEAN (Association of Southeast Asian Nations) Regional Forum (ARF)—"are a way to supplement our alliances and forward military presence, not supplant them." This was a clear statement for sustaining permanent military presence in the region and maintaining the cold war–era alliance structure rather than acceding to multilateral initiatives and force reductions.

Upon releasing its new strategy document, the United States launched efforts to strengthen the northern pole of its forward deployments in the Pacific. In northeast Asia, intense Pentagon pressure resulted in Japanese Prime Minister Ryutaro Hashimoto's agreement to an expansion of the U.S.-Japan Security Treaty of 1951 by adding, in 1996, an Acquisition and Cross-Servicing Agreement focusing the alliance away from the defense of Japan and toward cooperation in maintaining regional security. Although U.S. bases in Japan and Korea remain the critical component of U.S. deterrent and rapid response strategy in Asia, under the September 1997 Guidelines for U.S.-Japan Defense Cooperation, approved by both houses of Japan's parliament in mid-1999, there is to be "greater Japanese support for U.S. operations in a regional contingency." This is a major step toward Japan actually becoming involved in military operations, a major policy shift. Since the definition of a "regional contingency" includes Taiwan, China interprets this new focus as a major step toward a containment posture relative to them. China's anxiety was heightened in December 1998, when the Japan Security Council approved a plan for joint theater missile defense technical research with the United States, focusing on a sea-based system.[24]

Events momentarily heated up again at the Taiwan Straits in mid-1999, when Taiwan's president, Lee Tung-hui, made pro-independence statements. The evidence suggests that Lee's statements were more targeted at cultivating political support for the ruling Kuomintang (Nationalist Party or KMT) in the run up to presidential elections in March 2000 rather than any immediate plans to declare independence. While China made some bellicose statements, it did not move military forces into an offensive position.

The United States also moved to strengthen the southern pole of its forward perimeter by enhancing access arrangements with Southeast Asian countries to compensate for the loss of Subic and Clark military bases in the Philippines. These arrangements included formal access agreements, informal agreements for ship and/or aircraft repairs and maintenance, and maintenance and access arrangements with many countries for training and exercise purposes. In the Philippines, the United States has been seeking an agreement that would allow not only military exercises but also military operations to occur within the country as part, for example, of antiterrorist activities against alleged Muslim extremists.

Following the Taiwan Straits missile launch and the sharpening of the dispute between China and ASEAN over the Spratly Islands in 1996 to 1997, the Pentagon began to frame such incidents as clear evidence of Chinese expansionism, despite almost unanimous consensus among experts that China had neither the intention nor the capacity to invade Taiwan, a view shared by America's own National Defense University.[25] The dominant view within the Clinton administration that China has replaced the former Soviet Union as the major adversary of the United States and needs to be contained, ignores several other facts. Of China's nuclear arsenal of roughly 400 warheads, fewer than 24 are capable of reaching the United States (which has roughly 7,200 strategic warheads capable of targeting China). In assessing China's real military capacity, the London-based International Institute for Strategic Studies (IISS) notes that "China does not have the resources to project a major conventional force beyond its territory."[26]

While there is no significant evidence that any data the Chinese gained through spying has given them a strategic advantage over the United States, the espionage scandal does reveal security problems in the recently privatized management of U.S. nuclear weapons labs as well as in the growing dominance of commercial over security interests in shaping U.S. policy. The Chinese missile launches by U.S.-owned Loral and Hughes demonstrated the danger in allowing commercial diplomacy to dominate policy toward China.

Bolstering U.S. capacity in order to contain China and to be able to intervene in the region was only one objective of upgrading the bilateral defense relationships in the East Asia region; strengthening U.S. intervention capabilities in the Middle East and South and Central Asia was another. For example, *The United States Security Strategy for the East Asia-Pacific Region 1998* notes that as Asia becomes more dependent on oil supplies from the Persian Gulf, "crises outside the region, particularly in the Arabian Gulf, increasingly affect regional security."[27]

Arms sales have contributed to broader insecurity in the region, as commercial interests have overtaken U.S. security strategy in directing weapons acquisition. Through 1997, East and Southeast Asia formed the second-largest regional arms market after the Middle East, although the economic crisis has deferred a number of planned purchases in 1998 to 1999. Malaysia and South Korea have also either postponed or canceled weapons purchases.

In 1998, information surfaced about a previously little-known U.S. Department of Defense training program called Joint Combined Exchange and Training (J-CET). This program provides funds for U.S. troops to conduct "training exercises" with foreign militaries around the world, but it has not been reviewed by Congress. U.S. Special Forces were found to have provided training to military units in a number of countries including Indonesia, Pakistan, and Papua New Guinea despite congressional concern about the human rights records of these countries. Initially the program was designed primarily to train U.S. troops, but over time the bulk of the training shifted to other nations' military forces. The U.S. military was thereby able to provide lethal-tactics training to states that were prohibited by Congress from receiving training assistance under the traditional International Military Education and Training (IMET) program, which *is* subject to review by Congress.[28] In September 1998, Congress passed a legislative amendment prohibiting the training of foreign security forces that violate human rights and requiring the Department of Defense to prepare an annual report covering all military exercises and training involving foreign military troops.

To crack down on the illicit trade in arms, the United States enacted regulations in 1998 under the amended Arms Export Control Act requiring persons "engaged in the business of brokering activities with respect to the manufacture, export, import or transfer of any designated defense article or defense service or any foreign defense article or defense service" to register with and obtain a license from the Office of Defense Trade Controls.[29] This closed a gaping loophole—in the past, if weapons did not pass through the United States, the transaction was not regulated—that arms dealers and private military companies had used to evade government prohibitions on military transfers.

The Korean Peninsula

One of the Clinton administration's few foreign policy success stories was the negotiation of the Agreed Framework in 1994. North Korea agreed to freeze its nuclear program in exchange for the construction of two light-water nuclear reactors by 2003 and half a million tons of fuel oil annually until the reactors were finished. South Korea agreed to cover about 70 percent of the estimated $4.6 billion construction costs for the light-water reactors in North Korea, and Japan has pledged $1 billion in loans for construction of light-water reactors in support of the Agreed Framework.[30] These developments contributed to the convening of the Korean Peninsula Four Party Peace Talks between the United States, China, and the two Koreas. These talks are designed to lead to a negotiated conclusion of the formal state of war between South and North Korea and to the eventual peaceful unification of the Korean Peninsula. Given that this is the end game, U.S. policy, which has emphasized military expansionism, must also begin to address the likelihood of reunification within the next decade, a process that probably will include significant economic and social dislocation if it occurs suddenly.[31]

Unfortunately, Congress has consistently stalled implementation of the Agreed Framework by withholding appropriations of funds, and the Clinton administration has also been slow to meet its commitments. In mid-1998, North Korea announced that it was suspending implementation of the 1994 Agreed Framework due to Washington's unwillingness to keep its end of the bargain. But North Korea also announced that it was willing to negotiate an end to its missile tests and deployments, if the United States would end the economic embargo and compensate North Korea for the loss of one of its few sources of hard currency—the sale of missile equipment/technology abroad.

Then in August 1998, North Korea launched a Taepodong I Missile, and press reports appeared that the North Koreans were clandestinely reopening a "secret" nuclear plant. The United States used these activities as an excuse to hold back on meeting its obligations under the Agreed Framework, rather than recognizing that such actions likely reflect a particular style of bargaining brinkmanship, a type that North Korea believes is the only way to get U.S. attention. In November 1998, Clinton appointed former Secretary of Defense William Perry to coordinate policy with North Korea. His first trip to Pyongyang in late May 1999 followed on the heels of U.S. pledges of food aid and of a U.S. monitoring team sent to inspect the suspected nuclear weapons facility at Kumchangri.

It appears that the Clinton administration has recognized that the "muddling through" relationship between the United States and North Korea under the Agreed Framework has so far lurched from crisis to crisis and is not sustainable. After North Korea threatened to test the longer range Taepodong II Missile in mid-1999, Washington in effect (although not explicitly) agreed to Pyongyang's position of ending its missile development program in exchange for an easing of the trade embargo, some financial assistance, and taking steps towards normalization. In response to the food crisis that intensified in North Korea beginning in 1995, the Clinton administration has provided humanitarian aid (more than $170 million in 1998), and in April 1999, the U.S. government agreed to its first direct assistance to North Korea: 100,000 metric tons of food as well as a project coordinated with several U.S. nongovernmental organizations (NGOs) that will introduce new potato varieties to North Korean farms. Although the Clinton administration has stated it will renew sanctions if North Korea does proceed with a missile test, the shift in Washington's position is a de facto recognition that negotiation, rather than confrontation, has become the most effective means of lowering military tensions on the peninsula. This slight rapprochement remains threatened by hard-liners in the Congress, who continue to oppose any compromises with North Korea.

South Korean conventional military supremacy (the South spends three times as much as the North—See figure 12–4) was one of the spurs behind the North's now-suspended nuclear program. South Korea's current stance would have been impossible without President Kim Dae Jung's pursuit of the "sunshine policy" of normalizing relations toward the North. In contrast with the United States, Kim retained the normalization policy through the 1998 missile launch crisis. Previously, hard-liners within both Koreas played off each other, leading to a progressing ratcheting up of threats. The election of Kim Dae Jung marked the first transfer of political power to the opposition since Seoul's transition from military rule and is an important step for human rights in South Korea. The Kim administration has, however, come under criticism by human rights advocates for not freeing some of its longest-held political prisoners and for more than 240 arrests under a law that makes it illegal to "praise or encourage" North Korea.[32]

South Asia

South Asia, while largely a strategic and economic backwater in Washington's eyes during much of the cold war, became more central in the 1980s as the United States relied on Pakistan as a base of operations to channel support to the anti-Soviet Afghan guerrilla movements. With the partial exception of the India-Pakistan rivalry, which the United States helped accelerate by its historic "tilt" toward Pakistan throughout the cold war, most of the conflicts in South Asia (unlike in Pacific Asia) are not directly linked to the legacy of U.S. involvement in the region. The primary U.S. military presence in the region is the refueling facilities on the Indian Ocean island of Diego Garcia, positioned to support U.S. naval maneuvers in the Persian Gulf. Most U.S. forces in the Indian Ocean are commissioned for intervention in the Middle East and Central Asia, including Afghanistan.[33]

Figure 12.4   Military Expenditures and Budgets ($U.S. millions)

Country	1995	1996	1997
Japan	50,200	43,600	41,200
South Korea	14,200	15,500	15,500
North Korea (PPP[a])	5,200	5,200	2,400
China (PPP[a])	33,000	38,000	
China (official)	7,600	8,600	9,700
Indonesia	4,400[b]	4,700[b]	3,300
Laos	73	77	79
Malaysia	3,500[b]	3,600[b]	2,500
Mongolia	19	14	22
Philippines	1,400[b]	1,500[b]	1,100
Singapore	4,000	4,000	4,300
Taiwan	13,100	13,600[b]	11,300
Thailand	4,000	4,300	4,100
Vietnam	910	950	1,100

Source: International Institute for Strategic Studies, The Military Balance, 1998/99 (Oxford: Oxford University Press, 1998).
Note: Figures through 1996 are expenditures; 1997, unless noted, is budgeted. Procurement not included; 5-year procurement budget $1.9 billion for 1996 to 2000 approved December 1996.
[a]Expenditure figures include expenditures on procurement and defense industry; budgeted figure (1997) does not.
[b]PPP: Dollars expressed in Purchasing Power Parity

Following tit-for-tat nuclear tests in May 1998, India and Pakistan spurred their nuclear competition with ballistic missile tests in mid-April 1999. In keeping with the February 1999 Lahore Declaration, during this second round, both states informed each other—as well as the five permanent members of the UN Security Council—in advance of the tests.[34] The nuclear tests took place against a backdrop of renewed spending on conventional arms. Although conventional arms imports by India and Pakistan fell from $7 billion in 1990 to a low of $1 billion in 1994, they increased to $1.7 billion in 1996.[35]

The Indian and Pakistani tests violated the Non-Proliferation Treaty (NPT), of which all the declared nuclear powers (except India and Pakistan) and most developing countries are members. The objectives of that treaty were to freeze further expansion of the nuclear 'club' in exchange for steps toward disarmament on the part of the nuclear powers. India, Pakistan, and Israel remain the only nuclear powers outside the NPT regime. The Clinton administration imposed sanctions on both India and Pakistan in the aftermath of the tests (as required under law), but these were loosened and then lifted in December 1998. The collapse and then re-election of the Hindu nationalist BJP(Bharatiya Janata Party), coupled with the coup in Pakistan on October 12, 1999 have placed India and Pakistan's previous commitments to sign the Comprehensive Test Ban Treaty (CTBT) and to consider participation in other relevant multilateral nuclear arms control talks, in doubt.

Kashmir remains the most immediate regional flashpoint, with the most recent outbreak of fighting in May-June 1999. A Pakistani-backed insurgency, met by an Indian-led counterinsurgency, has killed more than 30,000 people since 1989.[36] Since 1998, both countries have effectively linked their nuclear escalations to the tensions in Kashmir, moving it onto the international agenda.[37] Conflict between the deposed Prime Minister Nawaz Sharif and the former army chief—now president—General Pervaiz Musharraf over policy towards Kashmir led to a coup d'etat in October 1999. Widespread dissatisfaction with the corruption of the Sharif administration appears to have most Pakistanis adopt a "wait and see" stance toward his regime, particularly since the new regime pledged to rid the country's political system of rampant corruption. New laws led to the arrest of hundreds of Pakistan's most powerful and wealthy people, hours after a deadline expired for debtors to state banks repay loans or face criminal charges. With Pakistan's political future uncertain, encouraging bilateral talks with India would be a useful step towards reducing tension.

U.S. security policy in South Asia is full of contradictions. In the nuclear realm, both India and Pakistan, justifiably, feel they are being held to double standards by the United States. India feels that Washington is willing to allow many more violations of nonproliferation in China, while placing sanctions on India. Pakistan feels that it is unfairly pressured to sign the Non-Proliferation Treaty as long as the United States does not require Israel to sign it. Pressure without an evenhanded, consistent global policy makes Washington's demands on India and Pakistan ring hollow. Now that India and Pakistan have committed to sign the Comprehensive Test Ban Treaty (CTBT) and the U.S. bilateral economic sanctions have been relaxed, pending their signing and ratification, the United States needs to act immediately to extend its own nonproliferation efforts, starting by ratifying the CTBT and taking clear steps toward disarmament as required under Article VI of the NPT. One step would be to declare that it is ready to de-alert all its nuclear weapons on a mutually verifiable basis and to challenge all other nuclear powers (including Israel) to sign a multilateral agreement to do likewise. At the bilateral level, the United States must move to the next phase in strategic arms control, should pressure Russia to ratify START II, and needs to encourage China to expand its participation in multilateral arms control regimes. Condemnations of India's and Pakistan's tests are rank hypocrisy without concrete U.S. steps toward disarmament as part of the NPT bargain.

Washington's War on Drugs in Asia

The other major justifications for extending U.S. military operations in South and Southeast Asia in the post–cold war period have been drugs and terrorism, areas in which Afghanistan and Burma feature prominently.[38] The State Department classifies Burma and Afghanistan as the first and second largest producers in the world of illicit opium and heroin. In Afghanistan, the U.S supports a poppy eradication/alternative development program in Helmand Province through Mercy Corps International, an American NGO. This dual-focused effort continued through 1998, and the Clinton administration agreed to provide $1 million for the program in fiscal year 1999. It is the only poppy reduction project being implemented by an NGO in Afghanistan.[39] Even though the United States has "decertified" Burma's military junta from receiving narcotics assistance, the Clinton administration decided in early 1998 to allocate up to $3 million toward a new crop-substitution program by the UN Drug Control Program in the Shan State, along the China border. Narcotics programs have generally entailed collaboration with the Burmese military, but it is not yet clear whether this assistance has involved closer cooperation with the authorities.[40]

The problems with drug-related programs in Asia are the same as with all efforts at interdiction—the strategies end up strengthening militaries in societies where civilian control over the military is weak or nonexistent. Sometimes such efforts actually create market incentives that boost the profits of the traffickers. Crop-substitution programs face numerous obstacles, from difficulties in finding viable alternatives to high-priced illegal crops, to trade barriers blocking access to the U.S. market for products that compete with U.S. growers. The reasonable alternative is to pursue demand-reduction efforts in the United States, cease all drug-related military efforts in Asia, and redirect those resources to programs that support sustainable agriculture and community-based resource management as part of integrated rural development programs.

FROM ECONOMIC TO POLITICAL CRISIS

The regional economic crisis has both sparked new political conflicts in Indonesia, Malaysia, and elsewhere and contributed to older, ongoing political crises in Burma and Cambodia. As a result, the United States has faced new obstacles in Asia and the Pacific, while expanding opportunities to support human rights and sustainable development efforts. The obstacles include long-standing U.S. support for authoritarian rule (Indonesia) and/or the military in new or weak civilian electoral regimes (the Philippines, South Korea, Taiwan, Thailand), the potential for heightened repression against labor unions, and the reality that the crisis will encourage a greater emphasis on the exploitation of natural resources (particularly forests and fisheries) to meet each country's foreign exchange and food security needs.

During the cold war, labor and human rights issues were regularly subordinated to broader U.S. military-strategic concerns; now they are subordinated to corporate interests. Labor rights issues have been integrated into the USTR's activities through the Generalized System of Preferences (GSP) program. GSP petitions and cases have covered internationally recognized labor rights, particularly in Indonesia, Malaysia, Thailand, and Indochina, but monitoring of labor rights issues and the overall priority of human rights in bilateral dialogues rank well below the attention allocated to intellectual property rights (IPR) issues, for example.[41]

Washington has been willing to impose economic sanctions only in cases where either security or corporate interests were threatened (e.g., against China for IPR violations) or where U.S. economic interests were slight, as in Burma. Burma continues to rank as one of the world's pariah states more than a decade after the 1988 prodemocracy uprising was crushed by the army and nearly ten years since the military prevented the National League for Democracy (NLD) from taking office after winning national elections. The continued standoff between the government and the opposition NLD (led by Daw Aung San Suu Kyi) along with other expressions of nonviolent dissent resulted in more than 1,000 detentions in 1998. Other human rights abuses—including extrajudicial executions, rape, forced labor, and forced relocations—drove thousands of Burmese refugees, many of them from ethnic minority groups, into Thailand and Bangladesh. The change in November 1997 from the State Law and Order Restoration Council (SLORC) to the gentler-sounding State Peace and Development Council (SPDC) had little impact on human rights practices and policies, and an economy in free fall just aggravated matters for the beleaguered population.

Extensive popular pressure persuaded the Clinton administration to enact economic and trade sanctions against the ruling junta in 1997, policies that continue to this day. The State Department has repeatedly condemned the political crackdown on the NLD, has warned that any moves against Aung San Suu Kyi would escalate the international response, and has urged other governments, including Japan, to impose sanctions. The U.S. Congress could do more, such as funding Burmese student groups and other NGOs along the Thai-Burmese border, ensuring that Thailand respects their rights as refugees, and pressuring other countries, including China, to withdraw support from Burma.

The Asian financial crisis triggered new opportunities in the struggle for human rights and democracy in the region. Through the late 1980s and early 1990s, the promotion of human rights and democracy was challenged by the so-called Asian values debate. That debate forged an alliance of convenience between some authoritarian Asian elites and U.S. policymakers and analysts who placed a higher priority on economic and political stability in Asia than on human rights and democracy. Others, such as the National Endowment for Democracy, defined human rights and democracy narrowly, emphasizing civil and political rights to the exclusion of economic, social, and cultural rights. Similarly democracy was designated as multiparty elections, without an examination of the nonelectoral conditions necessary for the effective exercise of democratic rights.

Although the Clinton administration has heralded its efforts to develop "democratization" programs around the world, U.S. foreign policy should not hinge on the promotion of democracy per se, since there is no international consensus as to what actually constitutes democracy. The criteria for evaluating the violations of particular rights, however, are fairly explicit and are internationally recognized. These explicit criteria should become the bases for unilateral, bilateral, and multilateral efforts. For example, the United States could support efforts to create a regional human rights mechanism, as proposed by prominent human rights groups in the region.

In terms of human rights, the Clinton administration has focused on child labor. In a June 1999 speech to the International Labor Organization (ILO) in Geneva, President Clinton urged the 174-member organization to put a "human face" on the global economy by adopting a treaty banning the "worst forms" of child labor, including labor that is harmful to children's health, safety, and morals.[42] In Pakistan, for instance, the United States is supporting an innovative model program designed to remove child labor in the carpet manufacturing sector by providing schools for the children and development projects for their communities. Managed by the ILO and funded by $1.5 million from the U.S. government and $900,000 from the carpet makers over the next three years, the program initially aims to help 8,000 children in some 30 villages; eventually, it will target all 30,000-plus children working at carpet looms. In 1998, President Clinton requested (and Congress approved) $30 million to spend on this and similar programs—ten times the previous year's budget.[43] However, some critics charge that banning imports of child labor products targets only the tiny export sector in developing countries, leaving untouched—and actually driving more children into— more dangerous and exploitative labor in domestic industries, agriculture, the informal market (i.e., begging), and illegal and criminal occupations (i.e., prostitution, drug trafficking, and child soldiering).

In addition, the Clinton administration has opposed, though less vigorously, other types of serious human rights abuses in Asia and the Pacific, including the repression of women by the ultraconservative Islamic movement, the Taliban, in Afghanistan, sectarian clashes between Sunni and Shiite Muslims in Pakistan, and ethnic conflict in Sri Lanka. The 15-year-old civil war in Sri Lanka between the government and the LTTE (Liberation Tigers of Tamil Eelam, the so-called Tamil Tigers) continues unabated. Human rights reports, including State Department documents, have detailed violations by both the Sri Lankan military and the LTTE,[44] but U.S. policy targets only the LTTE for blame. The United States has provided a small amount of resources for humanitarian assistance for war victims and displaced children as well as training for Sri Lankan troops. The Clinton administration has called on the LTTE to "cease all acts of terrorism" and has expressed unconditional support for the Sri Lankan government's proposals for a political resolution of the ethnic conflict. In October 1997, the Clinton administration included the LTTE on a list of 30 organizations banned under a 1996 antiterrorism law, which bars LTTE members from the United States, prohibits fund-raising for the organization, and permits the freezing of members' bank accounts.

The Taliban's gender policies have attracted widespread international condemnation, particularly from the European Union and from U.S. women's organizations. In response to pressure from these groups, Washington has also stepped up its criticism of the Taliban. Humanitarian assistance to Afghanistan and to the 1.2 million refugees in Pakistan remained the principal basis for most countries' relationship with the Afghans. Most neighboring countries provide financial or military support to one or more of the Afghan factions. The humanitarian effort is plagued with problems, since the UN and nongovernmental relief organizations must contend with new security concerns and the Taliban's restrictive gender policies.

The Clinton administration has participated in efforts to promote a negotiated settlement under the auspices of the Group of Six-plus-Two, composed of all the countries bordering Afghanistan (Pakistan, Iran, Turkmenistan, Uzbekistan, Tajikistan, and China) plus the United States and Russia. Operating under UN auspices, these eight countries stepped up efforts early in 1998 to initiate talks aimed at a settlement between the United Front and the Taliban. During an April 1998 visit by then-U.S. Ambassador to the United Nations Bill Richardson—the most senior U.S. official to travel to Afghanistan in 20 years—a cease-fire was announced, but plans for further talks between the two parties evaporated almost immediately. The Taliban's midyear offensive scuttled further progress, as did the U.S. bombing attack against a suspected terrorist camp in Afghanistan following the August 1998 bombings of U.S. embassies in East Africa. Since the bombings, Washington has only had a "get bin Laden policy," rather than a coherent Afghan policy. In mid-November, 1999 U.S.-backed UN sanctions went into effect to try and force the Taliban to turn over bin Laden.

A quarter century after the end of the U.S. war in Southeast Asia, Washington's policy in Indochina (Vietnam, Laos, and Cambodia) is still colored by people and policies from that era and remains dominated by concerns over prisoners of war and the interests of right-wing Indochinese exiles. In both Laos and Vietnam, for instance, broader U.S. economic development assistance and cultural ties as well as expanded support for land mine removal operations in all three countries and environmental clean-ups of Agent Orange and other defoliants could go a long way toward ending the legacy of the last "hot war" of the cold war in Asia. Indochina still suffers the effects of this war. Between 1962 and 1971, the United States sprayed 12 million gallons of defoliant over 10 percent of what was then South Vietnam. Vietnamese and Canadian researchers have found high levels of dioxin in soils, fish and animal tissue, and the blood of people born after the war. "If such data were collected in most Western jurisdictions, based on similar sampling levels, major environmental clean up and more extensive studies would be implemented," asserts a report by a Canadian consulting firm following a five-year study, completed in 1999, of the Aluoi Valley in central Quang Tri province.[45]

By mid-1999, Cambodia was effectively, albeit precariously, at peace for the first time in three decades. The Khmer Rouge guerrilla army—responsible for an estimated 1.5 to 2 million deaths between 1975 and 1978—has apparently been destroyed, its leader Pol Pot is dead, and, in November 1998, an agreement was reached on a coalition government. The current powersharing coalition is intended to last for five years until the next scheduled elections in 2002.

The United States bears heavy responsibility for Cambodia's initial slide into violence. During its "secret" bombing war between 1969 and 1973, Washington collaborated in a 1970 coup against the neutral government of Prince Norodom Sihanouk and helped install a pro-U.S. military government. The subsequent U.S. troop invasion to prop up General Lon Nol's right-wing government prompted a backlash that strengthened support for the radical Khmer Rouge guerrillas. When a 1978 Vietnamese invasion ended the horror of the Khmer Rouge's bizarre brand of radical communism, the United States shifted support (officially only "nonlethal" assistance) to an armed guerilla coalition that included the Khmer Rouge.

The Vietnamese troop withdrawal in 1989 set the stage for the signing, by all political factions, of the Paris Peace Accords in 1991. The United States played a key role in these UN-brokered negotiations and signed as one of the international guarantors of the accords, which led to years of unstable power sharing.[46] Given

America's long and nefarious track record in Cambodia, Washington should, at minimum, provide support for an international tribunal for the trial of Khmer Rouge leaders. It should also continue to exert pressure on the current Cambodian government to prosecute clear cases of executions that occurred during and since Prime Minister Hun Sen's extraconstitutional seizure of power in July 1997 in clear violation of the Paris Peace Accords. And the United States should publicly and promptly release information it has concerning the March 30, 1997, grenade attack on a peaceful political gathering in front of the National Parliament in Phnom Penh.

Indonesia

Nowhere else in Asia has the financial crisis led to such profound political upheavals than in Indonesia, the world's fourth most populous country and a critical U.S. ally throughout the last quarter century of the cold war. The July 1997 economic crisis wiped out three decades of material growth by what had been hailed as one of Asia's mightiest "Tigers," and the May 1998 forced resignation of President Suharto ended the military rule of Washington's longest-standing Asian ally. Since then, Indonesia's economic meltdown, human rights abuses, and man-made ecological disasters have continued to capture world headlines, and observers predict it is likely to remain a "black hole" economically, politically, and strategically for another decade.[47]

Indonesia, a former Dutch colony, was led from the time of its independence in 1945 until a military coup two decades later by Sukarno via an unusual political coalition that included factions of the military, the Indonesian Communist Party, and the nonaligned National Indonesian Party (PNI). Sukarno, a key figure in the founding of the Non-Aligned Movement, was replaced by Suharto in 1967 after two years of unrest beginning with a 1965 coup by military leaders. In the wake of the coup, Suharto, a military officer and staunch anticommunist, rose to power. His regime, known as the "New Order," was founded in part on a brutal campaign against the Indonesian Communist Party, during which an estimated 500,000 people were killed. He forged an occasionally uneasy coalition of neoliberal and nationalist technocrats, the military, crony businesspeople, and a national patronage party known as GOLKAR.

Washington endorsed General Suharto's rise to power and, in 1975, gave its tacit approval to Indonesia's invasion of the island of East Timor, which had just emerged from Portuguese colonial rule. In the wake of Indonesia's invasion and occupation, a third of East Timor's population—some 200,000 East Timorese—were murdered. The United States supplied weapons to the Indonesian military and vetoed any effective UN intervention. The Suharto regime's legitimacy—based on vigorous economic growth and backed by repressive military force—was gradually discredited by revelations of corruption and military links to systematic rapes, disappearances, tortures, and extrajudicial killings. Despite these human rights abuses, Washington supported Suharto and his New Order with generous military assistance, foreign aid, and trade preferences.

After the cold war, Suharto garnered further support from the United States for his opposition to anti-Western Islamist political movements in Indonesia, the world's most populous Islamic country. His family and other crony businesspeople provided political support in exchange for monopoly control of large sectors of the economy and access to public financing. The U.S. Commerce Department praised Indonesia as one of the world's "big emerging markets," and it became a favorite location for U.S. business, including 23 oil companies. As late as 1995, Suharto, while on a state visit to Washington, was described as "our kind of guy" by a senior Clinton administration official quoted in the *New York Times*.[48]

The Suharto regime remained relatively stable as long as oil prices were high and short-term capital inflows sustained growth at a level where something could trickle down. But the Asian crisis unraveled the fragile foundation of this military-political-business coalition. Between the neoliberal technocrats (allied with the IMF) on one side and popular outrage at Suharto's protection of his cronies (amid widespread misery) on the other, Suharto was caught in a bind. Other business elites, a segment of the military, the bureaucracy, and GOLKAR all persuaded him to step down in order to preempt the radicalization of popular opposition, which threatened the entire edifice constructed under the New Order. The United States, as well, weighed in with its support of a rapid handover of power in May 1998 to B. J. Habibie, the vice president and a Suharto protégé.

Since the fall of the Suharto regime, progress toward protecting human rights and sustainable development in Indonesia has been uneven. On the positive side, Habibie released several dozen political prisoners and allowed greater press freedom and the formation of new political parties. The June 1999 parliamentary election and October 20, 1999 election of Abdurrahman Wahid and Megawati Sukarnoputri as president and vice-president respectively have cooled political tensions. The cabinet of the coalition government is a rainbow coalition of hardcore Muslim politicians, military reformers, civilian progressives, bureaucrats, and former GOLKAR Party loyalists. Notably, two of the cabinet members are of Chinese descent. Three crucial matters will shape the prospects for democracy in Indonesia: a broad-based economic recovery; investigations of corruption and human rights violations under Suharto; and the military's future role in politics. The latter is the most contentious issue, since the Indonesian military shows no sign of relinquishing its *dwifungsi* (dual function): forcibly protecting the government while helping to operate it.

Ongoing violations of human rights include the continued imprisonment of some Suharto-era political prisoners, the repression of prodemocracy activists and workers, and military/paramilitary violence against independence activists in East Timor and Irian Jaya as well as autonomy movements in the province of Aceh. Major roadblocks to democratization include resolving the aforementioned independence and autonomy issues and addressing growing pressures for the renegotiation of relations between Jakarta and the Outer Islands. These resource-rich provinces want the Indonesian government to decrease taxes and revenue extraction, increase public spending, and decentralize government decisionmaking.

The Habibie administration tried to address autonomy demands with a decentralization law designed to provide something short of independence for East Timor and to undercut the widespread autonomy/secession demands by permitting more local control over government expenditures. The autonomy proposal was place before the Timorese voters in a UN-supervised referendum in August 1999, and 78.5 percent of Timorese voters chose independence, despite massive violence and intimidation by military-supported anti-independence militias.[49] After the vote, a carefully orchestrated campaign by militias and the military forced several hundred thousand Timorese into becoming refugees, the looting of the capital city, and the flight of the UN mission. Under international pressure, Habibie agreed to an Australian-led UN peacekeeping force to restore order. With the UN peacekeepers in place, the United States needs to convince the Indonesian government and military to respect the results of the referendum, disarm paramilitary groups operating from West Timor, support international efforts to conduct an investigation into human rights violations in East Timor, and provide assistance for political reconstruction and economic development. The United States halted military assistance and training as well as arms transfers to the Indonesian government in the aftermath of the paramilitary rampage in East Timor. The Clinton administration should not renew military assistance until clear steps are taken to ensure that military repression will not occur elsewhere in Indonesia. The United States should support the initial steps taken by the Wahid administration to pursue a non-violent political solution in Aceh, and encourage him to do so in Irian Jaya.

WEAK (AND WEAKER) MULTILATERALISM

The Asian financial and political crises exposed the weakness of regional institutions. Unlike the formal institutional structures that manage integration in North America under NAFTA or in the European Union, economic integration in East and Southeast Asia is not guided by structural accords. The inability of ASEAN (the Association of Southeast Asian Nations), the oldest regional multilateral organization, to respond effectively to the regional economic and environmental crises is reflected in the observation by Singapore's Premier, Goh Chok Tong, that ASEAN "is seen as helpless and worse, disunited in a crisis."[50] A major stumbling block is ASEAN's principle of nonintervention in the domestic affairs of member countries. More recent developments suggest that this principle is slowly being challenged. For example, the regional impact of the Indonesian forest fires of 1997 led Malaysia, Singapore, and the Philippines to pressure Indonesia to adopt policies to prevent a repeat occurrence, while Thailand and the Philippines initially opposed Cambodia's entrance into ASEAN.

When, on occasion, Asian governments have attempted collective action on economic issues without including the United States, as in the proposal Malaysian prime minister, Mohamed Mahathir, for an East Asian Economic Caucus or in the case of the ASEAN Free Trade Area, Washington has objected. For example, one early attempt at a regional response to the Asian economic crisis was Japan's August 1997 proposal for an Asian Monetary Fund. This would have created a fund to protect Asian currencies from speculative assaults in their financial markets. But the U.S. Treasury Department torpedoed the proposal, arguing that it was duplicating the efforts of the IMF.

The United States does not advocate multilateralism in Asia per se but uses multilateral institutions to advance U.S. corporate interests. The Clinton administration has relatively neglected the Asian Development Bank (ADB), which is unique among multilateral development banks for its policy on good governance and its requirement that projects do social impact assessments. The administration has also neglected the Asian Development Fund (ADF), the ADB's window for its poorest members. Similarly, the United States has taken a narrow interest in the Asia-Pacific Economic Cooperation forum (APEC), a rather lame-duck institution whose 21 members on both sides of the Pacific account for over half of world trade. APEC's three parallel purposes are economic and technical cooperation, promoting sustainable development, and trade and investment liberalization which has been pushed by the United States since 1993. The United States has used APEC countries to build support for free trade in the WTO. However, opposition from several other members—particularly Japan—to rapid liberalization of nine designated industry sectors has effectively blocked the process. With the U.S. liberalization agenda stalled and the United States unwilling to offer substantive new initiatives on the technical cooperation or sustainable development fronts, combined with APEC's ineffective response to the financial crisis, APEC now lies in a kind of diplomatic limbo.

Meanwhile, the main Asia-related issue for the United States at the WTO remains China's accession. Political scandals and tensions with China delayed the Clinton administration's plans to win Congressional approval of China's entry into the WTO and renewal of China's Normal Trade Relations. The United States and China concluded an agreement on accession shortly before WTO's Seattle Ministerial meeting in December 1999. The agreement involves significant concessions by China, granting foreign companies access in finance and other sensitive service sectors, and allowing the United States to use special programs to protect U.S. industries against import surges. But the agreement is just the beginning of contentious battles in both countries. The U.S. Congress needs to approve the agreement and also grant China permanent NTR status, difficult at any time, but particularly in an election year. The agreement is likely to have a more significant long-term political effect in China as its liberalization commitments will affect the large state-owned heavy manufacturing industries and the local small-scale consumer goods industries. The disruption that will occur in these politically sensitive sectors will have the long-term effect of weakening the power of the Communist Party relative to other social forces—both democratic and undemocratic.

Multilateral security institutions in Asia are also fairly weak. Currently, the only serious Asia-wide multilateral security framework is the ASEAN Regional Forum, which has assembled foreign ministers in annual meetings since 1994 to discuss security issues.[51] The current U.S. stance downplays ARF relative to America's bilateral alliances and forward-deployed forces tasked with waging a regional war and containing China. This stance continues the cold war legacy of emphasizing unilateral and bilateral approaches to advancing U.S. security interests in the region. If America needs to begin to redefine its security interests in Asia, it also needs to redefine the means by which they can be attained. The United States does participate in a number of smaller, "minilateral" efforts on the Korean Peninsula and in Afghanistan. These efforts are important and should be strengthened. The United States should also increase support for smaller, regional efforts by ASEAN and other countries.

A WAY FORWARD FOR U.S. POLICY: FROM
EXPORTING INSECURITY TO BUILDING PEACE

The U.S. drive to maintain the Pacific Ocean as an "American lake" remains the primary source of tension in the Pacific. The current rationale for the U.S.-Japanese military alliance in the Pacific basically revolves around containing China, maintaining the potential for military action against North Korea, and intervening in the Middle East. In South Asia, the Kashmir flashpoint has taken on new urgency in the context of the nuclear standoff between India and Pakistan and the military coup in Pakistan. But the main point is that there are few direct, immediate military threats to the security of the United States, and in this context the United States should be working to build the foundation for lasting security in the region.

The global economic crisis sparked by Asia's regional crisis exposed the weaknesses in the global economy and rolled back some of the significant gains in reducing poverty in the five most affected Asian countries while accelerating environmental degradation and unsustainable resource exploitation. Although the economic crisis has not yet seriously affected South Asia, the existing levels of poverty and the daunting challenges for sustainable development suggest that enlightened self-interest calls for an active U.S. response there as well. Asian countries will be key players in attempting to deal with global environmental problems that affect U.S. interests, such as climate change, ozone depletion, biodiversity loss, and overfishing. Asian consumers also represent a huge and growing market for U.S. goods and services.

Regarding the region as a whole, the United States should pay particular attention to the protection and/or advancement of fundamental human rights, such as freedom of association and speech, as well as basic labor rights. U.S. policy in this area will have greater legitimacy and effectiveness if it is applied consistently and is coupled with bilateral and multilateral efforts to reduce the social costs of the economic crisis, including debt reduction, support for safety nets and basic social services (including community-based resource management), and reduction of tariff and nontariff barriers to exports from the region.

The primary threat to the security of the United States and its citizens in Asia is not military. The intertwining of traditional security, economic, environmental, and health issues is a major challenge both for Asia and for the world. The overlap between these issues creates the possibility of a number of synergies. For example, if present trends continue, Asia will be the site of the fastest growth in nuclear power in the next two decades—appealing to some because nuclear power does not release greenhouse gases. The U.S. nuclear power industry has targeted Asia as a major growth area, given popular opposition in the United States and much of Europe. But expanding nuclear power poses both environmental and health risks and may also spur nuclear proliferation, if it is used without adequate safeguards. One win-win program that would address both some of the underlying proliferation issues while promoting sustainable development is the transfer (at other than commercial rates) of technology for renewable sources of energy, with the Export-Import Bank, Overseas Private Investment Corporation (OPIC), and U.S.-Asia Environmental Partnership as instruments for such transfers.

An alternative framework for U.S. policy in Asia and the Pacific already exists. It has three pillars: fully ending the cold war, creating sustainable prosperity, and supporting the construction of an Asia-Pacific community

Fully Ending the Cold War

The Clinton administration needs to take immediate steps to dismantle the legacies of the cold war in Asia. An important first step would be to rapidly declassify all documents relating to U.S. involvement in the region during the cold war period. This would set an important example regarding transparency and would assist grass-roots movements campaigning for similar transparency and accountability in government in Asia.

The initial steps taken in normalizing relations with Vietnam need to be deepened by expanding U.S. diplomatic engagement in Indochina, granting NTR status to Laos and Vietnam, and embarking on scientific and technical cooperation to address the legacies of the last Indochina war. This would include demining the region, addressing the continuing problems of unexploded ordnance, and taking responsibility for the environmental and health effects of extensive Agent Orange use.

Throughout Pacific Asia, the United States needs to take immediate steps to reduce its forward-deployed troops, close bases abroad, and transform its cold war–era military alliances into a multilateral framework for security in Asia. The Clinton administration must also agree to clean up all toxic and hazardous wastes in current and former military bases in Pacific Asia, which could simultaneously serve as a means of transferring "green technology" to the region and rebuilding relationships frayed by the cavalier attitudes and actions of some U.S. military personnel. Significant "collateral damage" from forward-deployed U.S. forces includes prostitution, stigmatized Amerasian children, and civilian casualties due both to military exercises and to off-duty crimes committed by U.S. troops. Washington must ensure that all U.S. troops respect human rights in Asia (especially women's rights) and that soldiers who violate laws of their host countries are prosecuted and held accountable for their actions. The military should actively promote employment opportunities for women—other than prostitution—and the United States should recognize the citizenship and immigration rights of Amerasian children.

On the Korean Peninsula, the easing of the embargo and reopening of negotiations led by former Secretary of Defense William Perry marks a positive step toward fulfilling the promise of the 1994 Agreed Framework. The United States should follow South Korean President Kim Dae Jung's lead regarding policy toward North Korea. Washington should meet its commitments under the Agreed Framework by ensuring progress in the construction of the reactor project and on-time delivery of heavy fuel oil. It should also support initiatives that seek to exploit renewable energy sources. Beyond its baseline commitments under the Agreed Framework, the United States should support overall efforts for maintaining peace on the Korean Peninsula by increasing economic cooperation and by supporting confidence building measures such as the Northeast Asia Cooperation Dialogue and the North Pacific Arms Control Workshop processes—upgrading them from a "Track II" (informal and nongovernmental) to a "Track I" (official) level.[52] Washington should also actively support the ongoing four-party talks involving the United States, China, and the two Koreas. America should not push for a rapid reunification but should instead make commitments to reduce the transition costs. Finally, the United States must champion demilitarization, including complete troop withdrawals and adequate financial support for demining efforts along the demilitarized zone as well as a comprehensive cleanup of toxics at all U.S. bases.

The United States should back away from its emerging "containment of China" strategy by halting efforts to build a theater missile defense system. In the Taiwan Straits, the United States should support the status quo: continued negotiations between Taiwan and the mainland, no military support to Taiwan for a declaration of independence, and opposition to an invasion by China.

In South Asia, the United States should expand its diplomatic presence and begin to develop a more ongoing relationship with India, the world's largest democracy. America must begin to move away from the legacy of its cold war–era support of Pakistan. Washington needs to recognize that China is a player in East, Southeast, *and* South Asia and that India may have legitimate concerns regarding China's role. Strengthening ties with India would be an important step in bolstering multilateral security efforts across Asia. The United States is paying the price in Afghanistan and Pakistan for its support of virtually any kind of anticommunist movements and regimes during the cold war. The Taliban emerged out of the Afghan guerrillas who fought against the Russians, and the United States continued to support these fighters even as veterans of those earlier battles started becoming active in terrorist organizations. Armed insurgents accused of terrorist attacks in China, Central Asia, and Pakistan have developed a symbiotic relationship with the Taliban: They help the Taliban militarily, the Taliban let them set up bases on Afghan soil.[53] From 1994 to 1997 the Clinton administration quietly allowed Pakistan and Saudi Arabia to back the Taliban, seeing it as a foil for Iranian influence in Central Asia. While some groups argue that the CIA should actively support moderate Taliban or opposition forces, such involvement would only further fragment Afghanistan and make things worse.[54] Instead, what the United States should do is pressure neighboring states to halt the supply of arms into Afghanistan—beginning with Pakistan.

Washington's tilt toward Pakistan during the cold war strengthened the military within Pakistan, vis-à-vis much weaker civilian-controlled institutions, and exacerbated the Indian-Pakistani rivalry. The United States should encourage the military government to set a timeline for a return to civilian rule and should actively support the government's efforts to prosecute the cronies of the previous administrations. In addition, the United States should encourage the ASEAN Regional Forum to adopt a range of confidence-building measures related to military transparency and conventional arms, including universal regional participation in the UN Register of Conventional Arms, voluntary submissions of additional information, and development of a regional register. ARF could also be an instrument to solicit support for universal adherence to the principles and commitments of the nonproliferation treaties and to engage other members not fully integrated into the global treaty regimes. Toward this end, the United States should advocate Pakistan's inclusion in ARF—to counterbalance India's existing membership—as a means of expanding the arenas for trust building ventures.

These multilateral efforts should be complemented by unilateral initiatives to reduce U.S. support for weapons suppliers and to implement the Arms Trade Code of Conduct, first introduced in Congress in 1993 (but not passed as of mid-1999), that would restrict official transfers of weapons to regimes that violate basic human rights. Recent gains in linking human rights issues to military aid and arms exports as an amendment to the House's Foreign Operations Act in 1997 must be extended.[55] The problem with these linkages, as with those regarding labor rights, is their perfunctory implementation by an unwilling Pentagon coupled with less-than-enthusiastic oversight by the Congress. Existing linkages need to be strengthened and supplemented by an arms trade code of conduct that would restrict weapons sales by U.S. companies to entities that respect basic human and democratic rights. Vigilant oversight by Congress is necessary to ensure that the Pentagon actually complies with restrictions proscribing training and support to the militaries of countries that systematically violate human rights.

Sustainable Prosperity

U.S. policy is at odds with enhancing sustainable and equitable development in the region. It currently privileges liberalization above concerns for sustainable development, concerns such as the pattern—as well as the pace—of growth. Instead of its fixation on economic liberalization, the United States must focus greater attention on the environmental costs of production and trade, especially in natural resource-intensive sectors such as forestry and fisheries. Unfortunately, despite growing recognition of the inherent dangers of liberalized capital flows, the Clinton administration argues that while the wiring in the international financial architecture may need some modernizing, the foundation is sturdy.

The Asian crisis and its echoes have exposed the weaknesses in both the foundation and the wiring of the global financial system, three of which are the lack of good international bankruptcy mechanisms designed to "bail in" the private sector, instability from unregulated short-term capital flows, and destructive pressure by the U.S. Treasury and the IMF to liberalize capital flows. Such issues transcend both Asia and the Pacific regions and the scope of this chapter.

So how does one enhance sustainable prosperity? Given the IMF's counterproductive role in Asia, increasing its resources without insisting on fundamental reform is both wasteful and harmful. Likewise, having recognized the importance of economic safety nets, it is not clear that the World Bank is the best channel to support such endeavors. While in 1999 the bank's chief economist at the time, Joseph Stiglitz, made statements supportive of Malaysia's capital controls, in practice it continues to advocate financial liberalization and structural adjustment policies. The United States must step back from pushing financial liberalization within the WTO and change its bilateral policies in the region so as not to exacerbate crises. Single-mindedly preaching economic liberalization may benefit U.S. corporations in the short term, but it undermines the medium- and long-term interests of building a shared prosperity for the majority of citizens in both the United States and Asia. The aftermath of the Asian crisis offers the United States an opportunity to rise above its vision of corporate-led integration and offer support for initiatives that enhance prosperity for all parties.

To achieve this end, U.S. foreign economic policy toward the region should embody three dimensions: (1) respect for a diversity of market economies; (2) a genuine and long-term commitment to confront the social crisis; and (3) promotion of sustainable resource management. The current opportunity should be seized, and bold action should be taken at the regional and global levels to address the roots of the crisis. This means ending U.S. pressure for continued economic liberalization, which only fuels anti-American sentiment. The long-term interests of the United States are best served by:

- A diversity of market economies. This would include extensive discussions on changing the international financial architecture to include greater democratization and accountability of international financial institutions and the development of mechanisms to regulate short-term capital flows. At the national level, it would mean supporting (or at least not opposing) capital controls and eschewing rapid liberalization in financial services.
- Focusing on the social costs of the crisis in Asia and the Pacific, especially the chronic poverty in South Asia. This would include support for expansionary fiscal and monetary policies and emphasis on rural development and agriculture in order to assure food security and a broad-based recovery, provision of safety nets for access to basic services, and support for redistributive programs like land reform, which lay the foundation for long-term sustainable growth and development guided by balancing domestic and international demand.
- Increased funding for community-based natural resource management programs that emphasize harvesting rather than mining of key natural resources such as forests and fisheries, and that can regulate such activities, especially in times of economic crisis.
- Forgiveness of official debt in exchange for commitments to respect human rights and reduce military expenditures.
- Strengthening the transparency of, the mechanisms for citizen participation in, and the sustainable development orientation of regional economic institutions in which the United States participates (e.g., APEC and the ADB).

- Supporting, or at least not opposing, independent regional initiatives by Asian countries striving to enhance regional cooperation. This would include supporting efforts by ASEAN and SAARC (South Asian Association for Regional Cooperation) to develop regional monitoring of and cooperation on environmental and economic issues.

Building Collaboration in Asia and the Pacific

The weakness of regional institutions and cooperation levels is a reflection, in part, of the lack of a sense of political community within which cooperation and nonviolent conflict resolution can take place. Let us be clear—it is unlikely that relations between the Asia region, the Pacific region, and the United States will ever be completely harmonious. Similarly, there is no reason to believe that a more democratic Asia will necessarily be totally peaceful. Conflicts that were kept under the surface through repression in Indonesia, for example, will emerge into open expression under democracy. It remains unclear how nonviolent those disputes will be, either within or between countries.

There will be routine tensions in Asian societies. The question is whether there will be mechanisms to prevent them from festering into violent conflicts and to resolve the more serious clashes as nonviolently as possible. The economic crisis and the increase in human rights activism and democracy movements throughout Asia have shifted the terms of the "Asian values" debate. It is clear that civil and political rights will be sought by Asian citizens regardless of whether their elites believe them to be "ready" for such rights. But economic, social, and cultural rights are equally important to these citizen movements, and the United States should acknowledge and affirm this sentiment. By doing so, Washington could help shift the terms of the debate from "Asian values" to the more expansive view of human rights articulated by prodemocracy and human rights movements in Asia and elsewhere. This will require a change from the more narrow focus on elections and civil and political rights that currently characterizes the official U.S. position.

A vibrant community in Asia and the Pacific is not something that can be created overnight; it requires a long-term perspective. Ignorance, for example, is a poor foundation upon which to build a community. Some simple and relatively cheap initiatives that could pay off in the long run include increasing funding of language training for U.S. students and expanding exchange programs to enhance cultural contacts between Asians and U.S. citizens. The Asian American community is an additional resource for expanding cross-cultural contacts.

In the short to medium term, there are some important (but distinctly "unsexy" areas) in which U.S. support could have significant positive effects in enhancing the global quality of life and laying the foundation for more long-term cooperation. These include scientific and technical cooperation in the areas of environmental technology and public health, which the United States provided through the Centers for Disease Control during the outbreak of a Japanese encephalitislike virus in Malaysia in early 1999. Supporting research into and treatments for infectious diseases, for example, enhances the health security of U.S.

citizens and supports broad-based growth in Asia, because poor people disproportionately suffer from infectious disease, and—in an age of globalization—
pathogens respect no borders. Encouraging the transfer of environmentally sound
technologies, including sustainable transportation and energy and ozone-safe
technologies to China, can bolster new industries in the United States and enhance the regional and global environment. Similarly, America could support such
initiatives as the multidonor environmental economics program for Southeast
Asia, which builds the capacity of local environmental economists and policymakers regarding sustainable development issues.

In general, human rights have taken a backseat to strategic and commercial
interests throughout the region. Human rights issues are occasionally acknowledged in less strategic or commercially unimportant countries, such as Burma and
Cambodia, or in speeches in which the United States comes across as preachy.
With China, the Clinton administration has continued a long-standing U.S. government policy of ambivalence on human rights questions regarding Tibet, Hong
Kong, and internal political and religious dissent and worker rights. Some human
rights organizations gave Clinton high marks for declaring during his state visit in
June 1998 that the Tiananmen crackdown was wrong and for arguing that "stability in the twenty-first century will require high levels of freedom" in China. But in
Tibet, the United States could support release of nonviolent political prisoners
and improved international press and human rights groups access to the region. In
Hong Kong, the United States and the international community must continue to
monitor the situation to ensure that China maintains its commitments to respecting democracy and human rights. More broadly, human rights could have a more
significant impact if the United States adhered to consistent criteria based on internationally recognized standards applied in a clear and transparent manner.

Exporting U.S. electoral institutions to Asian settings should not be America's
primary tool for advancing human rights. Although Washington should support
election monitoring efforts, the United States should shift its democracy agenda
away from a narrow focus on the stability of electoral institutions to embrace an
internationally recognized, broad-based human rights agenda that recognizes the
indivisibility of civil, political, economic, social, and cultural rights. This implies,
in the short-term, that America must place greater emphasis on monitoring
human rights violations in the region and pay more attention to both the achievements and violations of individual countries as they attempt to meet all their
human rights commitments. Specifically, the United States should disband Radio
Free Asia and shift support to human rights advocates and investigative journalists
in Asia through the Asia Foundation.

The United States should promote its human rights initiatives with more
carrots than sticks, building the capacities of governmental and nongovernmental organizations to monitor and implement human rights instruments and to
end impunity for human rights violators. The Clinton administration should ensure that the rule-of-law programs to which it is committed include a focus on
the rights guaranteed by the International Covenant on Civil and Political
Rights. In countries like China, Washington should encourage the ratification of
this covenant as quickly as possible, without reservations. It should also support

the efforts of Asian human rights organizations to create a regional human rights mechanism.

Finally, there is an issue of style. While the Clinton administration used rhetorical excess and missionary zeal, often devoid of substantive policy, future U.S. leaders would do better to favor humility and a pragmatic, results-oriented approach. For example, Vice President Al Gore's statement of support for *reformasi* (political reform) in Malaysia and Indonesia at the November 1998 APEC summit was widely perceived throughout the region as the action of a presidential candidate performing for a domestic audience, since it did not prefigure any real shift in U.S. policy in the region.

It Starts at Home

The most important contributions that the United States could make to greater peace and security in the Asia-Pacific region begin at home. As long as the U.S. government is unwilling or unable to exert leadership at home, its effectiveness abroad will be limited. Regarding human rights, the major issue is continued U.S. government hypocrisy in refusing to sign or ratify several human rights instruments, such as the basic International Labor Organization conventions, the Convention on the Elimination of Discrimination Against Women, the Convention on the Rights of the Child, and the International Covenant on Economic, Social, and Cultural Rights. Furthermore, reservations and restrictions placed on these covenants by Congress and the administration make a mockery of U.S. exhortations to other countries to recognize international law. Given the current leadership in the U.S. Senate, the likelihood that America will ratify these instruments anytime in the near future, absent public pressure, is low.

On the economic front, the United States needs to address the fact that the existing patterns of global trade and economic restructuring undermine the living standards of significant numbers of citizens worldwide. The administration needs to address the concerns of workers and communities displaced by economic transformation, whether due to imports or to technological change. With such safety nets in place, Washington can more appropriately accelerate the reduction of trade barriers to developing-country exports.

But citizens do not have to wait for governments to lead. Corporations know that they have been in the vanguard of advancing their own script for an Asia-Pacific "community" for years. Alternatively, NGO efforts in recent years have been critical to advancing a distinct vision in Asia. Citizen groups spearheaded base-closure movements in Pacific Asia and enhanced security in the Korean Peninsula by building direct links with North Koreans around alternative energy issues.[56] In addition, the antinuclear movement in the Pacific made significant gains in the 1980s, leading to the declaration of the South Pacific Nuclear Free Zone and the adoption of New Zealand's antinuclear policies in 1984. In recent years, labor and consumer groups have targeted transnational corporations through a number of campaigns against Nike, Unocal, and other corporations with a significant presence in the region. Such citizen campaigns can be important stepping stones in shaping an alternative vision for Asia and the Pacific.

Because local governments are expanding their own export and investment promotion activities, citizen efforts have also targeted state and local governments to promote these agendas.[57] One campaign involves the more than 20 cities engaged in some form of boycott of companies with operations in Burma. Direct assistance is another avenue for global betterment. The states of Oregon and California have contributed, under the auspices of APEC and the U.S.-Asia Environmental Partnership, respectively, to help develop local government capacities in Asia. Expanding these initiatives, which enhance mutual learning and capacity building, would be useful.

The dawn of the twentieth century was marked by America's first sustained military and economic engagement in the Pacific and Asia. Many of the institutions and policies established in that period still remain, along with others initiated 50 years later. Most, however, are poorly suited for the challenges of the twenty-first century. The dawn of the twenty-first century is an auspicious moment for writing a new chapter in relations between the United States and Asia. By forging new paths toward peace, security, and sustainable development, it may yet be possible to make the Pacific century a pacific century indeed.

NOTES

1. For the purposes of this chapter, "Asia" will be used to describe the entire region from Afghanistan in the west through the Philippines, Japan, and the Pacific Island states in the east. For shorthand purposes, South Asia includes Afghanistan, Pakistan, India, Nepal, Bangladesh, and Sri Lanka. Southeast Asia includes Burma, Brunei, Cambodia, Indonesia, Laos, Malaysia, the Philippines, Singapore, Thailand, and Vietnam—all of which are members of ASEAN. Northeast Asia consists of China, Mongolia, Japan, Taiwan, North and South Korea, and Russia. Oceania is made up of Australia, New Zealand, Papua New Guinea, Fiji, and the Pacific Islands. The Asia-Pacific region or Pacific Asia will be used to refer to countries in or along the Pacific Ocean, which excludes South Asia.
2. Shirley A. Kan, "Chinese Proliferation of Weapons of Mass Destruction: Current Policy Issues," Congressional Research Service, Issue Brief 92056, updated June 1, 1998.
3. The member countries of ASEAN (Association of Southeast Asian Nations) constitute America's fourth largest source of imports and its fourth largest export market. Since 1990, total U.S. trade with the ASEAN countries has grown at an average annual rate of 15 percent. The United States is the leading export market for the Philippines, Singapore, and Thailand and is the second largest export market for Malaysia and Indonesia. U.S. trade and investment in South Asia is much smaller, but U.S. direct investment increased following India's 1991 decision to pursue trade and investment liberalization.

    Although the United States continues to suffer merchandise trade deficits with Asia, America maintains a surplus regarding trade in services, including financial services, with the region. About 48 percent of the U.S. service trade surplus results from commercial relations with the Asia-Pacific countries. Data on services is from "U.S. International Sales and Purchases of Private Services: U.S. Cross-Border Transactions, 1996, and Sales By Affiliates, 1995," *Survey of Current Business*, October 1997.
4. Due to space limitations, Oceania is not a focus of this report.

5. World Bank, *World Bank Poverty Update*, (Washington, DC: World Bank), June 1999, p. 3.

6. See the discussions in "Asia: How Real Is Its Recovery," *Business Week*, May 3, 1999, pp. 24–27; "Asia Plots the Way Forward," *Asiaweek*, May 28, 1999, pp. 86–88; and Stanley Fischer, "The Asian Crisis: The Return of Growth," June 17, 1999. Fischer is the first deputy managing director of the International Monetary Fund. Available on the Internet at: http://www.imf.org/external/np/speeches/1999/061799.htm.

7. See, for example, Thomas Fuller, "Asia Pegs Its Recovery to a Lasting U.S. Boom," *International Herald Tribune*, May 18, 1999, pp. 1, 6.

8. *The Economist*, September 19, 1998, p. 51.

9. See the discussion in *Far Eastern Economic Review*, June 3, 1999, pp. 54–55; World Bank, *World Bank Poverty Update: Trends in Poverty*, (Washington, DC: World Bank, 1999).

10. Office of the United States Trade Representative, *1998 Trade Policy Agenda and 1997 Annual Report of the President of the United States on the Trade Agreements Program* (Washington, DC: U.S. Government Printing Office, March 1998), p. 9. Available on the Internet at: http://www.ustr.gov/reports/tpa/1998/contents.html. See, also, Testimony of Ambassador Charlene Barshefsky, United States Trade Representative before the House Ways and Means Trade Subcommittee, February 24, 1998, and Office of the United States Trade Representative, *USTR Strategic Plan, FY 1997-FY 2002* (Washington, DC: U.S. Government Printing Office, September 30, 1997), p. 151. Available on the Internet at: http://www.ustr.gov/reports/gpra.pdf.

11. As Kristalina Georgieva, head of environment and social development for the World Bank's East Asia and Pacific region, noted, "Logging, fishing, and mining activities have grown to generate export earnings and to support subsistence of the rural poor. Industrial and municipal treatment facilities have been forced to cut back operations, and untreated wastewater, solid waste discharges and illegal dumping have increased." Cited in Michael Richardson, "Fear of Fires Is Rekindled as Jakarta Copes with Turmoil," *International Herald Tribune*, April 30-May 2, 1999, p. 4.

12. Hong Kong and Singapore, as city-states and trading centers, are not reflective of the context of the majority of developing countries.

13. See, for example, the World Bank's belated recognition of the link between rapid growth and inequality, *Everyone's Miracle? Revisiting Poverty and Inequality in East Asia* (Washington, DC: World Bank, 1997).

14. According to a *U.S. News & World Report* account, "For months, Asian leaders have grumbled that the fiscal medicine administered by the International Monetary Fund has actually worsened the ailing economies of their region. Now a new report from the World Bank seems to agree. Without naming names, the bank's 186-page annual study of the global economy subtly suggests that the IMF and its backers in the U.S. Treasury Department may have paid too much attention to hiking interest rates and not enough to unemployment and the other social costs of fiscal austerity." Ben Wildavsky, "Curing the Asian Flu: Two Views on the Proper Medicine," *U.S. News & World Report*, December 14, 1998, p. 14. See also World Bank, *Global Development Finance* and *Global Economic Prospects and the Developing Countries* (Washington, DC: World Bank, 1999); Giovanna Prennushi et al., *Macroeconomic Crises and Poverty: Transmission Mechanisms and Policy Responses*, World Bank Working Paper, (Washington, DC: World Bank, 1999).

15. Paul Krugman, "Saving Asia: It's Time to Get Radical," *Fortune*, September 1998.

16. Office of the United States Trade Representative, *1998 Trade Policy Agenda and 1997 Annual Report of the President of the United States on the Trade Agreements Program*, pp. 180–81.

17. The others are Afghanistan, North Korea, Serbia, Montenegro, and Cuba.

18. Anya Schiffren, "Vietnam Says It May Face Debt Problem," *Asian Wall Street Journal*, May 5, 1999, p. 4.

19. The Department of Defense estimates Japan's cost-sharing in support of U.S. forces as somewhere from $3.7 to $4.3 billion, covering 75 percent of U.S. basing costs, while the Department of State estimates $4.9 billion. *A Report to the United States Congress by the Secretary of Defense: A Report on Allied Contributions to the Common Defense* (Washington, DC: U.S. Government Printing Office, March 1999), p. II-7. Available on the Internet at: http://www.defenselink.mil/pubs/allied_contrib99/

20. Ibid., p. II-8. These are in tune with previous expenditures. Under the 1995 agreement, South Korea was programmed to contribute $330 million in 1996, increasing to $399 million in 1998. But in the context of the Asian crisis, the 1998 payment was reduced to $314 million.

21. Stockholm International Peace Research Institute, *SIPRI Yearbook 1998: Armaments, Disarmament and International Security* (Oxford: Oxford University Press, 1998).

22. Vice Admiral Dennis C. Blair replaced Admiral Joseph W. Prueher in February 1999 as Commander in Chief, U.S. Pacific Command. Blair was serving as director of the Joint Staff at the Pentagon in Washington, DC. Preuher is the nominee to be the new U.S. Ambassador to China.

23. See Peter Hayes, Lyuba Zarsky, and Walden Bello, *American Lake: Nuclear Peril in the Pacific* (Penguin, 1986); Walden Bello, *People and Power in the Pacific* (San Francisco: Food First Books, 1994).

24. In the first step of what came to be known as the Nye Initiative (named after its architect, former U.S. Assistant Secretary of Defense for International Security Affairs Joseph S. Nye), the United States reaffirmed the American commitment to the defense of Japan and to the stability and security of East Asia. This phase of the process culminated in the April 1996 Tokyo Summit, with its security declaration introducing a plausible construct for the bilateral security relationship. The next step was to redefine Japanese contributions to the security relationship. This was necessary both because the United States needed the help and because the alliance could not withstand the criticism sure to ensue if Japan—no longer a lesser partner, as during the cold war—were to be seen as failing to pull its own weight. Moreover, it had become increasingly accepted that in the case of a conflict on the Korean Peninsula (hostilities appeared to be imminent in 1994), if Americans were dying in the defense of South Korea, the lack of Japanese involvement would spell the end of the bilateral security relationship. Thus, the work over the last several years has been to restore the U.S.-Japanese alliance to the point where new terms of bilateral cooperation could be constructed.

25. National Defense University Institute for National Strategic Studies, *1998 Strategic Assessment: Engaging Power for Peace* (August 1998), available on the Internet at: http://www.nyu.edu/globalbeat/usdefense/ndu0898.html.

26. International Institute for Strategic Studies, *The Military Balance 1997/98* (Oxford: Oxford University Press, 1997), p. 164.

27. Secretary of Defense, *The United States Security Strategy for the East Asia-Pacific Region* 1998 (Washington, DC: Department of Defense, 1998), Introduction. Available on the Internet at: http://www.defenselink.mil/pubs/easr98/easr98.pdf.

28. Human Rights Watch, *World Report 1999*, available on the Internet at: http://www.hrw.org/worldreport99/arms/arms5.html.

29. Ibid.

30. *A Report to the United States Congress by the Secretary of Defense*, p. II-9.

31. For an excellent discussion of the implications of reunification for U.S. policy, see Martin Hart-Landsberg, *Korea: Division, Reunification, and U.S. Foreign Policy* (New York: Monthly Review Press, 1999).

32. Pauline Jelinek, "S. Korea Rights Abuses Cited," Associated Press, Seoul, September 10, 1998.

33. See, for example, Peter Lavoy, "Learning to Live with the Bomb: India and Nuclear Weapons, 1947–1998," manuscript.

34. If the missiles are deployed with 1,000-kilogram or lighter warheads, the new systems would enable both states to reach important new targets: Islamabad would be able to strike Calcutta and Madras and potentially all of India; New Delhi would be able to reach Beijing and potentially Shanghai as well. Brahma Chellaney, Professor of Security Studies at the New Delhi-based Center for Policy Research, noted, "The [missile] tests have reinforced the deterrent relationship between India and Pakistan, while allowing India to deal with the third player in the regional strategic triangle— China." Quoted in Ajay Singh, "What a Big Mess," *Asiaweek*, April 30, 1999, p. 22.

35. International Institute for Strategic Studies, *The Military Balance, 1997/98*, p. 149. Available on the Internet at: http://www.sipri.se/projects/armstrade/atrec93_97.html.

36. Department of State, *Patterns of Global Terrorism*, Office of the Coordinator for Counterterrorism (Washington, DC: U.S. Government Printing Office, April 1999), available on the Internet at: http://www.state.gov/www/global/terrorism/1998Report/asia.html.

37. However, the renewed outbreak of hostilities in Kashmir in mid-1999, just four months after the signing of the Lahore declaration reflects domestic political considerations more than an escalation of tensions.

38. Department of State, *Patterns of Global Terrorism*; Department of State, *International Narcotics Control Strategy Report*, Bureau for International Narcotics and Law Enforcement Affairs (Washington, DC: U.S. Government Printing Office, February 1999), available on the Internet at: http://www.state.gov/www/global/narcotics_law/1998_narc_report/swasi98.html.

39. Department of State, *International Narcotics Control Strategy Report*, February 1999.

40. The United Nations Drug Control Program (UNDCP) is supporting an integrated rural development project in the southern portion of the Wa region to support the United Wa State Army's unilateral decision (announced in 1995) to establish five "opium-poppy-free zones" in its area of control, where opium cultivation will gradually be reduced. The project is part of a planned five-year, $15 million rural development project aimed at crop substitution and alternative development. At present, nine villages are scheduled to participate in the first stage of the activity. UNDCP has begun distributing seeds as part of the crop substitution aspect. The Wa project will incorporate a monitoring and evaluation component designed to measure progress in eliminating opium cultivation. As an integrated development scheme, this effort will also focus on developing the local infrastructure as well as providing educational and health facilities in the Ho Tao and Mong Pawk districts of the Wa region. The United Wa State Army is an ethnic-based military force of up to 5,000 soldiers. Subin Khernakaew, "Joint Hunt for New Drug Baron," *The Bangkok Post*, February 8, 1999.

41. Office of the United States Trade Representative, *USTR Strategic Plan, FY 1997-FY 2002*, pp. 29–30. Also see pp. 27–30 and 32–34. Available on the Internet at: http://www.ustr.gov/reports/gpra.pdf.

42. Jane Perlez, "Clinton Pushes for Treaty to Ban the Worst Child Labor Practices," *New York Times*, June 17, 1999, p. A17.

43. The funding is for programs sponsored by the International Labor Organization's International Program for the Elimination of Child Labor. Total combined funding from fiscal year 1995 through fiscal year 1998 was $8.1 million ($3 million in FY 1998; see website at http://www.dol.gov/dol/ilab/public/programs/iclp/crntprgs. htm). For further details, see Statement of Andrew James Samet, Deputy Undersecretary, Bureau of International Labor Affairs, U.S. Department of Labor, before the Congressional Human Rights Caucus, September 28, 1998, website at http://www.dol.gov/dol/ilab/public/media/speeches/chrc9–98.htm.

44. See the State Department's 1998 Human Rights Report, prepared by the Bureau of Democracy, Human Rights, and Labor, available on the Internet at: http://www. state.gov/www/global/human_rights/1998_hrp_report/98hrp_report_toc.html.

45. Seth Mydans, "U.S. Denials Over Agent Orange's Fallout Anger Vietnamese," *International Herald Tribune*, May 17, 1999, p. 4.

46. Phil Robertson, "Cambodia," *Foreign Policy In Focus*, Vol. 2, No. 52, December 1997.

47. Abigail Abrash, "Indonesia After Suharto," *Foreign Policy In Focus*, Vol. 3, No. 34, November 1998, available on the Internet at: http://www.foreignpolicy-infocus.org.

48. Edward Herman, "Words as Propaganda," presentation given at a congressional forum cosponsored by Dennis J. Kucinich (D-OH) titled "The Rhetoric of War," June 10, 1999.

49. Testimony by Sidney Jones, Executive Director, Human Rights Watch, Asia Division before the East Asia and Pacific Subcommittee of the Senate Foreign Relations Committee, *Violence and the Indonesian Elections*, March 18, 1999; *The Indonesian Army and Civilian Militias in East Timor*, available on the Internet at: http://www. hrw.org/hrw/press/1999/apr/etmilitia.htm.

50. Roger Mitton, "Now, ASEAN Becomes Ten," *Asiaweek*, April 30, 1999, p. 23.

51. Formed at the instigation of ASEAN, it has expanded to include not only ASEAN foreign ministers but also counterparts from Australia, Canada, China, India, Japan, Mongolia, New Zealand, Papua New Guinea, Russia, South Korea, and the United States as well as 18 representatives from the European Union.

52. There are two so-called Track II processes in Northeast Asia: the Northeast Asia Cooperation Dialogue (NEACD) and the North Pacific Arms Control Workshop (NPACW). The NEACD serves as the primary multilateral forum for regional participants to exchange views on confidence building measures and arms control. This process, which began in 1993, is managed by the Institute on Global Conflict and Cooperation at the University of California, San Diego. The NPACW, which includes members from South Korea, Japan, China, Russia, Canada, and the United States, is the only multilateral northeast Asia security forum dedicated solely to the promotion of regional arms control.

53. Ahmed Rashid in Kabul and Faizabad, "Heart of Darkness" *Far Eastern Economic Review* August 5, 1999.

54. Afghanistan Foundation, *White Paper on U.S. Policy Toward Afghanistan*, July 12, 1999, Washington, D.C. Available on the Internet at: http://www.afghanistanfoundation.org.

55. Section 570 prohibits the provision of any U.S. security assistance (funded by the foreign operations bill) to foreign military units that the secretary of state has credible evidence of having committed human rights violations. The appropriations act also (in section 571) requires that "any agreement for sale, transfer or licensing of any lethal equipment or helicopters" to Indonesia must explicitly warn that the United States expects such items not to be used in East Timor.

56. For a fascinating recounting of the story, see Leon V. Sigal, *Disarming Strangers: Nuclear Diplomacy with North Korea* (Princeton, NJ: Princeton University Press, 1998).
57. See, for example, Earl H. Fry, *The Expanding Role of State and Local Governments in U.S. Foreign Affairs* (New York: Council on Foreign Relations, 1998).

EDITORS AND CHAPTER AUTHORS

JONATHAN P. G. BACH is currently a postdoctoral fellow at the Saltzman Center for the Study of Constitutional Democracy at Columbia University. He received his Ph.D. from the Maxwell School of Citizenship and Public Affairs at Syracuse University. He is author of *Between Sovereignty and Integration: German Foreign Policy and National Identity* (St. Martin's Press, 1999).

TOM BARRY is a cofounder of the Interhemispheric Resource Center (IRC) and codirector of Foreign Policy In Focus. A senior analyst at the IRC, Barry has written extensively on U.S. relations with Mexico, Central America, and the Caribbean. He is author or coauthor of numerous books including *Zapata's Revenge: Free Trade and the Farm Crisis in Mexico; The Great Divide: The Challenge of U.S.-Mexico Relations for the 1990s; Central America Inside Out;* and *The United Nations: The Next Fifty Years.*

ROBERT L. BOROSAGE is codirector of the Campaign for America's Future. His writings on political, economic, and national security issues have been widely published in the *New York Times,* the *Washington Post,* the *Los Angeles Times,* the *Philadelphia Inquirer, The Nation,* and elsewhere. He was the founder and director of the Campaign for New Priorities, involving over 100 organizations in the call to reinvest in America in the post–cold war era. He has served as an issues advisor to progressive political campaigns, including those of Senators Carol Moseley-Braun, Barbara Boxer, and Paul Wellstone. In 1988, he was Senior Issues Advisor to the presidential campaign of the Reverend Jesse L. Jackson.

JOHN CAVANAGH is director of the Institute for Policy Studies (IPS) and has run the Institute's Global Economy Project since 1983. Prior to coming to IPS, he was an international economist at the United Nations Conference on Trade and Development (1977–1981) and at the World Health Organization (1981–1982). He has written widely in the fields of trade, debt, development, and other world economy issues. Mr. Cavanagh's most recent book, coauthored with Richard J. Barnet, is *Global Dreams: Imperial Corporations and the New World Order* (Simon & Schuster, 1994). The book, which has been translated into five languages, analyzes the rise of global firms and their impact on politics, workers, and the environment. He is coauthor of eight other books on the global economy.

JOHN FEFFER is the author of *Shock Waves: Eastern Europe after the Revolutions* (South End, 1992) and *Beyond Détente: Soviet Foreign Policy and U.S. Options* (Hill and Wang, 1990). He coedited both *Europe's New Nationalism* (Oxford University Press, 1996) and *State of the Union: The Clinton Administration and the Nation in Profile* (Westview, 1994). He has worked for the World Policy Institute and the American Friends Service Committee (AFSC). Based in Tokyo, he currently organizes regional exchanges for the AFSC.

JOHN GERSHMAN is a research associate at the Institute for Development Research and a visiting graduate student at the Woodrow Wilson School for Public and International Affairs at Princeton University. He is a coeditor of *Trading Freedom: How Free Trade Affects our Lives, Work, and Environment* (Food First Books, 1992) and of *Dying for Growth: Global Restructuring and the Health of the Poor* (Common Courage, 1999).

WILLIAM D. HARTUNG is an internationally recognized expert on the issues of the arms trade and the economics of military spending. He is a senior research fellow at the World Policy Institute of the New School for Social Research. He also serves as the director of the Institute's Arms Trade Resource Center. A former aide to New York Attorney General Robert Abrams, he is the author of *And Weapons for All* (Harper Collins, 1994) and *Welfare for Weapons Dealers*, an occasional paper published by the World Policy Institute.

MARTHA HONEY is director of the Peace and Security program at the Institute for Policy Studies and codirector of the Foreign Policy In Focus project. Before joining IPS in 1996 she worked for two decades as a journalist based in East Africa and Central America. She holds a Ph.D. in African history from the University of Dar es Salaam, Tanzania. Her most recent books include *Hostile Acts: U.S. Policy in Costa Rica in the 1980s* (University Press of Florida, 1994) and *Ecotourism and Sustainable Development: Who Owns Paradise?* (Island Press, 1999).

DAVID HUNTER is the executive director of the Center for International Environmental Law, and an adjunct professor at The American University's Washington College of Law, where he teaches international environmental law and comparative environmental law. A graduate of Harvard Law School, Hunter's research and advocacy work covers a broad range of global environment and development issues, including multinational corporate responsibilities, ozone depletion, and the role of international financial institutions. He coauthored *International Environmental Law Policy* (Foundation Press, 1998), a text for classroom and reference use for academics, practitioners, and policymakers.

RICHARD F. KAUFMAN is director of the Bethesda Research Institute and an associate of Economists Allied for Armed Reduction. He was formerly general counsel of the Joint Economic Committee of the U.S. Congress, and a fellow at the Woodrow Wilson Center for International Scholars. He specializes in international economics and national security and has written and edited many books, chapters in books, and articles for academic journals and popular magazines. He is presently engaged in a study of the U.S. defense budget under a grant from the Fund for Constitutional Government.

CHARLES WILLIAM MAYNES is president of the Eurasia Foundation. From April 1980 until April 1997 he served as editor of *Foreign Policy* magazine, one of the leading journals in the world on international affairs. Over the course of his career Mr. Maynes has held positions in the Department of State, U.S. Congress, and the foundation world.

WILLIAM MINTER is the senior research fellow at the Africa Policy Information Center in Washington, DC. He holds a Ph.D. in sociology from the University of Wisconsin. Minter is the author, among other works, of *King Solomon's Mines Revisited: Western Interests and the Burdened History of Southern Africa* (Basic Books, 1986) and coauthor of *Imperial Brain Trust: The Council on Foreign Relations and United States Foreign Policy* (Monthly Review Press, 1977). His most recent book is *Apartheid's Contras: An Inquiry into the Roots of War in Angola and Mozambique* (Zed Books,1994). He served in Tanzania and Mozambique as a teacher in the secondary school of the Mozambique Liberation Front (FRELIMO) from 1966–1968 and from 1974–1976, and worked with Africa News Service from 1976–1982.

JANINE R. WEDEL is an associate professor at the Graduate School of Public and International Affairs at the University of Pittsburgh. Her latest book is *Collision and Collusion: The Strange Case of Western Aid to Eastern Europe, 1989–1998* (St. Martin's Press, 1998). She holds a Ph.D. in anthropology from the University of California at Berkeley and is recipient of prestigious research awards. She has studied East Europe's evolving economic and social order for 20 years, conducted 8 years of fieldwork in the region, and published 3 books including *The Private Poland: An Anthropologist Looks at Everyday Life* (Facts on File, 1986) and *The Unplanned Society: Poland During and After Communism* (Columbia University Press, 1992). She has contributed congressional testimony and written articles for national newspapers and a number of scholarly and policy journals.

COLETTA YOUNGERS, a senior associate with the Washington Office on Latin America (WOLA), is an analyst of human rights and political developments in the Andes and of U.S. foreign policy toward the region, primarily Peru, Colombia, and Bolivia. She travels regularly to these countries. Frequently interviewed by Latin American and U.S. media, Younger writes and speaks widely on these issues and on U.S. international drug control policy. As a former project manager in the Peru-Chile office of Catholic Relief Services, she monitored and evaluated rural and urban development and human rights projects by Peruvian NGOs. She has also worked with the International Planned Parenthood Federation (Western Hemisphere Division) and the editorial staff of *Latinamerica Press/Noticias Aliadas* in Lima, Peru.

STEPHEN ZUNES is an associate professor of politics at the University of San Francisco and an expert on Middle Eastern history and politics. He holds a Ph.D. in government from Cornell University. Zunes served as director of the Institute for a New Middle East Policy, a resource center examining and proposing alternatives to Middle East policy of the U.S. Government, as well as associate scholar for the Institute for Global Studies. An author of dozens of scholarly articles and essays, he is completing two books, *Decision on Intervention: United States Response to Third World Nationalism, 1950–57*, and *Western Sahara: Nationalism and Conflict in Northwest Africa*.

ESSAY AUTHORS

SOREN AMBROSE is a policy analyst for 50 Years Is Enough: U.S. Network for Global Economic Justice, a Washington, DC-based coalition of over 200 organizations dedicated to the profound transformation of the IMF and World Bank.

PHYLLIS BENNIS, an expert on the United Nations and the Middle East, is a fellow at the Institute for Policy Studies, Washington, DC.

CARL CONETTA and CHARLES KNIGHT are the codirectors of the Project on Defense Alternatives at the Commonwealth Institute, Cambridge, Massachusetts.

KRISTIN DAWKINS, an analyst at the Institute for Agriculture and Trade Policy in Minneapolis, Minnesota, is author of *Gene Wars* (New York: Seven Stories Press, 1997).

ROBERT ENGELMAN is Vice President for Research at Population Action International in Washington, DC.

DAVID FELIX is Professor Emeritus at Washington University in St. Louis. This is an abridged version of a longer paper, David Felix, "Repairing the Global Financial Architecture: Painting over Cracks vs. Strengthening the Foundations," *Foreign Policy In Focus* Special Report #5, September 1999.

KIT GAGE is Washington representative of the National Committee Against Repressive Legislation as well as coordinator of the National Coalition to Protect Political Freedom.

ROBERT GREENBERG is an associate professor in the Department of Slavic Languages and Literatures at the University of North Carolina, Chapel Hill.

WILLIAM D. HARTUNG is a senior research fellow at the World Policy Institute, New York.

RICHARD F. KAUFMAN is director of Bethesda Research Institute, Maryland.

AILEEN KWA is with Focus on the Global South, Bangkok, Thailand.

ERIK LEAVER is a founding staff member of the Foreign Policy In Focus project. He compiled this essay from the project's several briefs on the international financial flows.

LISA LEDWIDGE is the editor of Science for Democratic Action and outreach coordinator with the Institute for Energy and Environmental Research (IEER), Takoma Park, Maryland.

JULES LOBEL is a professor of international law at the University of Pittsburgh Law School.

MIRIAM PEMBERTON is a research fellow at the Institute for Policy Studies. She is coauthor, with Michael Renner of the Worldwatch Institute in Washington, DC, of *A Tale of Two Markets: Trade in Arms and Environmental Technologies* (Washington, DC: Institute for Policy Studies, 1998) from which this essay was adapted.

MICHAEL RATNER is an international human rights attorney who works with the Center for Constitutional Rights in New York City.

JANICE SHIELDS is coordinator of the Corporate Welfare and TaxWatch projects of the Institute for Business Research, Washington, DC.

JOE STORK is advocacy director for the Middle East and North Africa division of Human Rights Watch, Washington, DC.

TOMÁS VALÁSEK is a research analyst at the Center for Defense Information, Washington, DC.

STACY D. VANDEVEER is a postdoctoral research fellow at the John F. Kennedy School of Government, Belfer Center for Science and International Affairs at Harvard University.

LYUBA ZARSKY is the co-executive director for the Nautilus Institute for Security and Sustainable Development in Berkeley, California and serves as the director for its Sustainable Development Projects.

PETER ZIRNITE is a Washington, DC-based freelance writer and author of *Reluctant Recruits: The U.S. Military and the War on Drugs* (Washington, DC: Washington Office on Latin America, 1997).

STEPHEN ZUNES is an assistant professor of politics at the University of San Francisco.

READERS AND CONSULTANTS

Steve Aftergood, Federation of American Scientists

Peter Andreas, Harvard University

Phyllis Bennis, Institute for Policy Studies

Robert A. Blecker, American University

Salih Booker, Council on Foreign Relations

Nicola Bullard, Focus on the Global South

Hugh Byrne, Washington Office on Latin America

John P. Caskey, Swarthmore College

John Cavanagh, Institute for Policy Studies

James Chace, *World Policy Journal*

Michelle Chan-Fishel, Friends of the Earth

Steve Charnovitz, Yale University

Terry Collingsworth, International Labor Rights Fund

Steve Daggett, Congressional Research Service

Herman Daly, University of Maryland

Mike Ettlinger, Citizens for Tax Justice

Richard A. Falk, Princeton University

Randall Forsberg, Institute for Defense and Disarmament Studies

Hilary French, Worldwatch Institute

Robert Goodland, World Bank

Rosemary Gutierrez, Office of Senator Tom Harkin

Peter Haas, University of Massachusetts

Karen Hansen-Kuhn, The Development GAP

John Hardt, Congressional Research Service

William D. Hartung, World Policy Institute

Pharis Harvey, International Labor Rights Fund

Robert Hayden, University of Pittsburgh

Adam Isacson, Center for International Policy

David A. Kideckel, Central Connecticut State University

Daryl Kimball, Coalition to Reduce Nuclear Dangers

Yukiko Koga, Columbia University

Arthur MacEwan, University of Massachusetts. at Boston

Arjun Makhajani, Institute for Energy and Environmental Research

Khaled Mansour, Middle East News Agency

Robert McIntyre, WIDER Institute, U.N. University, Helsinki

John D. Nagle, Syracuse University

Bob Naiman, Preamble Center

Michael O'Hanlon, Brookings Institution

Miriam Pemberton, Institute for Policy Studies

John Pike, Federation of American Scientists

Michael Ratner, Center for Constitutional Rights

Naomi Roht-Arriaza, University of California, Hastings College of Law

Dorothy Rosenberg, Russian Academy of Sciences, Moscow

Ranjit Sau, New Jersey Institute of Technology School of Management

Sherle Schwenninger, World Policy Institute

Frances Seymour, World Resources Institute

Michael Shifter, Inter-American Dialogue

Julianne Smith, British American Security Information Council (BASIC)

Lance Taylor, New School for Social
  Research
Karen Travis, U.S. Department of Labor
George Vickers, Washington Office on
  Latin America
Carol Welch, Friends of the Earth
Andrew Wells, Asia Pacific Center for
  Justice and Peace

Daphne Wysham, Institute for Policy
  Studies
Deborah Yashar, Princeton University
Coletta Youngers, Washington Office on
  Latin America
Vladislov Zubok, National Security
  Archive

FOREIGN POLICY IN FOCUS

THE FOREIGN POLICY IN FOCUS (FPIF) PROJECT, a joint venture between the Interhemispheric Resource Center (IRC) and the Institute for Policy Studies (IPS), examines U.S. foreign policy throughout the world, giving special attention to the need to shape a new vision of the U.S. place in global affairs. Begun in 1996, this multifaceted project is assembling a network of progressive experts and activists in the United States and abroad to analyze current U.S. foreign policy and define the principles that should guide U.S. international relations.

The Foreign Policy In Focus project—through its inclusive structure, multimedia character, comprehensive scope, and commitment to rethinking the operative principles of U.S. foreign policy—is playing a vital role in establishing a new vision and a cohesive policy framework for a more responsible U.S. role in the global community. The project's network of hundreds of advocates and scholars serves as a think tank without walls, functioning as a dynamic base from which to reach out to the constituencies that are essential to ensuring that U.S. foreign policy represents a more broadly conceived understanding of U.S. national interests.

The project reaches the public through:

POLICY BRIEFS

The project produces an average of one *Foreign Policy In Focus* brief per week. Written by regional or issue specialists, these four-page briefs provide the latest research and analysis on a wide variety of global affairs issues in an accessible format. Each briefing paper is distributed via e-mail, fax, and mail to policymakers, journalists, research institutes, academics, and to church, labor, arms control, environmental, consumer, and other organizations.

PROGRESSIVE RESPONSE

The *Progressive Response* is a weekly electronic magazine (ezine) that provides analysis about current foreign policy issues and attempts to stimulate global debate about U.S. international relations. To subscribe, send e-mail to: newusfp-manager@zianet.com with the words "join newusfp" in the body of the message.

WEBSITE

The website is a gateway to foreign policy information. In addition to the policy briefs, the site includes press releases, special reports, current affairs updates, and an extensive compilation of links to other organizations providing information and analysis about global affairs. If you want information about government agencies such as the U.S. Information Agency, countries such as Albania, or issues like human rights or economic integration, visit: http://www.foreignpolicy-infocus.org.

MEDIA GUIDE

Global Perspectives: A Media Guide to Progressive Foreign Policy Experts is a media guide to the thoughtful, critical, alternative voices of more than 300 progressive experts, academics, and activists. Organized into three easy-to-use sections, *Global Perspectives* is an invaluable tool for finding progressive people and organizations. Free to journalists; $10 for others. Also available on the FPIF website.

OTHER PUBLICATIONS

Global Focus is published every two years with the aim of presenting an up-to-date and comprehensive critique of U.S. foreign policy. FPIF also publishes occasional reports on topics such as U.S. police aid, the military-industrial project, and Latin America. In addition, the project assembles packets of briefs on such topics as women and U.S. foreign policy, international financial flows, global environment, and corporate welfare.

PUBLIC FORUMS, CONGRESSIONAL SEMINARS, AND PRESS BRIEFINGS

The FPIF project has organized dozens of panel discussions on a wide range of current affairs, including U.S. relations with China; the war on drugs; Colombia; NATO expansion; Kosovo; Iraq; India, Pakistan and the bomb; military base closures and clean up; and child labor.

For more information about the project, or to order materials contact:

Interhemispheric Resource Center (IRC)
FPIF Editorial Office
Box 2178
Silver City, NM 88062
Voice: (505) 388–0208
E-mail: resourcectr@igc.org
Fax: (505) 388–0619
Website: http://www.irc-online.org/

Institute for Policy Studies
FPIF Editorial Office/Outreach
733 15th St., NW, Suite 1020
Washington, DC 20005
Voice: (202) 234–9382
Fax: (202) 387–7915
E-mail: ipsps@igc.org or leaverfpif@igc.org
Website: http://www.ips-dc.org

IRC
FPIF Publication Ordering/Outreach
Box 4506
Albuquerque, NM 87196
Voice: (505) 842–8288
Fax: (505) 246–1601
E-mail: irc_alb@swcp.com

INSTITUTE FOR POLICY STUDIES

THE GREAT MUCKRAKING JOURNALIST I. F. STONE once said, "The Fortune 500 has the American Enterprise Institute; the right, the Heritage Foundation; and mainstream Democrats, Brookings. The Institute for Policy Studies is for the rest of us." Since 1963, IPS has been the nation's leading multi-issue, progressive think tank. Its public scholars have crafted policies to help those in society with the least power and to give their advocates intellectual ammunition to make changes in public policy consistent with the values of demilitarization, social justice, economic equality, environmental sustainability, and democratic participation. Over the years, IPS fellows and project directors have produced scores of books, reports, and video documentaries; they appear frequently in the media and lecture widely around the country and abroad.

IPS has four broad program areas: Global Economy, Peace and Security, Paths to the 21st Century, and Sustainable Communities. In addition to Foreign Policy In Focus, IPS projects include:

- *Global Economy* program, which supports activists in the labor, environmental, family farm, religious, consumer, and economic justice movements who seek more equitable and sustainable paths towards economic integration. It took a lead in the defeat of fast-track and monitors NAFTA and the Asian financial crisis, financial flows, and the impacts of economic globalization and integration.
- *Economic Conversion* project is dedicated to educating the public on the need and the means for an orderly transfer of military resources to civilian use.
- *Drug Policy* project seeks to broaden the public dialogue about the impact of the so-called war on drugs at home and abroad. The project promotes alternative drug policies based on education, treatment, and economic alternatives rather than a punitive, military response of arrest and incarceration.
- *The Sustainable Energy and Economy Network (SEEN)* provides ground-breaking research and support to activists, citizen groups, and policymakers around the world with the goal of steering investment of public funds away from fossil fuels and toward clean, safe, renewable forms of energy for human needs.
- *Campaign for Migrant Domestic Workers Rights* is assisting domestic workers employed by diplomats and officials with the World Bank, IMF, and other international agencies. It is involved in efforts to set up a monitoring system to ensure that grievances are dealt with justly and abusers are punished.
- *Middle East* project focuses on the U.S. role in the region, the Palestine-Israel conflict, and Washington's exclusion of the UN from political engagement in the conflict.
- *United Nations* project advocates real UN reform that goes beyond cutting cost and staff to include strengthening its conflict prevention and peacekeeping and monitoring

capabilities, ensuring that the United States and other members fully pay their dues, and democratizing the organization.

- *The Progressive Challenge* is a nation-wide coalition building project, based at IPS. This project organizes with hundreds of public interest, religious, labor, grassroots organizations as well as with policy-makers, around a broad-based domestic and foreign policy platform, entitled "The Fairness Agenda for America." The project also works on Capitol Hill with members of the Progressive Caucus on task forces and briefings on the various issues in the Fairness Agenda.

- *Paths to the 21st Century* is a collaborative project by a dozen scholars who are writing a series of books examining what has humanity learned from the twentieth century and what are the guideposts to bring about a multicultural and democratic society in the twenty-first century.

- *Bringing Pinochet to Justice* is coordinating public education and mobilization around the historic efforts to hold Pinochet and other dictators accountable for their crimes.

- *Social Action and Leadership School for Activists (SALSA)* provides evening classes to activists in how to manage, organize, communicate, and strategies more effectively.

- *Letelier-Moffitt Human Rights Awards* honoring outstanding human rights activists in Latin America and the United States are given each year in memory of two IPS staff members killed by a car bomb in 1976 under orders of the Chilean Secret Police.

INTERHEMISPHERIC RESOURCE CENTER

THE INTERHEMISPHERIC RESOURCE CENTER (IRC) celebrated 20 years as a research and policy institute in 1999. During this time, the IRC has monitored, researched, and analyzed worldwide events, and has provided people with the information they need to make informed decisions, to direct policy, and to be instruments for social change. On the eve of the millennium, we reflect on the changes that we have seen, both positive and negative, and we look ahead to a new century that we hope brings with it an era of peace, justice, human rights, education, economic security, and environmental stability throughout the world.

Foreign Policy In Focus is one of IRC's two main projects. The second main project, our U.S.-Mexico Borderlands work, puts our internationalist vision and principles to work in a region where the dynamics of economic integration and globalization are so evident. Our monthly publication, *borderlines*, provides an alternative voice (in Spanish and English) to borderlands actors on issues important in this physical juncture of North and South. The Border Information and Outreach Service (formerly INCITRA) works closely with a wide range of borderlands actors in Mexico and the United States to increase information sharing about sustainable development issues.

Utilizing research, analysis, and advocacy, the IRC forges the links necessary for social change and policy reform. Border *colonia* (settlement) organizers, national policymakers, church communities, labor unions, environmentalists, and scholars are among the diverse constituencies and sectors the IRC serves.

INDEX